T0212936

Lecture Notes in Computer Science 8611

Commenced Publication in 1973
Founding and Former Series Editors:
Gerhard Goos, Juris Hartmanis, and Jan van Leeuwen

Editorial Board

More information about this series at http://www.springer.com/series/7411

Ivan Ganchev · Marilia Curado
Andreas Kassler (Eds.)

Wireless Networking for Moving Objects

Protocols, Architectures, Tools, Services
and Applications

Springer

Editors
Ivan Ganchev
University of Limerick
Limerick
Ireland

Andreas Kassler
Karlstad University
Karlstad
Sweden

Marilia Curado
University of Coimbra
Coimbra
Portugal

ISSN 0302-9743
ISBN 978-3-319-10833-9
DOI 10.1007/978-3-319-10834-6

ISSN 1611-3349 (electronic)
ISBN 978-3-319-10834-6 (eBook)

Library of Congress Control Number: 2014948204

LNCS Sublibrary: SL5 – Computer Communication Networks and Telecommunications

Acknowledgement and Disclaimer
The work published in this book is supported by the European Union under the EU RTD Framework
Programme and especially the COST Action IC0906 "Wireless Networking for Moving Objects
(WiNeMO)". The book reflects only the author's views. Neither the COST Office nor any person acting
on its behalf is responsible for the use, which might be made of the information contained in this publication.
The COST Office is not responsible for external Web sites referred to in this publication.

Springer Cham Heidelberg New York Dordrecht London

Springer is part of Springer Science+Business Media (www.springer.com)

COST

COST - European Cooperation in Science and Technology is an intergovernmental framework aimed at facilitating the collaboration and networking of scientists and researchers at European level. It was established in 1971 by 19 member countries and currently includes 35 member countries across Europe, and Israel as a cooperating state.

COST funds pan-European, bottom-up networks of scientists and researchers across all science and technology fields. These networks, called 'COST Actions', promote international coordination of nationally-funded research.

By fostering the networking of researchers at an international level, COST enables break-through scientific developments leading to new concepts and products, thereby contributing to strengthening Europe's research and innovation capacities.
COST's mission focuses in particular on:

- *Building capacity by connecting high quality scientific communities throughout Europe and worldwide;*
- *Providing networking opportunities for early career investigators;*
- *Increasing the impact of research on policy makers, regulatory bodies and national decision makers as well as the private sector.*

Through its inclusiveness, COST supports the integration of research communities, leverages national research investments and addresses issues of global relevance.

Every year thousands of European scientists benefit from being involved in COST Actions, allowing the pooling of national research funding to achieve common goals.

As a precursor of advanced multidisciplinary research, COST anticipates and complements the activities of EU Framework Programmes, constituting a "bridge" towards the scientific communities of emerging countries. In particular, COST Actions are also open to participation by non-European scientists coming from neighbour countries (for example Albania, Algeria, Armenia, Azerbaijan, Belarus, Egypt, Georgia, Jordan, Lebanon, Libya, Moldova, Montenegro, Morocco, the Palestinian Authority, Russia, Syria, Tunisia and Ukraine) and from a number of international partner countries.

COST's budget for networking activities has traditionally been provided by successive EU RTD Framework Programmes. COST is currently executed by the European Science Foundation (ESF) through the COST Office on a mandate by the European Commission, and the framework is governed by a Committee of Senior Officials (CSO) representing all its 35 member countries.

More information about COST is available at www.cost.eu.

 ESF Povides the COST Office through an EC contract

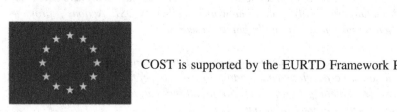 COST is supported by the EURTD Framework Programme

Preface

Wireless networks of moving objects have drawn significant attention recently. These types of networks consist of a number of autonomous or semi-autonomous wireless nodes/objects moving with diverse patterns and speeds while communicating via several radio interfaces simultaneously. Examples of such objects include smartphones and other user mobile devices, robots, cars, unmanned aerial vehicles, sensors, actuators, etc., which are connected in some way to each other and to the Internet. With every object acting as a networking node generating, relaying, and/or absorbing data, these networks may serve as a supplementary infrastructure for the provision of smart, ubiquitous, highly contextualized and customized services and applications available anytime-anywhere-anyhow. Achieving this will require global interworking and interoperability amongst objects, which is not typical today. To overcome current shortcomings, a number of research challenges have to be addressed in this area, ranging from initial conceptualization and modelling, to protocols and architectures engineering, and development of suitable tools, applications and services, and to the elaboration of realistic use-case scenarios by taking into account also corresponding societal and economic aspects.

The objective of this book is, by applying a systematic approach, to assess the state of the art and consolidate the main research results achieved in this area. It was prepared as the Final Publication of the COST Action IC0906 "Wireless Networking for Moving Objects (WiNeMO)." The book contains 15 chapters and is a showcase of the main outcomes of the action in line with its scientific goals. The book can serve as a valuable reference for undergraduate students, post-graduate students, educators, faculty members, researchers, engineers, and research strategists working in this field.

The book chapters were collected through an open, but selective, three-stage submission/review process. Initially, an open call for contributions was distributed among the COST WiNeMO participants in June 2013, and also externally outside the COST Action in September 2013 to increase the book quality and cover some missing topics. A total of 23 extended abstracts were received in response to the call. In order to reduce the overlap between individual chapters and at the same time increase the level of synergy between different research groups working on similar problems, it was recommended by the book editors to some of the authors to merge their chapters to ensure coherence between them. This way, 18 contributions were selected for full-chapter submission and 17 full-chapter proposals were received by the set deadline. All submitted chapters were peer-reviewed by two independent reviewers (including reviewers outside the COST Action), appointed by the book editors, and after the first round of reviews 16 chapters remained. These were revised according to the reviewers' comments, suggestions, and notes, and were resubmitted for the second round of reviews. Finally, 15 chapters were accepted for publication in this book.

The book is structured into three parts. Part I, entitled "Communications Models, Concepts, and Paradigms," contains seven chapters dedicated to these aspects of paramount importance for the successful functioning and operation of any type of network, and especially so of the new network types such as WiNeMO. A new generic techno-business model, based on a personal IPv6 (PIPv6) address embedded in an X.509 digital certificate, is put forward in the first chapter entitled "A New Techno-Business Model Based on a Personal IPv6 Address for Wireless Networks of Moving Objects." The authors argue that the new globally significant, network-independent PIPv6 address will enable real number ownership and full anytime-anywhere-anyhow portability for future generations of WiNeMO and could serve as a long-term node/object identity, thus enabling an advanced secure mobility and participation of the node/object in a variety of evolving dynamic, fluid wireless mobile network scenarios. The proposed model can also serve enhanced authentication, authorization, and accounting (AAA) functionality, through which commercially viable ad hoc and open mesh-networking solutions are realizable. The latter is an important result as commercially viable solutions are sorely lacking for these kinds of networks.

The next chapter, "Information-Centric Networking in Mobile and Opportunistic Networks," describes the emerging information centric networking (ICN) paradigm for the Future Internet, which could support communication in mobile wireless networks as well as opportunistic network scenarios, where end-systems have spontaneous but time-limited contact to exchange data. The authors identify challenges in mobile and opportunistic ICN-based networks, discuss appropriate solutions, and provide preliminary performance evaluation results.

This is followed by the chapter entitled "User-Centric Networking: Cooperation in Wireless Networks," which addresses the cooperation in wireless networks, based on the recently emerged, self-organizing paradigm of user-centric networking (UCN), whereby the user controls and carries wireless objects with integrated functionality, which today is part of the network core, e.g., mobility- and resource management. The user becomes more than a simple consumer of networking services, being also a service provider to other users. Resource sharing via cooperative elements, based on specific sharing incentives, is another aspect of this paradigm. The chapter provides UCN notions and models related to the user-centricity in the context of wireless networks. The authors also include recent operational data derived from the available user-centric networking pilot.

The concept of cooperation is also treated in the next chapter "Cooperative Relaying for Wireless Local Area Networks." By stating that future wireless systems will be highly heterogeneous and interconnected, which motivates the use of cooperative relaying, the authors describe the state of the art in this area with the main focus on media access control (MAC) layer design, analysis, and challenges, and go on to explain how cooperative networks can be designed as highly dynamic network configurations comprising a large number of moving nodes.

It is well known that clustering of moving objects in ad hoc wireless networks could increase the network scalability and improve efficiency, enabling the objects to simplify communication with their peers. While most of the clustering algorithms and protocols are applicable in WiNeMO, there are specific challenges induced by mobility. The next chapter, entitled "Clustering for Networks of Moving Objects," presents an overview of the technical challenges and currently available solutions to this problem. The chapter reviews the current scholarly works on clustering for moving objects, identifies the main methods of dealing with mobility, and analyzes the performance of the existing clustering solutions for WiNeMO.

As node mobility heavily influences the operation of wireless networks, where signal propagation conditions depend on the nodes' location and thus may cause drastic changes in data transmission and packet error rates, the authors of the next chapter, entitled "New Trends in Mobility Modelling and Handover Prediction," argue that the accurate representation of the user mobility in the analysis of wireless networks is a crucial element for both simulation and numerical/analytical modelling. The chapter discusses mobility models used in simulating the network traffic, handover optimization, and prediction, along with alternative methods for radio signal propagation changes caused by client mobility.

Analytically capturing the operation of carrier sense multiple access with collision avoidance (CSMA/CA) networks is the theme of the next chapter entitled "Throughput Analysis in CSMA/CA Networks Using Continuous Time Markov Networks: A Tutorial." The authors use a set of representative and modern scenarios to illustrate how continuous time Markov networks (CTMN) can be used for this. For each scenario, they describe the specific CTMN, obtain its stationary distribution, and compute the throughput achieved by each node in the network, which is used as a reference in the discussion on how the complex interactions between nodes affect the system performance.

Part II, entitled "Approaches, Schemes, Mechanisms and Protocols," contains four chapters. The first two chapters address energy saving and awareness, which are particularly important for mobile devices with limited energy capability, because battery lifetime is expected to increase only by 20 % in the next 10 years. The chapter entitled "Energy-Awareness in Multihop Routing" discusses how the current multihop routing approaches could still be utilized by enriching them with features that increase the network lifetime, based on the energy-awareness concept. The authors cover notions and concepts concerning multihop routing energy-awareness, show how to develop and apply energy-awareness in some of the most popular multihop routing protocols, and provide input concerning performance evaluation and realistic specification that can be used in operational scenarios, demonstrating that the proposed approaches are backward compatible with the current solutions.

Considering the energy as the most prominent limitation of end-user satisfaction within the anytime-anywhere connectivity paradigm, the next chapter, "An Overview of Energy Consumption in IEEE 802.11 Access Networks," provides readers with insights on the energy consumption properties of these networks and shows the way for further improvements toward enhanced battery lifetime. Through experimental energy assessment, the authors demonstrate the effectiveness of the power-saving mechanisms and the relevance of wireless devices' state management in this regard.

By identifying the need for capacity increase in 4G cellular systems for the support of a diverse range of services, the chapter "Resource Management and Cell Planning in LTE Systems" introduces a new soft frequency reuse (SFR) scheme, which is able to increase the cell capacity, by considering the impact of different scheduling schemes and user mobility patterns. The authors describe an implementation of a consistent SFR scenario in both NS-3 and OMNeT++ environments, and propose an analytical approach for the evaluation of the cell capacity with SFR.

Another example of WiNeMO are the networks involving unmanned aerial vehicles (UAV), which are growing in popularity along with the video applications for both military and civilian use. A set of challenges related to the device movement, scarce resources, and high error rates must be addressed in these networks, e.g., by implementing adaptive forward error correction (FEC) mechanisms to strengthen video transmissions. In the next chapter, "Improving Video QoE in Unmanned Aerial Vehicles Using an Adaptive FEC Mechanism," such a mechanism is proposed. It is based on motion vector details to improve real-time UAV video transmissions, resulting in better user experience and usage of resources. The authors consider the benefits and drawbacks of the proposed mechanism, based on analysis of conducted test simulations with a set of quality of experience (QoE) metrics.

Part III, entitled "M2M Aspects of WiNeMO," contains four chapters dedicated to machine-to-machine (M2M) communications. This is a specific strand of WiNeMO communications, which opens new horizons to the current concept of smart environments by enabling a new set of services and applications. One of the main M2M features is the large number of resource-constrained devices that usually perform collective communication. This particular feature calls for network solutions that support the data aggregation (DA) of groups of low duty cycling (LDC) devices. In relation to this problem, in the chapter entitled "Group Communication in Machine-to-Machine Environments," - abbreviated as GoCAME, an architecture is set out that enables joint execution of DA and LDC. This is achieved by taking into account the two-way latency tolerance and multiple data types, and assuring concurrent execution of data requests and management of groups of nodes, thereby providing the best strategy for replying to each data request.

It is well established that a successful simulation platform should be based on a user-friendly framework and models that support virtualization in order to enable the incorporation of simulations into day-to-day engineering practice and thereby shrink the gap between real and virtual developing environments. With this in mind, the next chapter, "Simulation-Based Studies of Machine-to-Machine Communications," presents two showcases – of using the ultra-wide band (UWB) and the IEEE 802.15.4a-based radio technologies in M2M applications – highlighting the necessity of trustworthy simulation tools for M2M communications. A novel open-source simulation framework "Symphony" is presented at the end as a possible solution for bridging the gap between simulation and real-world deployment.

Important participants in making M2M systems widely used and applicable in numerous real-life scenarios are the standardization organizations, which develop technical specifications addressing the need for a common M2M service layer, realized through various hardware and software implementations. The next chapter, "Communication and Security in Machine-to-Machine Systems," presents current M2M standards and architectures with the focus on communication and security issues, while also discussing current and future research efforts addressing important open issues both with respect to aspects not covered by the current standards and in relation to research proposals, which could be integrated in the future versions of the M2M standards. A scheme that enables a unique identification of heterogeneous devices regardless of the technology used is also presented by the authors.

Continuing with security aspects, the final chapter, entitled "MHT-Based Mechanism for Certificate Revocation in VANETs," introduces a public-key certificate revocation mechanism based on the Merkle hash tree (MHT), which allows for the efficient distribution of certificate revocation information in vehicular ad hoc networks (VANETs). Within the WiNeMO paradigm, this is another example involving M2M communications. The proposed mechanism allows each node, e.g., a road side unit or intermediate vehicle possessing an extended-CRL − created by embedding a hash tree in each certificate revocation list (CRL) − to respond to certificate status requests without having to send the complete CRL, thus saving bandwidth and time. The authors describe the main procedures of the proposed mechanism and also consider the related security issues.

The book editors wish to thank the reviewers for their excellent and rigorous reviewing work and their responsiveness during the critical stages to consolidate the contributions provided by the authors. We are most grateful to all authors who have entrusted their excellent work, the fruits of many years of research in each case, to us and for their patience and continued demanding revision work in response to the reviewers' feedback. We also thank them for adjusting their chapters to the specific book template and style requirements, completing all the bureaucratic but necessary paperwork, and meeting all the publishing deadlines.

July 2014

Ivan Ganchev
Marilia Curado
Andreas Kassler

Organization

Reviewers

Sergey Andreev	Tampere University of Technology, Finland
Francisco Barcelo-Arroyo	Universitat Politècnica de Catalunya, Spain
Boris Bellalta	DTIC, Universitat Pompeu Fabra, Spain
Vinicius Borges	Federal University of Goiás, Brazil
Torsten Braun	University of Bern, Switzerland
Raffaele Bruno	IIT-CNR, Italy
Koen De Turck	Ghent University, Belgium
Trcek Denis	University of Ljubljana, Slovenia
Desislava Dimitrova	University of Bern, Switzerland
Orhan Ermiş	Boğaziçi University, Turkey
Dieter Fiems	Ghent University, Belgium
Ivan Ganchev	University of Limerick, Ireland
Giovanni Giambene	University of Siena, Italy
Rossitza Goleva	Technical University of Sofia, Bulgaria
Krzysztof Grochla	Institute of Theoretical and Applied Informatics of PAS, Poland
Zoran Hadzi-Velkov	Ss. Cyril and Methodius University, The Former Yugoslav Republic of Macedonia
Toke Høiland-Jørgensen	Karlstad University, Sweden
Georgios Karagiannis	University of Twente, The Netherlands
Andreas Kassler	Karlstad University, Sweden
Solange Lima	University of Minho, Portugal
Ian Marsh	SICS, Sweden
Maja Matijasevic	University of Zagreb, Croatia
Jose Luis Muñoz	Universitat Politècnica de Catalunya, Spain
Dusit Niyato	Nanyang Technological University, Singapore
Máirtín O'Droma	University of Limerick, Ireland
Evgeny Osipov	Luleå University of Technology, Sweden
Andreas Pitsillides	University of Cyprus, Cyprus
Jacek Rak	Gdansk University of Technology, Poland
Veselin Rakocevic	City University London, UK
Laura Ricci	University of Pisa, Italy
Laurynas Riliskis	Luleå University of Technology, Sweden
Vasilios Siris	Athens University of Economics and Business/ ICS-FORTH, Greece
Martin Slanina	Brno University of Technology, Czech Republic
Enrica Zola	Universitat Politècnica de Catalunya, Spain

Contents

M2M Aspects of WiNeMO

Communications Models, Concepts and Paradigms

A New Techno-Business Model Based on a Personal IPv6 Address for Wireless Networks of Moving Objects

Ivan Ganchev[✉] and Máirtín O'Droma

Telecommunications Research Centre (TRC),
University of Limerick, Limerick, Ireland
{Ivan.Ganchev,Mairtin.ODroma}@ul.ie
http://www.trc.ul.ie

Abstract. A new techno-business model, based on a personal IPv6 (PIPv6) address embedded in an X.509v3 digital certificate, is described in this chapter. The new globally significant, network-independent PIPv6 address class will enable real number ownership and full anytime-anywhere-anyhow portability for future generations of wireless networks of moving objects, such as those in vehicular ad hoc networks (VANETs), mobile ad hoc networks (MANETs), and other types of ad hoc networks. The unique PIPv6 address of the network node (object) could serve as its long-term identity, and enable its advanced secure mobility and participation in the variety of evolving dynamic, fluid wireless mobile network scenarios. It can also serve enhanced authentication, authorization and accounting (AAA) functionality, through which commercially viable ad-hoc networking and open mesh-networking solutions are realizable. In these latter, a mobile node (object) acting as a gateway (or a relay) may offer (or facilitate) wireless Internet access services casually or persistently to other mobile nodes or objects and receive credits for this service. This solution is exactly the kind of incentivised one that is required for cooperative relaying over multiple hops, i.e., that available idle mobile nodes and objects are incentivised to operate and offer service as relay nodes for other objects which are trying to reach a gateway for access to specific or general telecommunications services, such as the Internet. The idle nodes may provide this access directly if that is possible or in a dynamic collaboration via a multi-hop link.

Keywords: Techno-business model · Personal IPv6 address · X.509 certificate · VANETs · MANETs · WiNeMO

1 Introduction

Many scenarios of evolving dynamic, fluid, wireless mobile networks have been conceived and described in the ESF "Wireless Networking for Moving Objects" (WiNeMO) COST IC0906 project (http://cost-winemo.org/index.html), [1].

© Springer International Publishing Switzerland 2014
I. Ganchev et al. (Eds.): Wireless Networking for Moving Objects, LNCS 8611, pp. 3–13, 2014.
DOI: 10.1007/978-3-319-10834-6_1

Within the context of this chapter and book we use the acronym WiNeMO as a communication paradigm which encompasses these scenarios and related concepts, ideas and solutions which have emanated within the studies in this project. The WiNeMO concept, therefore, envisages a framework and environment to advance the state-of-the-art concerning all networking aspects and scenarios of integrating moving objects of any kind into the 'Internet of the Future.' It concerns that evolution of the Internet where large numbers of autonomous wireless objects moving with diverse mobility and functional patterns and speeds while communicating via several radio interfaces simultaneously are incorporated [1].

Through standard communication protocols and unique addressing schemes, these objects should be able to interact with other objects in an autonomous way in order to provide information and services to the end users (e.g., object owners) [2]. Examples of such objects include robots, cars, unmanned aerial vehicles, smartphones and other personal devices, sensors, actuators, electronic tags, etc. The generic object communications profile is that any and every object may act as a networking node generating, relaying and/or absorbing data [1].

The WiNeMO paradigm encompasses the existing mobile ad hoc networks (MANETs), wireless mesh networks, vehicular ad hoc networks (VANETs), and some types of wireless sensor networks (WSN). The endpoint entities and network objects in these networks are typically organized according to the peer-to-peer (P2P) principle. Such nodes, or objects, then are equal and hence, peers, with equivalent capabilities and responsibilities to cooperate to achieve basic and balanced communication in the network, with benefits such as potential to increase the network performance perceived by the nodes. Each node may act both as consumer and provider of a communication service at the same time. Cooperation -and mechanisms used to achieve it- is one of the major issues in such networks.

The downside of such balanced communication interaction and collaboration among peers is the open potential for the opposite. As nodes are concerned primarily about their own benefits, cooperation and fairness cannot be guaranteed at the same time [3]. There is always possibility that some nodes will behave selfishly, maliciously, faultily or uncooperatively.

Further, this openness and balanced peer relationship has significant potential for security problems through the launching a variety of attacks by individual nodes or a groups of nodes operating in concert. Types of attacks include but are not limited to the following:

- *Sybil attacks*: This is where a node generates multiple identities for itself and pretends to be several nodes at the same time for its own benefit, e.g. to receive more requests for relaying/forwarding of packets of other nodes and gain more money/credit from them. This kind of behaviour, on the one hand, can undermine fairness which could have further consequences of disincentiving users to make their idle mobile devices available, and on the other hand could reduce the potential 'ad hoc' networking performance and throughput by reducing the visibility of idle and available objects, and hogging of traffic through a node which will become loaded. If the 'Sybil' nodes have malicious intentions which threaten security and privacy, the attacks take on a more serious character. To deter these types of attack, a registration system, with a certification authority, could be employed. Mobile nodes would register themselves with the authority in such a way that each node could only have one identity. Also, the authority could impose a minimum time period before a node may change its identity [4]. Authentication procedures with each node would be part of the standardized protocol exchange in the provision of services such as relay services. The outline of a scheme is proposed in the next section. However as in entering Internet sites, users, by the nature of them being balanced peers, will have, and will want to have, the last say on whether or not to use another node as a relay whether or not that node has acceptable certification. This would be quite the case in consumer-centric networking [5,6]. In subscriber-based networks such controls can be more stringently enforced.

- The *whitewashing attack* allows some mobile nodes (whitewashers) to leave and re-join the network just to get rid of all drawbacks - e.g. bad reputation, payment debt, etc. - accumulated under an old identify or to get extra benefits from a cooperation system that rewards newly joined nodes. Apart from adding to the overall network instability, these whitewashing nodes may also decrease the efficiency of the cooperative incentives used in the network by repeatedly getting the benefits of a blank state without being detected [4]. This type of node behaviour cannot be distinguished from the newcomers' behaviour unless the node identities are persistent over a long period of time. Further, the incentive to acquire a good standing for a node only providing service over a certain (long) period of cooperation in the network is not a satisfactory solution due to diminishing the initiative to participate in the network at all, especially for short transactions [4].

There are other security problems specific to the WiNeMO paradigm (e.g., misbehaviour, malicious attacks, etc.). With these also, the use of a proper *node identity* is very important as it could help identify the node that misbehaves or behaves suspiciously, or is responsible for launching a particular attack. This identity must persist long enough to cast the so called *shadow of the future*, i.e., to allow for repeated interactions and opportunities for cooperation in the future [4] and to facilitate the prevention or limiting the effect of some types of attacks, including those described above.

A brief history and the state-of-the-art of the node identity is provided in the next section.

The node identity management is a key ingredient for establishing a secure communication between networked objects along with the trust management. The aim is to enhance the level of trust between objects, which are 'friends' in the network [2]. The trust can be established by using a centralized trusted third party (as proposed in this chapter) or by using a distributed trust negotiation algorithm [1].

2 Node Identity

The idea of having a unique identification is not new. In 1995 the International Telecommunication Union's Telecommunication Standardization Sector (ITU-T) proposed a personal telephone number to be used for *unique user identification* irrespective of the terminal used as part of the ITU-T vision for Universal Personal Telecommunication (UPT) [7]. The concept of *node identifier*, e.g. [8], authors Chelius and Fleury, was proposed to support IP routing for ad hoc connectivity by uniting all physical-layer multi-hop topologies in a single multi-graph topology. The node identifier serves to unify a set of wireless interfaces and identify them as belonging to the same ad hoc node. It consists in a dynamic assignment of a new non-permanent IPv6 local-use unicast address which would serve as an ad hoc connector. However, the proposal for static, permanent, personal IPv6 address [9] gives more flexibility to set up and operate ad hoc networks because the node/object can use the same IP address in every case and in any communication scenario. Further, the commercial dimension and viability of ad hoc networking (as well as mesh networking e.g. in a transportation environment) can be realized and served through this personal address.

Another approach to *mobile node identifier* is treated in [10]. It arose as a direct response to the need of a Mobile IPv6 (MIPv6) node to identify itself using an identity other than the default home IP address during the first registration at the home agent. For this, a new optional data field within the mobility header of MIPv6 packets was defined. The proposal for personal IPv6 address [5,6,9] described in the next section, however, provides the opportunity for more flexible control over mobility/roaming, e.g. by end-to-end execution of handovers by users/end-nodes in collaboration with service providers, and independently of the access network providers, through the use of the multi-homed functionality of the Mobile Stream Control Transmission Protocol (mSCTP) [11]. Implicit here is a greatly multiplied functional capability and intelligence at the edge, i.e. in mobile devices, objects, service entities, etc.

The concept of using a personal address associated with a person instead of a device was considered in [12,13]. In [12] a networking model is proposed which treats the user's set of personal devices as a single logical entity. In effect individually or collectively they appear as a point of presence for this user to the rest of the Internet. All communication destined for that person is addressed to a unique identifier (a single IP address). This identifier is mapped to the actual device(s) preferred by the user in a particular scenario.

This idea of an invariant address was also proposed to identify users in [5,13]. That proposed in [5] is described in detail in the next section. In [13] the ideas of [12] are developed further, by re-iterating the driving principle that the external world does not need to know which particular user's device is used for communication, but needs to address "the person" involved in communication.

The main advantage of such a personal address, as described in [14], is that the correspondent node involved in a communication session sees at any time the same address, independently of the other node's/user's movements and the device currently utilized for communication. This way, any migration (handoff and/or session transfer) will be transparent to the remote application, which thus will not require any specific functionality. Additional flexibility could be to have a personal address being specific for each device, or even for each communication session and associated with the currently utilized device(s), in order to prevent the risk to use the same address in multiple contexts [14]. This however implies that, if the user sets up more than one communication session simultaneously with multiple other communication entities, s/he will need multiple personal addresses [14]. The proposal for a personal IPv6 address, described in the next section, caters for this flexibility.

The idea of personal address has evolved towards the user-centric paradigm where users play the leading roles - they are the session end-points, while their devices act as physical terminals only [14,15]. For this, Bolla et al. [15] proposes the use of static and invariant identifiers, in the form of Universal Resource Identifiers (URI), which are then translated into temporary personal addresses depending on the underlying network technology. In contrast to these schemes, the PIPv6 address proposal described in the next section is both network-independent and topology-independent.

3   Personal IPv6 (PIPv6) Address

The globally significant, network-independent, *personal IPv6 (PIPv6) address*, described here, was first proposed in [5] and later discussed in more details in [9]. It could be used as a long-term identity solution that can prevent impersonation, Sybil and other types of attacks, can help distinguish whitewashers from newcomers in WiNeMO, and be useful in schemes to deter security attacks. This static, permanent, PIPv6 address will give more flexibility to set up and operate these types of networks because a node (object) can use the same address (identity) in every case and in any communication scenario. In addition, the uniqueness of the PIPv6 address (managed and allocated by a global address supplier) will eliminate the need for duplicated address detection, which is compulsory in IPv6 networks with stateless address autoconfiguration (SLAAC) [8]. This could be useful in developing WiNeMO scenarios, where it would greatly simplify the establishment and functioning of a network without a need for IP address allocation by some authority, access network provider, etc., and with the possibility for each of the network nodes (objects) participating in separate IP-based service sessions over the network. As the PIPv6 address is network-independent, a new responsibility arises for the networks providing access service in that their infrastructure itself must provide some kind of delivery functionality to locate the node/object and deliver IP packets to it from the Internet [14]. Such a requirement can be satisfied by a number of different solutions.

A new IPv6 address class should be identified for this new PIPv6 address by appropriately assigned *class prefix*. Figure 1 shows a possible format, with the space including this field and three other fields, described below. A further small version field may also be advisable to allow greater restructuring flexibility into the future.

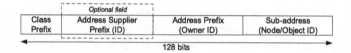

Fig. 1. The proposed personal IPv6 address class format

The *Address Prefix* is the primary field in the PIPv6 address which could be used to identify the owner (user) of the address. Having the length of the *Owner ID* field ranging from 34 to 37 bits will allow addressing of 17–137 billion owners. This may seem plenty in a world population context of 7 billion. However, perhaps a longer length, such as 40 bits, would be advisable to increase the duration before a long-lease address automatically reverts to the pool, and to reduce the cost (e.g., of enforcing leases), stress or necessity on returning addresses over a few generations. An additional *Sub-address* field is owner/user assignable and could be used by the owner for a range of sub-addresses (each for use in a separate transition scenario or developing wireless scenario). The assignable sub-address part may also be used as a node/object identifier to facilitate its smooth participation in MANETs, VANETs, and other WiNeMO types. The length of this field should be sufficiently large to allow addressing of hundreds of nodes/objects belonging to the same owner. For instance allowance can be made for narrowcast addresses which may find use in corporations and various community and social groupings.

Key to any network-independent personal address is the prevention of duplicates, whether by accident or (malicious) design. A second issue is the eventual return of unused addresses or addresses whose use has ceased or become defunct. In the case of the PIPv6 address proposal, this could be achieved by a centralized purchased scheme through authorized address suppliers, each of which owning a portion/subset of this new IP address class' space and identified by an optional *Address Supplier ID* field and/or by characteristics in the *Owner ID* field in the address. The selling of PIPv6 addresses within a 'renewable lease-based' system would also facilitate unused or defunct addresses being returned to the pool of available addresses.

Obtaining PIPv6 addresses would be a commercial transaction. In addition, as there is no reason why owners might not engage in address trading, the commercial legal arrangements should allow for this, e.g. ownership should be legally verifiable and transferable without difficulty. Perhaps this responsibility would ultimately fall to an IANA/ICANN type organization. Address trading would also incentivize use or return of addresses.

There would be privacy concerns with this permanent PIPv6 address employed by users for node/object identification and addressing, authentication, authorization and network access admission. These reflect on possible compromise of privacy related to the potential for tracking of, and gathering statistics about, a user/node/object as s/he/it moves through different locations. However, some of the existing mechanisms for privacy protection, c.f. [10], may still be used in this case, e.g., encrypting the traffic at the data link layer, encrypting the IP traffic, use of temporary and changing "pseudonyms" as identifiers, etc.

There is also a need for this new PIPv6 address to be securely 'locked' to enable the user/node/object to be uniquely identified and authenticated during communication. This is a key attribute. It could be achieved by embedding the PIPv6 address into a X.509 public-key digital certificate [16]. The ITU-T's X.509 authentication framework defines a good model for strong secure authentication with a minimum number of exchanges. The authentication is performed through simple automatic exchange of X.509 digital certificates between communication parties (network nodes, objects, entities, etc.). It seems reasonable to employ the three-way option for mutual authentication, as it does not require the communication parties to have synchronized clocks. The exchange of certificates will enable trusted relationship and secure payment of (micro) transactions in WiNeMO. The extensions defined in the current version 3 of X.509 standard (X.509v3) provide methods for associating additional attributes to carry information unique to the owner of the certificate [16]. In particular, the *Subject Unique Identifier* field (Fig. 2), which allows additional identities (e.g. e-mail address, DNS name, IP address, URI etc.) to be bound to the owner, can accommodate the proposed PIPv6 address. This, however, must be clearly marked as a critical X.509v3 extension in order to be used in a general context. Because the *Subject Unique Identifier* is definitively bound to the public key, all parts of it (including the PIPv6 address) will be verified by the certificate authority (CA).

A universal X.509-based Consumer Identity Module (CIM) card is proposed in, through which an owner would use his/her PIPv6 address with whatever mobile device s/he chooses and through which the usage of services may be paid. Through the relevant CAs' public key infrastructures (PKIs), the validity of the certificates of all parties to a transaction may be mutually checked as required. To achieve this in the formally infrastructure-less wireless networks, such as the voluntary dynamic and temporary composition of an ad hoc chain of wireless relay nodes to serve specific end nodes (objects) gaining 'short-stay' access to a legacy access network, each party must supply its complete chain of certificates up to the root, or at least may be required to so provide their certificates in order to be included as one of the relay nodes.

The CIM card can be developed by using the Java Card technology [17], which provides highly secure, market-proven, and widely deployed open-platform architecture for the rapid development and deployment of smart card applications meeting the real-world requirements of secure system operations. The Java card may typically be a plastic card containing an embedded chip. A possible CIM card architecture is described in [9].

4   Generic Communication Scenario

A generic WiNeMO communication scenario using PIPv6 addresses is depicted in Fig. 3. The scenario imagines a mobile node (object) seeking and finding a gateway (GTW) among or through those mobile nodes (MNs) available to it as

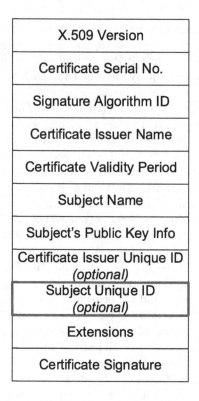

Fig. 2. The X.509v3 certificate format

relays either directly or through other mobile nodes. The GTW is defined as an access point to connect directly to the Internet and through it - to a particular correspondent node (CN). First a mutual authentication procedure is executed-of the object and all other supporting relay nodes in this WiNeMO scenario, including the GTW; this along with any other procedures to enable authorization and admission of and by each of the nodes in this cooperative ad hoc network. This being successfully completed, the GTW decides to allow (or not) the object to use its Internet connection for a particular period of time. Then the GTW accepts the PIPv6 address supplied by the object and stores it in its Network Address Translation (NAT) table along with the corresponding IPv4 address to be used for this new Internet session for the duration of communication between the object and CN. Then GTW confirms to the object that it may start using the Internet for communication with CN. After that, following the standard Network Address Translation IPv6 to IPv4 (NAT64) procedure, each IPv6 packet originating from the object will carry its PIPv6 address in the Source Address field. When this packet reaches the GTW, the PIPv6 address of the object (used only locally) will be translated into the IPv4 address allocated by the GTW for global routing on the Internet. In other words, as the IP traffic passes from this WiNeMO to the Internet, the GTW translates 'on the fly' the source

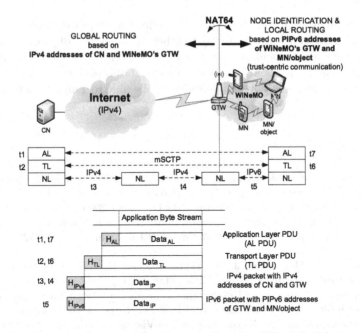

Fig. 3. A generic communication scenario using PIPv6v6 addresses

address in each packet from the PIPv6 address of the particular object engaged in communication to (one of) its IPv4 address(es). The reverse address translation is performed in the opposite direction of communication.

5   Conclusion

A new personal IPv6 (PIPv6) address class together with a secure universal Consumer Identity Module (CIM) card utilizing X.509v3 digital certificate security have been considered in this chapter for use in wireless networks of moving objects (WiNeMO). The new globally significant, network-independent PIPv6 address class will enable real number ownership and full anytime-anywhere-anyhow [5,6] portability for WiNeMO scenarios. It is proposed and envisaged that in future generations of wireless networks, nodes (objects) will have a unique PIPv6 addresses. These will serve also as a means of long-term node identity in the network.

The chapter has described a novel techno-business model, based on this PIPv6 address concept. This model will enable the object to use its PIPv6 address for advanced mobility, i.e. in ways not presently possible, and will enable continued participation in various evolving WiNeMO scenarios. An example of a generic communication scenario has been described here.

Through an enhanced authentication, authorization and accounting (AAA) functionality, this PIPv6-based model has also the potential to enable commercially viable ad-hoc and/or open mesh-networking solutions, where a mobile node (object) acting as a gateway (or relay) may offer (or facilitate) wireless Internet access services casually or persistently to other mobile nodes/objects and be paid for this service, e.g. through a third-party AAA service provision [5,6]. Realization of this would bring about a radical change to the access network business, and add many new ways whereby mobile users will be able to gain access to network services.

References

1. WiNeMo Members: Memorandum of understanding for the implementation of a European Concerted Research Action IC0906 Wireless Networking for Moving Objects (WiNeMO), Brussels, Belgium, 14 December 2009
2. Atzori, L., Iera, A., Morabito, G.: From 'smart objects' to 'social objects': the next evolutionary step of the internet of things. IEEE Commun. Mag. **52**(1), 97–105 (2014)
3. Buchegger, S., Mundinger, J., Le Boudec, J.-Y.: Reputation systems for self-organized networks. IEEE Technol. Soc. Mag. **27**(1), 41–47 (2008)
4. Buchegger, S., Chuang, J.: Encouraging cooperative interaction among network entities: incentives and challenges. In: Fitzek, F., Katz, M. (eds.) Cognitive Wireless Networks: Concepts, Methodologies and Visions Inspiring the Age of Enlightenment of Wireless Communications, pp. 87–108. Springer, Amsterdam (2007)
5. O'Droma, M., Ganchev, I.: Toward a ubiquitous consumer wireless world. IEEE Wirel. Commun. **14**(1), 52–63 (2007)
6. O'Droma, M., Ganchev, I.: The creation of a ubiquitous consumer wireless world through strategic ITU-T standardization. IEEE Commun. Mag. **48**(10), 158–165 (2010)
7. ITU-T Recommendation F.851: Universal Personal Telecommunication (UPT) Service Description - Service Set, 1 February 1995. http://www.itu.int/rec/T-REC-F.851-199502-I/en
8. Chelius, G., Fleury, E.: RFC Draft: IPv6 addressing architecture support for mobile ad hoc networks, September 2002. http://www1.ietf.org/mail-archive/web/manet/current/msg00923.html
9. Ganchev, I., O'Droma, M.: New personal IPv6 address scheme and universal CIM card for UCWW. In: Proceedings of the 7th International Conference on Intelligent Transport Systems Telecommunications (ITST 2007), Sophia Antipolis, France, pp. 381–386, 6–8 June (2007)
10. Patel, A., et al.: RFC 4283. Mobile Node Identifier Option for Mobile IPv6 (MIPv6), November 2005. http://www.networksorcery.com/enp/default0802.htm
11. Ma, L., Yu, F.R., Leung, V.C.M.: Performance improvements of mobile SCTP in integrated heterogeneous wireless networks. IEEE Trans. Wireless Commun. **6**(10), 3567–3577 (2007)
12. Kravets, R., Carter, C., Magalhaes, L.: A cooperative approach to user mobility. Comput. Commun. Rev. **31**(5), 57–69 (2001)
13. Niemegeers, I.G., Groot, S.M.H.D.: Research issues in ad-hoc distributed personal networking. Wirel. Pers. Commun. **26**(2–3), 149–167 (2003)
14. Bolla, R., Rapuzzi, R., Repetto, M.: A user-centric mobility framework for multimedia interactive applications. In: 2009 6th International Symposium on Wireless Communication Systems, pp. 293–297, 7–10 September 2009

15. Bolla, R., Rapuzzi, R., Repetto, M.: User-centric mobility for multimedia communications: experience and user evaluation from a live demo. In: International Symposium on Performance Evaluation of Computer and Telecommunication Systems (SPECTS), pp. 210–217, 11–14 July 2010
16. Housley, R., Polk, W., Ford, W., Solo, D.: Internet X.509 public key infrastructure certificate and certificate revocation list (CRL) profile. In: Internet Engineering Task Force (IETF), United States, RFC 3280, April 2002. http://tools.ietf.org/html/rfc3280
17. (U)SIM Java Card Platform Protection Profile Basic and SCWS Configurations: Evolutive Certification Scheme for (U)SIM cards (PU-2009-RT-79) (2010)

Information-Centric Networking in Mobile and Opportunistic Networks

Carlos Anastasiades[1]([✉]), Torsten Braun[1], and Vasilios A. Siris[2]

[1] Institute of Computer Science and Applied Mathematics, University of Bern,
Neubrückstrasse 10, 3012 Bern, Switzerland
{anastasiades,braun}@iam.unibe.ch
[2] Department of Informatics, Athens University of Economics and Business,
Patission 76, 10434 Athens, Greece
vsiris@aueb.gr

Abstract. Information Centric Networking (ICN) as an emerging paradigm for the Future Internet has initially been rather focusing on bandwidth savings in wired networks, but there might also be some significant potential to support communication in mobile wireless networks as well as opportunistic network scenarios, where end systems have spontaneous but time-limited contact to exchange data. This chapter addresses the reasoning why ICN has an important role in mobile and opportunistic networks by identifying several challenges in mobile and opportunistic Information-Centric Networks and discussing appropriate solutions for them. In particular, it discusses the issues of receiver and source mobility. Source mobility needs special attention. Solutions based on routing protocol extensions, indirection, and separation of name resolution and data transfer are discussed. Moreover, the chapter presents solutions for problems in opportunistic Information-Centric Networks. Among those are mechanisms for efficient content discovery in neighbour nodes, resume mechanisms to recover from intermittent connectivity disruptions, a novel agent delegation mechanisms to offload content discovery and delivery to mobile agent nodes, and the exploitation of overhearing to populate routing tables of mobile nodes. Some preliminary performance evaluation results of these developed mechanisms are provided.

Keywords: Information-Centric Networking · Mobility · Opportunistic networks

1 Introduction and Motivation

Information Centric Networking (ICN) is a new paradigm for the Future Internet architecture given that the Internet is increasingly used for the dissemination and retrieval of information rather than just interconnecting a pair of particular end-hosts. The most important features of ICN are the usage of content or application-level names/identifiers for addressing, the possibility to cache content

© Springer International Publishing Switzerland 2014
I. Ganchev et al. (Eds.): Wireless Networking for Moving Objects, LNCS 8611, pp. 14–30, 2014.
DOI: 10.1007/978-3-319-10834-6_2

in routers as well as the integrated content discovery mechanisms. Employing content-awareness in the network can help to address a number of limitations in the current Internet's architecture, including mobility support, efficient content distribution and routing, and security.

While most research work investigated the use of ICN in wired networks [1–3] ICN provides some interesting and beneficial features for wireless networks, especially when users are mobile and have rather temporary connectivity with the Internet and between each other, as in opportunistic networking scenarios. This chapter introduces and motivates the usage of ICN in mobile and opportunistic networks and reviews the basic ICN approaches proposed so far. Name resolution (content discovery) and content transfer can be separated as proposed in decoupled ICN approaches or might be integrated as in coupled ICN approaches, each having implications for mobility support.

Related work on ICN and especially for mobile and opportunistic networks is discussed in Sect. 2. ICN concepts nicely support mobility of content consumers, i.e., receivers of content, since no receiver host address information must be updated in case of receiver mobility as it is required in today's Internet mobility solutions such as Mobile IP. However, if content is moving, e.g., when moved from one source to another, or when the source of content is moving, e.g., when content is stored on mobile users' smart phones or on devices located in cars, there are certain issues to be solved. Solutions to address the source mobility problem are extensions of ICN routing protocols, indirection of content discovery messages, and resolution of location-independent identifiers. These are discussed in Sect. 3.

In opportunistic networking scenarios connectivity and contact durations between devices are unpredictable and intermittent. To avoid beaconing and establishing connections among specific end systems, content discovery messages can be transmitted (possibly using broadcast) to find relevant content at neighbour nodes. Section 4 discusses various options for efficient discovery of content on neighbour nodes as well as other issues related to content transfer. To overcome possible connectivity disruptions between devices, we propose to integrate resume functions into ICN, which allows content transfer to continue after connectivity disruptions. Moreover, the chapter discusses the idea of delegating content discovery and retrieval to agents. Also, it investigates the use of unicast and multicast/broadcast for content transfer. Finally, Sect. 5 summarizes and concludes the chapter.

2   Information-Centric Networking

2.1   Coupled and Decoupled ICN Approaches

Information-Centric Network (ICN) architectures depart from the current Internet's host-centric end-to-end communication paradigm and adopt an information (or content) centric communication paradigm, where information objects, rather than host end-points, are named. Receivers (or subscribers) request information objects by their names and the network is responsible for locating the sources (or publishers) of the information objects and transporting the objects from the sources to the receivers. Three key functions of Information-Centric Networks are the following:

- **Name resolution** involves resolving (or matching) the name of an information object with its location or its source. Name resolution can be performed in a hop-by-hop manner or by an independent name resolution system. The name resolution system can have a hierarchical structure: subscribers and publishers communicate with a local name resolution server, which in turn communicates with other name resolution servers if necessary.
- **Topology management/routing** involves determining a path from the source to the receiver. Different domains can implement different topology management and routing procedures. Similar to the name resolution system, topology management can be performed in a hierarchical manner.
- **Forwarding** involves moving information from the sources to the receivers along the determined path. Possible forwarding mechanisms include hop-by-hop forwarding based on end-system IDs, label switching, and forwarding based on a series of link identifiers selected by the source.

Different ICN proposals involve a different degree of coupling between name resolution and routing/forwarding [4]. At one extreme (tight coupling), the same network nodes perform both functions in an integrated manner. This is the approach followed by Content Centric Networking (CCN)/Named Data Networking (NDN) [5,6]: Receivers express their request for content using Interest packets, which serve for content discovery. Such Interest packets are routed based on the name of the requested content, using longest prefix matching, either to the source that contains a data packet with the requested name or to an intermediate network node that has cached the requested data packet. Once the data packet is found, it is returned to the requester following the reverse path of the received Interest packet.

At the other extreme (decoupled), the functions are implemented in different network nodes and/or different modules. This is the approach followed by architectures such as PSIRP/PURSUIT's PSI (Publish-Subscribe Internet) [4,7] and 4ward/SAIL's NetInf architecture [1,8]. With such an approach, the name resolution system is independent and operates as an overlay of the routing/forwarding network, which transfers content from the source to the receiver. This has similarities with the current Internet's Domain Name System. Proposals such as DONA [3] and COMET [9] describe overlay solutions that run on top of an IP infrastructure, hence inherit IP's routing and forwarding functionality. A more detailed survey and comparison of the similarities and differences of the most important ICN proposals can be found in [4].

Decoupling the resolution and routing/forwarding functions allows more flexibility in where and which entities implement this functionality. This flexibility can allow existing or new mechanisms, e.g., for routing and forwarding, to be used in different domains that have specific characteristics or restrictions, such as satellite networks or home networks. Decoupling allows usage of separate paths for control traffic and data traffic. Moreover, data transfer can utilize multiple paths (multi-path) from one or more information publishers (multi-source) to a subscriber. Another property of decoupling name resolution and routing/forwarding is that the resolution layer can employ a receiver-driven (pull-based) communication mode, whereas the routing/forwarding layer can employ either a receiver-driven (pull-based) or sender-driven (push-based) communication mode. This, for example, allows a receiver to declare (through a subscription message) its interest in receiving future content related to some content category. Once the publishers (sources) create such content, they can send it (push-based) to the receiver without requiring requests for each individual content object. On the other hand, when resolution and routing/forwarding are coupled, then implementation of sender-driven (push-based) functionality requires either overlay solutions to inform receivers of the availability of content, or polling-based solutions where the receivers periodically poll the sources for new content. It is interesting to note that for architectures that employ a similar level of coupling between name resolution, topology control/routing, and forwarding, the same mechanisms and algorithms can be implemented for the same functionality.

2.2   Related Work in ICN for Mobile and Opportunistic Networks

CCN in mobile networks has already been the subject of several studies [10]. Early works investigated the applicability of existing MANET routing protocols for mobile CCN based on analytical models [11]. A hierarchical CCN routing scheme based on distributed meta information has also been implemented [12]. The Listen First, Broadcast Later (LFBL) [13] algorithm limits forwarding of interests at every node based on its relative distance to the content source. However, all these works assume continuous network connectivity and do not consider intermittent connectivity.

Opportunistic and delay-tolerant communication has been investigated extensively in the last decade. The Bundle Protocol [14] describes a delay-tolerant protocol stack to support intermittent connectivity. The destinations of messages, i.e., bundles, are identified by endpoint identifiers. To receive bundles, nodes can register in endpoint identifiers and these registrations are exchanged when two devices meet. Thus, bundles are transmitted in bursts and stored locally until the next forwarding opportunity arises. Haggle [15] describes a data-centric network architecture for opportunistic networks. The platform uses device discovery to establish point-to-point connections between devices. Data is described by meta data composed of multiple key words. Users express and forward interests containing keywords when connected to other devices. All data objects that match the keywords are forwarded to the requesting node by a push-based dissemination model. The successor project of Haggle, called SCAMPI [16], developed a service-oriented platform for mobile and pervasive networks, which benefits from opportunistic communication paradigms. Routing and opportunistic networking is hidden from applications through a middleware. It contains a communication subsystem, which is responsible for detecting neighbouring peers and exchanging messages. Direct peer sensing mechanisms are applied to discover peers and services within communication range based on IP multicast or static IP discovery. To discover nodes further away, the platform defines transitive peer discovery, where nodes exchange information about other nodes they have discovered. Routing of messages in the network is based on discovered peers and controlled by the routing subsystem.

CCN can support opportunistic networking without device (or peer) discovery because data transmissions are based on content names available in the current environment. Investigations [17] already identified the potential of CCN for delay-tolerant networking (DTN). The effectiveness of CCN for opportunistic one-hop content discovery has been investigated in an earlier work [18]. There are also related efforts in creating a new content-centric opportunistic networking architecture inspired by CCN [19].

3   Mobility Support in Information-Centric Networking

This section considers mobility support in ICN architectures in more detail. Mobility support is particularly important within the context of moving objects and things that are network connected. Receiver mobility and sender mobility are discussed separately, since they have different requirements and can involve different mechanisms.

3.1   Receiver Mobility

ICN architectures promote a receiver-driven information request model, where nodes receive only the information which they have requested or subscribed to. This is in contrast to the current Internet's model, where the sender has full control of the data he/she can send. Additionally, ICN's request model and content transfer from sources to receivers is connectionless, in contrast to TCP's connection-oriented (stateful) end-to-end control, which involves location-dependent addresses. Both the above features allow mobile devices that have changed their positions (network attachment points) to simply re-issue requests for information objects they did not receive while they were connected to their previous attachment point or while they were disconnected [20]. Hence, delay/disruption tolerant operation in addition to mobility is supported without requiring cumbersome solutions such as Mobile IP.

Specific schemes for enhancing mobility support have also been proposed in the context of ICN architecture proposals. In rendezvous-based schemes the rendezvous service has the major role. The (moving) receiver upon re-location and re-attachment to the network needs to re-issue a subscription for the content he/she did not receive due to their movement. Upon receipt of this subscription the rendezvous service returns the new path for connecting the receiver with a sender (either the same or a new one). Depending on the service (streaming or file transfer), lost packets (those that were being transferred during the hand-off) may need to be recovered or not. If packets need to be recovered, then the new subscription may also contain a hint about the last successfully received chunk of content, which the rendezvous service communicates to the newly chosen source, so that lost packets can be recovered. If it is useless to recover packets (e.g., if the subscription is for a real-time video stream and the play-out time for the frames contained in the lost packets has passed) then the rendezvous service simply returns the new path from the source to the re-located receiver. Some approaches, such as CCN/NDN, require that subscriptions (or interests) have to be issued for every packet, so in this case the receiver upon re-attaching to a new location simply re-issues the non-satisfied interests. In addition to the inherent support for mobility, additional mechanisms, such as proactive caching [21], can be further utilized to reduce the delay for obtaining time-critical information.

3.2   Source Mobility

Unlike receiver mobility, source mobility in ICN architectures requires additional mechanisms. In particular, the following two issues need to be addressed with source mobility: (a) find the source's location, which includes finding the source's location in the beginning of communication but also tracking the source when it moves, and (b) session continuity, which involves reducing the impact of mobility, such as reducing disconnection periods, minimizing/avoiding data loss during mobility, and supporting graceful disconnection and fast reconnection.

How source mobility can be supported depends on whether name resolution and data transfer are coupled or decoupled. In CCN/NDN, where name resolution and data transfer are coupled, receivers issue Interest messages, which contain the name of the requested content; these Interest messages are routed towards the source based on FIB (Forward Information Base) entries. If the source changes its location, it will need to issue a new prefix announcement from its new location. These prefix announcements are distributed (e.g., flooded using a link state protocol) to other CCN/NDN nodes in the network, which update their FIB tables. Note that the above approach can have some similarities with service advertisement and discovery; specifically in wireless networks, the broadcasting nature of the wireless channel can be used to advertise services locally. Nevertheless, updating routing information in large networks with multiple domains requires mechanisms for disseminating location information across multiple domains.

On the other hand, in architectures where name resolution and data transfer are decoupled, source mobility requires updating the resolution information, which maps names to locators. In cases where multiple sources offer the same content as the source that moved, the rendezvous service may also choose to assign some (or all) of the receivers that were served by the source that moved to other new sources that are closer to the receivers.

There are three approaches for supporting source mobility: (1) the routing-based approach, (2) the indirection approach, and (3) the resolution approach.

The *routing-based approach* involves updating the routing tables that are used to forward information requests, as in the case of CCN/NDN. Issues with this approach include convergence time and scalability of the routing tables. The approach can be enhanced to reduce the routing convergence time by using a proactive prefix advertisement scheme, similar to the proposal in [22]. Additionally, if mobility prediction information exists, then proactive actions along the lines of [21] can be utilized.

The *indirection approach* is based on home agents, which forward interests to the mobile device and are updated with the mobile device's current point of attachment, similar to Mobile IP. The approach also requires agents in the visited network and location-based identifiers. An advantage of this approach is that there is no overhead due to a resolution phase. A disadvantage is that all requests and data packets go through the home agent. Moreover, home agents would require names with topological/location information to be able to forward requests to the mobile source.

The *resolution approach* involves a separate resolution phase: the receiver first sends a request containing the name of the requested content; it gets a response containing the location-dependent name or address to use for obtaining the requested content. Hence, this involves a location-identity split and has similarities with HIP (Host Identity Protocol) [23]. The resolution approach adds overhead, which however is limited to the first packet. Also, this approach requires some form of agent in the visited network. If a name resolution function already exists, then the approach can be implemented by updating the name to locator binding that is used for resolution. On the other hand, if a resolution system does not exist, such as in CCN/NDN, then a resolution phase can be added in two ways: use names that contain location/topology information [22] or add a locator field in Interest messages [24].

The source mobility solution depends on whether the particular ICN architecture supports only names (location independent identifiers) or both names and locators (location or topology dependent addresses). If only names are supported, then only the routing-based approach can be applied. If names are generic, then some form of location dependence can be added to names, e.g. exploiting some hierarchical structure of names [22]. In this case, the indirection approach can be applied. However, note that the addition of location dependence to names can have implications to mechanisms such as in-network caching and content-aware processing, which assume that names are location independent. If both names and locators exist, as advocated by recent proposals [2], then the resolution approach offers higher flexibility.

4   ICN in Opportunistic Networks

Opportunistic networking defines communication in challenged networks, where connectivity and contact durations between devices are unpredictable and intermittent. The main goal is to exploit contact opportunities between users to support best-effort content and service interactions when fixed network infrastructures may not be available. Based on exchanged beacons, users detect neighbouring devices as communication opportunities and need to connect to neighbours individually to perform content discovery and file transmissions. ICN can support opportunistic networking because all communication can be performed inside the local network environment. No device discovery is required, because content availability may be independent of neighbouring devices. Mechanisms for content discovery are described in Subsect. 4.1, whereas content transfer techniques are discussed in Subsect. 4.2. All investigations are done using a CCN/NDN implementation based on the CCNx software [25].

4.1   Content Discovery

Nodes need to transmit requests, i.e., Interest messages, to find available Data. Therefore, transmissions are only performed if there is a node interested in it. If a requester moves within the network, the recipients of Interest messages will change and new content sources or forwarders are discovered automatically. Content discovery is performed using multicast to quickly detect nearby available content sources. If a multicast Interest message is not answered by a neighbouring node, no matching content is available, which - in terms of content retrieval - is equivalent to the unavailability of neighbouring devices. Content discovery is required in distributed environments without centralized directories to learn about available content or service options without demanding the content or service completely. In the following we describe two different discovery approaches and an extension to ensure flexibility of content discovery.

Discovery Algorithms. In opportunistic ICN, we assume that content names follow a hierarchical structure comprising multiple name components. Each data file consists of one or several segments similar to chunks in Bittorrent. The hierarchical name structure may not indicate the location of content objects and content may be stored on one or multiple hosts. The first name component may be based on the identity of a content publisher and the following components are arbitrarily chosen based on the publisher's naming scheme. We designed two discovery mechanisms: *Enumeration Request Discovery* and *Regular Interest Discovery* [18].

Enumeration Request Discovery (ERD) requires the expression of enumeration requests, which are addressed to local and remote repositories only. A name enumeration request for a certain prefix /A requests next level components that are available in a repository, e.g., {*a1, b1, c1, d1*}. To discover the entire name space, the algorithm starts from the top of the name tree with the shortest possible prefix and sequentially moves down to the leaves by extending the prefix with the discovered name components, e.g., /A/a1 in the next step. At every iteration and level, the requesting user receives a list of available next-level components at a specific repository. We assume that mobile repositories are not synchronized among each other. Therefore, the requesting user has to address each repository that holds content with a specific prefix separately until no information is received anymore, i.e., timeout event.

Regular Interest Discovery (RID) is based on recursive expression of regular Interest messages. The user expresses an Interest in a prefix */A* and receives the first data segment of a content object in response, e.g., */A/B/C/segment_0*. Although this leads to overhead because only the content name and no data is required, it is still more efficient than retrieving all segments in complete file downloads. The requester knows the complete name of a content file at the leaf of the tree after only one content request and can sequentially browse its way up to the root. In contrast to ERD, where every component list is unique due to the repository that created it, although it may contain the same information, duplicate content transmissions can be identified and suppressed.

Evaluations have shown that multicast discovery is advantageous in wireless environments, because it addresses multiple content sources simultaneously. If nearby content sources provide different diverse content, a single discovery Interest can pull multiple content objects at the same time. Only exact duplicates of the same content are suppressed. ICN systems enforce one-to-one relations between Interest and Data messages. However, in wireless networks it is beneficial to keep unsolicited content for a short time in the cache so that it can be retrieved in follow-up requests resulting in fewer transmitted messages and higher discovery efficiency.

Two delay values are important for multicast discovery: *transmission delay (TD)* and *requesting delay (RD)*. The transmission delay defines the transmission interval $[\text{TD}, 3 \cdot \text{TD}]$ within which each host randomly selects a time to reply with a content object. Once scheduled, the content object stays in the senders' send queue until the transmission delay is due enabling duplicate suppression by removing overheard content from the send queue. Larger TD values result in fewer collisions and duplicate content transmissions but increase discovery time. However, even large TD values result in non-negligible duplicate content transmissions. To reduce duplicate content transmissions to nearly zero, a requesting delay of $2 \cdot TD$ is required. The requesting delay defines the delay between subsequent Interest requests and equals the maximum difference in the transmission interval $[\text{TD}, 3 \cdot \text{TD}]$ to ensure that another response is received and can be found in the cache without additional re-expression. If a requester transmits the next request quicker, not all answers from other content sources may have been received yet. If the next Interest arrives at a content source just after it has answered the previous request, the same content object will be returned since content sources do not memorize recently transmitted content.

ERD is independent of the number of content objects but it depends on the number of content sources and may, therefore, be inefficient in mobile networks where neighbours change frequently. Compared to RID, the ERD content lists of all repositories need to be processed and accumulated to know which content names are available. If all hosts store the same content, ERD requires all nodes to request and process all content lists without learning anything new. RID is more efficient to detect small differences in collections, because it can ask specifically for new content: redundant information can be avoided via duplicate suppression. RID is also faster in finding content names in highly structured name spaces with many name components where ERD would require subsequent traversing through all name components until reaching the content objects. Therefore, a combination of both approaches may be promising: an initial RID request may quickly find the full name of a content object and subsequent ERD requests discover all available name components on the same level.

Alias Mapping. To support communication during short opportunistic contacts, it is important that nodes discover available resources quickly. The hierarchical name structure may not be flexible enough to support location-based discovery. Hereafter, we describe how CCN can be used to detect local services or content independently of the publisher that provides it but based on local context. This can be achieved with temporary broadcast names that can be mapped locally to available unique names, i.e., alias mappings.

Broadcast components can be temporarily used by many publishers to describe content, e.g., via */<content_description>/<node_type>/ <node_Id>/*, and are not bound to the public key of a specific unique publisher so that everybody can publish within the name space *content_description/node_type*. Published content objects are signed by the corresponding publishers. A sample data name that follows that structure is */temperature/sensors/sensor_A/*. If connectivity to sensor_A breaks, requesters can quickly find alternative sensors in the vicinity by shortening the prefix to */temperature/sensors/* addressing all nearby sensors that provide temperature.

Alias mappings map names that use broadcast components to unique names. To ensure flexibility in the content description, a content source may map multiple broadcast components to the same unique content name or a list of locally available unique names. For example, a sensor node may use the broadcast components */weather* and */temperature* for the same content. To identify redundant content transmissions for multicast and ensure efficient storage, name aliases link broadcast components to unique names in the form */node_Id/name*. Subsequently, the unique content name is used during data transmission enabling duplicate suppression because the same content can be identified.

4.2   Content Transfer

Content transmissions are only performed in response to a received Interest message. A requester needs to transmit Interests in every segment to receive the complete content. By that, content transmissions are only performed in the vicinity of an active requester. Received segments are first included in temporary cache (content store) and complete files are stored on persistent storage (repository). This subsection describes a cache extension for intermittently connected networks and introduce an agent-based approach that can be used if requester and content source would never meet or to increase content density. Finally, the benefits and disadvantages of multicast communication and overhearing are discussed.

Resume Functions for Intermittent Connectivity. During short opportunistic contacts and, hence, intermittent connectivity between content requesters and content sources, file transmissions may not be completed. If no alternative content sources are available, content is kept in the requester's cache until it can be completed and properly stored. Unfortunately, persistence of data in CCN caches is not guaranteed since they are limited in size and can be overwritten by other files depending on the cache replacement strategy. Caches are built upon high-speed memory to support quick forwarding. In delay-tolerant networking, memory speed is not important since delays between successive requests are high. Therefore, in case of disruptions, partial data can be stored on and loaded from secondary storage.

Content-centric overlays to existing DTN protocols such as the Bundle protocol would experience multiple drawbacks. First, multiple Interests would be required to obtain all segments. Since requesters do not know the file length until receiving the last segment, proactive transmission of Interests would be required. If Pending Interest Table (PIT) entries are valid for a long time as required in DTN networks, the PIT size would drastically degrade lookup performance. Second, long-living Interests prevent forwarding of similar Interests for the entire lifetime period even if the environment has changed and the content becomes available. Therefore, the Interest lifetime should be limited to a rather small value but Interests can be re-expressed periodically to account for changes in content availability.

Every segment is named individually with a segment number. Thus, disrupted downloads can be precisely resumed from where they were stopped. For every incomplete and aborted file, the received partial data is stored in the file *name.part* and the meta information in the file *name.meta*. The meta information includes name and version of the content, the segment number that is expected next, the file position in the partial file *name.part* and the publisher's public key digest. To avoid incomplete files that never get completed or storing data of real-time traffic, an expiration time indicates a timeout value after which the partial files can be deleted. The expiration time can be based on the *reception time* and the *freshnessSeconds* values of the first received segment. In case of real-time traffic, content would only be valid for a few seconds and no partial information would be stored. While strategies without resume operations may never be successful, resumed file transmissions result in constant effective transfer times independent of the time they where disrupted.

Evaluations on wireless mesh nodes showed that the processing and storage overhead is negligible and does not affect file transfers without disruptions in any way. If content sources are unknown, transfers need to be performed by multicast because no unicast addresses can be statically configured. Unfortunately, multicast transfer rates are considerably lower than unicast rates. Additionally, no MAC layer acknowledgements are transmitted during multicast communication. Thus, missing segments, e.g., due to collisions, are detected only after the Interest lifetime has passed and the Interest is re-expressed. However, since opportunistic communication is performed via one hop, the Interest lifetime can be decreased to a lower value to reduce retransmission delays. Evaluations have shown that this strategy can increase the multicast throughput by a factor of 7.2 without significantly increasing the number of transmitted messages [26].

Transfer Agents. In situations where a requester never meets a valid content source, it cannot request content. The proposed solution for this problem is agent-based content retrieval, where requesters can delegate content retrieval to agents, which retrieve content on behalf of the requesters. Communication exploits the agents' mobility. The approach comprises three phases. In the agent-delegation phase (phase I), the requester needs to find an agent and delegate content retrieval to it. In the content retrieval phase (phase II), the agent is looking for the content and retrieves it. In the notification phase (phase III) the requester asks available agents whether they retrieved the complete content. The requester can then retrieve the content from the agent node.

Phase I: Agent Delegation. If a requester cannot find the desired content in its environment, content retrieval can be delegated to an agent. In phase I, the requester finds and assigns an available agent based on a three-way handshake protocol. An agreement between requester and agent can be enforced by signing the exchanged Interest and Data messages with the sender's private key so that both nodes know the identity of each other. Because available agents in the neighbourhood are not known and can change, agent discovery and delegation is performed via multicast. The requester transmits first an *Exploration Interest* in the name space */ferrying/%C1.<namespace>~<param>*. Every agent application listens to Interests for */ferrying* followed by the *namespace* of the content to be found and optional additional parameters. Parameters may describe an area where content retrieval should be performed and agents can decide whether to respond based on locally collected mobility traces. Agents return an *Exploration Response*, which is a Data message including the requested prefix name and appending their */nodeId* at the end. Exploration Responses have short lifetimes of only a few seconds to avoid usage of old information from the cache. Since Exploration Interests are transmitted via multicast, they trigger potentially many answers and the requester can subsequently poll its content store for other responses. The requester can then create an agent list that includes all available agents and selects one from it for delegation. The requester assigns an agent by transmitting a *Delegation Interest* with the name prefix */ferrying/nodeId/%C1.<namespace>~<param>/rTime/groupId*. The nodeId is included right after the /ferrying prefix so that all nodes receive it and know whether they have been selected or not. *rTime* defines the remaining time, i.e., how long the requester is still interested in the content. This is an upper limit for content retrieval and after this time has passed, the agent does not look for the content anymore. *groupId* is a random nonce, which is created by the requester for every delegation in order to create a multicast group of agents. Assigned agents will listen to Interests with the */groupId* to receive notification requests from the requester in phase III.

Phase II: Content Retrieval. After receiving the Delegation Interest in Phase I, the agent registers the */namespace* to the multicast face using a lifetime based on *rTime*. Then, it can probe the environment for the availability of a content source similar as explained above for resumed transfers. An agent needs to replicate the received content including all CCN header information and original signatures so that the requester can verify that the content is authentic and produced by the original publisher. Therefore, as soon as connectivity to a content source has been detected, the agent delegates content retrieval to its mobile repository, which is an application running on the same device as the agent. The repository can then request all content objects via the multicast face. When the content transfer is complete, the agent can answer notification requests in phase III.

Phase III: Notification and Content Distribution. Since notifications can only be transmitted in response to Interests, the requester needs to request content notifications from any agent in the vicinity that has retrieved a content object completely. The pull-based approach is advantageous in mobile networks with multiple agents. Since only requesters periodically ask for notifications instead of multiple agents transmitting beacons, fewer notification messages need to be transmitted, i.e., only in the requester's vicinity. The Notification Request is an Interest message with the name */groupId/namespace* and is transmitted periodically until a *Notification Response* is received. By using the groupId, all assigned agents in the requester's transmission range receive the request and only agents that have completed phase II will respond by a Notification Response, which is a Data message that uses the same name as the Notification Request. The payload of the Notification Response comprises the current IP address of the mobile agent so that the requester can create a unicast face to the agent's mobile repository. The IP address can be viewed as locator of the content, which is not part of the routable prefix included in Interest packets. After the requester creates a new unicast entry with a short lifetime, the content can be requested directly via unicast from the mobile repository.

Evaluations on Android smart phones showed that the overhead for agent-based content retrieval compared to two hop forwarding can only be measured for very small files of 1 MB or less. For files larger than 4 MB, agent-based content retrieval resulted in 20 % higher throughput than with two-hop forwarding although content is stored at intermediate nodes on secondary storage but not in the cache. Because the maximum number of concurrently transmitted Interests is limited by the pipeline size, the overall transfer rate during multi-hop forwarding is limited by the slowest link. This means that transmissions via unicast on the first hop can never exceed multicast throughput on the second hop. With agent-based retrieval, content is transmitted subsequently via multicast and unicast over both hops, and, thus, every link can reach its maximum capacity. Moreover, multi-hop forwarding over multiple hops may not be possible (or only at very low rates) due to intermittent connectivity between the network nodes [27].

Multicast and Overhearing. CCN Forwarding is based on registered prefixes in the Forwarding Information Base (FIB). In opportunistic networks, forwarding tables cannot be configured statically and multicast communication is required to find suitable content sources. Since topologies can change, proactive exchange of all content information from all nodes may overload the network. In static networks or networks with limited mobility, delegating content retrieval to one-hop neighbours as described above may not be enough. In such situations, it is required to forward Interests over multiple hops to discover content on nodes, which are just outside the requesters' transmission range.

To enable wireless multi-hop communication in content-centric networks, it is required to configure two faces, one for receiving and one for transmitting. Interests can then be forwarded via alternating faces, e.g., via face 2 if received on face 1 and vice versa. Nodes that overhear content transmissions on a specific face can include this information in the FIB to forward Interests received from others to this face. To ensure that every node can always try to request content from its neighbours and, thus, enable overhearing of Data, Interests from local applications need to be forwarded via a multicast face if no matching FIB entry is configured, i.e., pass-through. If the content is available at a neighbour, the requester overhears the response and registers this information in the FIB. After that, the requester can also forward Interests received from other nodes to the content source via the newly created FIB entry. If the content is not available at neighbours, and neighbours have no FIB entry configured, they discard the received Interest to avoid unbounded forwarding. The registered FIB entry is valid for a limited time but is updated with successive content receptions.

To limit update and processing operations, only every *nth* received content object is processed. By using modulo operations on the received segment number included in the name, only the *1st* and every *(n+1)-th* content object during a transmission is processed not requiring the maintenance of additional state information. Processing the *1st* object is important since it indicates that a content source is available. Every other *nth* content object results in a FIB update. Entries that are not updated will expire automatically after time.

Evaluations on wireless mesh nodes have shown that processing overhead is only measurable for very small files and becomes negligible for files of 10 MB or larger. This is because in the beginning of every file transfer when receiving the first segment, a new FIB entry needs to be included in the FIB. Later, only life-time values of existing FIB entries need to be updated. During large file transfers, the ratio of entry updates vs. entry creations increases and, therefore, the relative processing overhead decreases. Since overhearing is a passive activity, it has no impact on the number of transmitted messages. Energy measurements revealed that a content source has the largest power consumption but the power over-head is only marginal. A requester with enabled overhearing functionality has a 1.3 % higher power consumption, because received prefixes need to be extracted and included in the FIB. The largest power overhead of 4.6 % is measured at a passive listener, which moves from a passive to a more active role when adding prefixes to the FIB. Compared to the unicast case, where passive nodes can stay in idle mode, the energy overhead of passive listeners not participating in the communication is 22 % higher.

However, overhearing can help to increase multi-hop throughput since retransmissions can be performed quicker from cache, similar to [28]. Additionally, in contrast to caches, which are limited in size and where cache replacement strategies make content disappear quickly, the RAM memory requirements for a content name is considerably lower than for the full content. For example, a 5 MB file may require 5.5 MB storage in the cache, i.e., including CCN headers and signatures, whereas the FIB entry requires only a few bytes depending on the length of the content name. Therefore, FIB entries based on overheard content names indicate a node whether it is worth to forward received Interests to a nearby content source if the cache entry has already been cleared. A combination of multicast discovery and subsequent unicast data transmissions after the content source has been identified may further improve energy efficiency and throughput but it requires modifications of the current CCNx daemon.

5   Conclusions and Outlook

This chapter discussed the use of ICN in mobile and opportunistic networks. Although ICN in such environments seems to have huge potential and benefits, there are still some problems and issues to be optimized. In mobile networks, the problem of source mobility is challenging and requires an appropriate solution for scenarios where content is located in mobile user devices or at devices deployed in vehicles. Moreover, the chapter discussed several problems in opportunistic network scenarios such as the problem of intermittent connectivity between devices or the problem that two devices might never be in contact to each other. Solutions such as suspending and resuming content transfer between devices and delegating content retrieval to agents have been proposed and preliminary evaluations in small-scale testbed scenarios have been performed.

References

1. Ahlgren, B., Aranda, P.A., Chemouil, P., Oueslati, S., Correia, L.M., Karl, H., Sollner, M., Welin, A.: Content, connectivity, and cloud: ingredients for the network of the future. IEEE Commun. Mag. **49**(7), 62–70 (2011)
2. Baid, A., Vu, T., Raychaudhuri, D.: Comparing alternative approaches for networking of named objects in the future internet. In: Proceedings of IEEE INFOCOM NOMEN Workshop, March 2012
3. Chun, B., Ermolinskiy, A., Kim, K.H., Shenker, S., Stoica, I.: A data-oriented (and beyond) network architecture. ACM SIGCOMM Comput. Commun. Rev. **37**(4), 181–192 (2007)
4. Xylomenos, G., Ververidis, C.N., Siris, V.A., Fotiou, N., Tsilopoulos, C., Vasilakos, X., Katsaros, K.V., Polyzos, G.C.: A survey of information-centric networking research. IEEE Commun. Surv. Tutor. **16**(2), 1024–1049 (2014)
5. Jacobson, V., Smetters, D.K., Thornton, J.D., Plass, M., Briggs, N., Braynard, R.: Networking named content. In: Proceedings of ACM CoNEXT, December 2009

6. Named Data Networking project. http://www.named-data.net/index.html
7. PURSUIT Project. http://www.fp7-pursuit.eu/PursuitWeb/
8. SAIL Project. http://www.sail-project.eu/
9. Chai, W.K., Wang, N., et al.: CURLING: content-ubiquitous resolution and delivery infrastructure for next-generation services. IEEE Commun. Mag. 49(3), 112–120 (2011)
10. Tyson, G., Sastry, N., Cuevas, R., Rimac, I., Mauthe, A.: A survey of mobility in information-centric networks. Commun. ACM 56(12), 90–98 (2013)
11. Varvello, M., Rimac, I., Lee, U., Greenwald, L., Hilt, V.: On the design of content-centric MANETs. In: 2011 Eighth International Conference on Wireless On-Demand Network Systems and Services (WONS), pp. 1–8, January 2011
12. Oh, S.Y., Lau, D., Gerla, M.: Content centric networking in tactical and emergency MANETs. In: IFIP Wireless Days (WD), pp. 1–5 (2010)
13. Meisel, M., Pappas, V., Zhang, L.: Listen first, broadcast later: topology-agnostic forwarding under high dynamics. In: Annual Conference of International Technology Alliance in Network and Information Science, London, pp. 1–8 (2010)
14. Scott, K., Burleigh, S.: Bundle protocol specification. RFC 5050, November 2007. http://tools.ietf.org/html/rfc5050
15. Su, J., Scott, J., Hui, P., Crowcroft, J., de Lara, E., Diot, C., Goel, A., Lim, M.H., Upton, E.: Haggle: seamless networking for mobile applications. In: Krumm, J., Abowd, G.D., Seneviratne, A., Strang, T. (eds.) UbiComp 2007. LNCS, vol. 4717, pp. 391–408. Springer, Heidelberg (2007)
16. Pitkänen, M., Karkkainen, T., Ott, J., Conti, M., Passarella, A., Giordano, S., Puccinelli, D., Legendre, F., Trifunovic, S., Hummel, K., May, M., Hegde, N., Spyropoulos, T.: SCAMPI: Service platform for soCial Aware Mobile and Pervasive computIng. In: Proceedings of Mobile Cloud Computing (MCC), Helsinki, Finland, August 2012
17. Tyson, G., Bigham, J., Bodanese, E.: Towards an information-centric delay-tolerant network. In: Proceedings of 2nd IEEE INFOCOM Workshop on Emerging Design Choices in Name-Oriented Networking (NOMEN), Torino, Italy, April 2013
18. Anastasiades, C., Uruqi, A., Braun, T.: Content discovery in opportunistic content-centric networks. In: Proceedings of 5th IEEE WASA-NGI, Clearwater, FL, pp. 1048–1056, October 2012
19. Batista, B., Mendes, P.: ICON - an information centric architecture for opportunistic networks, Poster. In: 2nd IEEE INFOCOM Workshop on Emerging Design Choices in Name-Oriented Networking (NOMEN), Italy, Torino, April 2013
20. Xylomenos, G., Vasilakos, X., Tsilopoulos, C., Siris, V.A., Polyzos, G.C.: Caching and mobility support in a publish-subscribe internet architecture. IEEE Commun. Mag. 50(7), 52–58 (2012)
21. Vasilakos, X., Siris, V.A., Polyzos, G.C., Pomonis, M.: Proactive selective neighbor caching for enhancing mobility support in information-centric networks. In: Proceedings of ACM SIGCOMM Workshop on Information-Centric Networking (ICN), Helsinki, Finland, pp. 61–66, August 2012
22. Ravindran, R., Lo, S., Zhang, X., Wang, G.: Supporting seamless mobility in named data networking. In: Proceedings of IEEE FutureNet V, Ottawa, Canada, June 2012
23. Moskowitz, R., Nikander, P.: Host Identity Protocol (HIP) Architecture. IETF RFC 4423, May 2006

24. Hermans, F., Ngai, E., Gunningberg, P.: Global source mobility in the content-centric networking architecture. In: Proceedings of 1st ACM workshop on Emerging Name-Oriented Mobile Networking Design - Architecture, Algorithms, and Applications (NoM), pp. 13–18, June 2012
25. CCNx. http://www.ccnx.org/
26. Anastasiades, C., Schmid, T., Weber, J., Braun, T.: Opportunistic content-centric data transmission during short network contacts. In: Proceedings of IEEE WCNC, Istanbul, Turkey, April 2014
27. Anastasiades, C., El Maudni, W., Braun, T.: Agent-based content retrieval for opportunistic content-centric networks. In: Proceedings of 12th WWIC, Paris, France, May 2014
28. Shen, S.-H., Gember, A., Anand, A., Akella, A.: Refactoring content overhearing to improve wireless performance. In: Proceedings of 17th ACM MobiCom, Las Vegas, USA, pp. 217–228, September 2011

User-Centric Networking: Cooperation in Wireless Networks

Rute Sofia[1]([✉]), Paulo Mendes[1], Huiling Zhu[2], Alessandro Bogliolo[3],
Fikret Sivrikaya[4], and Paolo di Francesco[5]

[1] COPELABS, University Lusófona, Building U First Floor,
Campo Grande 388, 1749-024 Lisbon, Portugal
{rute.sofia,paulo.mendes}@ulusofona.pt
[2] University of Kent, Canterbury, UK
h.zhu@ac.kent.uk
[3] University of Urbino, Urbino, Italy
alessandro.bogliolo@uniurb.it
[4] DAI-Labor, Technical University of Berlin, Berlin, Germany
fikret.sivrikaya@dai-labor.de
[5] Level7 S.p.A., Rome, Italy
paolo.difrancesco@level7.it

Abstract. This chapter addresses cooperation in wireless networks, based on the recent, self-organizing paradigm of User-centric Networking. In user-centric networking, the Internet user controls and carries networking wireless objects, usually located in customer premises. Some of such objects integrate functionality that is today part of the network core, such as mobility management, or resource management. The chapter provides notions and models concerning user-centric networking, as well as notions and models directed to user-centricity in the context of wireless network. We also include recent operational data derived from available user-centric networking pilots, as well as a market analysis with a wholesale model analysis example.

Keywords: User-centric networking · Wireless networks · Cooperative networking

1 Introduction

The flexibility inherent to wireless technologies is giving rise to new types of access networks and allowing the Internet to expand in a user-centric way. This is particularly relevant if one considers that wireless technologies such as *Wireless Fidelity (Wi-Fi)* are preferential solutions to complement Internet access broadband technologies, forming the last hop to the end-user. The density derived from such deployment, in particular in urban environments, must be considered when developing future Internet networking architectures. *User-centric networks (UCNs)* [1,2] are wireless networking architectures that integrate a self-organizing, even viral behavior in terms of connectivity models and topology, as these two aspects

© Springer International Publishing Switzerland 2014
I. Ganchev et al. (Eds.): Wireless Networking for Moving Objects, LNCS 8611, pp. 31–49, 2014.
DOI: 10.1007/978-3-319-10834-6_3

are developed based on the willingness of the Internet end-user to trade resources and services. In UCNs, users own devices that are part of the network. Therefore, UCNs exhibit a highly dynamic topological behavior, as the objects that compose the network roam frequently, and are in some cases solely controlled by the Internet end-user (e.g. a residential *Access Point*, AP; a smartphone).

In the networking models that UCNs integrate, the end-user is one of the Internet stakeholders, ceasing to simply be a consumer of Internet services (be it connectivity or content). The user becomes an active hop of the connectivity distribution chain. Such empowerment is a natural step of the Internet architectural evolution, as in Internet services, a similar paradigm shift has already emerged as a wave of open-source software and of new licensing models which culminated in the *Creative Commons (CC)* licensing. CC licensing allows authors to define the details of licensing rights regarding attribution, commercialization, derivative works, as well as distribution. In the beginning, CC licenses were used only in blogs or Web sites such as Flickr; today the Internet holds millions of sites whose content is protected under CC. This means that Internet users are no longer mere consumers.

The grassroots movement that was the basis for Web2.0 and also the key aspect in CC licensing is today being applied to the networking layers of the OSI protocol stack, e.g. via *Software Defined Networking (SDN)*, and thus create opportunities to further evolve the Internet value chain.

All of the paradigm shifts that we are witnessing are based upon a specific form of cooperation between end-users towards network access or towards Internet services/providers [3]. Cooperation, as well as cooperation incentives, is therefore modeling a new category of Internet community and impacting social and business behavior [4]. However, technical limitations of today's technologies, as well as a lack of understanding on how such micro-business models may evolve and impact current Internet wholesale models still undermine the potential impact of networks where the user becomes an active link in the provision chain. There is neither a clear modeling of incentives nor clear mechanisms to develop cooperation incentives on the fly, incentives which are prerequisite to the growth of such types of networks.

This chapter is focused on UCNs and explores features and concepts of cooperation in heterogeneous wireless networks. The chapter gives insight not only to the most technological advances of UCNs, as well as onto the market aspects concerning UCN usage. The chapter covers also different aspects concerning cooperation incentives, which are essential to assist UCNs in becoming adequately integrated into the existing infrastructures.

The work and research that the chapter is focused upon derives from the research developed in the context of the European Project ULOOP (*User-centric Wireless Local Loop*) [2]. ULOOP tackled several aspects of UCNs, both from a technical and socio-economic perspective, having as main goal to assist a robust and yet self-organizing deployment of UCNs.

The chapter is organized as follows. Section 2 goes over UCNs notions and terminology, covering the main functional blocks of a UCN model, as well as a socio-economic feasibility analysis for the ULOOP UCN model. Section 3 goes over cooperation aspects in UCNs, namely, incentives and crediting aspects, as well as explaining models. Section 4 is dedicated to operational aspects, and describes results of UCN live usage derived from the ULOOP pilot, which is a tool that is open to the global community. The chapter concludes in Sect. 5, providing a few guidelines for future work.

2 UCN Background

UCNs relate to a recent trend in spontaneous wireless deployments where individual users or communities of users share subscribed access in exchange of specific incentives. In literature, names that relate with the UCN concept are *personal hotspot, spontaneous user-centric networks.*

UCNs explore and integrate functional solutions to allow user-centric wireless (Wi-Fi) local loops to form and to develop in an autonomic and user-friendly manner. *User-centric* refers to a community model which extends the reach of a high rate, multi-access broadband backbone by means of communication opportunities provided by end-users, based upon cooperation incentives. Such incentives may relate to an individual or a community of individuals, as well as to access stakeholders. Moreover, user-centricity can be discussed from two different perspectives. Firstly, the user is in power of assisting the network in terms not only of its deployment, but also of its proliferation. Secondly, services to be provided by the end-user are assisted by an access infrastructure that is engineered towards assisting the user in terms of *Quality of Experience (QoE)*. In regards to the first aspect, deployment refers to assisting in sharing equipment that makes the network scale. Deployment per se does not suffice for this type of architectures to grow.

2.1 Notions and Terminology

In UCNs, there are two fundamental networking roles: *node* and *gateway*. A UCN node concerns a role (software functionality) that a wireless capable device takes. Concrete examples of nodes can be specific user equipment, access points, or even some management server. A UCN gateway is a role (software functionality) that reflects an operational behavior making a UCN node capable of acting as a mediator between UCN systems and non-UCN systems – the outside world. The gateway role may or may not be owned and controlled by a UCN user; it may also or only be controlled by an access operator. The key differentiating factor of the role of gateway, in contrast to a regular UCN node, is the operational intelligence and mediation capability. Similarly to UCN nodes, the UCN gateway functionality may reside in the user-equipment, in APs, or even in the access network. Hence, they exhibit a feature that is key in user-centric environments: their behavior as part of the network is expected to be highly variable. Gateways will be active or inactive based on several conditions such as users' wishes and network load.

As previously mentioned, each UCN node has a unique *owner, micro-provider (MP)*, assigned. An owner is an entity (end-user, operator, virtual operator) that is responsible for any actions concerning his/her device. The term "responsible" reflects liability, i.e., from an operator's perspective the owner is the single responsible for the adequate/inadequate usage of the user's device within a specific, trust-bounded community.

A *community* in UCN is a set of UCN nodes that hold common interests (such as sharing connectivity or resources/peripherals) at some instant in time and space. In other words, nodes exhibit a space and time correlation that is the basis to establish a robust connectivity model. This is expected to be extrapolated by adequately modeling trust associations between nodes. We highlight that the notion of community does not have any relation whatsoever to an *Online Social Network (OSN)*, or even to some specific OSN subset.

An interest is here defined as a parameter capable of providing a measure (cost) of the "attention" of a node towards a specific location in a specific time instant. In other words, an interest is a parameter that provides a node with a measure of a specific time and space correlation. For instance, assuming that a user goes each Saturday morning to the coffee-shop on the neighborhood corner, an interest here could be "having a coffee". Other users in the same location (exhibiting a similar time and space correlation) are in the same place during an overlapping period of time. They all share an interest as they are all collocated in the same location for a specific period of time. The shared interest here is: attending the same coffee-shop. Therefore, owners may be complete strangers and yet, connectivity may be set across the devices, based on parameters such as specific *Quality of Experience (QoE)* metrics; node movement history; roaming and service sharing patterns.

In terms of generic model, UCN stakeholders are Internet users and Internet providers. These two stakeholders can, however, assume several of four main roles: user; micro-provider; provider; *Over-the-Top (OTT)* service provider.

The *user* is a role assigned to an entity that wants to use shared services at some instant in time and space. The *micro-provider* is a role assigned to an entity that is willing to share, at some instant in time and space, resources in exchange of specific cooperation incentives, or rewards. The provider is a role assigned to an entity that is responsible for direct Internet access, while the usual *Over the Top (OTT)* role relates with management of credentials or trust circles; initial authentication; gateway registration. As a coordinating role, the OTT does not have any impact on the way traffic is transmitted in the communities or across the Internet. Moreover, the OTT does not account for any end-to-end measures, such as data privacy, liability of the traffic source(s), or traceability. However, our research has shown that there are benefits in terms of market for an OTT to have responsibilities that go beyond initial setup and will become service differentiators, e.g. distributed mobility management across communities.

The roles of UCN stakeholders (users, and providers) and their relationships shape the Internet design, as these relationships impact the communication in ways that were not foreseen, e.g., by placing both the *upstream* (from user to network) and *downstream* (from network to user) flows at an equal level.

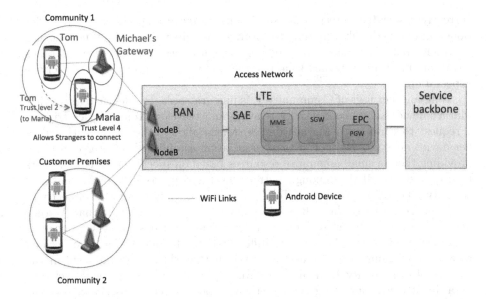

Fig. 1. Scenario example derived from the ULOOP project.

2.2 UCN Global Use-Cases

Figure 1 (a) illustrates a UCN where two different communities are represented, Community 1 and Community 2 [5]. The term community in this example is simply representative and identifies a set of users within the same WLAN. It could be, for instance, a mesh network in a city, or a hotspot at a coffee-shop.

Community 1 therefore represents an example of a dense wireless network, infrastructure mode (e.g. shopping-mall, football stadium, indoor spaces in a school campus). By dense it is meant that several users may activate devices in AP mode and therefore, there is a strong signal overlap. Hence, the result of this is that despite the fact that spectrum abounds, *Signal to Noise Ratio (SNR)* can be very low in some areas (known as gray areas) [6].

As for Community 2, it stands for a mesh network also interconnected to the same LTE provider. There is no strict relation between a community and a geographic location.

Maria is a user in Community 1 carrying her Android smart-phone (*User Equipment, UE*). Maria's UE selects a specific gateway (AP or UE) to be associated with in a certain location. After the reception of her association request, the gateway broadcasts a query both via the Wi-Fi interface and the LTE interface (to reach the backend) in order to figure out whether Maria is or not an authorized and trusted user. At the same time, the chosen gateway also triggers an adequate gateway selection mechanism that takes into consideration not only Maria's expectations, but also the potential overlap and electromagnetic noise in the area, as well as the optimization of the load across the entire network. While Maria roams in Community 1, the gateway onto which Maria's UE is currently associated detects that she is on the move (e.g. due to SNR variations) and immediately attempts to estimate/anticipate a potential new anchor for connectivity (new gateway). Upon agreement between the gateways, Maria's UE is automatically attached to a new gateway which can fulfill Maria's service expectations.

Tom, another user of Community 1, is in a gray area. His device realizes that Maria's device allows connectivity relaying and therefore Tom's device triggers a request to connect to Maria's device. Maria allows other users with whom her device does not yet have a trust association established to interconnect by providing them a small amount of resources based on specific QoE requirements (e.g. only if her UE has enough battery level and up to 20 % of Maria's link capacity). Therefore, Maria and Tom's UE automatically negotiate connectivity and Tom goes online through Maria's device. We also highlight that Maria's device is already using shared Internet access via Michael's gateway. Michael is a subscriber of a network operator different than the one Maria is subscribed to and also belongs to Community 1. Given that they share interests in the context of Community 1, Michael and Maria are able to connect and exchange data directly, without going through their respective operators. Thanks to the resource optimization and load-balancing features of gateways within Community 1 continuously exchange data and thus offload/transfer some UE's to other elected gateways.

UCN communities are also the basis to derive local services, based on entities that are willing to provide services on exchange of specific incentives. In such cases, the ultimate goal is not to expand coverage but instead to consider UCN functionality as an enabling technology platform for cooperative data dissemination. In regular deployments, such data cannot be available, as it is simply the result of a cooperative effort based on a self-organizing system. Moreover, end-user devices that are UCN enabled may be able to gather open data (data collected from the users' surrounding environment). To illustrate the concept, we again refer to Maria, who now needs to print her boarding pass at an airport with Wi-Fi coverage. Due to the UCN functionality implemented in gateways and also provided directly by other users, Maria can print her boarding pass through John's device, a user that Maria's device trusts through a bi-directional trust association.

2.3   UCN Model Functional Blocks

UCNs assume that an existing infrastructure is available and that Internet users are willing to expand such infrastructure in a way that is user-friendly and self-organizing. UCNs assumes also that within specific trust circles some form of cooperation incentives can be provided in order for both the access and the end-user to cooperate and assist in further developing Internet architectures. In order for that to happen, our UCN model considers three main functional blocks: *trust management and cooperation incentives*; *resource management*; *mobility aspects* [7].

In this section we briefly explain the main functional blocks for a UCN model that has been conceived, validated, as well as implemented in the context of the European project ULOOP, being currently available to the community as open-source LGPLv3.0 software [8,9].

Trust Management and Cooperation Incentives. Trust management and cooperation incentives relate with understanding how to define and build circles of trust on-the-fly [10]. Such circles of trust are capable of sustaining an environment where stakeholders share some form of Internet resources in order to support the dynamic behavior of UCN. Trust management is based on reputation mechanisms able to identify end-user misbehavior and to address social aspects, e.g., the different types of levels of trust users may have in different communities (e.g., family, affiliation) [11]. In situations where the created network of trust is not enough to allow resources to be shared, devices are able to use a cooperation incentive scheme based on the transfer of credits directly proportional to the amount of shared resources [12,13].

Motivating Usage via Cooperation. Cooperation incentives in UCN are considered both from a specific technology perspective, as well as from a business perspective. Technical incentives may relate to natural features of the technology that result in a win-win match when cooperation is applied [14]. A concrete example of a technical incentive relates to potential improvements of the 802.11 MAC layer, namely, UCN engineers the MAC layer in a way that mitigates problems related with low data rate stations, as low data rate stations and high data rate stations can simultaneously profit from the shared medium as shall be explained in Sect. 2.3. While as for a business incentive, we can think of a specific peering scheme that may assist the access operators in understanding how to obtain revenue based on UCN architectures.

As part of communities and also as individual nodes, cooperation must consider the willingness of owners/nodes in participating in communication. Willingness can be driven by different facts such as energy saving, low processing power, and/or lack of storage. Although a node is not willing to share resources due to one of the aforementioned facts, the cooperation functionality should encourage such user in doing it so, as he/she can get an immediate return (e.g., more processing) while sharing that resource it has the most (e.g., storage) [15]. Instead of simply paying users with the same "currency", e.g., you get more bandwidth if you give more bandwidth, the cooperation functionality should reward involved entities with the type of resource the user wants and at the moment the user needs (i.e., immediately or later on).

The User Perspective. The lack of trust between users can influence their level of willingness and our belief is that motivation should be based on shared interests. Users sharing the same interest (e.g., movies), although being completely unknown to one another, can be easily encouraged in carrying information on behalf of others. A user interested in comedy movies surely won't mind to carry a copy of a movie destined to some other user if he/she is able to get a copy also. At this point, cooperation not only helps users disseminate information quickly and seamlessly (as the movie will reach different interested users other than the destination) as it also contributes to sparing resources from users who are not interested in that specific content. Cooperation shall be easily encouraged if users share some social relationship. Thus, social ties have an important role in making cooperation among users even more reliable. Software functionality in UCN nodes is expected to track user expectations and service response. In this case, users are expected to cooperate in order to provide surrounding UCN nodes with information that not only can improve their own but also the other users' network experience. Users can exchange: (i) SNR information, e.g., to aid in the handover process; (ii) behavior information, to strictly penalize malicious/greedy users; (iii) connectivity quality levels, to aid in load balancing and interference reduction.

The Provider Perspective. UCN is a perfect solution for operators who are looking for higher density at limited cost, letting them to rely on created communities, in order to provide the required resources to demanding users at specific instants in time. This will offer an energy-efficient and cost optimized solution to increase density of the operators' networks. Moreover, the subscription relation between the end-user and the access operator can be strengthened by having the access operator empowering the end-user with partial networking functionality, in a way that is completely transparent to the end-user. In other words: such cooperative model (based upon Internet service micro-generation) gives the means for the access operator to provide value-added services that are more appealing to the end-user and that go beyond regular subscriptions, common today both in the bundled and in Service Provider centric models such as the one embodied today by e.g. FON, when used in strong cooperation with access providers, give the means to access providers to offer Internet access. For instance, access operators can take advantage of UCN capabilities to further expand its control towards the customer premises devices.

Some reasons for UCN adoption (and hence for the relevancy of operator-based incentives) are: to provide adequate feedback to customers; to ensure an optimal network operation, where expanded coverage is also offered; to be able to deal with interference in dense areas; to provide residential areas with the same authentication/authorization model used in UCN coverage and thus, reduce CAPEX; to gain in reputation by supporting communities, following what is today common practice in open-source business models.

An "Open Source" model with "some limitation" can favorite a win-win equilibrium between UCN and operator's competitiveness goals. Hence, operator's based incentives are expected to improve the potential of interoperability and of business opportunity for access and service stakeholders.

Augmented Resource Management. As UCN relies on wireless infrastructures that are often deployed in an ad-hoc way, resource management optimization is a key aspect to pursuit. UCN has as purpose to assist in developing robust and high debit wireless local-loops in a way that meets current broadband access technologies debit as possible, and in a way that reduces the chances for bottlenecks to occur [16, 17]. Throughput maximization is to be addressed across more than one hop by means of cooperative networking techniques of which one possibility is relaying. In regards to resource management, and to achieve a fair and self-organizing network operation, there are aspects to be looked for such as the need to adequately and dynamically be able to control growth of UCN communities; dynamic fluctuations of the network both in terms of traffic due to stations joining and leaving frequently, as well as due to the movement of stations. Another aspect that is considered crucial to look for is to develop cooperative and distributed mechanisms that assist the network in adequately selecting nodes that are willing to be micro-providers. Such selection is to be performed in a way that considers not only throughput maximization, but also the lowest-cost in terms of energy-efficiency.

Dealing with Frequent Roaming: Anchor Point Control and Movement Estimation. UCN is based on the notion of users carrying (or owning) low-cost and limited capacity portable devices which are cooperative in nature and which extend the network in a user-centric way, not necessarily implying the support for networking services such as multi-hop routing. For instance, in UCNs transmission may simply be relayed based on simple mechanisms already existing in end-user devices. These emerging architectures therefore represent networks where the nodes that integrate the network are in fact end-user devices which may have additional storage capability and which may or may not sustain networking services. Such nodes, being carried by end-users exhibit a highly dynamic behavior. Nodes move frequently following social patterns and based on their carriers interests; inter-contact exchange is the basis for the definition of connectivity models as well as data transmission. The network is also expected to frequently change (and even to experience frequent partitions) due to the fact that such nodes, being portable, are limited in terms of energy resources.

In terms of mobility and adding to the currently available solutions, UCN is focused on two main aspects: mobility tracking and estimation, as well as handover support. The purpose is to assist in improving the underlying connectivity model, and hence overall network operation. Social mobility modeling is an aspect that assists in deriving algorithms and functionality that can anticipate the way nodes move based on analysis and tracking of node movement through time.

A final aspect to consider is to ensure that the functionality to be developed can assist in dealing with the unmanaged aspects of UCN architecture and should get rid of anchors in the network. This may be required, for instance, if a UCN community is not capable of providing a node with adequate mobility management e.g. due to trust aspects.

2.4   Regulatory and Socio-Economic Implications

The potential of UCNs can be exploited both to complement broadband access (by increasing capillarity/coverage and by providing 3G to Wi-Fi offloading) and to implement a self-adapting territorial platform for collaborative data gathering and dissemination. These two broad application scenarios correspond to the use-cases described in Sect. 2.2 and which were considered in the context of the ULOOP project to establish realistic boundaries and requirements for UCNs.

Methodology to Analyze the Impact on Regulation. UCNs are a relatively new concept which is not yet included in regulatory frameworks. Still, the impact on regulation is a determinant for the diffusion of any new technology or model. This is particularly true for community-scale models which need to reach a high penetration in order to trigger the positive externalities which can make them profitable. In order to evaluated the impact of UCNs both at a national and international level, the ULOOP project considered a methodology based on questionnaires and scoring sheets, questionnaire which is illustrated in Fig. 2. The questionnaire encompasses 14 questions covering the main relevant regulatory aspects, divided into five groups. Questions Q01 and Q02 are about the general principles of *Net Neutrality* and *Universal Service*, which might contribute to the diffusion of the UCN model, if properly adopted. Questions Q03 to Q06 relate with electronic communications, with particular emphasis on the definitions and possible limitations which apply to *"non/public networks"*, as opposed to public communication networks managed by operators and established service providers.

Questions Q07 to Q09 cover the definition of *"operator"* and the exclusive rights and obligations coming from the so called *general authorization*, which are essential to understand whether and to what extent allow UCN users are allowed to provide associated services and facilities without being established service providers. Questions Q10 to Q12 concern the bureaucracy required to install/activate/manage a public Wi-Fi access point, which might limit the diffusion of UCNs. Questions Q13 and Q14 are about e-commerce regulation.

As for the scoring sheet, it considered the relevance of each question within the context of the two use-cases described in Sect. 2.2. Answers to the questionnaire were collected via involvement of several European regulation authorities from several European countries: Italy, Spain, France, Switzerland, and Finland.

Socio-Economic Analysis. The socio-economic sustainability of a UCN depends on the diffusion of UCN devices which, in its turn, depends on the capability of the model to attract people. Hence, the sustainability analysis has to start from the key features of a UCN, which have to be perceived as added-value or differentiators to the stakeholders involved in the model. For the socio-economic analysis we grouped the distinguishing features of UCNs into four main categories: resources; information; availability; protection. The scenes introduced to represent the potential of the two use cases ULOOP-1 and ULOOP-2 were

Questionnaire on Regulatory aspects

QIs network neutrality officially adopted/enforced as a principle?
QIs Internet access officially considered to be a "universal service"?
QIs there any specific definition/rule for "non-public networks"?
QIs there any requirement of logical/physical separation between public and private networks?
QIs it possible (and under which conditions) for a private network to transport third-party traffic?
QIs it possible (and under which conditions) to interconnect two private networks without going through a public network?
QIs there any specific definition of "operator"?
QIs there any authorization required to become an operator?
QWhich rights and obligations come from the authorization?
QIs there any bureaucracy required to install a Wi-Fi hot spot in a public place?
QIs there any specific rule which applies to the management of public hot spots?
QHow is criminal liability distributed between operators (IDP and/or SP) and subscribers?
QIs there any specific rule for electronic commerce?
QIs there any specific type of contract to be applied to exchange or provide electronic services?

Fig. 2. Questionnaire used in the ULOOP project to cover the main regulatory aspects for UCNs.

then weighted in terms of each of the features described. We summarize the main results of the analysis by means of Fig. 3, which illustrates a bar graph showing, for each category of players, the number of scenes in which the category take advantages or disadvantages from their involvement in UCN. Whenever all UCN users fall within the same category they are simply denoted as users without further distinction. Two categories are used for operators, since the benefits they take depend on their degree of involvement in UCN. Special categories are used for malicious users, attackers, and untrusted users.

According to Fig. 3, the only players who are truly damaging to the UCN model are untrusted users, malicious users, and attackers who do not need to be motivated. On the contrary, UCNs can help in inducing these users to behave properly in order to start taking advantage of UCNs, as regular users can.

3 Cooperation Models and Incentives

In usual deployments of UCNs, spontaneous wireless access points and mobile devices have incentives to cooperate by: (i) sharing Internet connectivity; (ii) extended access to shared services by few-hop relaying; (iii) sharing wireless resources based on incentives; (iv) providing monitoring and user traceability. In recent years, research has been directed towards cooperative networking mechanisms capable of assisting data transmission under circumstances where the channel experiences interference. For instance, by controlling medium access

42   R. Sofia et al.

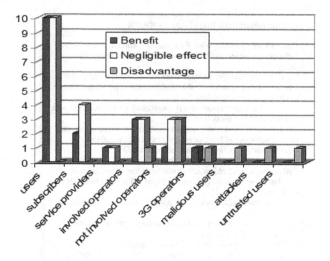

Fig. 3. Socio-economic analysis of use-cases ULOOP-1 and ULOOP-2, two representative use-cases of UCNs.

between source and relay terminals, it has been found that the diversity of the communication system can be improved. By leveraging the broadcast nature of the wireless channels, cooperative networking significantly improves system performance. While scientific results abound in what concerns cooperative networking, the feasibility of applying it beyond cooperative wireless transmissions is not yet fully understood.

One key aspect to address relates with incentive mechanisms to boost cooperation [13–15]. Another key aspect relates with the potential compatibility of the developed cooperative networking mechanisms, across existing infrastructures. In the context of UCNs, a cooperative networking model must be based on effective incentives for cooperation, and on an efficient improvement of networking experience for all of the UCN model stakeholders.

3.1 Cooperation and Sharing

Cooperation is a central feature of user-centric systems aiming to compensate for the lack of a central and dedicated controlling entity. In spontaneous networks, such as UCNs, users need to cooperate in order to help one another aiming to mitigate the constraints posed by the dynamic networking environment. Such cooperation can be achieved by sharing available resources (e.g., bandwidth, processing power, memory, battery) and/or effort.

The success of a cooperation process may be diminished by the fact that users have full control on their devices and may try to maximize the benefits they get from the network. In general, the cooperative behavior of a device will indeed result in an increase in resource consumption to take more than its fair share of a resource (e.g., network, CPU, storage). Knowing that mobile devices have scarce resources, each of these devices should better not cooperate from its point of view. Despite the potential advantages of enrolling in a cooperation process, it is imperative to give users the option to participate or not in cooperation. That is, user willingness to cooperate must be considered.

Three reasons may discourage willingness to participate in cooperation: (i) lack of trust on other users, which can be mitigated by a mechanism able to manage trust; (ii) users are running out of resources, which can be lessened if offering users resources that may improve (e.g., increase battery lifetime, processing power, storage room) their own operation; and (iii) users' egoistic behavior, that is easily diminished once users know they will have resources available upon their needs. However, independently of what is increasing/decreasing their willingness level, users will easily engage in cooperation if they know that they will get resources whenever they need them.

In what concerns the type of shared resources, related literature is usually focused on cooperation related with sharing of the same category of resources, e.g. storage by storage; processing by processing; roaming now by roaming later. However, it is envisioned that UCNs, being software based, provide the grounds to exchange resources based on different categories as this is a main feature to ensure an efficient usage of networking resources in wireless heterogeneous networks. This can be achieved via a cooperation model/mechanism that provides a direct exchange of networking resources, for instance, connectivity time against bandwidth, or networking storage vs. Quality of Service.

3.2   Cooperation Models

In a UCN, cooperation incentives are implemented as a combination of: trust-based, in which incentives for cooperation are created by adopting policies that are based on the threat of retaliation for non-cooperating nodes; reward-based, in which nodes get a virtual payment for cooperating. Such incentives are used to motivate nodes to cooperate in order to augment their networking experience. This section provides two examples for potential cooperation models that have as motivation to improve resource management via the combination of social parameters (such as trust) with networking aspects.

A Direct Exchange Cooperation Framework Model, USWAP. As explained, UCNs are expected to profit from integrating a framework that can assist direct exchange of different types of (networking) resources. To provide an example, Table 1 contains several networking resources, some of which are traffic-related resources, while others are in categories such as storage, or time (e.g. lifetime). The third column explains the mapping of the resource to one or more OSI Layers.

In this section we describe a potential example of such a framework, the *USWAP - Cooperative Network Resources Swapping in User-centric Networks* software-defined framework, a software-defined solution that is being devised to run on UCN nodes, on OSI Layer 7. The USWAP resource manager (RM) is

Table 1. Potential resources to be considered under a direct exchange framework.

Resource	Description	Related OSI Layers
Traffic rate	Number of bits sent per second	1, 2, 3
Coverage	Radius of coverage associated to the signal power and measured	3
Connectivity	Internet access time (e.g. seconds)	1,2
Storage	Memory to be shared e.g. for the purpose of caching, in bytes	7
Lifetime	Period of time since a node (or network) becomes active until the node is said to be dead. Associated to the node energy consumption	1
Bandwidth	Wireless capacity chunk	1,2
Frequency chunk	A sub-frequency range or an aggregation of sub-frequencies	1
Duty cycle	The time a node takes to serve one request	2
Density	Number of nodes in a network or neighbors of a specific node. The higher that number the more dense the node/network is	1,2

an entity based on the ULOOP Resource Management entity, extended via the inclusion of two additional modules: a *Cooperative Resource Exchange (CRE)* module, and the *Self-organizing Swapping* (SOS) entity. CRE deals with the optimization of the proposed exchanges, for instance, by considering relaying, or offloading to multiple nodes around (instead of onto a single node). The SOS entity is responsible for ensuring that the swapping done is beneficial both from a node and from a network perspective, to prevent nodes from becoming greedy or jeopardizing the whole system.

The USWAP *Network Resource Exchange Mapper (NREM)* is an abstraction entity that assists in the direct exchange of networking resources.

The USWAP *Exchange Adaptation (EXA)* entity is a module that assists the exchange, by considering algorithms that assist in a dynamic exchange. For instance, if a device intends to swap network storage per connectivity time, then this entity shall analyze the cost efficiency of accepting such a request. If there are different possibilities offered, this entity shall optimize and prioritize the exchange possibilities via the Policy Interface which shall be developed in a way that is easily extendable, e.g. XML.

Let us provide an example considering two different USWAP nodes (e.g. an end-user device and an access point), which engage in active communication, to exchange resources. The UCN node wants to access the Internet freely for 60 min and in order to do so, is offering to swap two different types of networking resources: 200M bytes of network storage, or 30 minutes of relaying to others. The AP, via e.g. a resource management entity, gets the request, and asks the NREM entity to wrap adequately the type of resources being offered. This wrapping implies that the NREM shall analyze whether or not the node contemplates the type of offer being done, via both local policies and eventually network policies. For instance, this may be a node that is not willing to consider network storage as a networking good. This mediation implies that both the NREM and EXA become involved in this process. Then, the EXA entity provides the adequate negotiation and adaptation, via self-organizing and cooperative mechanisms to ensure an optimal mapping of resources offered. EXA then provides an answer to RM, stating that the node accepts the offer of exchanging network storage per connectivity time. RM then replies to the requester, in order to trigger the regular connection process. This means that, for instance, RM interfaces with the node captive portal to allow the requester to access the network in exchange of connectivity time.

Cooperation-Based Resource Management. The management of network resources takes advantage of the willingness that users have in cooperating, based on the mentioned two types of incentives: trust-based and reward-based. Cooperative based resource management has three components: call admission control, resource allocation and load balancing. Call admission control decides whether a new request from an end-user can be accepted or not. In one gateway, resource allocation assigns resources among all accepted and active end-users. Load-balancing can be used to react to congestion or to prevent congestion in the presence of a prediction mechanism. Call admission control in is innovative since once a request for specific resources arrives to a gateway, the gateway will take into consideration not only the available resources, but also the requesting end-user's credits, which are gained by the end-user through its previous cooperation and behavior (e.g. by sharing services and resources). The allocation of resources can, for instance, be done according to the type of requested resources (e.g. real-time vs non real-time) and the amount of credits own by the end-user (requester). Based on these two criteria, resources (e.g. bandwidth, power and bit rates) are allocated fairly among users aiming to guarantee the quality level required by them, while weighting users based on they cooperation level within the community. For instance, a user with a high quality demand with a cooperation deficit in a UCN community (few earned credits) may get fewer resources than another user with a lower quality demand, but with a higher cooperation index (more earned credits) in case of scarcity of resources. That is to say that resource allocation does not consider only the service quality obtained by each individual end-user, but also the whole performance of the community: network capacity can be maximized by increasing the incentives for nodes to share services and/or resources by providing them higher priority to access shared services/resources. In the presence of congestion, load balancing aims to provide a more efficient usage of resources by different gateways. A congested gateway may decide to shift traffic towards another gateway based on local measurements and by analyzing the measurements of neighbor gateways. The latter cooperate with

Table 2. ULOOP Pilot sites, where specific UCN functional blocks are available to the global community.

Site	Country	Type	Partner	Description
L7	Italy	Tests	Level7	Commercial
UWIC	Italy	Tests	University of Urbino	Neutral access network for students and urban communities
BOWL	Germany	Tests	Technical University of Berlin	Campus testbed for wireless technologies
FON	Spain	Pilot	FON	FON commercial network
ZON	Portugal	Pilot	ZON	ZON commercial network

the congested gateway by deciding to receive some of its traffic, since they will get extra credits for that. The decision to help balancing the load of a congested gateway is done based on a cooperation index, which is locally computed based on the analysis of the trade-off between accepting traffic from neighbors and the advantage of having more credits. Based on the list of neighbor gateways that are willing to cooperate with the congested gateway, the later will select a neighbor based on the trust level that the users, trying to access the congested gateway, have on the potential new gateway.

4 Operational Aspects, the ULOOP Pilot

The ULOOP project has deployed a model of UCNs and built a pilot composed of different sites as presented in Table 2 [18]. Test sites are open to the global community and have been used during the project lifespan to test and to validate software developed. Pilot sites were used to gather results concerning operational UCN usage.

The ULOOP partners ZON and FON were responsible for setting up the pilot sites. These two entities have past experience working together, with FON's Community Wi-Fi software already deployed in ZON's residential customers, serving more than 500.000 Wi-Fi users all over Portugal.

The two sites were installed in real environments within ZON's and FON's commercial networks. Taking advantage of the above mentioned ZON and FON commercial relationship, FON provided the access points, acting as UCN gateways, to ZON, ensuring that the same equipment was used in both sites, in order to minimize the changes required to both sites. Nonetheless, both sites present different targeted users: FON gateways are located in public places while in the ZON site the gateways are in a residential area. The statistics gathered during a fixed observation period allow direct comparison between both sites.

The FON site consists on an area of one square kilometer, where the shortest distance between access points is 60 m. ZON's pilot locations are spread around the City of Lisbon, mostly in the vicinities.

The statistics concerning usage have been collected during a period of two weeks, between 9th of September 2013 and 20th of September 2013. ULOOP requires the installation of an Android plugin provided via a regular captive portal methodology. Public places show a higher volume of users increasing the heterogeneity of the samples. On the other hand, residential areas have less activity but show more predictable habits. A relevant aspect to consider is the group of users/devices that these deployment sites are targeting. The statistics have been collected with the help of the Google Analytics dashboard and summarize different usage reports. There are two data segments for each graph related to the FON and the ZON demo sites. To measure the user acceptance of the ULOOP experience, ZON has conducted a small survey with their customers on the pilot site. This survey was conducted at the end of the statistics gathering [16]. For the questions provided and which intended to understand the satisfaction of users concerning connection, installation, configuration, usage, a scale of 0 to 5 was used, being 0 the most negative aspect on the scale, and 5 the most positive. Moreover, the users were previously informed that this was an experience based on a proof-of-concept technology.

In regards to the user-friendliness of the ULOOP Android plugin, required to be part of the ULOOP UCN community, users rated such friendliness with a total of 3.33. Some problems were detected concerning the identity validation process, which in ULOOP is a one-step only process required to ensure liability of the involved users.

In regards to Internet access, 66 % of the universe automatically obtained Internet access immediately after the configuration of the application. This is the usual process in the ULOOP UCN model, as after the initial setup, users are not required to use credentials to access the Internet, given that ULOOP identifies users via a unique mobile token, the crypto-id.

Concerning whether or not the experience with ULOOP was better than without a UCN model, the users replied with a tendency to a positive experience in a total of 3.2 out of 5.

The users were asked whether or not they would recommend the service to other users, and 50 % replied that they would recommend the service. ZON also asked users whether or not they would engage commercially with such a service, and 66 % replied they would.

5   Conclusions and Future Research

This chapter is dedicated to raise awareness, as well as to give insight into the growing trend of user-centricity in the form of user-centric networking models. The chapter provides notions and concepts concerning UCNs, including description of existing examples, stakeholders, as well as roles in UCN models. The chapter then debates aspects concerning cooperation models and incentives for sharing in the context of wireless networks, proposing to revisit current paradigms to consider heterogeneous exchange of resources. An operational perspective of UCNs is provided via a description of a specific UCN pilot, developed in the context of the ULOOP project, which is available to the community. Such description explains some of the results that were gathered during a live experiment on two operational networks from ZON and FON. The chapter contains also a market analysis for a concrete example of a potential cooperation, explaining how current Internet access stakeholders can profit from considering wholesale models that integrate UCN concepts.

The expectations concerning UCNs are, from a business perspective, that these networking architectures must not be overlooked. The chapter provides market exercises that show the benefits that may arise for Internet stakeholders. From a technological and scientific perspective, the concepts that have been so far validated corroborate the potential that these networking architectures introduce in regards to network operation improvement e.g. in regards to spectrum usage or energy-efficiency.

Relevant research opportunities in the context of UCN relate with the application of trust as a potential parameter stemming from social sciences and which can be applied to QoS as a way to create more robust Internet architectures. Another relevant field to be addressed is direct trading of resources on the network, as a way to develop new business models, an aspect that we are currently pursuing.

Acknowledgments. The research leading to these results has received funding from the EU IST Seventh Framework Programme (FP7/2007–2013) under grant agreement number 257418, project ULOOP (User-centric Wireless Local Loop), participants: Alcatel-Lucent Bell Labs, (FR), COFAC c.r.l./University Lusófona (PT), Huawei Technologies Duesseldorf GmbH (DE), ARIA S.p.A (IT), Caixa Mágica Software, Lda (PT), FON Wireless Ltd (UK), Technische Universität Berlin (DE), University of Kent (UK), Université de Genève (CH), Level7 srlu (IT), University of Urbino (IT). We thank in particular all of the authors involved in deliverables D2.2, D5.4, D5.5, D3, and in the ULOOP white papers number 01, 05, and 09, and the Cost Action WiNeMo - IC0906.

References

1. Sofia, R., Mendes, P.: User-provided networks: consumer as provider. IEEE Commun. Magazines, Feature Top. Consum. Commun. Networking - Gaming Entertainment **46**(12), 86–91 (2008)
2. Eu IST FP7 ULOOP - User-centric Wireless Local Loop project, grant number 257418 (2010–2013). http://uloop.eu/
3. Murray, D.G., Yoneki, E., Crowcroft, J., Hand, S.: The case for crowd computing. In: Proceedings of the Second ACM SIGCOMM Workshop on Networking, Systems, and Applications on Mobile Handhelds, August 2010
4. Aldini. A., Bogliolo, A.: Modeling and verification of cooperation incentive mechanisms in user-centric wireless communications. In: Rawat, D.B., Bista, B.B., Yan, G. (eds.) Security, Privacy, Trust, and Resource Management in Mobile and Wireless Communications. IGI Global (2013)
5. Moreno, V. (Editor, FON Wireless Ltd.), ULOOP Consortium: D2.1: ULOOP Use-cases, Assumptions, and Requirements. EU FP7 IST ULOOP project (grant number 257418) deliverable, March 2011

6. Pong, D., Moors, T.: Fairness and capacity trade-off in IEEE 802.11 WLANs. In: 29th Annual IEEE International Conference on Local Computer Networks. IEEE (2004)
7. Aldini, A., Bogliolo, A. (eds.): User-centric Networking - Future Perspectives. Springer Lecture Notes in Social Networks. Springer, Heidelberg (2014)
8. Mendes, P. (ed.): D3.8: ULOOP Framework Specification and validation, ULOOP European project deliverable (gr. Nr 257418), October 2013
9. Matos, A. (ed.): D3.9: ULOOP Software Suite. ULOOP European project deliverable (gr. Nr 257418), October 2013
10. Ziegler, C.-N., Lausen, G.: Propagation models for trust and distrust in social networks. Springer Sci. Inf. Syst. Front. **7**(4/5), 337–358 (2005)
11. Ballester, C., Seigneur, J.-M., di Francesco, P., Moreno, V., Sofia, R.C., Bogliolo, A., Martins, N., Moreira Jr., W.: A user-centric approach to trust management in Wi-Fi networks. In: IEEE INFOCOM - Demos Track (2013)
12. Fang, Z., Bensaou, B.: Fair bandwidth sharing algorithms based on game theory frameworks for wireless ad-hoc networks. In: Twenty-Third Annual Joint Conference of the IEEE Computer and Communications Societies, INFOCOM 2004, vol. 2. IEEE (2004)
13. Bogliolo, A., Polidori, P., Aldini, A., Moreira, W., Mendes, P., Yildiz, M., Ballester, C., Seigneur, J.-M.: Virtual currency and reputation-based cooperation incentives. In: Proceedings of the IWCMC (2012)
14. Neely, M.J.: Optimal pricing in a free market wireless network. Wireless Netw. **15**(7), 901–915 (2009)
15. Biczók, G., Toka, L., Vidács, A., Trinh, T.A.: On incentives in global wireless communities. In: Proceedings of the UNET 2009 Workshop, CoNext 2009 (2009)
16. Haci, H., Zhu, H., Wang, J.: Resource Allocation in User-Centric Wireless Networks, VTCSpring (2012)
17. Jamal, T., Mendes, P., Zúquete, A.: Analysis of hybrid relaying in cooperative WLAN. In: Proceedings of Wireless Days (2013)
18. Matos, A. (Editor, Caixa Mágica Software Lda), ULOOP Consortium: D4.2: Pilot Deployment and Validation. EU FP7 IST ULOOP project (grant number 257418) deliverable, October 2013

Cooperative Relaying
for Wireless Local Area Networks

Tauseef Jamal[(✉)] and Paulo Mendes

Copelabs, University Lusofona, Lisbon, Portugal
{tauseef.jamal,paulo.mendes}@ulusofona.pt

Abstract. The concept of cooperation in wireless communication networks has drawn significant attention recently from both academia and industry as it can be effective in addressing the performance limitations of wireless networks due to user mobility and the scarcity of network resources. Future wireless systems are provisioned to be highly heterogeneous and interconnected, motivating cooperative relaying to be applied to future mobile networks. This chapter describes the state of the art in this area classified in different families. The main focus is the Medium Access Control (MAC) layer design, analysis, challenges and how cooperative networks can be designed for highly dynamic networks comprising large number of moving nodes.

Keywords: Wireless networks · Cooperative diversity · MAC protocols · Wireless resource management

1 Introduction

The growth of wireless networks in the last decades is motivated by their ability of providing communication anywhere and anytime. Because of the importance of this aspect on the modern society, a high proliferation of wireless services and devices, such as mobile communications, WiFi or cordless phones has emerged. This increasing trend is the main motivating factor for development of novel wireless technologies for reliable and cost efficient transmissions, among the cooperative networks.

Cooperative networking can find its niche in diverse applications, from increasing capacity or extending coverage in cellular networks, to enhancing transmission reliability and network throughput in Wireless Local Area Networks (WLANs); from offering more stable links in volatile and dynamic propagation conditions in vehicular communications, to saving energy and extending network lifetime in wireless Ad-hoc networks.

While cooperative networking has a rich theoretical history in the literature, efforts to actually implement cooperative systems have been much more limited. Cooperative networking refers to the sharing of resources and the realization of distributed protocols among multiple nodes in a network. Cooperation in communications is achieved in various ways such as cooperation by relay to forward

© Springer International Publishing Switzerland 2014
I. Ganchev et al. (Eds.): Wireless Networking for Moving Objects, LNCS 8611, pp. 50–69, 2014.
DOI: 10.1007/978-3-319-10834-6_4

source's data, cooperation among nodes in a cluster and cooperation between source and relay to transmit together to achieve diversity. There are numerous cooperative techniques for physical layer (cooperative communications) but to get the most out of the system it requires the support of MAC layer. Cooperation can be incorporated at MAC layer. This is achieved by cooperative MAC protocols (cooperative relaying).

Over the past decade, Internet access became essentially wireless, with 802.11 technologies providing a low cost broadband support for a flexible and easy deployment. However, channel conditions in wireless networks are subjected to interference and fading, decreasing the overall network performance [6]. Fading effects in a wireless environment can be classified as either fast or slow [29]. While fast fading can be mitigated by having the source retransmitting frames, slow fading, caused by obstruction of the main signal path, makes retransmission useless, since periods of low signal power last for the entire duration of the transmission. Moreover, the interference from other transmitters also affects the communication quality severely. Because of the constant change of the environment and the mobility of the terminals (transmitter or receiver or both) the signal is scattered over many objects in the surroundings. Such channel impairments can be mitigated by exploiting cooperative diversity [22].

In what concerns WLANs, they suffer among other issues from scarcity of bandwidth, which limits the network throughput and requires efficient utilization of this valuable resource. One example of these issues is from the existing WLANs, where the performance of the whole system degrades greatly once low data-rate nodes become dominant. Cooperative relaying may mitigate this problem by allowing low data-rate devices to finish their transmission faster by using a pair of wireless links (relays) that provide better wireless conditions than the direct channel to the destination. High data-rate stations have a high incentive to cooperate by relaying messages from low data-rate stations, since such cooperation may increase their probability to grab the wireless channel faster.

This chapter is organized as follows: Sect. 2 describes cooperative networking in general. In Sect. 3 we explain cooperative relaying and provides analysis of prior art. Section 4 discusses open research issues. Finally Sect. 5 presents the summary.

2 Cooperative Networking

Extensive research has been done to achieve better throughput and reliability in wireless networks, being mostly focused on MIMO systems. Recently, cooperative networking techniques have been investigated to increase the performance of wireless systems by using the diversity created by different single antenna devices. In cooperative networking, intermediate nodes (relays) help source-destination transmission forming dual-hop communication. This unique solution provides a response to the majority of the concerns in an efficient way. However, most of the cooperative solutions rely upon Channel State Information (CSI), explicit notifications and additional broadcast information, which incur overheads and complexity.

Current cooperative networking proposals are characterized by their limited focus. Most of the research being done focuses on the physical layer, by exploiting spatial diversity to increase system reliability of cellular networks [22]. In its simplest version, a terminal trying to reach a base station is assisted by a relay terminal. Due to the broadcast nature of the wireless channel, the relay can overhear the sender's transmission, decode it, and, if correctly received, repeat it. The base station combines these two copies of the same transmission, reducing the packet error-rate. This results in larger reliability gains than simple retransmission due to the exploitation of spatial diversity, in addition to time diversity.

From an implementation perspective, cooperative systems can be classified accordingly to different ways of utilizing relays, as shown in taxonomy given in Fig. 1. Cooperative networking can be designed with physical layer approaches (cooperative communications) or with higher layers (relay stages or cooperative relaying). The main focus of this chapter is cooperation at MAC layer (relaying). Since considerable research has been done on physical layer we explain cooperative communication in the following.

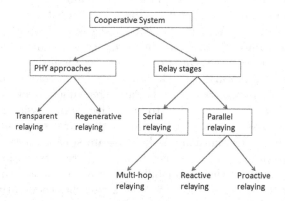

Fig. 1. Classification of cooperative systems.

2.1   Cooperative Communications

The basic ideas behind cooperative communication can be traced back to the groundbreaking work of Cover and El Gamal [5] on the information theoretic properties of the relay channel. The transmission of different copies of the same signal from different locations, generating spatial diversity allows the destination to get independently faded versions of the signal that can be combined to obtain an error-free signal.

In a cooperative communication system, each wireless user is assumed to transmit its own data as well as acting as a relay for another user. Figure 2 shows single antenna devices able to act as relays of each other by forwarding some version of "overheard" data along with its own data. Since the fading channels of two different devices are statistically independent, this generates spatial diversity.

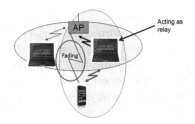

Fig. 2. Mitigating fading effects by relaying.

At PHY layer, cooperative diversity is usually modeled as a MIMO system. Some designs aim at full diversity: For N-antenna virtual array, the outage probability decreases asymptotically with SNR^{-N}. Other designs set their performance criteria according to the well-known trade-off between diversity and multiplexing gain: for N-antenna array, the multiplexing gain r and the diversity gain d, as defined in [2], are complementary and upper bounded by $d(r) \leq N + 1 - r$.

There are two main categories of PHY relaying approaches, i.e., transparent and regenerative relaying (c.f. Fig. 1). In transparent relaying the relay does not decode data from the signal received from the direct link; examples are Amplify and Forward (AF) and Store and Forward (SF) [25]. In regenerative relaying, relays decode received packets, recode the information and forward it to the destination; example is Decode and Forward (DF) [17].

2.2 Cooperative Relaying

The choice of relay stages is very important, because relays can operate either in series or in parallel (see taxonomy in Fig. 1). On the one hand, increasing the number of serial relaying nodes reduces the path-loss along each transmission hop. On the other hand, increasing the number of parallel relaying nodes increases potential diversity gains. Parallel relaying is implemented at PHY/MAC layers (single-hop), while serial relaying can be implemented with combination of both MAC and routing layers (multi-hop). There are two types of approaches for implementing parallel relaying, i.e., proactive and reactive relaying, which are explained in Sect. 3. In case of multi-hop relaying, the relays help more than one transmission requiring routing information.

Recently, the exploitation of link-layer diversity (cooperative relaying) in cellular and multi-hop wireless networks has attracted considerable research attention. The first attempts have been done in cellular networks by devising cooperative relaying systems with single-hop relays: the MAC allows the usage of relays that can help the source-destination transmission with one retransmission. Cellular networks generally suffer from three fundamental problems: interference, limited coverage and capacity shortage. To alleviate these problems, it is proposed that communication between a Base Station (BS) and a Mobile Station (MS) can be performed not only directly but also (or exclusively) via a Relay Station (RS), as shown in Fig. 3. Such a deployment can yield significant gains, which can boost performance of users that are capacity-limited (bottom-left cell in Fig. 3); coverage-limited (top-left cell) or interference-limited (middle-right cell) [24]. The case of multi-hop networks is more complex since such networks are still a challenging target for the design of MAC protocols. The challenge increases when terminals or objects move, resulting in time-selective fading channels.

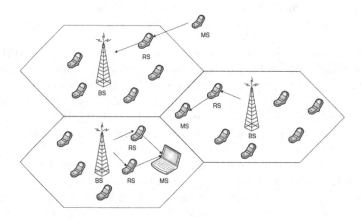

Fig. 3. Cooperative relaying in cellular networks.

Relaying can benefit not only the nodes involved, but the whole network in many different aspects. Many MAC protocols have introduced rate adaptation to overcome adverse channel conditions. Due to its distance from the AP, a wireless node can observe a bad channel as compared to other nodes that are closer to the AP, leading to the use of 802.11 rate adaptation schemes. Figure 4 illustrates the transmission characteristics of wireless nodes, as a result of the rate adaptation functionality of 802.11: nodes closer to the AP transmit at high data-rates, while nodes far away from the AP decrease their data-rate after detecting missing frames. Figure 4 also shows the role that relaying may have increasing the performance of the overall wireless network, helping low data-rate nodes to release the wireless medium sooner, helping high data-rate nodes to keep the desirable performance, and the network to achieve a good overall capacity. In this case the total transmission time for the dual-hop transmission is smaller than that of the direct transmission, cooperation readily outperforms the legacy direct transmission, in terms of both throughput and delay perceived by the source S.

Cooperative transmissions require unique features from MAC, which should be distributed and cooperative for a multipoint-to-multipoint environment. There are noteworthy issues that must be taken into account while designing cooperative diversity MAC: relay selection, cooperation decision, cooperation notification and cooperative transmission design [16].

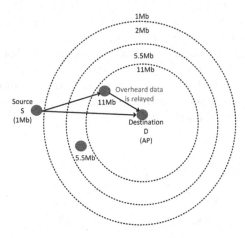

Fig. 4. Helping low data-rate nodes by cooperative relaying.

In what concerns the relay selection, there is broad horizon of selection parameters, mostly based on channel information. Such parameters are complex and
unstable. Moreover, the selected relay may be the best for the transmission pair
that is helped but may be the worst in terms of the overall network capacity.
Therefore, there is need to design hybrid techniques that allow simultaneous
optimization over several parameter domains. In what concerns the relay failure
issues, there are many situations when the relay may fail or when the poor relay
is selected.

In what concerns the cooperative transmission design: the first issue is the
relay discovery. Most of the protocols require an image of neighborhood implemented in a table, normally based on channel qualities. Most of the protocols use
periodic broadcast for this purpose. Such periodic broadcast needs to be very
frequent to cope with network variations, in any case it limits the performance
of cooperative system. Another issue is coordination with relays; most of the
protocols use additional control messages for relay management in a centralized
manner. Such explicit notifications affect the gain of cooperation. Yet, in some
scenarios, it is infeasible to have such a centralized coordination [23]. The challenge is how to identify the cooperation capabilities of the possible relays in a
distributed manner.

2.3   Potential Benefits and Limitations of Cooperation

Spatial diversity is the main advantage provided by cooperative communications.
This property can be expressed in terms of increased diversity order [17]. As a
simple example (c.f. Fig. 5), if the channel quality between source node S and destination node D degrades severely, a direct transmission between these two nodes
may experience an error, which in turn leads to retransmissions. Alternatively,
S-D can exploit spatial diversity by having a relay R1 overhear the transmissions

and forward the frame to D. The source S may also use another relay R2 for helping in forwarding the information, or use both relays together. So, compared with
direct transmission, the cooperative approach enjoys a higher successful transmission probability. Therefore, cooperative communications have the ability to
mitigate the effects of shadow fading better than MIMO since, unlike MIMO,
antenna elements of a cooperative virtual antenna array are separated in space
and experience different shadow fading.

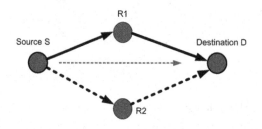

Fig. 5. Increasing diversity order.

Cooperative communications also ease the roll-out of a system that has no
infrastructure available prior to deployment. For instance, in disaster areas,
relaying can be used to facilitate communications even if existing communication
systems such as cellular systems are out of order.

Due to relaying, a node can reach to AP even via a relay, extending range and
avoiding handovers. In the case of pedestrian mobile networks, mobile devices
may perform pendular movements at the edge of an AP with high probability,
where devices will spend too much time performing handovers between neighbor
APs, leading to performance degradation. To avoid such situation, another device
can act as relay allowing the moving node to stay always associated to the same
AP, avoiding handovers (c.f. Fig. 6).

The limitations of cooperation can be as significant as the advantages. Therefore, cooperative network design needs to be performed carefully in order to

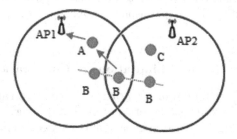

Fig. 6. Avoiding unwanted handovers.

achieve the full gains of cooperation and at the same time to ensure that cooperation does not cause degradation of system performance. As cooperative transmissions involve additional transmissions via relays, therefore, it always introduces some additional overhead and interference as compared to non-cooperative transmission. Thus, the benefits brought by cooperation can be diminished if relaying mechanism is not cleverly designed. There are many other constrains such as concurrent transmissions and mobility etc., which can affect the performance of cooperative networks [11]. Therefore, the implementation of cooperative relaying implies additional design constraints so that cooperative transmissions do not interfere with other direct transmissions. In cooperative systems, not only the traffic of different sources but also the relayed traffic needs to be scheduled. Thus, more sophisticated scheduling is required.

3   Analysis of Cooperative Relaying

Both the telecommunications operators and the end-users would reject a wireless network with cooperative diversity if the PHY layer requires manual configuration. So the role of the MAC layer is essential. In addition to cooperation control, the MAC layer must support error recovery, dynamic optimization, mobility support, relay selection and cooperation decision [11].

Cooperative relaying at MAC layer comprises two phases: relay selection and cooperative transmission. In the first phase a relay or group of relays are selected, while in the latter phase the transmission via relay(s) takes place. The relays can be selected either by source (source-based), destination (destination-based), or by the relay itself (relay-based). At MAC layer we can classify cooperative protocols as proactive and reactive. In the proactive protocols, the cooperation is based on some pre-arranged optimal or random format. In proactive relaying the source, destination or potential relay replaces the slow direct transmission with a fast, one-hop relayed transmission, aiming to improve the data-rate [27]. These protocols are time critical and incur higher overheads. They require frequent information exchange for timely delivery of data. Whereas, in reactive protocols, the cooperation is initiated with a Negative ACK (NACK) due to collision or error [16]. Reactive protocols are appropriate for applications that are delay tolerant and incur lower overhead.

In what concerns the 802.11 MAC, Fig. 7 shows a basic 802.11b system where nodes have different transmission rates at different distance from AP. Cooperation at MAC enables source node to find a relay node and transmit via that relay. The relay node must be within the cooperation area to rectify the impact of low rate nodes. In Fig. 7, R_{11} is the distance from AP to transmit at 11 Mbps, while r_{11} is the distance from a source node to transmit at 11 Mbps and d is the distance from source to AP. The cooperation area is the intersection of two circles (R_{11} and r_{11}), defined as follows [31]:

$$CooperationArea = r^2 cos^{-1}(\frac{d^2 + r^2 + R^2}{2dR}) + R^2 cos^{-1}(\frac{d^2 + R^2 + r^2}{2dR}) -$$
$$\frac{1}{2}\sqrt{(-d+r+R)(d+r-R)(d-r+R)(d+r+R)} \qquad (1)$$

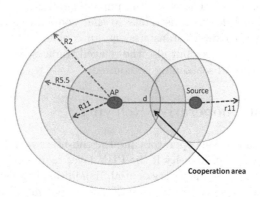

Fig. 7. Sample 802.11b network.

Such cooperation may also bring some extra overhead, mainly due to the high interference levels. In this case, the interference caused by relay transmissions will be, in the best case, directly proportional to the relay degree (i.e., number of neighbors). The situation may get worse in the presence of multi-hop networks, where the usage of hop-by-hop cooperation will increase the network cost (e.g., number of transmissions).

3.1 Taxonomy

As discussed, cooperative MAC can be classified as proactive and reactive. Proactive protocols work if the direct link between source and destination exists. Whereas, reactive protocols are initiated when the direct link fails. Hence, proactive relaying aims to increase the throughput of wireless networks while reactive relaying aims to decrease degradation by avoiding retransmissions. Proactive relaying can be further split into broadcast-based protocols, and opportunistic protocols, as illustrated in Fig. 8.

Broadcast-based protocols represent a relatively simple strategy by utilizing the broadcasting nature of the wireless medium. While broadcast-based protocols offer more control due to its centralized nature, opportunistic relaying is the one where nodes can independently make cooperation within certain time constraint under some conditions. Such relaying does not require extra control messages. The reactive protocols can be further classified as broadcast-based protocols, opportunistic protocols, and multi-hop protocols.

From the classification of cooperative MAC protocols shown in Fig. 8, it is apparent that most of the literature focuses on the broadcast-based protocols due to their easy implementation and backward compatibility. Multiple relay broadcast protocols, though not very well researched, require better coordination among the multiple relays, thus increasing the complexity. In the next section, we provide details of some existing protocols.

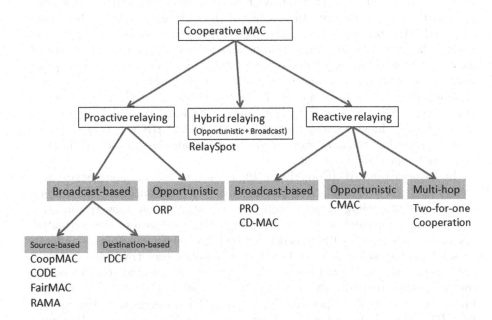

Fig. 8. Cooperative MAC classifications.

3.2 Cooperative Relaying Protocols

In general, both proactive and reactive approaches have their pros and cons, which greatly depends on individual mechanisms. Therefore, it is important to study individual protocols irrespective of their class. Following we describe cooperative MAC protocols grouped into families as mentioned in Fig. 8.

3.2.1 Broadcast-Based Protocols

In this type of protocols normally sources or destination or potential relays maintain a table which is updated periodically based on broadcasting. The limitations of this sub-class are periodic broadcasts, maintenance of table and extra control overhead which effect the performance. These protocols can be proactive as well as reactive.

Relay-enabled DCF (rDCF) protocol was developed by Zhu and Cao [32] based on Distributed coordination function (DCF), where a high data-rate dual-hop path is used instead of a low data-rate direct path between the source and destination. For a given flow between a pair of sender and receiver, with the measured channel quality, if a relay finds that the data can be transmitted faster, it adds the identity (e.g., MAC address) of the sender and the receiver into its willing list. Periodically, each relay node advertises its willing list to its one-hop neighbors, from where the source picks a relay. rDCF proposed a triangular handshake mechanism for source-relay-destination transmission. First source node send Relay Request To Send (RRTS). After reception of RRTS, the relay and destination can measure the quality of the channel. The relay then sends another RRTS to destination with a piggybacked measurement information of source-relay channel. The destination measures the quality of relay-destination channel and sends Relay Clear To Send (RCTS) to the source including rate information of source-relay and relay-destination channels.

However, rDCF is only suitable if the frame size is larger than 400 bytes. Otherwise, rDCF gives worse performance when compared to DCF because of its relatively higher overhead. Another drawback of rDCF is that when the relay is forwarding the data frame, it does not include the duration field, which increases the probability of collisions.

In Cooperative MAC (CoopMAC) [19], the source uses an intermediate node (relay) that experiences relatively good channel with the source and the destination. Instead of sending frames directly to the destination at a low transmission rate, the source makes use of a dual-hop high data-rate path to the destination via a relay. Based on the CSI broadcasted by potential helpers, sources update a local table (cooptable) used to select the best relay for each transmission. CoopMAC performs 3-way handshakes, which require the selected relay to send a control message Helper ready To Select (HTS) between RTS and CTS messages. First, source sends a Cooperative RTS (CoopRTS) message with the selected relay ID. If the selected relay is willing to cooperate, it then sends an HTS message back to source. If destination overhears an HTS message, it transmits a CTS. After receiving CTS, the source sends the data frame to destination via selected relay.

The solution CODE [30] uses two relays to form the virtual antenna array and additionally makes use of the physical layer network coding technique to achieve the gain. For bidirectional traffic between the source and destination, network coding is applied at the relay node to increase system throughput. In CODE all nodes overhear RTS/CTS frames, and if they find that they can transmit data faster than the source, they add the identity of source and destination to their willingness list. Once the source finds its address in the willing list of relay(s), it adds those relay(s) into its cooperation table.

FairMAC, presented in [3], concerns about the energy cost of cooperation, since there is a trade-off between energy per transmitted bit and achieved throughput. FairMAC, allows the selection of the desired cooperation factor, which represents the limit of frames to be relayed for each own frame transmitted.

Relay-Aided Medium Access (RAMA) [33] protocol proposed the relay-based transmission to improve the performance and reduce the transmission time. RAMA consists of two parts: first is the invitation part which is used to configure the relay and second is the transmission part. RAMA allows only one relay in a transmission and in case of collision of the invitation, the relay node does not need to transmit and wait for the next transmission.

In Opportunistic Retransmission Protocol (PRO) [20] a potential relay may retransmit on behalf of a source when it detects a failed transmission. In PRO the potential relays broadcast their channel information allowing other relays to set their priority level. Based on priority level relays then select their contention window in order to increase chances of retransmission. Thus, each node maintains a table to keep the channel information (priority levels) of neighbors. Such maintenance operation consumes power, resources and affects the network capacity. Another problem is the occurrence of unnecessary retransmissions, if eligible relays do not overhear an ACK frame of successful transmission.

In Cooperative Diversity MAC (CD-MAC) [21], when the direct link fails, retransmission takes place via a relay. First the source and its preselected relay send a Cooperative RTS (CRTS) to the destination. Destination and its preselected relay respond with Cooperative CTS (CCTS). After receiving a CCTS, the source and its relay cooperatively transmit the data frame to destination and its relay. After receiving data frame, destination and its relay cooperatively transmit Cooperative ACK (CACK). There is high overhead of control frames as source, destination and relay repeat the whole control and data frames in different codes.

3.2.2 Opportunistic Protocols

These protocols do not maintain tables, therefore, a relay can forward data opportunistically without prior coordination.

Opportunistic Relaying Protocol (ORP) [7] is a relaying solution where nodes are able to increase their effective transmission rate by using dual-hop high data-rate links. ORP does not rely on the RSSI for relay selection. It opportunistically makes a frame available for relaying and all nodes try to forward that frame within the time constraint. However, the relays back-off every time they forward. Another drawback of this approach is that the source does not know about the availability of a relay, so it does not know rates of source-relay and relay-destination channels.

Cooperative Communication MAC (CMAC) [28] introduces spatial diversity via user cooperation. In case of CMAC each node stores the source node data frame. If no ACK is overheard the relay forwards the stored data frame on behalf of source. Due to usage of additional queues and channel estimations, CMAC faces the challenges of overhead.

3.2.3 Multi-hop Protocols

In the two-for-one cooperation approach [18], cross layering is used to provide routing information to the MAC layer in order to allow simultaneous relaying over two hops. The two-for-one cooperation is particularly suited to achieve high diversity with little bandwidth expansion. At a given Packet-Error-Rate

(PER), the gain of the two-for-one approach can be used to reduce transmit power, improving network capacity. However, it presents the problem of unnecessary transmissions. Another multi-hop relaying approach is proposed by H. Adam el al. [1]. It exploits synergy between single-hop relays (helping only one transmission) and multi-hop relays (helping two transmissions simultaneously) taking into account information provided by a link-state routing protocol. The used scenario excludes a potential (even if weak) direct link between source and destination. Still, as occurred with the proposal presented by H. Lichte et al. [18], the presented solution depends on a global topological view of the network provided by the routing protocol. Moreover, it is not justified why is the usage of a single-hop relay over the destination link, and not the source link, the best choice: considering that a bad channel from source to relay will jeopardize the effort applied from the relay to the destination, it could make sense to have the single-hop relay helping the source transmission.

3.2.4 Hybrid Relaying

Hybrid relaying improves the performance of wireless networks by an efficient combination of proactive (broadcast-based and opportunistic) and reactive relaying [10,16]. With hybrid approaches such as RelaySpot [11,12] a relay is chosen for a cooperative transmission opportunistically, without any broadcast overhead. The relay is selected cooperatively without maintaining any table. The cooperative transmission takes place without any further contention or handshake messages. Poor relay selection and relay failures are adjusted dynamically without expecting the relay selection procedure. Therefore, we conclude that such hybrid behavior has potential to rectify drawbacks that occur in prior art, in what concern broadcast-based and opportunistic relaying.

RelaySpot comprises four building blocks: Opportunistic relay selection, cooperative relay scheduling, chain relaying and cooperative relay switching, as explained below:

- Opportunistic relay selection: Intermediate nodes may take the opportunity to relay in the presence of local favorable conditions (e.g., no concurrent traffic) after detecting one of two situations: (i) a broken communication; (ii) a poor direct transmission, by analyzing the wireless data-rate;
- Cooperative relay scheduling: The destination node will be able to cooperate in the relay selection procedure by electing one over several potential relays, based on the quality of the relays. In RelaySpot, the cooperative scheduling mechanism can create diversity higher than two, by selecting more than one relay.
- Relay switching: This functionality aims to compensate unsuccessful relay transmissions. Relay selection faces several optimization problems that are difficult to solve, which means that the best relay may be difficult to find by the destination based on the set of potential relays. Hence, aiming to be suitable for dynamic scenarios, RelaySpot allows the destination to select the best possible relaying opportunity even if not the optimal one (e.g., in terms

of CSI). In order to keep a good quality level in case of a bad decision from the destination, RelaySpot allows potential relays to take over the control of the relay operation, by asking the source to switch the relay for the subsequent data frames.

RelaySpot can also be extended to multi-hop [14] by using chain relaying. With the usage of chain relaying, the relaying will be triggered over relay-destination link. This leading to serial relaying, i.e., multi-hop relaying. Such relaying can be beneficial only if the relay is aware of next hop. Hence, the relay can forward the frame to next hop. This way complexity of hop-by-hop relaying can be mitigated. In chain relaying, the destination node may receive more than two independent signals of the same frame (e.g., directly via the source, via the intermediary node identified by the routing protocol and via the selected relay node). This extra spatial diversity increases robustness and performance. However, the price to pay is the extra network overhead to transmit redundant information, and the cross layering needed to collect routing information, which may not be updated with the frequency required to react in environments with mobile devices.

3.3   Cooperative Relaying Functionalities

All proposed solutions have their benefits and drawbacks, and none of them is completely superior to the others. In this section, we identify the common functionalities that the protocols follow. In [4] the cooperation process is proposed into four phase process, which are (i) discovery and request, (ii) negotiation, (iii) transaction, and (iv) evaluation and feedback. The first phase is cooperation initiation, negotiation refers to conditions, transaction refers to rewards while last phase refers to quality of experience.

From the analysis of cooperative MAC protocols, it is clear that cooperation brings benefits to the operation of wireless networks but its usage over large networks may introduce undesirable levels of overhead and complexity. The complexity is mainly due to the number of channel estimations, while the overhead is mainly due to the multiple copies of data messages and feedback signals. The complexity may increase due to the number of times relay transmission fail. Moreover, waiting for optimal relay to assist one transmission degrades the overall performance of the network and decreases its capacity.

Before investigating suitable solutions, we need to answer the following questions: (i) when do we really need to use cooperative relaying? (ii) how to coordinate? and (iii) whom to cooperate with? For cooperation to be triggered, we need to compare the transmission throughput achieved by proposals that take advantage of spatial diversity (cooperative relaying) over the direct link. The coordination between cooperative nodes can be done implicitly or with minimum feedback. To devise a cooperative relay solution able to achieve a good balance between interference and transmission throughput it is important to start by investigating the choice of relay selection parameters, as well as consideration of evaluation scenarios. The performance of cooperative relaying greatly depends upon the used scenario, on the other hand it gives opportunity to analyze various aspects, such as concurrent transmissions.

As mentioned before, cooperative relaying comprises of relay selection and cooperative transmission as explained below.

3.3.1   Relay Selection

With cooperative relaying, the relay selection process requires special attention, since it has a strong impact on network and transmission performance. Independently of operating only at the link layer or in combination with cooperative diversity schemes at the physical layer, the performance of cooperative relaying strongly depends upon the efficiency of the process used to select one or more relays.

It is clear that the major challenge in cooperative relaying is to select a node, or set of nodes, which can effectively improve data transmission. Although most of the current schemes envision operation under a single AP, relay selection mechanisms should be carefully defined thinking about large networks. A reason is the impact that one relay may have on concurrent transmissions.

The first aspect that needs to be considered when analyzing relay selection mechanisms is related to the selection criteria. The most common in the literature are: CSI, SNR and Bit-Error-Rate (BER). Since such parameters need to be measured in both sender-relay and relay-receiver links, relay selection may require the exchange of meta-data, usually transported within RTS and CTS frames.

The second aspect is the impact on the overall network. Normally, relays are selected to improve the performance of a source-destination communication [19], but no consideration is taken about the impact over the overall network capacity. Such selfish behavior may lead to higher probability of transmission blocking and interference.

In what concerns the level of interaction, relay selection mechanisms has two categories: *Distributed or Opportunistic Relay Selection* (ORS) and *Centralized or Cooperative Relay Selection* (CRS) [9].

With ORS each potential relay decides about forwarding frames, based on the information that it has about the network. This may lead to a high probability of selecting more than one relay whose transmissions end up competing for the wireless medium. Such mechanisms present a high probability of collisions.

While CRS process encompasses two phases: In the first phase relays broadcast willingness to relay and local information that will be useful for relay selection. Such information is overheard by other nodes, which can then participate in the selection of one or more relays in a second phase. One drawback of cooperative relay selection is the potential lack of synchronization between the two operational phases. As a consequence, relaying may not occur if a node that was selected as relay is not available when transmission occurs, due to mobility or lack of energy. Another problem with this class are the periodic broadcast and extra handshaking signals which can limit the efficiency.

3.3.2   Cooperative Transmission

Since the wireless channel condition varies from time to time, a source node may not always need help from relay nodes. Therefore, the first issue is when cooperative transmissions should be enabled. To initiate cooperation, implicit or explicit notifications are required, such signaling overhead should be considered in making a decision on whether or not to use cooperation. It is necessary to compare the non-cooperative scenario with the cooperative options in terms of proficiency and cost.

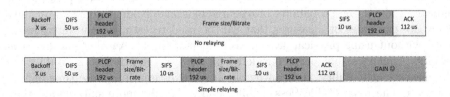

Fig. 9. Simple relaying gain.

Relaying involves transmission of two data frames separated in time and space; therefore, it introduces overhead, which increases due to additional control messages. However, significant gain can be achieved by a careful selection of reservation duration and back-off timings. Figure 9 shows the gain of cooperative relaying in 802.11 (when there is no extra control message). As seen in Fig. 9 a regular data transmission with acknowledgment takes longer to send data when compared to the data transmission based on a relay protocol. With a relay protocol the relatively slow nodes would reserve the channel for a duration of *frame_size/(fast_data_rate=11Mbps)* instead of *frame_size/(slow_data_rate=1Mbps)* and the other nodes will benefit from this with higher probability of accessing the channel.

Irrespective of relay selection mechanism, one of the important issue is relay management. Most cooperative MAC protocols require an image of their surroundings, typically implemented through a neighbor table, possibly featuring estimates of link qualities and cooperation possibilities. The neighbors discovery mechanism, either passive (overhearing) or active (polling), leads to creation of willing list. Unfortunately, even if a relay is being able to cooperate, it might refuse to do so due to changes in network conditions etc. Therefore, the relaying protocol needs to track the network changes and relying over stable parameters.

4   Open Research Issues

From the realized analysis we make two strong observations: (i) all approaches assume static devices, small networks with high probability or a direct source-destination link usage, and the need to use always one relay; (ii) there is no single approach that presents good behavior in terms of both transmission and network capacity. These observations lead to the identification of two important research issues: (i) achieve a good balance between interference and transmission throughput; (ii) improve the capacity of large mobile networks.

To limit communication overhead, especially in large networks, it is important to investigate the intelligent usage of thresholds over local variables, since they can filter out poor relays as well as unwanted transmissions.

In what concern the parameters themselves, majority of previous work uses local variables such as SNR, BER, CSI (with the exception of RelaySpot). Since these are very unstable parameters, we propose the usage of less volatile parameters, namely interference level, and stability. Interference level provides an indication about the probability of resource blockage. Node degree and queuing delay are examples of measures that can be used to estimate the interference level, without using physical layer measurements [13,15]. Another parameter is stability, which has not been considered by most of the prior work. Stability is the measure of mobility, and can be obtained by estimating pause time or link duration. The more stable (less mobile) nodes are, the more suitable are they to operate as relays. So, this investigation leads to the conclusion that the most suitable parameters for large scale networks are devised by using local parameters characterized by being less volatile than the usual SNR, BER and CSI parameters.

Apart from stability and interference, there are other issues we identified, such as usage of multiple relays, protocol overhead, energy efficiency and multi-hop relaying.

With the exception of CODE and RelaySpot, all analyzed proposals rely upon the usage of one relay to help one transmission. However, the advantage of selecting more than one relay to help the same transmission (even if in different time frames), should be further investigated. The presence of multiple relays over the same link requires the analysis of the gains that physical layer coding offers in comparison to a full link layer approach.

While relaying in wireless communication networks can improve network performance, such protocols can incur a considerable overhead. This overhead includes signaling and network control overhead for cooperative transmission, relay selection and coordination, additional required resources such as radio bandwidth for relay transmission. Another form of cooperation overhead is the incurred delay of the whole communication process which includes the time consumed in selecting the relays and establishing the cooperative paths. Finally, this cooperation overhead also includes the overall added complexity to the networking process. The cooperation overhead affects the decision of whether or not cooperation should proceed. In literature, only signaling overhead for relay selection and coordination is considered in the decision process [26]. Other forms of cooperation overhead should be appropriately modeled and taken into account in the cooperation decision.

Introduction of power control and rate adaptation in relay based MAC protocols to increase spatial reuse, reduce interference and improve energy efficiency. Most of the relay selection is based on the available rates only and may result in reuse of the same relay again and again. This would drain the energy of this relay thus lose a potential cooperative partner. This requires the design of efficient and fair relay selection algorithms that can select the potential relays based on energy consumption and network throughput together. This would result in network lifetime maximization and fairness.

Although significant efforts have been made on the study of cooperative systems, there has been very little work on cooperative routing. Some of the relevant studies focus on the theoretical analysis on routing and cooperative diversity [8]. With regard to the implementation of a cooperative routing protocol, the theoretical optimal route is too complicated and therefore unsuitable for the current status of ad-hoc and sensor networks.

An alternative way to extend cooperative relaying to the routing layer (multiple-hops between source and destination), it would be beneficial to further exploit the selection of relays that can help over multiple hops simultaneously (multi-hop relay selection), namely trying to identify the most suitable relay/hops ratio. However, current multi-hop relay selection approaches rely on link-state routing information, which means that they are not suitable for scenarios with intermittent connectivity. Hence the investigation of the usage of multi-hop relay selection in the presence of more opportunistic routing is an important research topic.

5 Summary

Cooperative Networking is a very active research area with promising developments. The MAC layer is the most important for a cooperative networking (relaying), as this relies on identifying alternative ways of transmission within a networked context. Therefore, for cooperation to be implemented at the link layer, link layer needs to be changed in order to allow indirect transmission between source and destination.

The development of cooperative relaying raises several research issues, including the performance impact on the relay itself, and on the overall network, leading to a potential decrease in network capacity and transmission fairness. Such research issues can be influenced not only by fading, but also by other performance constrains in wireless networks, such as the distance at which wireless nodes are from APs, as well as the mobility of such nodes.

This chapter discussed the topic of cooperative networking with emphasis on cooperative relaying. We proposed a taxonomy for cooperative systems comprising of PHY approaches and relaying stages. We further provided a taxonomy for cooperative relaying (MAC). This chapter has addressed a number of significant issues such as analysis and performance of relay based MAC protocols.

The advantage of cooperative relaying is possible if MAC layer is cleverly designed. Most relaying protocols rely on handshake messages, modifying the DCF of 802.11 MAC, either in cooperative or opportunistic way. Relaying protocols are expected to minimize signaling exchange, remove estimation of channel conditions, and improve the utilization of spatial diversity, minimizing outage and increasing reliability even in mobile environments.

References

1. Adam, H., Bettstetter, C., Senouci, S.M.: Multi-hop-aware cooperative relaying. In: Proceedings of IEEE VTC, Barcelona, Spain, April 2009
2. Azarian, K., Gamal, H., Schniter, P.: On the achievable diversity multiplexing tradeoff in half-duplex cooperative channels. IEEE Trans. Inf. Theory **51**(12), 4152–4172 (2005)
3. Bocherer, G., Mathar, R.: On the throughput/bit-cost tradeoff in CSMA based cooperative networks. In: Proceedings of ITG Conference on Source and Channel Coding (SCC) (2010)
4. Bogliolo, A., Polidori, P., Aldini, A., Moreira, W., Mendes, P., Yildiz, M., Ballester, C., Seigneur, J.: Virtual currency and reputation-based cooperation incentives in user-centric networks. In: Proceedings of IEEE IWCMC, Cyprus, August 2012
5. Cover, T., El Gamal, A.: Capacity theorems for the relay channel. IEEE Trans. Inf. Theory **IT–25**, 57284 (1979)
6. Elmenreich, W., Marchenko, N., Adam, H., Hofbauer, C., Brandner, G., Bettstetter, C., Huemer, M.: Building blocks of cooperative relaying in wireless systems. Electr. Comput. Eng. **125**(10), 353–359 (2008). (Springer)
7. Feeney, L.M., Cetin, B., Hollos, D., Kubisch, M., Mengesha, S., Karl, H.: Multi-rate relaying for performance improvement in IEEE 802.11 WLANs. In: Boavida, F., Monteiro, E., Mascolo, S., Koucheryavy, Y. (eds.) WWIC 2007. LNCS, vol. 4517, pp. 201–212. Springer, Heidelberg (2007)
8. Gui, B., Dai, L., Cimini, L.: Routing strategies in multihop cooperative networks. IEEE J. Wirel. Commun. **7**(8), 3066–3078 (2008)
9. Jamal, T., Mendes, P.: Relay selection approaches for wireless cooperative networks. In: Proceedings of IEEE WiMob, Niagara Falls, Canada, October 2010
10. Jamal, T., Mendes, P.: Analysis of hybrid relaying in cooperative WLAN. In: Proceedings of IFIP WirelessDays, Valencia, Spain, November 2013
11. Jamal, T., Mendes, P.: Cooperative relaying for dynamic networks. EU Patent, (EP13182366.8), August 2013
12. Jamal, T., Mendes, P.: Cooperative relaying in wireless user-centric networks. In: Aldini, A., Bogliolo, A. (eds.) User Centric Networking - Future Perspectives. LNSN, pp. 171–195. Springer, Heidelberg (2014)
13. Jamal, T., Mendes, P., Zúquete, A.: Interference-aware opportunistic relay selection. In: Proceedings of ACM CoNEXT Student Workshop, Tokyo, Japan, December 2011
14. Jamal, T., Mendes, P., Zúquete, A.: RelaySpot: a framework for opportunistic cooperative relaying. In: Proceedings of IARIA ACCESS, Luxembourg, June 2011
15. Jamal, T., Mendes, P., Zúquete, A.: Opportunistic relay selection for wireless cooperative network. In: Proceedings of IEEE IFIP NTMS, Istanbul, Turkey, May 2012
16. Jamal, T., Mendes, P., Zúquete, A.: Wireless cooperative relaying based on opportunistic relay selection. Int. J. Adv. Netw. Serv. **5**(2), 116–127 (2012)
17. Kramer, G., Gastpar, M., Gupta, P.: Cooperative strategies and capacity theorems for relay networks. IEEE Trans. Inf. Theory **51**, 3033–3063 (2005)
18. Lichte, H.S., Valentin, S., Karl, H., Loyola, L., Widmer, J.: Design and evaluation of a routing-informed cooperative MAC protocol for Ad hoc networks. In: Proceedings of IEEE INFOCOM, Phoenix, USA, April 2008
19. Liu, P., Tao, Z., Narayanan, S., Korakis, T., Panwar, S.: CoopMAC: a cooperative MAC for wireless LANs. IEEE J. Sel. Areas Commun. **25**(2), 340–354 (2007)

20. Mei-Hsuan, L., Peter, S., Tsuhan, C.: Design, implementation and evaluation of an efficient opportunistic retransmission protocol. In: Proceedings of IEEE MobiCom, Beijing, China, April 2009
21. Moh, S., Yu, C., Park, S., Kim, H., Park, J.: CD-MAC: cooperative diversity MAC for robust communication in wireless Ad hoc networks. In: Proceedings of IEEE Conference on Communications, Glasgow, Scotland, pp. 3636–3641, June 2007
22. Nosratinia, A., Hunter, T., Hedayat, A.: Cooperative communication in wireless networks. IEEE Commun. Mag. **42**, 74–80 (2004)
23. Ozgur, A., Leveque, O., Tse, D.L.: Hierarchical cooperation achieves optimal capacity scaling in Ad hoc networks. IEEE Trans. Inf. Theory **53**(10), 3549–3572 (2007)
24. Pabst, R., Walke, B.H., Schultz, D.C., Herhold, P., Yanikomeroglu, H., Mukherjee, S.: Relay-based deployment concepts for wireless and mobile broadband radio **42**, 80–89 (2004)
25. Sendonaris, A., Erkip, E., Aazhang, B.: User cooperative diversity, part ii: implementation aspects and performance analysis. IEEE Trans. Commun. **51**(11), 1939–1948 (2003)
26. Shan, H., Wang, P., Zhuang, W., Wang, Z.: Cross-layer cooperative triple busy tone multiple access for wireless networks. In: Proceedings of IEEE Globecom, New Orleans, USA, December 2008
27. Shan, H., Zhuang, W., Wang, Z.: Distributed cooperative MAC for multi-hop wireless networks. IEEE Commun. Mag. **47**(2), 126–133 (2009)
28. Shankar, S., Chou, C., Ghosh, M.: Cooperative communication MAC (CMAC): a new MAC protocol for next generation wireless LANs. In: Proceedings of International Conference on Wireless Networks, Communications and Mobile Computing, Maui, Hawaii (2005)
29. Stallings, W.: Wireless Communication and Networks. Pearson Prentice Hall, NJ (2005)
30. Tan, K., Wan, Z., Zhu, H., Andrian, J.: CODE: cooperative medium access for multirate wireless Ad hoc network. In: Proceedings of IEEE SECON, California, USA, June 2007
31. Weisstein, E.W.: Circle-circle intersection. From MathWorld-A Wolfram Web Resource. http://mathworld.wolfram.com/Circle-CircleIntersection.htm
32. Zhu, H., Cao, G.: rDCF: a relay-enabled medium access control protocol for wireless Ad Hoc networks. In: Proceedings of IEEE INFOCOM, pp. 12–22 (2005)
33. Zou, S., Li, B., Wu, H., Zhang, Q., Zhu, W., Cheng, S.: A relay-aided media access (RAMA) protocol in multirate. Wirel. Netw. **5**, 1657–1667 (2006)

Clustering for Networks of Moving Objects

Veselin Rakocevic[✉]

Department of Electrical and Electronic Engineering,
City University London, London, UK
Veselin.Rakocevic.1@city.ac.uk

Abstract. This chapter presents the problem of clustering of moving objects in ad hoc wireless networks. The networks of moving objects include networks of flying objects, networks of cars and other vehicles, networks of people moving in the cities, and networks of robots sensing the environment or performing coordinated actions. Clustering of such objects increases the scalability of the network and improves efficiency, enabling the objects to simplify the communication with their peers. Clustering of static network objects has been analysed in great detail in the literature. While most of the clustering algorithms and protocols are applicable in the networks of moving objects, there are specific challenges produced by the mobility. This document will present a rich body of currently available scholarly work on clustering for moving objects, focusing on the case when all network nodes (both clusterheads and cluster members) are moving. Most of the research works presented in this Chapter aim to predict the movement of the networked nodes, or to measure the relative mobility between the nodes, in order to optimise the processes of clusterhead election and cluster maintenance.

Keywords: Clustering · Ad hoc networks · Mobility

1   Introduction

The modern world has witnessed a significant increase in the number and the complexity of electronic objects which move and have a need to be networked. These objects include a variety of robot devices, sensors, small flying machines, vehicles and smart telephones and handheld devices carried around by millions of people. Networks of these devices are built on wireless communication channels, which are unstable. Further to this, the fact that the network nodes (objects) are constantly moving implies that their point of attachment to the network is constantly changing, and their neighbours are not fixed. Designing networks for moving objects is complex; it requires fresh solutions to the problems that have already been solved for networking of fixed objects.

The design of ad hoc networks for moving objects is the main subject of this Chapter. Clustering of distributed network nodes can be defined as the generation of groups of nodes which share some common features and communicate to the rest of the network via their leader (often called the clusterhead), rather than

© Springer International Publishing Switzerland 2014
I. Ganchev et al. (Eds.): Wireless Networking for Moving Objects, LNCS 8611, pp. 70–87, 2014.
DOI: 10.1007/978-3-319-10834-6_5

individually. The common feature of the network elements is typically their geographic location, although other features, such as speed of movement, application interest or established trust agreements can be considered. Clustering is important in distributed networks, as it contributes to improved network efficiency, connectivity and saves the cost of networking communication with regard to resource utilisation, power consumption and signalling overhead. In the process of clustering we can identify the following two processes: (1) clusterhead election process; (2) cluster maintenance. Clusterheads are typically elected using a distributed algorithm in which all nodes follow a predefined sequence of steps and elect the clusterhead based on a predefined election rule. Cluster maintenance process deals with the life of cluster, with the routing of packets inside the cluster and the processes that take place when cluster members have to leave the cluster or new cluster members join the cluster.

Clustering in wireless ad hoc networks and more specifically in wireless sensor networks has been analysed extensively over the last few decades. A number of clustering solutions for sensor networks have been designed, showing major performance improvements in terms of network efficiency (i.e. the number of routing messages, or the number of retransmissions due to unnecessary collisions), or power consumption. Significant theoretical work in leader election algorithms and connected dominating set establishments have paved the way for numerous protocols and algorithms that have been designed and tested in the simulation and experimental environments over the past decades. Some of the most important of these solutions will be presented in this Chapter as they typically form the basis of the mobility-aware clustering network designs. It is well known that clustering combined with data aggregation mechanisms can significantly improve the overall network efficiency.

During the last decade we have witnessed the emergence of a new generation of electronic systems which have potential to have a significant impact on everyday life and industry. This new generation includes various so-called cyberphysical systems: robots, small quadcopters or similar unmanned small flying objects, networked intelligence integrated in our cars, wearable sensor networks, etc. These devices form what is known today as the Internet of Things. These devices typically require communication and naturally form networks. Networks that can be small, consisting of only a few moving robots investigating a difficult terrain, or can be large, with thousands or tens of thousands little sensors forming huge networks, very difficult to manage. Clustering these objects to simplify their communication is not only a useful add-on to the operation of these networks, but an absolute necessity.

The objective of this Chapter is to present the problem of clustering in distributed networks of objects that may be moving. Contrary to many existing research surveys, we focus here on the movement of all network nodes, both the clusterhead nodes and the 'standard' nodes. The movement generates the following problems:

– The clusters become unstable, because members of the clusters move and can often disappear out of the range of the clusterhead. For this reason, it is often that the slowest moving element is elected as the clusterhead.
– In the case the clusters perform some data aggregation, the lack of stability of the cluster can have a major impact on the quality of the aggregated data.
– The movement of the networked objects means that clusterheads cannot count on the connectivity of the nodes, and the amount of time the nodes are not connected into the networks increases.

Considering the listed problems, it will come as no surprise that the majority of researchers today tend to think towards predicting the movement of the networked objects, in order to predict the next step of the clustering process before any damage is created by the movement of the nodes.

However, before we get more into the detail of clustering for mobility, it is necessary to remind ourselves about the nature of the distributed networks, the principles and ideas for clustering, and the modelling techniques we can use to model the networks we discuss.

2   Topology Management in Distributed Networks

We define distributed networks as networks without a clear point of centralised control. In communication literature, such networks are often called ad hoc networks, to emphasise the temporary and random process of network formation. In such networks, typically all nodes are at equal hierarchical level. Depending on the geographical distribution of nodes and the communication requirement of such a network, the number of potential direct communication links between nodes can be very large. In these networks, when a node needs to transmit data packets to another node, it can do this directly in the case the receiving node is in the range of the sending node, or indirectly, by using other network nodes as routers. For this reason, routing procedures and protocols are required in ad hoc networks. Considering the fact that ad hoc networks can grow very large, one of the main challenges is how to operate an efficient network service in such a network. It is clearly not optimal to broadcast all data packets to all nodes in the networks, as this will have major implications on the resource utilisation and energy consumption (often these networks are energy-limited). A certain level of the control over the network structure (topology) is required.

Topology control in ad hoc networks can be done in many ways. Over the past few decades, two main directions of topology control in ad hoc networks have been identified: hierarchical topology organisation and power control.

In the hierarchical topology organisation the network nodes are grouped together (clustered) in smaller networks. One of the network nodes is elected to be a clusterhead, and all packets communicated from or to other nodes in the group (cluster) have to go through the clusterhead. We can see an example of a clustered network in Fig. 1. The white nodes on Fig. 1 represent clusterheads, and the blue nodes represent the standard nodes. We can see how the clustering process introduces a clear structure into the network.

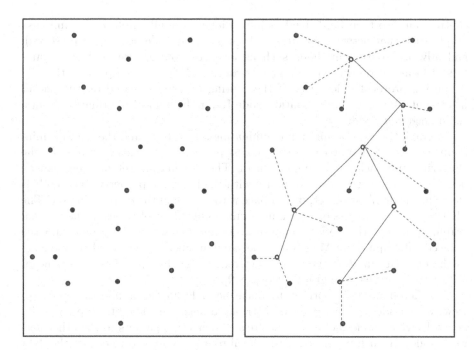

Fig. 1. Ad hoc network: unconnected (left) and fully connected and clustered (right) (Color figure online)

Topology control using power control is based on the idea that network nodes can have different transmission ranges - this can be controlled by varying the signal strength at transmission. Performing careful power control can establish communication patterns in the network that can increase the efficiency of the network communication. We can consider that the fewer the incidents when network nodes receive packets that are not destined for them, the more efficient the network is.

It is worth remembering that clustering is not a technique that is only used in distributed communication networks. As described in the work of [1,2], given any data set of connected elements, the goal of clustering is to divide the data set into clusters such that the elements assigned to a particular cluster are similar or connected in some predefined sense.

In general, the topology of an ad hoc network can be presented by an undirected graph $G = (V; E)$, where V is the set of network nodes, and $E \subseteq V \times V$ is the set of links between nodes. Nodes in an ad hoc network communicate through a common broadcast channel using omni-directional antennas with the same transmission range. For any two nodes u and v that are within the packet-reception range of each other, u and v are called one-hop neighbours of each other. Two nodes that are not connected but share at least one common one-hop neighbour are called two-hop neighbour of each other. The challenge in topology control can also then be defined as [3]: to identify a subgraph of the unit disk graph, such that network features such as bounded node degree are preserved, and advance routing methods such as localized routing are enabled. Examples of localized routing include greedy routing [4–6], and compass routing [7]. A routing protocol is localized if the routing decision is based on the packet header information (i.e. destination node ID) and the local information from a small neighbourhood.

In graph theory, the minimum dominating set problem and the relevant minimum connected dominating set (MCDS) problem most closely represent the clustering approach to topology control. The dominating set problem can be described as finding a subset of nodes with the following property: each node is either in the dominating set, or is adjacent to a node in the dominating set. The MCDS problem consists of obtaining a minimum subset of nodes in the original graph, such that the nodes compose a dominating set of the graph, and the induced subgraph of an MCDS has the same number of connected components as the original graph. Although attractive, finding the MCDS is a well-known NP-complete problem in graph theory [8,9].

Another point is important to make here. From the application point of view, we can identify two types of distributed networks. The first type includes networks where nodes act as routers/relays, delivering packets to the other network nodes. In such networks, hierarchical routing is applied to ensure the data reaches their destination. Clustering in such networks is very important, as it enables hierarchical routing and optimises the routing process. An example of such a network would be a standard wireless sensor network, or a large-scale ad hoc network of everyday electronic appliances. When it comes to the issue of mobility in such networks, the challenge is great, as there is a critical requirement for fast reclustering of moving nodes to ensure packets are routed through the network in an efficient way.

The second network type is a network in which the nodes are required to communicate their location information and potentially some basic information about their environment, in order to help other nodes to get a better understanding of the environment around them. Typical examples of such networks are vehicular ad hoc networks for traffic information dissemination, or dissemination of safety-related information from a particular geographic location.

Whatever the service the network delivers and the requirement for clustering is, all clustering methods have several features in common. Cluster members all share a common feature, which can be location (cluster members are close to each other, often within a transmission range of the clusterhead), speed and direction of movement, or some application-level information. Clustering in mobile ad hoc networks is an area that has been analysed in the literature. Yu and Chong give a good survey on clustering algorithms in [11]. They investigate the cost of clustering and identify the following types of clustering solutions: (1) Dominating Set based clustering; (2) Low maintenance clustering; (3) Mobility-aware clustering; (4) Energy-efficient clustering; (5) Load Balancing clustering and (6) Clustering based on combined metrics. Their paper gives a good overview of representative algorithm that fit this classification. Similarly, Vodopivec et al. [12] give a short survey of clustering schemes focused on vehicular networks. One-hop clustering algorithms and their performance are surveyed in [13].

This Chapter will focus on how movement and mobility is represented in the clustering algorithms and protocols. We start the analysis by introducing the basic principles of cluster formation (Sect. 3). This is followed by an overview of mobility-aware clustering solutions in Sect. 4. Section 5 introduces the cluster maintenance processes, and briefly discusses the performance evaluation methods.

3   Cluster Formation

This section analyses the most important methods for cluster formation. While clustering - as we have already mentioned earlier in this document - is a generic method with many applications in data processing and in the analysis of live organisms and biological processes, here we focus on the cluster formation in wireless ad hoc networks. As we have seen earlier in the Chapter, clusters are typically formed in a distributed process of leader (clusterhead) election. This process requires all nodes to be able to identify themselves and all nodes to follow a pre-defined procedure. Early leader election algorithms chose the clusterheads on the basis of a given ID, or on the basis of the number of neighbours nodes have. We will see that mobility-aware clustering algorithms typically use the detailed information about the movement of the nodes to elect a clusterhead. But, firstly we need to introduce the basic leader election algorithms that have been proposed to use in ad hoc networking.

The *leader election* algorithm is a standard algorithm for distributed systems, often found in theory and practice. The classical definition of the leader election problem is to elect a unique leader from among the elements of a distributed system. In a mobile ad hoc network, we can expect that the network topology will change frequently, so the definition of the leader election algorithm can be modified, as it was done by Vasudevan et al. in [14]: the requirements for the leader election algorithm are: after topological changes stop sufficiently long, every connected component will eventually have a unique leader with maximum identifier from among the nodes in that component. Vasudevan et al. in [14] present a leader election algorithm which is based on a process of growing and then shrinking of a spanning tree that is rooted at the node that initiates the leader election process. In this algorithm, in the Election phase, the node sends Election message to its neighbours. The receiving nodes identify the sending node as a parent node. For each node there can be only one parent node. In the acknowledgement phase, an ack message is sent to each node from which Election message is received, apart from the parent node. Nodes respond to their parents only when all of their children have responded to them. In these acknowledgement messages nodes will announce to their parents the maximum identity node among all downstream nodes. Finally, in a phase that is called Leader, once the root node has received all acknowledgements rom all the children, it will broadcast a leader message to all nodes announcing the identity of the leader. Other proposals for leader election algorithms can be found in the work of Royer and Perkins [16], and Malpani et al. [17].

One of the best known simple clustering algorithms in the *lowest-ID* algorithm. In this algorithm, the node with the lowest identification number has the highest priority to be selected as the clusterhead. The lowest ID algorithm was originally proposed by Baker and Ephremides in [18,19]. The neighbouring nodes with higher IDs assume the role of cluster members and form the cluster. The clusterhead selection procedure is repeated for the remaining nodes until either each node is selected as a cluster-head or a cluster member. The lowest ID is known to be a two-hop cluster formation algorithm, since the distance between each node and every other node in a cluster is at most two hops. In its basic form, the algorithm assumes that all nodes are given some IDs before the network is set up. The nodes exchange the IDs and the nodes with larger IDs back up and declare themselves as network nodes, while those with higher ID become clusterheads. This algorithm in its basic form show no appreciation of the topology changes in the networks and it is expected that the level of reclustering is larger compared to the e.g. highest degree clustering.

A somehow natural extension of the lowest ID algorithm is the so-called *node-weight clustering* concept, where nodes are given weights (in a sense equivalent concept to Ids), but not randomly - the weights are given based on some specified feature of the nodes. Basagni [20] generalized the lowest-ID algorithm proposed by Gerla and Tsai [22], by using a generic weight as a criterion for cluster-head selection. In his distributed and mobility adaptive clustering (DMAC) algorithm, a weight is associated with each host in the network. This weight corresponds to the suitability of the host to be selected as a clusterhead. The weight was originally thought to represent the residual energy of the host, but as we will see in the next section, it can also represent the mobility level. In [21], Ghosh and Basagni investigated the impact of the different mobility degrees and mobility patterns of the mobile hosts on the performance of DMAC protocol. They showed that the cluster reorganization rate of DMAC protocol considerably increases in the presence of the host mobility. To address the negative impact of the host mobility on the performance of DMAC, Ghosh and Basagni proposed a generalization of DMAC protocol called GDMAC in which the clusters are more stable against the host mobility. GDMAC reduces the rate of unnecessary cluster updates by applying two limiting rules: (1) controlling the rate of reclustering by reclustering only when the weight of the new clusterhead exceeds the weight of the current one; (2) controlling the spatial density of the cluster-heads.

Another standard method for clustering is the *highest degree* algorithm. This algorithm, with its application to mobile ad hoc networks originally proposed by Gerla [22] and Parekh [23], is based on the idea that the node with a maximum number of neighbours is chosen as clusterhead. In this algorithm, the clusterhead is directly connected to all nodes in the cluster, so the maximum distance between two nodes is two hops, similarly to the lowest ID algorithm. This results in a typically lower throughput than other clustering algorithms, as the degree (the number of neighbours) for some of the clusterheads may be large.

Clustering algorithms do not have to support two-hop solutions only. We can take the example of a d-hop cluster formation given by Amis, Prakash, Vuong, and Huynh. In their paper [9] they first give a proof that the minimum d-hop dominating set problem is NP-complete, and then present an interesting heuristic for the construction of d-hop clusters in a network. In their heuristic, the clusters are formed following $2d$ rounds of broadcasting hello-type messages in the network. The basic idea is that each node maintains two arrays of nodes - WINNER and SENDER. Initially, each node sets WINNER to be equal to its ID, and then messages are broadcasted to all neighbours. Each node chooses the largest ID from all the received messages and puts it into the WINNER array. This process is called *Floodmax*. After d rounds of *Floodmax*, a separate process called *Floodmin* is performed, where, following a similar message broadcast, the smallest IDs are chosen and remembered. The *Floodmin* phase allows the relatively smaller clusterheads the opportunity to regain the nodes from the neighbourhood. The clustering algorithm follows these two message propagation processes with the next two stages: (a) determination of clusterheads and (b) linking of clusters. The determination of clusterheads happen based on simple rules - e.g. if a node received its own ID in the second round of flooding, the node immediately declares itself as a clusterhead. Otherwise, if a node finds another node in the WINNER arrays for both rounds of flooding, the node declares will declare that node as clusterhead. Finally, if neither of these two cases happens, the node will declare the maximum ID from the first round of flooding as clusterhead.

Another example of clusterhead formation where cluster size is not limited to two hops is the work of Er and Seah [33]. In their solution, the diameter of clusters is flexible and determined by the stability of clusters.

It is easy to see from these cluster formation examples, what may be the natural design idea for mobility-aware clusterhead formation. Rather than basing the clusterhead election decision on the ID of the node, or the node's degree, or an arbitrary weight, the idea would be to identify the nodes by their mobility level and/or movement direction, which can be measured in many different ways, as we will see later in this chapter. The idea then is to choose for the clusterheads those nodes that have a specific mobility pattern; in most of the works we can notice that there is an attempt to choose for the clusterhead the node that is the least mobile.

Finally, it is worth noting that clustering and cluster formation are not only applications of complex mathematical theory, but are networking techniques that needs to be designed to satisfy an application requirement. The work of Reumerman et al. [24] gives an interesting insight into what is called application-level clustering. They present a concept where each application can set up its own virtual cluster in order to optimise the information exchange relevant for that application. It is interesting to note that they distinguish between two cluster types (they mostly observe vehicular networks) - the 'moving cluster', where all cluster members move more or less together, in a group; and the 'quasi static cluster', where the identity of the cluster head and the cluster members is not important - the application requires a clusterhead and cluster members at a certain geographical location, to be able to disseminate certain information. This would typically be applied for applications on traffic information and safety-related information in vehicular networks.

4   Considering Mobility in Clustering Solutions

In the previous section we have seen that clustering formation algorithms typically support a distributed election process where all nodes follow a pre-defined rule when electing the clusterhead. In this section we will review the existing solutions for mobility-aware clustering. We will see that the majority of solutions attempt to predict the position of mobile nodes and perform clustering with this knowledge. This typically means that the clusterhead election focuses on the choice of a clusterhead that will ensure maximal stability for the network. The estimation of mobility focuses on the *local* mobility, i.e. the relative position of the nodes compared to their neighbours, rather than on the *global* mobility which can be accurately measured using GPS or other satellite-based global systems.

In the analysis given in this section, we focus on the case when all nodes in the network (both clusterhead nodes and non-clusterhead nodes) are moving. With this in mind, the focus on the analysis is to identify the existing solutions for clusterhead selection and cluster formation in the case when all nodes in the network are moving. A similar analysis can be made on the network connectivity for moving nodes when clusterheads are fixed and uniformly distributed. For more details about this, we refer to the excellent paper of Wang et al. [42].

In this section different methods for mobility consideration will be presented. We are interested to analyse the ways mobility can be measured and what parameters can be used in the process of clustering. We are looking at a simple basic case of nodes as presented in Fig. 2. There we have two nodes, x and y, which are changing their locations $l(x,t)$ and $l(y,t)$, using speed $v(x,t)$ and $v(y,t)$. We will see that mobility is used in clustering solutions in one of the following three ways: (1) by measuring the relative mobility of node x in comparison to node y; (2) by identifying similarities in the movement pattern of x and y; (3) by predicting the next locations of nodes x and y.

The general idea for using the relative mobility measure for cluster formation in network of moving objects typically follows a well-known MOBIC protocol [10], where estimation of node's speed variance is used in the clusterhead election process, with nodes with low speed variance having a better chance of becoming clusterheads. Basu et al. point out in [10] that correct estimation of local mobility is critical for the clustering process. A number of works investigate global mobility, by assuming the existence of the GPS or some other method of accurate positioning of the nodes. As clusters need to form and reform quickly, especially in the presence of high mobility, it is the local mobility, the relative speed/location difference between the nodes that is of interest. Basu et al. use the received power as the estimate of the distance between the nodes. While the received power is not the most accurate method of estimating the distance considering the wireless channel fading and other constraints to signal propagation, it is usually assumed that clustered nodes share the environmental constraints and the received power is often used as the estimate of the distance. Basu et al. introduce what they call the *relative mobility metric*, which is in essence the ratio of the received signal power between the old and the new packet that was exchanged between two nodes. The relative mobility metric can be defined as

$$M_y^{Rel}(x) = 10log_{10}\frac{Pr_{x->y}^{new}}{Pr_{x->y}^{old}} \tag{1}$$

For this to work, regular exchange of the packets is necessary. Regular exchange of packets is a feature of ad hoc networks, where periodic 'Hello' packets are exchanged between the neighbours. The aggregated local mobility for any node is then the variance with regard to zero of all relative mobilities for the neighbouring nodes:

$$M_y = var_0(M_y^{Rel}(x_1), M_y^{Rel}(x_2), M_y^{Rel}(x_3), ..., M_y^{Rel}(x_m)) = E[(M_y^{rel})^2] \tag{2}$$

Basu et al. continue to suggest that the node with the smallest variance of relative mobilities should be identified as the clusterhead, as this would maximise the cluster stability.

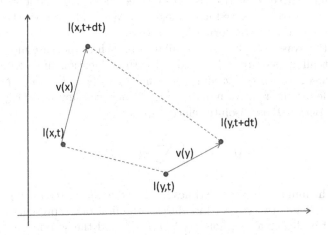

Fig. 2. Simple model of movement of two nodes, x and y

Other research presents similar approach to the problem. One of the first mobility analyses was performed in the well-known work of Johansson et al. [25]. They present a global mobility metric where the speed of node is measured relative to the other moving nodes. A mobility metric is proposed which is geometric in the sense that the speed of a node in relation to other nodes is measured. Johansson et al. propose a simple model where the relative velocity $v(x, y, t)$ at time t between node x which is at location $l(x, t)$ and node y which is at location of $l(y, t)$ (like in Fig. 2) can be expressed as $v(x, y, t) = \frac{d}{dt}[l(x, t) - l(y, t)]$. The mobility measure M_{xy} is defined as the absolute relative speed taken as average over the time period:

$$M_{xy} = \frac{1}{T} \int_{t_0}^{t_0+T} |v(x, y, t)| dt \tag{3}$$

Many other variations of the basic mobility analysis given by Basu et al. exist. For example, Wu et al. [37] use mobility index to characterize the mobility of each node. This index is shared in the hello messages and can be used to improve the stability of the clustering process. The mobility index is expressed as

$$M_y = \sum_{i=1}^{n} W_i * D_y^{x_i} \tag{4}$$

where W_i is a weight parameter defined as

$$W_i = \frac{(M_{x_i})^{-1}}{\sum\limits_{j=1}^{n} (M_{x_j})^{-1}}, \sum_{i=1}^{n} W_i = 1, \tag{5}$$

and $D_y^{x_i}$ is the relative geometric distance between node y and node x_i, calculated from two consecutively received hello messages. Wu et al. propose the use of the mobility index in the cluster formation process.

An and Papavassiliou [30] use a similar approach to measure mobility. They assume that all nodes are able to identify their location and define relative velocity between two nodes x and y at time t as $v(x, y, t) = v(x, t) - v(y, t)$. They then define the relative mobility $M_{x,y,T}$ between any pair (x, y) of nodes during time period T as absolute relative speed:

$$M_{x,y,T} = \frac{1}{N} \sum_{i=1}^{N} |v(x, y, T)| \tag{6}$$

where N is the number of discrete times the speed is calculated during the period T. Then they define two cluster mobilities - the first one represents the motion behaviour of a cluster as a whole, $\frac{1}{M} \sum v(i, T)$, and the second one represents the motion behaviour of nodes within the cluster, $\frac{1}{N} \sum M_{x,y,T}$, where M is the number of nodes in the cluster, and N is the number of node pairs in the cluster. The clusters are then formed by nodes exchanging the velocity information, calculating their mobility metrics and then the clusterhead can be elected only if its relative mobility is below a threshold.

Measuring relative mobility is done in a slightly different way by Er and Seah in [33]. They attempt to measure the variation of distance between nodes over time in order to estimate the relative mobility of two nodes. Their idea is to cluster together nodes that have a similar moving pattern. This idea is later used for clustering in vehicular networks, where there are several attempts to cluster the nodes based on their speed (e.g. [43,44]), so that the nodes that move at similar speeds are clustered together. Er and Seah, similarly to some other works we have seen here, use the received power strength to estimate the distance between two nodes in the network. The estimated distance between two nodes x and y:

$$E[D_{xy}] = \frac{k}{\sqrt{P_r}} \tag{7}$$

is used only as an approximation of the 'closeness' of the nodes. The relative mobility is defined as:

$$M_{xy}^{t-1} = E[D_{xy}^t] - E[D_{xy}^{t-1}] \tag{8}$$

In the algorithm they estimate the stability of a node by observing the standard deviation of the variations in mobility to all other nodes in the network.

We can see in all of the presented examples that the objective of clusterhead election process in mobile networks is to elect for clusterheads the nodes that are the least mobile, in expectation that the relative lack of movement of such nodes will increase the stability of the clusters.

Identifying similarities in the moving patterns of networked nodes often leads to *group mobility*, which is a frequent event in the real world and is also naturally linked to the concept of clustering. Within group mobility modelling, the work of Hong et al. [26] is especially important. Hong et al. investigate the movement of groups of mobile nodes and make an assumption that each group needs to have a logical centre, with the group movement being defined by the movement of the centre node. They introduce a novel group mobility model - Reference Point Group Mobility (RPGM) - to represent the relationship among mobile hosts.

Work of McDonald and Znati [27] is also very important, as they attempt to bound the probability of path availability for moving nodes. They look at the problem that is often found is the research on the networks of moving objects: developing a model that derives expressions for the probability of path availability as a function of time. In other words, the aim was to determine the conditional probability that the nodes will be within range of each other at some time $t + \delta t$ given that they are located within range at time t.

Zhang et al. in [31] propose a revised group mobility metric, the linear distance based spatial dependency (LDSD), which is derived from the linear distance of a node's movement instead of its instantaneous speed and direction. Their work also assumes the nodes node their exact physical location. The linear distance is a square root of the sum of the changes in geometric x and y coordinates of a node. If the node's linear distance D is greater than some threshold D_{thr}, the mobility history information is updated correspondingly. Based on the information in the history cache, a node calculates its linear distance based total spatial dependency with respective to its neighbours.

In a number of works researchers attempt to predict the mobility of the moving nodes, in order to improve the cluster stability. In their excellent paper,

Konstantopoulos et al. [36] present an algorithm that estimates the probability of neighbourhood stability (which is for them the product of nodes' stabilities). They make an assumption that a mobile node can be considered a good candidate for the clusterhead if its neighborhood is relatively stable in comparison to the neighborhoods of other candidate hosts. In their paper a detailed algorithm for estimating neighbourhood stability is presented.

Leng et al. [35] use the node connectivity and node mobility jointly to select clusterheads. Their approach is based on availability of position information using GPS or similar technology. They then consider the *link expiration time*, defined as the time after which two nodes will leave each other's transmission range. They use simple geometry for this, assuming that the velocity does not change during the link expiration process. After this, they define average link expiration time for each node, by averaging link expiration times. The node with a large value of average link expiration time is able to maintain relatively long connection with their neighbouring hosts. Such a host should more likely be selected as a clusterhead than the host with a short link expiration time. In the clusterhead election process, the nodes use the combined metric of node degree (i.e. the number of neighbours) and the node's average link expiration time.

Finally, it is worth noting that, while the clustering solutions are required to consider the mobility of the nodes, for the correct clustering solution it is important that the mobility of the nodes in modelled the right way. Mobility modelling has been observed over many decades in the research community. An excellent survey of mobility modelling for ad hoc network research has been done by Camp, Boleng and Davies in [38]. In addition to this, a lot work has been done on modelling specific mobility patterns, such as the one identified in vehicular networks, where cars and other vehicles are constrained by the transport network. The work of Fiore and Harri in [39] is typical for mobility analysis of vehicular network. This paper gives a detailed analysis of the topological properties of a vehicular network. Similarly, Wang and Tsai in [40] present an interesting study of the mobility of vehicles in urban environments and develop algorithms for the estimation fop traffic congestion based on vehicle mobility patterns.

Comparing the approaches presented here is not easy. The accuracy of mobility measurements is only one performance aspect, because design of the networks of moving objects often has to follow a tailored-made approach, where rarely we have the case when one solution fits all problems. This is why full understanding of all presented approaches is important in the design process, to help us make the correct design decision.

5   Cluster Maintenance and Reclustering

For the majority of clustering solutions, the clustering process is based on the fundamental algorithms presented earlier in Sect. 3. The distributed process begins with nodes broadcasting the information about themselves. This is followed by an election process where all nodes identify their position as clusterheads or cluster members, depending on the node features which were included in the broadcasted message. While in the traditional clustering algorithms this feature was typically node ID or the node degree (number of neighbours), in the mobility-aware clustering solutions, the nodes distribute information about their mobility, and clusterheads are chosen on the basis of the mobility information. Typically, the clusterhead is chosen as a node that is the least mobile; this is done in attempt to increase cluster stability. A typical example of the mobility aware clustering algorithm is the DMAC algorithm presented by Basagni in [20].

Once the clusters are set up, and each node knows its role in a clustered network (clusterhead or cluster member), the critical issue with regard to the operation of network of moving objects is cluster maintenance. If we consider a network with moving nodes, we can assume that the cluster members will frequently leave the transmission range of clusterheads. This can cause a significant problem, especially if we are observing a network of nodes expecting support for complex data transfer application. For these networks, to minimise the effect of clustering on the quality of service, it is essential that alternative routes are identified when the nodes change clusters. For the type of network where routing is not the main challenge (i.e. the networks where nodes exchange location information, rather than acting as relays for data traffic), the problem is smaller, but is still important.

Basagni [20] gives a simple procedure for dealing with moving nodes. The movement of the nodes can result in link failure, and the idea is that the clustering process reacts on link failure, as a trigger that a node has left the cluster. When this happens, the clusterhead removes that node from a list of nodes in the cluster. For the departed cluster member, there is an immediate need to find a new clusterhead. This node would then listen to incoming messages from clusterheads, and would perform a clusterhead check, similar to the one that was done at the cluster formation process. In the case of the DMAC algorithm, for example, this means the weight assigned to new clusterheads needs to be checked. If the weight of the newly arrived node is greater than the weights of the potential new clusterheads, the new arrival will announce itself as clusterhead. Otherwise, it will accept the clusterhead with the greatest weight as its new clusterhead.

Similar approach is taken by other algorithms. For example, Konstantopoulos [36] present a solution where the moving node chooses the clusterhead that has the highest probability of still being the neighbour in the immediate future. An et al. [30] expect the moving node to choose the clusterhead with the highest mobility index and Zhang et al. [31] expect the node to choose the clusterhead with the largest linear distance based spatial dependency. We can notice that for the majority of existing solutions the idea is that the choice of the new clusterhead is done on the basis of the mobility metric and/or weight assigned to the nodes. For Ni et al. [34] in the initial clustering stage, the nodes having the smallest relative mobility in their neighbourhoods are selected as the clusterheads. In the cluster maintaining stage, mobility prediction strategies are introduced to handle the various problems caused by node movements, such as possible association losses to current clusterheads and clusterhead role changes, for extending the connection lifetime and providing more stable clusters.

We have seen in this Chapter that various parameters can be used to identify optimal clusterheads and that various methods can be used to establish and maintain clusters in networks of moving objects. The current research attempts to evaluate the presented clustering solutions, by identifying the performance evaluation parameters most suited for these dynamic solutions. The main performance parameters that can be used to evaluate clustering techniques for networks of moving objects include the following: the number of formed clusters in a network; the clusterhead duration; the reaffiliation rate, and signalling overhead.

Clustering is done to simplify the network operation, and to find the optimal subset of the network graph which can deliver full network connectivity. Therefore, the objective of cluster formation is to strike a balance between the number of clusters (the fewer, the better) and achieving network connectivity. Measuring the number of active clusterheads is a good measurement of the efficiency of the clustering scheme. For example, the simulation results shown in [36] show that the lowest ID and the highest degree clustering solutions results in the largest number of clusterheads. This result is expected, as the two algorithms have not been designed to minimize the number of clusterheads.

Similarly, the clusterhead duration can be used as a performance parameter, as a measurement of how long on average clusterheads keep their role. Fewer changes in clusterheads are desirable in order to increase the network stability. In power-based topology control, changes in clusterheads may be desirable, to increase the fairness of the power consumption across the network, but in the hierarchical topology control we can look at this measurement in a different way. This is especially interesting when moving nodes are considered. In the simulation results presented in [36], for high average speeds of node movement, the 'traditional' clustering algorithms (the lowest ID, the highest degree), perform worse that the algorithms that are specifically designed to deal with mobility. This shows again why designing for mobility is important, as movement of nodes presents a new set of challenges.

Finally, measuring the reaffiliation rate, we can find out the average number of times a mobile node has to change the clusterhead. This is an important measurement, as it can show why when designing clustering schemes for moving nodes it is important to specify carefully when reafilliation can take place. Many traditional clustering algorithms are designed for nodes to identify the optimal clusterhead based on the ID, or node degree, or some other parameter, and are designed for static networks where the risk of mobility is minimal.

6   Conclusion

This Chapter presented the current research work on clustering for moving nodes in distributed wireless networks. Clustering is a process of grouping the nodes in network subsets, in order to simplify network operation and ensure network connectivity. This Chapter introduces topology control in ad hoc wireless networks, and introduced the standard techniques for hierarchical topology control. It then presents how mobility is considered in clustering solutions. The first generation of clustering solutions was focused on optimisation of the choice of network subset, without detailed consideration of topology dynamics or node movement. The Chapter presents a number of ways mobility can be considered. All the solutions have in common the design principle that they attempt to predict the mobility of the nodes and to integrate the mobility information in the clusterhead election process, typically by choosing the least moving node to be a clusterhead. For most of the presented solutions, the reafilliation and cluster maintenance should be based on minimising the number of clusterhead changes and simplifying the control overhead.

References

1. Schaeffer, S.E.: Graph clustering. Comput. Sci. Rev. **1**, 27–64 (2007)
2. Boccaletti, S., Latora, V., Moreno, Y., Chavez, M., Hwang, D.-U.: Complex networks: structure and dynamics. Phys. Rep. **424**(45), 175–308 (2006)
3. Basagni, S., Conti, M., Giordano, S., Stojmenovic, I.: Mobile Ad Hoc Networking. IEEE Press, New York (2004)
4. Bose, P., Morin, P., Stojmenovic, I., Urrutia, J.: Routing with guaranteed delivery in ad hoc wireless networks. Wireless Netw. **7**, 609–616 (2001)
5. Stojmenovic, I.: Position-based routing in ad hoc networks. IEEE Commun. Mag. **40**(7), 128–134 (2002)
6. Karp, B., Kung, H.T.: GPSR: greedy perimeter stateless routing in wireless networks. In: Proceedings of the 6th Annual ACM/IEEE International Conference on Mobile Computing and Networking (2000)
7. Kranakis, E., Singh, H., Urrutia, J.: Compass routing on geometric networks. In: Proceedings of 11th Canadian Conference on Computational Geometry (1999)
8. Bao, L., Garcia-Luna-Aceves, J.J.: Topology management in ad hoc networks. In: Proceeding MobiHoc '03, Proceedings of the 4th ACM international Symposium on Mobile Ad Hoc Networking and Computing, pp. 129–140 (2003)
9. Amis, A.D., Prakash, R., Vuong, T.H.P., Huynh, D.T.: Max-Min D-cluster formation in wireless ad hoc networks. In: Proceedings of IEEE INFOCOM (2000)
10. Basu, P., Khan, N., Little, T.D.C.: A mobility based metric for clustering in mobile ad hoc networks. In: Proceedings of IEEE ICDCSW' 01, pp. 413–418 (2001)
11. Yu, J.Y., Chong, P.H.J.: Survey of clustering schemes for mobile ad hoc networks. IEEE Commun. Surv. **7**(1), 32–48 (2005)
12. Vodopivec, S., Bester, J., Kos, A.: A survey on clustering algorithms for vehicular ad-hoc networks. In: 2012 35th International Conference on Telecommunications and Signal Processing (TSP) (2012)
13. Chinara, S., Rath, S.K.: A survey on one-hop clustering algorithms in mobile ad hoc networks. J. Netw. Syst. Manage. **17**, 183–207 (2009)
14. Vasudevan, S., Kurose, J., Towsley, D.: Design and analysis of a leader election algorithm for mobile ad hoc networks. In: Proceedings of the 12th IEEE International Conference on Network Protocols, ICNP 2004 (2004)
15. Malpani, N., Welch, J., Vaidya, N.: Leader election algorithms for mobile ad hoc networks. In: Fourth International Workshop on Discrete Algorithms and Methods for Mobile Computing and Communications (2000)

16. Royer, E., Perkins, C.: Multicast operations of the ad hoc on-demand distance vector routing protocol. In: Proceedings of Fifth Annual ACM/IEEE International Conference on Mobile Computing and Networking (MOBICOM), pp. 207–218 (1999)

17. Malpani, N., Welch, J.L., Vaidya, N.: Leader election algorithms for mobile ad hoc networks. In: Proceeding DIALM '00, Proceedings of the 4th International Workshop on Discrete Algorithms and Methods for Mobile Computing and Communications, pp. 96–103 (2000)

18. Baker, D.J., Ephremides, A.: The architectural organization of a mobile radio network via a distributed algorithm. IEEE Trans. Commun. 29(11), 1694–1701 (1981)

19. Ephremides, A., Wieselthier, J.E., Baker, D.J.: A design concept for reliable mobile radio networks with frequency hopping signaling. Proc. IEEE 75(1), 56–73 (1987)

20. Basagni, S.: Distributed clustering for ad-hoc networks. In: Proceedings of International Symposium on Parallel Architectures, Algorithms and Networks (I-SPAN99), pp. 310–315 (1999)

21. Ghosh, R., Basagni, S.: Mitigating the impact of node mobility on ad-hoc clustering. J. Wirel. Commun. Mob. Comput. 8, 295–308 (2008)

22. Gerla, M., Tsai, J.: Multicluster, mobile, multimedia radio network. ACM/Baltzer J. Wirel. Netw. 1(3), 255–265 (1995)

23. Parekh, A.K.: Selecting routers in ad hoc wireless networks. In: Proceedings of the SET/IEEE International Telecommunication Symposium (1994)

24. Reumerman, H.-J., Roggero, M., Ruffini, M.: The application-based clustering concept and requirements for intervehicle networks. IEEE Commun. Mag. 43(4), 108–113 (2005)

25. Johansson, P., Larsson, T., Hedman, N., Mielczarek, B., Degermark, M.: Scenario-based performance analysis of routing protocols for mobile ad hoc networks. In: Proceedings of ACM Mobicom, Seattle WA (1999)

26. Hong, X., Gerla, M., Pei, G., Chiang, C.-C.: A group mobility model for ad hoc wireless networks. In: Proceedings of ACM/IEEE MSWiM 99 Workshop, Seattle WA (1999)

27. McDonald, B., Znati, T.F.: A mobility-based framework for adaptive clustering in wireless ad hoc networks. IEEE J. Sel. Areas Commun. 17(8), 1466–1486 (1999)

28. Lin, C.R., Gerla, M.: Adaptive clustering for mobile wireless networks. IEEE J. Sel. Areas Commun. 15(7), 1265–1275 (1997)

29. Torkestani, J.A., Meybodi, M.R.: A mobility-based cluster formation algorithm for wireless mobile ad-hoc networks. Cluster Comput. 14(4), 311–324 (2011)

30. An, B., Papavassiliou, S.: A mobility-based clustering approach to support mobility management and multicast routing in mobile ad-hoc wireless networks. Int. J. Netw. Manage. 11, 387–395 (2001)

31. Zhang, Y., Mee Ng, J., Ping Low, C.: A distributed group mobility adaptive clustering algorithm for mobile ad hoc networks. Comput. Commun. 32, 189–202 (2009)

32. Chatterjee, M., Das, S.K., Turgut, D.: WCA: a weighted clustering algorithm for mobile ad hoc networks. Cluster Comput. 5, 193–204 (2002)

33. Er, I.I., Seah, W.K.G.: Mobility-based d-hop clustering algorithm for mobile ad hoc networks. In: IEEE Wireless Communications and Networking Conference 2004, pp. 2359–2364 (2004)

34. Ni, M., Zhong, Z., Zhao, D.: MPBC: a mobility prediction-based clustering scheme for ad hoc networks. IEEE Trans. Veh. Technol. 60(9), 4549–4559 (2011)

35. Leng, S., Zhang, Y., Chen, H.-H., Zhang, L., Liu, K.: A novel k-hop compound metric based clustering scheme for ad hoc wireless networks. IEEE Trans. Wireless Commun. **8**(1), 367–375 (2009)

36. Konstantopoulos, C., Gavalas, D., Pantziou, G.: Clustering in mobile ad hoc networks through neighborhood stability-based mobility prediction. Comput. Netw. **52**, 1797–1824 (2008)

37. Wu, H-T., Ke, K-W., Chen, C-H., Kuan, C-W.: Mobile awareness based cluster selection mechanisms in wireless ad hoc networks. In: Proceedings of IEEE Vehicular Technology Conference (Fall), vol. 4, pp. 2774–2778 (2004)

38. Camp, T., Boleng, J., Davies, V.: A survey of mobility models for ad hoc network research. Wireless Commun. Mob. Comput. **2**(5), 483–502 (2002)

39. Fiore, M., Harri, J.: The networking shape of vehicular mobility. In: Proceedings of the 9th ACM International Symposium on Mobile Ad Hoc Networking and Computing (2008)

40. Wang, C., Tsai, H-M.: Detecting urban traffic congestion with single vehicle. In: Proceedings of the 3rd International Conference on Connected Vehicles and Expo (2013)

41. Gutting, R.F., de Almeida, T., Ding, Z.: Modeling and querying moving objects in networks. Int. J. Very Large Data Bases **15**(2), 165–190 (2006)

42. Wang, X., Lin, X., Wang, Q., Luan, W.: Mobility increases the connectivity of wireless networks. IEEE/ACM Trans. Netw. **21**(2), 440–454 (2013)

43. Ucar, S., Ergeny, S.C., Ozkasap, O.: VMaSC: vehicular multi-hop algorithm for stable clustering in vehicular ad hoc networks. In: Proceedings of IEEE Wireless Communications and Networking Conference (2013)

44. Hassanabadi, B., Shea, C., Zhang, L., Valaee, S.: Clustering in vehicular ad hoc networks using affinity propagation. Ad Hoc Netw. Part B **13**, 535–548 (2014)

New Trends in Mobility Modelling and Handover Prediction

Francisco Barcelo-Arroyo[1], Michał Gorawski[3], Krzysztof Grochla[3]([✉]),
Israel Martín-Escalona[1], Konrad Połys[3],
Andrea G. Ribeiro[2], Rute Sofia[2], and Enrica Zola[1]

[1] Universitat Politècnica de Catalunya (UPC), Barcelona, Spain
[2] COPELABS, University Lusofona, Lisboa, Portugal
[3] Institute of Theoretical and Applied Informatics of PAS, Gliwice, Poland
kgrochla@iitis.pl

Abstract. A wireless network may include fixed nodes and mobile nodes
that change the location during data transmission. The node mobility
influences heavily the operation of a wireless network, as the signal propagation conditions depend on the location of the nodes and may cause
dramatic changes in the data transmission rates and packet error rates.
Because the network performance is influenced by the location and signal
propagation conditions between network nodes, accurate representation
of the user mobility in the wireless network analysis is a crucial element
in both simulation and numerical or analytical modelling. This chapter
discusses mobility models used in simulating network behaviour. Further, the handover optimization and prediction are discussed, along with
alternative methods of radio signal propagation changes caused by client
mobility.

Keywords: Mobility modelling · Prediction · Handover optimization

1 Introduction

Wireless networks are omnipresent in current telecommunication technology,
and are used to cover a wide range of telecommunication needs ranging from
infrastructure-mode hotspots to pervasive mesh networks. Nowadays, wireless
networks are not only used as a complimentary technology for network access.
Also the deployment of wireless community networks relies on short- and long-
range wireless technologies. Reasons for going wireless include the low cost of
short-range wireless links, the evolution of wireless end-user devices, as well as
the emergence of smart Access Points (APs) that allow for spontaneous growth
of community networks.

From the operational perspective, these network architectures should not over-
see an important component: wireless devices are carried by humans, thereby inher-
iting human mobility patterns which impact network operation and performance.

First and foremost, mobility heavily impacts path recomputation as multihop
routing is based on the single-source shortest path paradigm. Secondly, resource

© Springer International Publishing Switzerland 2014
I. Ganchev et al. (Eds.): Wireless Networking for Moving Objects, LNCS 8611, pp. 88–114, 2014.
DOI: 10.1007/978-3-319-10834-6_6

management is affected, particularly in dense networks which naturally arise in highly populated areas such as cities. Here, it is not uncommon to have an AP per household, which serves a few users and a few devices.

Besides the path re-computation, predictability of the location of mobile nodes (MNs) can help in adaptation of the mobile service, which should be flexible enough to work with different transmission links, all the more so because a single user can have a device with more than one wireless interface.

In a mobile network environment, the MNs' movement path has impact on several aspects of networking, which range from location update and paging, radio resource management (e.g. dynamic channel allocation schemes), to technical network planning and design (e.g. cell and location area layout, network dimensioning).

This chapter discusses trends in mobility modelling as a tool that is currently being applied in simulations concerning experimentation of mobile network behaviour, as well as in handover optimization and prediction along with alternative methods of radio signal propagation changes caused by personal mobility.

The chapter is organized as follows. Section 2 introduces relevant aspects to the context of mobility modelling, while Sect. 3 describes related work focused on obtaining good quality movement traces that can be used in modelling mobility in cellular networks. Section 4 is dedicated to prediction aspects applied to cellular networks. In Sect. 5 we also propose methods to simplify performance evaluation of the wireless networks by directly modulating the transmission bitrate and packet loss rate in the simulation without full representation of client location. Section 6 summarizes the chapter.

2   Background on Mobility Modelling

A better understanding of the node movement and, if possible, the transfer of specific and common properties to the several aspects of network operation will facilitate optimization of the network performance. Traces, investigated and gathered by the scientific community, will assist in understanding the mobility behaviour of nodes under different conditions and, from the analytical perspective, may be useful when modelling such movement behaviour. From the perspective of wireless and cellular network operation, it is essential to quantify the human movement behaviour, given that the paradigms described are based on Internet end-users carrying and/or owning a multitude of wireless enabled devices. These devices have a movement pattern similar to their human carriers, therefore the movement of these devices is affected by the human interest to socialize and cooperate.

In addition to obtaining the node behaviour from real traces, for many years there has been an attempt to define the movement of nodes synthetically. In networking, most of such attempts are based on the Bayesian [20] models mostly because of its randomness. These models show some features which were considered relevant for the movement of nodes, e.g. variability.

Accurate representation of the user mobility in wireless networks analysis is a crucial element in both simulation and numerical or analytical modelling. The mobility models allow generation of the changing location of the network nodes in time. In most cases, the network area is represented by a two dimensional plane [5], although some of the models (e.g. [28]) represent the user mobility in three dimensions. The mobility model provides the coordinates of the modelled nodes in space and their evolution in time. Traces of the real devices' location are now easy to acquire due to the popularization of the GPS devices. However, the main drawbacks are the limited and constant number of devices which can be monitored and the repeatability of the conditions under which traces are acquired. Moreover, the real data from mobile devices is hard to find in the public space, especially for a large number of devices. Synthetic models provide better flexibility and parameterization in terms of the number of devices, the number of MNs, location intervals, among others. They are also more practical to use with discrete event simulations, thus the need for synthetic models and their data is substantial.

Simulations of mobile wireless networks allow testing of the developed protocols in various conditions, represented in the computer memory. The simulation must have representation of the location in space for every network node to calculate the radio signal propagation. Mobility models are used for this purpose. In discrete event simulation, the model generates location of every device in the network for the time of each event in the simulation.

The mobility models are needed both in the analysis of the networks with mobile clients and fixed Base Stations (BSs) (where only location of some network nodes changes) and in the evaluation of mobile ad-hoc networks (where all the nodes may move).

The mobility pattern should mimic the movements of real MNs. Both trace-based models and synthetic models can be used. Traces are these mobility patterns which are observed in real-life systems. They provide accurate information, especially when they involve a large number of participants and an appropriately long observation period. Traces can be derived from observation of real movements. To achieve this, the user log traces should be collected during a period which is long enough to capture periodical behaviours. However, exhaustive traces are hard to capture and as consequence, most models derived from traces are only applicable in specific contexts. While synthetic models attempt to statistically capture movement behaviour of MNs. Speed; direction; pause time; inter-contact times are often parameters used in modelling movement. Of course, the mobility pattern derived from this analysis is quite simplistic and hence, today are models - social mobility models - that attempt to integrate social aspects into models, such as social attractiveness, as discussed in Sect. 3.2.

The first goal is to achieve the statistical properties of the movement as similar to the ones observed in the real world as possible. The second goal is to keep the model relatively simple and easy to implement. Selection of the model has significant influence on the results. When the model is too simple or represent some properties which are not observed in the real network, its results can lead to false conclusions. The mobility models are also used while selecting parameters for the networking devices. In LTE networks, the handover (HO) thresholds and neighbour relations are configured by the network administrator. They may be selected based on the observed traffic and network statistics or by offline analysis, which requires the modelling of the people movement.

Another application of mobility models relates with their capability to assist in estimating specific aspects of future roaming behaviour. Dynamic wireless environments of today are based on the notion that users carry low-cost and limited capacity portable devices which are cooperative in nature and which extend the network in a user-centric way, not necessarily implying the support for networking services such as the multihop routing [12]. For instance, in the user-centric networking, transmission can simply be relayed as based on simple mechanisms that already exist in end-user devices. In terms of mobility and addition to the currently available solutions, the user-centric networking is focused on two main aspects: mobility tracking and estimation, and HO support. One of the aspects described through the subsequent sections of this book is the ways of addressing patterns of node movement to estimate mobility patterns based on the existing or novel social models.

A final thing to consider is ensuring that the functionality to be developed can assist in dealing with the unmanaged aspects of dynamic wireless architectures, which requires more support for the management of mobility anchor.

HOs across user-centric networks require more support than the ones available in today's wireless technology. For instance, the regular 250 m range of Wi-Fi is small compared to the geographic distances that users are expected to travel in user-centric scenarios. Hence, performing a complete HO would impose strong requirements on the speed of message exchange. One way to tackle this issue is to consider the regularity (routine) of the users' movement, which may facilitate determining the place and type of resources that may be required for seamless HOs. For example, based on movement analysis, the system may determine with a high probability that the user will hand over towards the range of specific mobility anchor points. In this case, specific functions may assist in defining the next adequate target and the way of handing over to it. The challenge here is to identify with enough accuracy and reliability the gateways which a wireless node should connect to while moving.

3   Review and Comparison of Available Mobility Models

In this section we try to enumerate most widely used and representative models which have been categorized into different groups. For instance, Bai et al. consider mobility models to be divided into 4 categories [3]: random models; models with temporal dependencies; models with spatial dependencies; models with geographic restrictions. While pure random models are incapable of simulating complex human movement faithfully, models with certain types of dependencies provide some representation of rational human behaviours, like grouping, inertia or avoiding obstacles; but they do not model social interactions. Thus we divide the models into the ones based on randomness (*random models*); the ones based on social interaction (*social mobility models*) and the models which merge these two approaches (*hybrid models*), describing each category in Sects. 3.1, 3.2 and 3.3 respectively.

3.1   Random Models

The random models consider movement to be a random process. The periods of movement may be interrupted by periods of inactivity. The most widely used models are the basic ones. They focus mostly on randomness of human walk, like *Markovian mobility, Random Waypoint (RWP)* model or *Random Walk (RW)* [3, 40] model, and clearly are not precise enough. There are several studies [36, 37] which prove that human walk resembles Lévy flight, which has been identified initially in animal movement patterns (e.g. albatrosses, insects, jellyfish, sharks) [22, 42]. Individual walking is hardly random incorporating instead some characteristics of a Lévy flight [36]. Moreover, Mascolo et al. addressed social notions such as social attractiveness [32] to bring mobility modelling closer to human movement and incorporated features concerning social interaction to provide clustering of nodes in movement. Lee et al. propose several enhancements of the Lévy flight pattern to give a more realistic representation of human walk [30, 36, 37] including pause-time, LATP (Least Action Trip Planning), hotspots attraction and social dependencies. Further research [14] shows that it is quite possible to obtain a mobility model with a high predictability rate, as human movement is actually less random and more regular than we think.

Random Walk Model. The simplest random mobility model is the RW model [3, 40] which was commonly used to mimic random behaviour of particles in physics. It is characterized by pure randomness of both the movement speed and direction. The speed is selected from the $[V_{min}, V_{max}]$ set and the direction is selected from $[0, 2\pi]$ using uniform distribution. Typically, MNs move in one direction for a determined distance or in a fixed time interval and during each step, the speed and direction are chosen randomly. The RW is a memoryless process, where the next action is irrelevant to the previous speed and direction. No information about the previous movement is stored. It leads to obtaining totally unrealistic routes with common rapid movement along and sudden directional changes.

Random Waypoint Model. According to the RWP mobility model [3, 40, 47], a MN moves at constant speed and on a straight line between two waypoints (i.e., random locations in the selected area of movement, WPs). By reaching a WP, the node will choose a new WP and a new speed, according to given distributions. The MN can also wait a certain time before moving on to next WP; however, if pause time is set to zero we actually obtain a movement very similar to random walk). The movement of a MN from a starting WP to its destination WP is called in the literature *movement epoch, transition* or *movement period*.

The RWP and RW models provide non-uniform spatial distribution of nodes [7]. Other related work [6,47] list some statistical properties and possible flaw results when those two simplest models are used in simulations. In particular, there is much higher probability of the node to be in the middle of the modelled area than near to its borders. Some modifications to the original RWP have been proposed, e.g. the *Random Direction Model* [3,13], that overcomes the non-uniform spatial distribution problem and provides more distributed paths. Another problem of the RW and RWP is the emulation of sharp turns or rapid speed changes that do not happen for real objects, which have some inertia. However, the RWP is one of the most used mobility models in simulation studies [1,45].

Gauss-Markov Mobility Model. The *Gauss-Markov Mobility Model* (GMMM) takes into consideration how speed changes in time and smoothes out rapid changes of speed and direction during subsequent iterations. Contrary to the RW and RWP, the GMMM is not memoryless. It assumes that a MN has an initial speed and direction, and takes this fact into consideration while computing these values for the next step:

$$S_n = \alpha S_{n-1} + (1 - \alpha)\overline{S} + \sqrt{(1 - \alpha^2)}S_{xn-1} \tag{1}$$

$$d_n = \alpha d_{n-1} + (1 - \alpha)\overline{d} + \sqrt{(1 - \alpha^2)}d_{xn-1} \tag{2}$$

where:
α - tuning parameter
$\overline{S}$ and $\overline{d}$ are mean values of speed and direction
S_{xn-1} and d_{xn-1} are Random Variables from Gaussian distribution

The turning parameter α is used to vary the randomness of changes. There can be 3 cases:

$$\begin{cases} \alpha = 0 \\ 0 < \alpha < 1 \\ \alpha = 1 \end{cases} \tag{3}$$

$\alpha = 0$ means that the model has no memory and the movement is totally random, $\alpha = 1$ means strong memory which results in linear movement. The ideal case is when $0 < \alpha < 1$ which means that the model has some memory and the randomness is intermediate – no sharp turns and rapid directional changes. The GMMM does not only model different types of movement depending on its memory strength, but also includes a Brownian motion model when $\alpha = 0$.

S_{xn-1} and d_{xn-1} are calculated based on the previous speed and direction. In time moment n its position is calculated:

$$x_n = x_{n-1} + S_{n-1} \cos d_{n-1} \tag{4}$$

$$y_n = y_{n-1} + S_{n-1} \sin d_{n-1} \tag{5}$$

where:

(x_n, y_n) - MN's coordinates in time moment n

(x_{n-1}, y_{n-1}) - MN's coordinates in time moment n

(S_{n-1}, d_{n-1}) - MN's speed and directions in time moment $n-1$

To make sure that the MN does not leave the simulation area, or it will not stay close to simulation space borders for too long, the d parameter is forced to change by 180° when the node is close to simulation space borders. The GMMM solves the problem of rapid speed and direction changes unlike the RW and RWP models, however it still lacks the ability to mimic actions like grouping or avoiding obstacles.

Truncated Lévy Walk Model. While researching the traces of foraging animal patterns [22,42], the authors revealed clear Lévy flight characteristics in their movements (a flight is a Euclidean distance between two waypoints visited in succession by the MN). The research was followed by studies on human movement traces [11,17,36,37] which gave some interesting results. According to these studies, human movement characteristics are quite similar to one of the characteristics found in movement of jackals [2] and spider monkeys [35]. To simplify, the Lévy walk is a series of short trips with occasional longer ones.

The simple *Truncated Lévy Walk* (TLW) Model [8] that gives heavy-tailed characteristics of human motion. The model is described with 4 variables $(l, \theta \Delta t_f \Delta t_p)$ where:

l is a heavy-tailed variable that describes the flight length. It is obtained from the Lévy distribution:

$$p(l) \sim |l|^{-(1+\alpha)}, l < l_{max} \tag{6}$$

θ is the movement direction taken from $(0, 2\pi)$

$\Delta t_f > 0$ is the flight time

Δt_p is the pause time that follows a truncated power law

$$p(\Delta t_p) \sim |\Delta t_p|^{-(1+\beta)}, 0 < \Delta t_p < l_{max} \tag{7}$$

Using this simple model, the authors were able to obtain synthetic traces with the power-law distribution of inter-contact times. The authors related their research to rather small sets of traces on a bounded space. The traces which they generated using the TLW are quite similar to the collected real traces [37].

Group Mobility Models. There are several models used for modelling group mobility. The *Column Mobility Model* represents a movement of several MNs in a line towards a common goal in an orderly fashion. The authors of [3] suggest that such movement can be used as searching and scanning activities of military robots in, for example, mine searching. If the MN is due to leave the simulation area, similarly to the GMMM, its direction is flipped by 180°. The next example of group mobility is the *Pursue Model*, where one node moves freely according to, for example, the RWP and the other nodes are "pursuers" which follow the "escaping" node. This model can be used in scenarios for race, tracking or police pursuit. The nomadic *Community Mobility Model* introduces a group movement, where a group of MNs move together towards a common waypoint, however individual nodes can deviate from the original, straight-to-goal path and move using, for example, the RWP in the vicinity of the moving group. Such behaviour can be observed during organized tours in a zoo or a museum, where the whole group follows a general sightseeing pattern, however individual people move independently inside the group and move toward different points of interest.

3.2   Social Mobility Models

Barabási et al. analysed human movement [4], showing that there is an increasing evidence that the human activity routine exhibits properties that follow the non-Poisson model, as the traces could be characterized by bursts of rapidly occurring events separated by long periods of inactivity. Hence, this was the first proof that humans do not move randomly.

Another trace analysis, which was based on a data set obtained from over one million users for several years [11], showed that such traces follows the power-law characteristics. Although the traces were exhaustive, they represent mobile roaming users in specific settings and as such we cannot apply such analysis to all potential movement cases. A third study comprises monitoring of movement of 100,000 people, also based on cellphones [17]. Such a study has proven that travel patterns of an individual human follow simple reproducible patterns in spite of the diversity of roaming.

Social mobility modelling considers movement aspects derived from the way humans move and hence, derived from social behaviour. For instance, moving to a restaurant implies an interest. The relevancy of such interest impact speed (e.g. acceleration); social interaction impacts the direction as well as stationary time of a node in specific places.

In social mobility modelling, a relevant aspect is the daily routine of citizens, as it has been observed, as described, to have some repeating features. The second relevant aspect is that while moving, users are often involved with other users, be it passively or actively. Humans as social beings are always part of a group which can be virtual in the sense that there may or may not be an association between humans. From the mobility modelling perspective, the relevant aspect to consider is a correlation between the space and time, where different and possibly not acquainted persons cohabit the same space and time due to a temporary (or permanent) routine overlap. For instance, this is the case of two strangers who regularly share the same subway line for a specific period of time every week. To simplify, individual movement exhibits a correlation between time and space. When different people exhibit a similar correlation, then it means that they form a cluster of nodes with the same group (social movement). From the networking perspective, this correlation is relevant to model time and space.

Sociological Interaction Mobility for Population Simulation - SIMPS.
SIMPS [10] is a mobility model that incorporates recent findings in sociological research on human interaction, assuming that each person has specific social needs derived from their societal posture, as well as assuming that people interact to meet their specific social needs. These two features lay the groundwork for the SIMPS behavioural model which is based on two social actions: *socialize* - to move toward acquaintances - and *isolate* - to escape from the undesired presence.

The MN contacts are modelled using a social graph, which represents relationships among people. While the graph does not give information about human proximity, people that are socially attracted tend to meet more often. SIMPS does not model grouping behaviour, however the individual mobility patterns tend to naturally converge, and give collective motion features.

Community-Based Mobility Models – CMM and HCMM. The *Community-based Mobility Model (CMM)* [33] bases on *social attractiveness (SA)*, which evolved from the relevancy parameter of social networking. This notion was the predecessor of the SIMPS socialize notion, being a more simple translation of a social belief into a networking parameter. Considering the *deterministic* mechanism, the cells are simply selected based on their overall social attractiveness. The probabilistic mechanism is more realistic, given that the selection of the next target becomes proportional to the social attractiveness of each cell for a specific node i, based on the roulette-wheel selection, which gives the possibility to choose an empty cell. While the CMM is interesting, it still falls short in some aspects, such as proximity (considering that humans prefer short distances to long ones), pause time, and collision avoidance.

MNs movement can be described as follows: for a node i located in a specific cell $S_{p,q}$, the computation of the next target involves computing SA towards node i for each set of nodes positioned in different cells. The SA function is provided in Eq. 8.

$$SA_{p,q_i} = \frac{\sum_{j \in C_{S_{p,q}}} m_{i,j}}{\omega} \tag{8}$$

Where:
SA_{p,q_i} - the social attractiveness towards the MN i
$C_{S_{p,q}}$ - the set of the hosts associated to square $S_{p,q}$
$m_{i,j}$ - the interaction between two individuals, i and j
ω - the cardinality of $C_{S_{p,q}}$ (i.e. the number of hosts associated to the square $S_{p,q}$).

The SA_{p,q_i} corresponds to the social attractiveness that a specific set of nodes has towards the node i. Such attractiveness is a product of the nodes that are, at a specific moment in time, in such a cell. The $S_{p,q}$ represents a cell in the grid, p being the row and q being the respective column representation. The n parameter denotes the total number of nodes in $S_{p,q}$, while $w_{i,j}$ represents the cost of the association (social attractiveness) of the node j in the cell $S_{p,q}$

towards the node i. This weight is in fact related to the potential time and space correlation of nodes, which is called social interaction.

The *Home-cell Community-based Mobility Model (HCMM)* [9], is based on the social model of the CMM but it presents a different approach to model movement. In the HCMM, nodes are attracted by their home cell (the specific community's cell). The nodes are attracted to places swarmed with other nodes from their community. Occasionally, they visit other communities and then return home, so the HCMM reproduces an environment where nodes are attracted towards places selected from places which are popular among their friends.

3.3   Hybrid Models

Hybrid models combine various features of human movement, such as its limited randomness, social ties and daily routines. They try to merge the random and social models. Since this approach is relatively new, in this section we present four most interesting propositions of the human movement modelling.

Self-Similar Least-Action Human Walk - SLAW. SLAW [30] is a mobility model based on traces, where the authors extracted some important features from the collected data to define the behaviour of nodes. The pause time and flight length should represent the truncated power-law behaviour. The waypoints can be modelled by fractal points, assuming that people are always more attracted to more popular places.

SLAW introduces TLW movement characteristics with heterogeneously bounded mobility areas and truncated power law intercontact times. The topology of the SLAW model is defined by the Delaunay triangulation on the fractal waypoints using the Brownian Motion generation technique (fBm). After the waypoints are defined over a 2-D area, the movement of MNs is defined by the LATP (Least Action Trip Planning) algorithm, where the distance between all unvisited waypoints is calculated - people choose their destination based on the distance and tend to visit waypoint nearest to their destination. The waypoints are defined as self-similar, which creates more crowded, popular waypoint clusters. The authors assign a weight to each cluster, proportional to the total number of waypoints. Each MN chooses from 3 to 5 clusters randomly based on a given probability, proportional to these weights. The main objective in the allocation of weights is the ability to build some sense of community, making the choice of the same clusters possible for many MNs, with regards that each MN has its own mobility area, and moves mainly in its boundaries. To increase randomness, each day MN picks additional waypoints from a different cluster, also respecting from 5 % to 10 % of waypoints in the new cluster. When MN reaches each waypoint (its destination), it pauses for a period of time which is predefined, considering that the whole trip should be completed in 12 h (T = 12 h), and that the node comes back to its starting point within this period.

Working Day Movement Model. While SLAW points out that inter-contact times can be modelled by a truncated power-law distribution with the power-law head and the exponentially decaying tail after a certain time, other work proposes the cut-off period to consist of roughly 12 h. *The Working Day Movement Model* (WDMM) the authors simulate a real-life situation of the "going to work-staying at work-going home" cycle. we can see that the exponential cut-off appears roughly after 12 h, what could suggest the influence of people daily routines on the inter-contact times. This model can be characterized by three activities: working, staying at home, evening activities with friends. These three main activities are connected via the transport submodel. The daily routine is as follows: each node starts its "life" in a fixed location marked as home location. Home is a place which obviously simulates home activities, e.g. the mobile device stays in one place until the wakeup time. After wakeup, the node travels to work where it spends a certain amount of time (which can be configured adequately). During the office hours, the node walks short distances along the office waypoint to simulate movement around the office (this is simulated by an office activity submodel). After the office hours, the node can choose to participate in evening activities or return home. In case of going home, the node stops at a home location, moves a small distance to simulate entering the home and stays inside until wakeup. Evening activities are considered group activities done after work. The node can choose to move to its favourite meeting point, wait there for all other nodes from a group to join in. The group moves together randomly. After these activities the group splits and the nodes return to their home locations. Travelling between activities is done by a transport submodel, which includes a car, bus or a walking submodel. The node that does not own a car chooses whether it travels by a bus or walks. The WDMM can be further improved by additional real-life features such as pause time, clear definition of a workday/weekend routines, speed variations in all the travel submodels. Also, if the submodels of vehicular movement are part of the model, it is crucial to include a set of rules of vehicular movement different than walking (the only difference in the model is the speed of travelling).

The Hybrid Mobility Model Based on Social, Cultural and Language Diversity. This hybrid model [27] is based on a framework which integrates social, cultural and linguistic factors which impact human mobility, including the temporal and spatial features in the model. The model is based on real traces obtained from the IEEE INFOCOM 2006 conference [16, 21]. The data was collected using the IEEE 802.15.4 or 802.11 communication protocols and devices. It includes information about the participant's nationality, spoken language and the number of contacts with other participants. Based on these pieces of information, the authors created a contact graph which represents forming of social activities of groups, communities and participants depending on their social and cultural features. The most common features for MNs are grouped into clusters that impact human mobility, e.g. demographic information (country of citizenship and residence, language) and professional information (affiliation, area of expertise). The model uses the individual MN's features and preferences like the spoken language and citizenship, but also takes into consideration the influence of high –impact groups (like the most popular language group) on the mobility pattern. Although the idea of modelling mobility this way is interesting, still it is based on traces obtained from a very characteristic event, like a conference, and there is no data how such a model relates to everyday situations.

The Real-Life Mobility Model – RLMM. RLMM model [19] tries to give a representation of natural life cycles of a working human, including the division on workday/weekend activities, and to simulate basic activities like sleeping, working, shopping, going to popular places, weekend travels. The model is based on cycles that are repeated through the whole simulation and are composed of several states that can exist in a MN's life. The assumptions made in RLMM model are consistent with characteristics observed by the authors of WHERE model [25], which is based on probability distribution drawn from empirical data from Call Detail Records (CDRs) from cellular network. RLMM's basic states are: at-home, at-work, at-popular-place, regular-travel, and alternative-travel. The model assumes that every MN has a fixed position of work and home, and that some popular places are defined. The regular travel is executed between these points with the user-defined pause times and commute distances. The alternative-travel is used to break the ordinary routine of "life" and add random, often longer travels to the weekend activity point. Such an approach also gives the MN's path the Lévy walk characteristics [17,36,37]. In this model, time is strictly regulated to assure a cyclic and repetitive behaviour for the whole scenario, e.g. a real-life scenario where day lasts 24 h and week lasts 7 days. The travel is realized in a semi-random manner: the goal and source of the travel are known, however to randomize the travel movement, the RLMM offers a possibility to add a certain, user defined number of semi-waypoints along the travel path to avoid generating straight lines. The algorithm chooses a random point in a rectangle's diagonal created using two given points – source and destination (the distance from the source and the new semi-waypoint is user defined; by default it is $\frac{1}{4}$ of the original source-destination distance). Within the created rectangle, it randomly designates a semi-waypoint, which becomes the new source. The new rectangle is created within the boundaries of the original one and the new semi-waypoint is designated recursively until the adequate source-destination distance is achieved. Such an approach enables us to obtain the curve path with relatively little deviations from the original direction. The node's life follows certain routines repeated through the entire workweek, with some deviations to implement randomness of the human behaviour.

The standard routine is:

1. Waking up and travelling to work
2. Working
3. Returning home for a short stay
4. Travelling for a short visit in a popular place (pub, mall, etc.)
5. Returning home to sleep.

During the weekend this routines are a little different:

1. The wake up time is later than usual.
2. The MN can travel to a popular place or a weekend travel place
3. The MN returns home for a short stay.
4. Visit in a popular place lasts longer than in the workweek
5. The MN returns home to sleep.

The weekend location set in a simulation tends to have a longer drive distance than the standard commute distance done by the MN, which, to some extent, gives the Lévy walk characteristics to such movement traces. The RLMM model is based on the WDMM and SLAW. It extends these two models with modifications which more faithfully represent life periodic cycles and differences in human actions between different days of the week. The RLMM mobility model can be used in various environments connected with human traces, like wireless mobile networks, gathering measurement from a distributed system [18], or in location prediction [46]. The simulation analysis of the RLMM model shows that it provides more realistic values in the number of created links and the average link duration than other models which are currently available.

4   Prediction Applied to Cellular Networks

In cellular networks, a layout for the BSs to which the mobile devices are connected must be designed. There are several well established patterns, including hexagonal (typical for suburban areas), Manhattan (urban) and linear (highways). The possibility of having several connection layers must also be considered, e.g., microcells as the first choice and macrocells as umbrellas for overflowing traffic. The problem of the cell borders is related to the layout. For simplicity, it is possible to consider a network in which each device is covered only by the BS closest to it. This assumption is simple and allows direct conclusions; however, it is not realistic. When the radiation patterns and random nature of the radio channel are taken into account, the borders are not regular shapes and may change along time (i.e. cell breathing, random fading). This increases the complexity of the analysis significantly; however, it offers realistic results, although they are more difficult to interpret.

The mobile behaviour of devices within the cellular network can be characterized in a variety of ways, with each of them corresponding to a different scenario and environment. Experimental research has been conducted during the last two decades to determine the statistical properties of each representative user class, e.g., public networks, Local Area Networks (LANs), indoors, outdoors, cars, pedestrians, etc. Depending on the network technology, geographical area and type of user, it is possible to characterize users' movements in such a way that the resulting pattern will be similar to the real one. Mobility models play a key role in the analysis of planning issues in a cellular network. Knowledge about the pattern followed by the MNs in a given scenario may help network planning to guarantee service along the pathway followed by each user.

The purpose of a cellular network is to provide coverage to moving users while their connections are transferred between cells. As the user moves, the quality of the signal received from the current cell may decrease below the acceptable threshold. This event will trigger the HO procedure [41]. The time needed to transfer the ongoing communications to the new cell is crucial since if this process lasts too long, the user may suffer degradation in the quality of the ongoing services. In some cases, it may lead to a drop in the communication [24]. This issue is particularly important for delay-sensitive applications such as video and audio streaming. Mobility prediction techniques allow the network to be prepared for the HO in advance (e.g., booking resources for the expected HO in the destination cell) [43]. Resource demands could fluctuate abruptly due to the movement of high data rate users. If one can predict requests of bandwidth at a cell, the overall network performance would improve.

Some research has been targeted to develop models that predict the users' trajectory, which can be used to allocate resources at the new cell and to aid the HO process. The technique proposed in [43] uses real-time mobile positioning information and previous HO locations reported by other nodes in order to predict the HO event. With mobility prediction, the resources reservation at each BS can dynamically be adjusted. They demonstrate that reservation efficiency improves as the knowledge incorporated into the scheme increases. Joshi et al. [26] aim to exploit the notion of predictability and propose algorithms to achieve low latencies while minimizing the message overhead. Prediction of users' movement is also possible using trace data [31]. For HO success, the most important predictions occur when moving into highly populated cells. Other studies exploit real traces to analyse the predictability of users' movements inside the network. Sricharan and Vaidehi [44] examine real-time mobility traces and identify key mobility parameters. A generic framework for mobility prediction is described in [34], where a model is proposed to predict the sequences of user's paths from observed sequences.

Structural approaches study mobility through mathematical models that try to represent human or vehicle mobility. Mobility models play a key role when planning a wireless network (i.e., resource allocation, location updating, and channel holding time). The RWP mobility model is simple and has extensively been used in simulation studies. Kurkowski et al. [29] analyse MANET simulation studies published in a premiere conference for the MANET community between 2000 and 2005. They found that 66 % of the studies involving mobility used the RWP mobility model. Despite it has been criticized for not being representative of how humans actually move, it is still largely used in many studies [1, 45]. Rojas et al. [38] validate the RWP against real mobility data. With small changes to the distributions used in the model (e.g., non-uniform distribution of the waypoints), the authors show that it can be used as a good model for mobility in large geographic areas such as a city. Considering that extracting a mobility pattern from real traces is complex and, anyway, it would be specific to the environment and conditions from which it has been extracted, the use of the RWP mobility model in simulation studies is widely accepted.

Recently, we provided a detailed description of the analytical framework to forecast the next cell to which a user moving according to the RWP mobility model handovers within a certain period of time [49]. The details of the movement pattern according to the RWP are given in Sect. 3.1. The movement between two WP is called a leg and its length is represented here by l. The assumption behind the proposed framework is that the user knows its current position and the position and time of the last change of speed and direction (i.e., the last WP). This analysis follows previous research on statistical characteristics of the RWP mobility model (i.e., length and duration of the straight movement between two waypoints [6], node distribution [23]). By assuming a symmetrical layout (i.e., any symmetrical layout is valid, e.g. 4 APs providing coverage to a circular area as presented here), our framework is able to predict the HO to each APs in a given interval of time. This time interval Δt is short enough so to guarantee that the node will reach no more than one waypoint ($X(\Delta t) \leq 1$). In this way, the probability of HO in Δt can be written as the sum of the probability of HO in case a WP is reached during Δt (which we call $Pr\{HOa\}$) plus the probability of HO in case the node does not change direction and speed during Δt (which we call $Pr\{HOb\}$), as shown in Eq. 9:

$$
\begin{aligned}
Pr\{\text{HO in } \Delta t\} = {} & Pr\{X(\Delta t)=1\} \cdot Pr\{\text{HO in } \Delta t | X(\Delta t)=1\} + \\
& Pr\{X(\Delta t)=0\} \cdot Pr\{\text{HO in } \Delta t | X(\Delta t)=0\} = \\
& Pr\{X(\Delta t)=1\} \cdot Pr\{HOa\} + Pr\{X(\Delta t)=0\} \cdot Pr\{HOb\}
\end{aligned}
\tag{9}
$$

The following parameters are considered:

- γ_j: represents the current angle of direction and v_j the current speed.
- Y is the distance between the last WP and the current position (P_t) at time t (i.e., the distance already travelled at speed v_j in direction γ_j).
- x_t is the distance of P_t from cell boundaries in current direction γ_j.
- x_A is the distance of P_t from whole area in direction γ_j.

The flow chart in Fig. 1 provides the algorithm used to estimate the probability of HO, the probability of no HO and the expressions used in each case. It is easy to understand that $Pr\{HOb\}$ is easy to evaluate if the geometry of the layout and the current position, speed and direction of movement are known (as assumed). A more complex calculation is needed for $Pr\{HOa\}$, instead. The correspondent equations and a brief explanation are given hereafter. Different formulations can be applied to $Pr\{X(\Delta t)=1\}$ or $Pr\{X(\Delta t)=0\}$ according to the geometry (i.e., relationship among x_t, x_A, and $\Delta t \cdot v_j$), as shown in Fig. 1. The final expression for $Pr\{HOa\}$ is:

$$
Pr\{HOa\} = \begin{cases}
\displaystyle\int_{x_t}^{v_j \cdot \Delta t} Pr\{HOa|r\} \cdot f_R(r)dr & \text{if } x_t \geq v_j \cdot \Delta t \text{ and } x_t < x_A \\
\displaystyle\int_{0}^{x_t} Pr\{HOa|r\} \cdot f_R(r)dr & \text{if } x_t < v_j \cdot \Delta t \text{ and } x_t < x_A , \\
\displaystyle\int_{0}^{x_A} Pr\{HOa|r\} \cdot f_R(r)dr & \text{if } x_t \geq x_A
\end{cases}
\tag{10}
$$

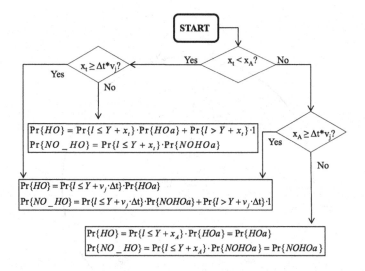

Fig. 1. Formulas used to determine the probability of HO and NO HO.

where $Pr\{HOa|r\}$ represents the probability of HO given that the next WP is at the generic point $S(r)$ at distance r from P_t, which is reached at the generic time $(t+r/v_j)$; $f_R(r)$ is the pdf of the possible positions $S(r)$. A graphical example of how to evaluate $Pr\{HOa|r\}$ in case $S(r) = P_t$ (i.e., $r = 0$) is provided in Fig. 2. Two circles can be drawn around $S(r)$, each representing the distance reached in any direction if the minimum speed (red circle) or maximum speed (blue circle) is selected. Then, the points falling inside the crown and the area of movement (black circle) represent all the possible locations that can be reached in Δt; those falling outside the coverage of AP1 (black discontinuous line) represent the probability of HO (green area).

We run simulations to validate the proposed analytical model and to test the loss of accuracy produced by the necessary simplifications to the analytical model. The results from the numerical evaluation of the analytical model and those from simulation are presented for ten different cases in Table 1. For each scenario, the probability of HO to AP1, AP2, AP3 and AP4 are displayed ($Pr\{HO1\}$, $Pr\{HO2\}$, $Pr\{HO3\}$ and $Pr\{HO4\}$, respectively). Values in bold stand for the probability of remaining in the current cell (i.e., $Pr\{NO\text{-}HO\}$). It is shown that the error is always smaller than 2 %.

The importance of this study is twofold. First, it provides a deeper insight into the statistics of the RWP mobility model, extending previous analysis. This statistical knowledge provides a better understanding of the interplay of the mobility pattern with network parameters. Second, and from a more practical perspective, the HO prediction is useful to manage resource allocation and reservation strategies. For example, these results can be applied in studies on allocation strategies for QoS improvement in cellular networks.

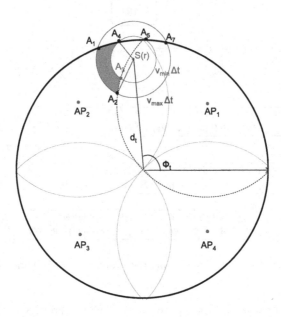

Fig. 2. Area representing the $Pr\{HOa|r\}$ when $S(r) = P_t$. At time t, the node is associated with AP1 (color figure online).

We also applied the model in a simulation study through which the implications of different HO strategies (i.e., aggressive vs. conservative) and of more complex radio patterns (i.e., shadowing) can be analysed [48]. Under non-ideal channel conditions, the HO probability generally increases when the shadowing effect is taken into account; the shadowing has an effect on the borders of the current cell which now change over time, thus making higher probable that the node exits its cell if compared to the ideal channel situation. However, depending on the geometry, shadowing can result in a "capture effect" in the current cell, especially when the node is located close to the cell borders. Moreover, it has been proven that the impact of the HO strategy is stronger in non-ideal channel conditions [48].

5   Alternative Methods for Simulation of Changes in Radio Signal Propagation

The transmission performance in mobile wireless networks is determined by two dominant factors: the bitrate of the communication and the packet loss ratio. Typically, locations of access points and BSs are given. The locations of clients are emulated by the mobility model. The radio signal propagation model, such

Table 1. Numerical and simulation results for the ten cases analysed. Values in bold stand for the probability of remaining in current cell.

Case	Pr{HO1}		Pr{HO2}		Pr{HO3}		Pr{HO4}	
	Num.	Sim.	Num.	Sim.	Num.	Sim.	Num.	Sim.
1	0.83	0.64	**98.28**	**98.76**	0.83	0.58	0.06	0.02
2	0.62	0.46	97.43	98.08	0.62	0.49	**1.32**	**0.98**
3	**70.06**	**73.80**	0.00	0.00	0.00	0.00	29.94	26.20
4	99.90	99.65	0.02	0.0	0.04	0.1	**0.04**	**0.16**
5	**100**	**100**	0.00	0.00	0.00	0.00	0.00	0.00
6	0.75	0.35	**98.46**	**99.21**	0.78	0.44	0.01	0.00
7	**20.77**	**22.02**	68.20	70.76	2.04	0.96	8.99	6.27
8	**3.78**	**2.73**	90.43	93.66	2.48	1.20	3.31	2.40
9	0.02	0.01	0.14	0.06	**18.66**	**15.06**	81.18	84.87
10	**63.85**	**57.00**	19.59	25.30	5.35	3.21	11.21	14.50

as Okumura-Hata, together with the MAC layer simulation are used to calculate the effective data throughput and packet loss rate. We try to simplify this by creating a model that generates the bitrate and the packet loss ratio directly. We based our work on the GPS traces gathered from multiple travels along the same path by the same person. This provides a good representation of the rate of changes during a typical way to work, or a travel on a predefined path. We defined some location of the Wi-Fi access points and calculated the distributions of time in which the client enters the range of the access point and crosses the borders of areas with different signal levels. To model an effective data rate, the AP coverage is divided into areas of relatively constant transmission conditions representing an area in which a specific modulation (and effectively bitrate) is used. The measured distributions of the passage time per area were matched with common statistical distributions, and showed to fit into normal distribution in most cases. In some cases, the location of the AP influences heavily the distribution of change time, e.g. when an AP is located near the traffic lights, the change must be modelled using the bimodal or multimodal distribution. The model can be parameterized to represent such locations correctly. The model is verified by comparison to the GPS, signal level and transmission rate traces gathered in the real life conditions.

5.1 Proposed Model of Wireless Network Throughput

We assume that within the area on which a single coding rate is used, a client is offered a constant throughput which depends only on the packet size and the number of other clients connected to the same AP. This is a simplification based on assumptions made already by most of the discrete event simulation models, such as neglecting the influence of interferences. To determine the data rate

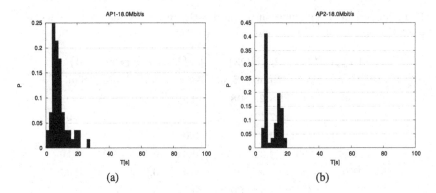

Fig. 3. Distribution of the passage time of a single coding rate for a client moving along a straight road in the AP range (a) and for a client moving through a crossing in the AP range (b).

Fig. 4. Map of a simulated AP with the marked path and points at which the coding rate changes.

offered to a client, we need to define the moments at which it enters and leaves the area with a particular coding rate. We used the distances provided in [39].

In the simulation model, we propose the transmission time of a packet is determined by the client bitrate (which is selected according to the area in which currently the client is). A guard time representing the MAC layer activity is added between two consecutive packet transmissions. It is calculated based on the packet size and the number of clients connected to the same AP, according to the values provided in [15]. When multiple clients are using the same AP, the traffic is served using the round robin scheme, which represents a fair allocation of radio resources.

To select moments at which clients move into or out of the area with a specific coding rate, we gathered GPS traces of multiple travels along a single path by the same person. The GPS traces are used to collect the distribution of passage time between points in space, which represent the change in transmission conditions (the moments of entering and leaving the area). The points in time have been selected according to the signal propagation model to calculate the maximum and minimum distance at which a specific coding scheme is optimal. We defined some location of the Wi-Fi access points and calculated the distributions of time in which the client enters the range of the access point and crosses the borders of areas with different signal levels.

5.2   Sample Results

The measured distributions of the passage time per area were matched with the common statistical distributions. In most cases they fit into the normal distribution. In some cases, the location of the AP influences heavily the distribution of the change time, e.g. when the AP is located near to the traffic lights, the change must be modelled using the bimodal or multimodal distribution. Such distributions for a straight road within the AP access are present if there is a road crossing. They are shown in Fig. 3. The model can be parameterized to represent elements like road crossing and traffic lights correctly.

The GPS trace represents a typical path taken by a single mobile client. It provides a good representation of the rate changes during a typical way to work, or a travel on a predefined path. The sample track that we used in the simulation, with marked points at which the coding rate changes, is shown in Fig. 4. It represents a single path for a single client. To model multiple clients we need to use multiple instances of the same node (it will represent multiple clients using the same path) or gather GPS traces from multiple clients.

The results for the model showing the coding rate simulated in time for a sample path is presented in Fig. 5. This is an input for the packet delay model, which also takes into account the packet size and the number of clients connected to the same AP and calculates the packet delay.

5.3   Validation of the Simplified Model

To validate the proposed simplified representation of bitrate change, we have created a discrete event simulation model using the ns-3 environment with the full representation of layer 2. The simulation consists of 3 Wi-Fi Access Points and a single client, which was moving according to the GPS trace imported into the simulation. The Access Points were connected to a PC by a simulated Ethernet link (using a CSMA NetDevice), which was flooding the client with packets. The FreeSpace signal propagation was used.

We have collected the Wi-Fi bitrate of packets transmitted in the simulation and compared it to the bitrate generated by the proposed simplified model.

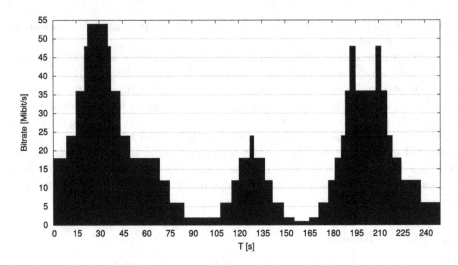

Fig. 5. Sample simulation results with the model of the coding rate changes in time.

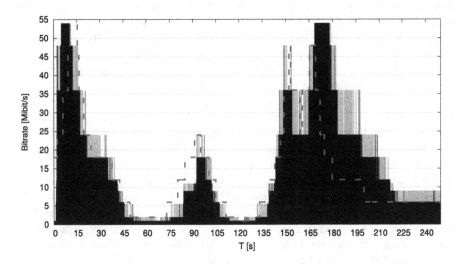

Fig. 6. Comparison of the bitrate generated by the proposed simplified model (red) and the bitrate used in the ns-3 simulation (black) (color figure online).

The Fig. 6 shows how both bitrates changed in time for sample simulation run. In the simplified models, the results provide similar values of the bitrate in time, however the simulation shows that in some cases the modulation and coding scheme in Wi-Fi jumps constantly between two values, what is not captured by our model.

To evaluate quantitatively the difference between proposed simplified model and the full simulation with radio signal propagation model we have executed the simulation 30 times for different random seeds over a sample path presented

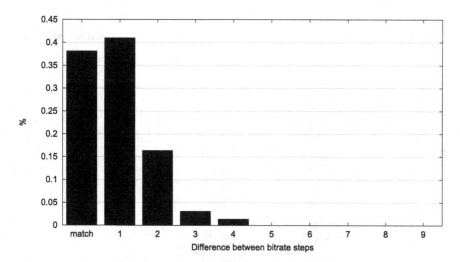

Fig. 7. Distribution of difference in bitrate steps between the simplified and full signal propagation model

on Fig. 4. We have measured at what percentage of time the bitrates provides by both models match, when they differ by one or more steps. The results presented on Fig. 7 show that at 80 % of time the simplified model provided values which were the same or different only by one step.

5.4 Computational Complexity

To evaluate the computational complexity of the model we have implemented three models representing a node moving along the same path: full simulation in ns-3 with packet transmission, MAC layer model and radio signal propagation calculations, simulation with packet transmission through channel with modelled bitrate changes according to the proposed method and calculation only of the bitrate changes in time within the proposed model. The simulations were executed 30 times for different random seeds. The average execution time of the generation of bitrate changes was below 2 s for the sample path presented on the map, what is shown on the right bar on Fig. 8. The execution of the simulation with packet transmission over wireless network with emulated bitrate according to the presented model required on average 16 s to execute, while the ns-3 simulation of the full WiFi MAC model with signal propagation calculation required more than 45 s (left bar on Fig. 8). It shows that the simulation that uses our model is approximately 3 times faster than the traditional method, and the computational complexity of the bitrate calculation is more than one order of complexity lower than the calculation of the full client mobility model: it requires less than 2 s comparing to 29 s required for the calculation of bitrate using full signal propagation model (calculated as the difference between full and simplified simulation).

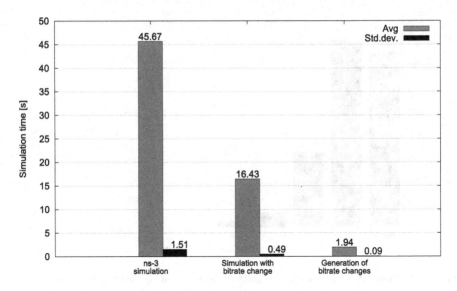

Fig. 8. Computation time for models with different representation of WiFi bitrate changes.

6   Conclusions

The problem of mobility modelling is one of the most important parts of the network performance evaluation. Good quality traces are the basis of a network simulation, thus choosing the adequate mobility model for generating these traces is crucial. In this chapter, we briefly presented large variety of mobility models available in the literature. Mobility modelling of mobile devices movement correlates with modelling of a human-like movement and it is still under research. The Hybrid models proposed in Sect. 3.3 are a good basis for modelling such a movement in a cellular network environment.

We also discuss two novel approaches to the mobility models: using it to handoffs optimization and replacing it by a bitrate modelling. In mobile communications, the probabilistic knowledge of the terminals movement and the subsequent prediction of their position are useful to improve several processes such as HO and paging and the signalling associated with them. In this chapter, some advances towards improving these processes have been presented along with the mobility models for synthetic trace generation. An analytical framework for the estimation of the probability of a node handoff to its neighbour cells has been presented. The analysis is useful for simple scenarios, such as RWP mobility, a simple symmetrical layout, position and time of the last known change in transition. The model can be generalized to other symmetrical layouts and the comparison of the analysis and simulation proves the validity of the analytical framework. The terminal ends up at the expected cell in a significant proportion of predictions, hence the needed capacity for HO can be correctly reserved most of the times. The above-mentioned prediction algorithm needs to be fed with accurate historical data that reflects the movement and use of capacity by the nodes.

The statistical analysis of actual bandwidth traces for moving terminals and the changes of involved available bandwidth can sometimes substitute the actual traces in simulations. The results presented in this chapter show that changes of the available bandwidth versus movement of the terminal generally follow the common probability distributions. The use of such distributions in the simulations leads to more compact simulation models, requiring less computations. In the Sect. 5 of this chapter the simplified model is presented. It simulates bitrate changes without the need to perform complex computations (running mobility and signal propagation models). The use of such a model can significantly decrease the simulation execution time at the costs of lower accuracy of the model.

Acknowledgement. This work was partially supported by the grant of the Polish National Centre for Research and Development, No. LIDER/10/194/L-3/11.

We thank the team of the *User-centric Mobility Management* project funded by Fundação para a Ciência e Tecnologia, (UMM, http://copelabs.ulusofona.pt/~umm), reference PTDC/EEA-TEL/105709/2008.

References

1. Ali, T., Saquib, M., Sengupta, C.: Vertical handover analysis for voice over WLAN/cellular network. In: Proceedings of the IEEE International Conference on Communications, pp. 1–5 (2010)
2. Atkinson, R.P.D., Rhodes, C.J., Macdonald, D.W., Anderson, R.M.: Scale-free dynamics in the movement patterns of jackals. OIKOS **98**(1), 134–140 (2002)
3. Bai, F., Helmy, A.: A survey of mobility models. Wireless Adhoc Networks, vol. 206. University of Southern California, USA (2004)
4. Barabási, A.L.: The origin of bursts and heavy tails in human dynamics. Nature **435**, 207–211 (2005)
5. Bettstetter, C.: Mobility modelling in wireless networks: categorization, smooth movement, and border effects. ACM SIGMOBILE Mob. Comput. Commun. Rev. **5**(3), 55–66 (2001)
6. Bettstetter, C., Hartenstein, H., Perez-Costa, X.: Stochastic properties of the random waypoint mobility model. ACM/Kluwer Wirel. Netw. (Special Issue on Modelling and Analysis of Mobile Networks) **10**(5), 555–567 (2004)
7. Bettstetter, C., Wagner, C.: The spatial node distribution of the random waypoint mobility model. In: Proceedings of WMAN, Ulm, pp. 41–58 (2002)
8. Birand, B., Zafer, M., Zussman, G., Lee, K.-W.: Dynamic graph properties of mobile networks under Lévy walk mobility. In: IEEE 8th International Conference on Mobile Adhoc and Sensor Systems, MASS 2011, Valencia, Spain, 17–22 October 2011, pp. 292–301 (2011)
9. Boldrini, C., Passarella, A.: HCMM: modelling spatial and temporal properties of human mobility driven by users' social relationships. Elsevier Comput. Commun. **33**, 1056–1074 (2010)

10. Borrel, V., Legendre, F., de Amorim, M.D.: Simps: using sociology for personal mobility. IEEE/ACM Trans. Netw. **17**, 831–842 (2009)
11. Brockmann, D., Hufnagel, L., Geisel, T.: The scaling laws of human travel. Nature **439**, 462–465 (2006)
12. Cai, X., Chen, L., Sofia, R.: A dynamic and user-centric network selection in heterogeneous wireless networks. In: IEEE International Performance, Computing, and Communications Conference, 2007, IPCCC (2007)
13. Camp, T., Boleng, J., Davies, V.: A survey of mobility models for ad hoc network research. ACM Comput. Surv. (CSUR) **37**(2), 164–194 (2005). ACM, New York, NY, USA
14. Chaoming, S., et al.: Limits of predictability in human mobility. Science **327**, 1018–1021 (2010)
15. Chatzimisios, P., Vitsas, V., Boucouvalas, A.C.: Throughput and delay analysis of IEEE 802.11 protocol. In: Proceedings of 2002 IEEE 5th International Workshop on Networked Appliances, 2002, Liverpool, pp. 168–174. IEEE (2002)
16. CRAWDAD - A Community Resource for Archiving Wireless Data at Darthmouth. http://crawdad.org/. Accessed Nov 2012
17. Gonzalez, M.C., Hidalgo, C.A., Barabási, A.L.: Understanding individual human mobility patterns. Nature **453**, 779–782 (2008)
18. Gorawski, M., Marks, P., Gorawski, M.: Collecting data streams from a distributed radio-based measurement system. In: Haritsa, J.R., Kotagiri, R., Pudi, V. (eds.) DASFAA 2008. LNCS, vol. 4947, pp. 702–705. Springer, Heidelberg (2008)
19. Gorawski, M., Grochla, K.: The real-life mobility model: RLMM. In: Proceedings of FGCT 2013, London, pp. 12–14 (2013)
20. Einstein, A.: Investigations on the Theory of the Brownian Movement. Dover Publications Inc., New York (1956)
21. Hossmann, T., Spyropoulos, T., Legendre, F.: A complex network analysis of human mobility. In: IEEE Conference on Computer Communications Workshops (INFOCOM WKSHPS), 10–15 April 2011, pp. 876–881 (2011)
22. Humphries, N.E., Weimerskirch, H., Queiroza, N., Southall, E.J., Sims, D.W.: Foraging success of biological Lévy flights recorded in situ. In: Proceedings of the National Academy of Sciences of the U.S.A. (2012)
23. Hyttiä, E., Lassila, P., Virtamo, J.: Spatial node distribution of the random waypoint mobility model with applications. IEEE Trans. Mob. Comput. **5**(6), 680–694 (2006)
24. Iraqi, Y., Baoutaba, R.: Handoff and call dropping probabilities in wireless cellular networks. In: Proceedings of IEEE International Conference on Wireless Networks, Communications and Mobile Computing, vol. 1, pp. 209–213 (2005)
25. Isaacman, S., Becker, R., Cáceres, R., Martonosi, M., Rowland, J., Varshavsky, A., Willinger, W.: Human mobility modeling at metropolitan scales. In: Proceedings of the 10th International Conference on Mobile Systems, Applications, and Services (MobiSys'12), pp. 239–252. ACM, New York (2012)
26. Joshi, T., Mukherjee, A., Agrawal, D.P.: Exploiting mobility patterns to reduce reauthentication overheads in infrastructure WLAN networks. In: Proceedings of IEEE Canadian Conference on Electrical and Computer Engineering, pp. 1423–1426 (2006)
27. Karim, L., Mahmoud, Q.H.: A hybrid mobility model based on social cultural and language diversity. In: 9th IEEE International Conference CollaborateCom (2013)
28. Kim, T.S., Kwon, J.K., Sung, D.K.: Mobility modelling and traffic analysis in three-dimensional high-rise-building environments. IEEE Trans. Veh. Technol. **49**(5), 1633–1640 (2000)

29. Kurkowski, S., Camp, T., Colagrosso, M.: MANET simulation studies: the incredibles. SIGMOBILE Mob. Comput. Commun. Rev. **9**(4), 50–61 (2005)
30. Lee, K., Kim, S.J., Rhee, I., Chong, S.: SLAW: self-similar least-action human walk. IEEE/ACM Trans. Netw. **20**(2), 515–529 (2012)
31. Michaelis, S., Wietfeld, C.: Comparison of user mobility pattern prediction algorithms to increase handover trigger accuracy. In: Proceedings of IEEE Vehicular Technology Conference, vol. 2, pp. 952–956 (2006)
32. Musolesi, M., Hailes, S., Mascolo, C.: An ad hoc mobility model founded on social network theory. MSWiM **2004**, 20–24 (2004)
33. Musolesi, M., Mascolo, C.: A community based mobility model for ad hoc network research. In: Proceedings of the 2nd International Workshop on Multi-Hop Ad Hoc Networks: From Theory to Reality (REALMAN '06), pp. 31–38. ACM Press (2006)
34. Prasad, P.S., Agrawal, P.: Movement prediction in wireless networks using mobility traces. In: Proceedings of the 7th IEEE Conference on Consumer Communications and Networking Conference, pp. 1–5 (2010)
35. Ramos-Fernandez, G., Morales, J.L., Miramontes, O., Cocho, G., Larralde, H., Ayala-Orozco, B.: Lévy walk patterns in the foraging movements of spider monkeys (ateles geof-froyi). Behav. Ecol. Sociobiol. **273**, 1743–1750 (2004)
36. Rhee, I., Lee, K., Hong, S., Kim, S.J., Chong, S.: Demystifying the Lévy-walk nature of human walks. Technical report, CS Department, NCSU, Raleigh, NC (2008). http://netsrv.csc.ncsu.edu/export/Demystifying_Levy_Walk_Patterns.pdf
37. Rhee, I., Shin, M., Hong, S., Lee, K., Chong, S.: On the Lévy-walk nature of human mobility: do humans walk like monkeys? IEEE/ACM Trans. Netw. (TON) **19**(3), 630–643 (2011)
38. Rojas, A., Branch, P., Armitage, G.: Validation of the random waypoint mobility model through a real world mobility trace. In: Proceedings of IEEE Region 10 TENCON, pp. 1–6 (2005)
39. Romano, P.: The range vs. rate dilemma of WLANs (2004). http://www.eetimes.com/document.asp?doc_id=1271995
40. Roy, R.R.: Handbook of Mobile Ad Hoc Networks for Mobility Models. LXIV, 1st edn, 1104 p. Springer, Boston (2011)
41. Sgora, A., Vergados, D.: Handoff prioritization and decision schemes in wireless cellular networks: a survey. IEEE Commun. Surv. Tutor. **11**(4), 57–77 (2009)
42. Sims, D.W., et al.: Scaling laws of marine predator search behaviour. Nature **451**, 1098–1102 (2008)
43. Soh, W.S., Kim, H.S.: QoS provisioning in cellular networks based on mobility prediction techniques. IEEE Commun. Mag. **41**(1), 86–92 (2003)
44. Sricharan, M.S., Vaidehi, V.: A pragmatic analysis of user mobility patterns in macrocellular wireless networks. Elsevier Pervasive Mob. Comput. **4**(5), 616–632 (2008)
45. Tong, C., Niu, J.W., Qu, G.Z., Long, X., Gao, X.P.: Complex networks properties analysis for mobile ad hoc networks. IET Commun. **6**(4), 370–380 (2012)
46. Tong, L., Bahl, P., Chlamtac, I.: Mobility modelling, location tracking and trajectory prediction in wireless ATM networks. IEEE J. Sel. Areas Commun. **16**(6), 922–936 (1998)
47. Yoon, J., Liu, M., Noble, B.: Random waypoint model considered harmful. In: Proceedings of INFOCOM 2003, San Francisco, April 2003

48. Zola, E., Barcelo-Arroyo, F.: Probability of handoff to neighbor cells for random waypoint mobility and non-ideal conditions. In: Proceedings of IEEE 2nd Baltic Congress on Future Internet Communications (BCFIC'12), pp. 162–169 (2012)
49. Zola, E., Barcelo-Arroyo, R., Martín-Escalona, I.: Forecasting the next handoff for users moving with the random waypoint mobility model. EURASIP J. Wirel. Commun. Netw. **2013**, 16 (2013)

Throughput Analysis in CSMA/CA Networks Using Continuous Time Markov Networks: A Tutorial

Boris Bellalta[1]([⊠]), Alessandro Zocca[2], Cristina Cano[3], Alessandro Checco[3], Jaume Barcelo[1], and Alexey Vinel[4]

[1] Universitat Pompeu Fabra, Barcelona, Spain
boris.bellalta@upf.edu
[2] Eindhoven University of Technology, Eindhoven, The Netherlands
[3] Hamilton Institute, Maynooth, Ireland
[4] Halmstad University, Halmstad, Sweden

Abstract. This book chapter introduces the use of Continuous Time Markov Networks (CTMN) to analytically capture the operation of Carrier Sense Multiple Access with Collision Avoidance (CSMA/CA) networks. It is of tutorial nature, and it aims to be an introduction on this topic, providing a clear and easy-to-follow description. To illustrate how CTMN can be used, we introduce a set of representative and cutting-edge scenarios, such as Vehicular Ad-hoc Networks (VANETs), Power Line Communication networks and multiple overlapping Wireless Local Area Networks (WLANs). For each scenario, we describe the specific CTMN, obtain its stationary distribution and compute the throughput achieved by each node in the network. Taking the per-node throughput as reference, we discuss how the complex interactions between nodes using CSMA/CA have an impact on system performance.

Keywords: CSMA/CA · Markov Networks · WLANs · VANETs · PLC

1 Introduction

The presence of devices that use the license-exempt spectrum to communicate is increasing everyday. Those devices range from that of personal and multimedia use (including smart-phones, laptops and storage units, among others) to environment-interactive ones (such as sensors, that gather environmental data, and actuators, that apply a certain action based on given inputs). In between, there is also a plethora of heterogeneous mobile objects, such as vehicles and robots.

Most of those wireless devices access the channel to transmit data using CSMA/CA, as it offers a good tradeoff between performance and simplicity of implementation. However, when those devices are nearby placed and share the same spectrum band, the use of CSMA/CA creates some complex interactions between their operation, which may also affect their performance. Moreover,

© Springer International Publishing Switzerland 2014
I. Ganchev et al. (Eds.): Wireless Networking for Moving Objects, LNCS 8611, pp. 115–133, 2014.
DOI: 10.1007/978-3-319-10834-6_7

those interactions might happen between devices belonging to the same or different networks. For instance, in the former, interactions may occur among two-hop neighbors in a multi-hop network [1], while in the latter, there may be an interplay between multiple co-located WLANs belonging to different owners [2].

Analytical models help in improving our understanding of those interactions and allow us to evaluate their impact on system performance. This knowledge should yield to the design of more adequate settings (i.e., parameter configurations) and the development of new mechanisms able to ameliorate the negative effects of such interactions. In this book chapter, we show that CTMN models are able to capture those interactions and provide accurate predictions of their effect on system performance.

To illustrate how CTMN can be used to model the coupled operation between nodes using CSMA/CA, we consider three representative scenarios. For each scenario, we describe the analytical model that captures the behavior of the network, obtain the stationary distribution of the CTMN and compute the per-node throughput. As we discuss in this tutorial, the number of states of the CTMN depends on the number of nodes, their location, the spectrum band they use, and the channel characteristics of the scenario under study. Moreover, the transitions between states are based on the CSMA/CA parameters, such as the backoff-related settings, the packet size and the transmission rate.

This book chapter is structured as follows. First, we present the basic operation of CSMA/CA networks, detailing all assumptions considered in this work. Then, we briefly introduce the required background to understand how the dynamics of CSMA/CA networks can be modelled using CTMN. After that, we model three representative scenarios as use-cases. Finally, we conclude the tutorial summarizing the lessons learned.

2   Related Work

The use of CTMN models for the analysis of CSMA/CA networks was originally developed in [3] and further extended in the context of IEEE 802.11 networks in [1,4–6], among others. Although the modeling of the IEEE 802.11 backoff mechanism is less detailed than in the work of Bianchi [7], it offers greater versatility in modeling a broad range of topologies. Moreover, experimental results in [6,8] demonstrate that CTMN models, while idealized, provide remarkably accurate throughput estimates for actual IEEE 802.11 systems.

Boorstyn et al. [3] introduce the use of CTMN models to analyze the throughput of multi-hop CSMA/CA networks. They apply these models to study several network topologies, including a simple chain, a star and a ring network. In [4], Wang and Kar, extend the work done in [3] by considering also the fairness between the throughput achieved by each node. Moreover, they connect the parameters of the CTMN with the ones defined by the IEEE 802.11 standard, such as the contention window or the use of RTS/CTS frames. They also provide several approximations with the goal of reducing the model complexity by using local information only. In [5], Durvy and Thiran, also use CTMN models to characterize the behavior of wireless CSMA/CA networks and explore their spatial reuse gain. Nardelli and Knightly [6] extend previous models to specifically consider the negative effect of collisions and hidden terminals. They evaluate several multi-hop topologies and compare the results with experimental data, showing that CTMN models can provide very accurate results. In [8], Liew et al. also validate the accuracy of CTMN to model CSMA networks using both simulations and experimental data. Besides, they introduce a simple but accurate technique to compute the throughput of each node based on identifying the maximal independent sets of transmitting nodes. Recently, Laufer and Kleinrock [1] have extended such CTMN models to support non-saturated nodes. Finally, the CTMN model presented in [1] is used in [9] to evaluate the performance of a vehicular video surveillance system.

3 CSMA/CA Networks

In this section, we describe the node characteristics and the operation of the considered CSMA/CA protocol.

3.1 CSMA/CA Protocol

The MAC protocol defines the rules used by nodes to transmit packets to the channel. The basic principle of CSMA is to listen to the channel before transmitting a packet. In case the channel is detected busy, the transmitter defers its transmission until the channel is sensed idle again. To avoid that all nodes with at least a packet pending for transmission collide as soon as the channel is sensed idle, a collision avoidance (CA) mechanism is introduced. In our case of interest, the CA mechanism is known as the backoff procedure, and it is basically a timer.

The operation of the backoff timer considered in this work is as follows. The backoff timer is initialized to a random value every time the node starts a new transmission attempt. Then, while the channel remains idle, the backoff timer is decreased until it reaches zero, time at which the node transmits the packet to the channel. In case the channel is detected busy before the backoff timer has expired, the node defers the transmission and pauses the backoff timer until the channel becomes idle again.

We also assume that the backoff countdown is continuous in time, and that every time it is initialized, an exponentially distributed random value is selected, with an average duration of $E[B]$ seconds. Therefore, the attempt rate for every node is equal to $\lambda = E[B]^{-1}$, and the potential[1] activation epochs (i.e., when a node starts a transmission) occur as a Poisson process with rate λ.

3.2 Node Characteristics

Each node implements the CSMA/CA protocol previously described. A node detects the channel busy if the energy level in the channel is equal or higher

---

[1] Potential since the node may be transmitting or overhearing.

than the Carrier Sense threshold. However, it will only be able to recover the transmitted data if the energy level has an energy equal or higher than the Data Communication threshold. Based on both thresholds, the carrier sense and data communication ranges are defined. In Fig. 1, we can see two nodes communicating. The green circles represent their data communication ranges, and the blue ones their carrier sense ranges.

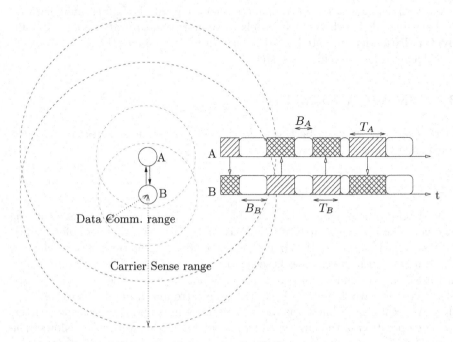

Fig. 1. Two nodes exchanging data using the basic CSMA/CA protocol. B_i indicates the duration of a single backoff instance, and T_i the duration of a packet transmission from node i.

In this work, we assume that the carrier sense range is at least two times larger than the data communication range. We also assume that the propagation delay between two nodes inside the carrier sense of each other is negligible.

The Data Communication threshold depends on the transmission rate. It is defined as the required received signal level to guarantee a certain packet error probability when a modulation and a coding rate are employed. Here, we consider that all nodes use a single transmission rate, R, and we assume that the considered data communication threshold guarantees an error free transmission regardless the packet size.

All nodes are assumed to be saturated. It means that all nodes have always packets waiting for transmission, and therefore, after transmitting one packet successfully, they will try to start the transmission of the next one. All nodes transmit packets of random size L, where L is a random variable exponentially distributed, with average $E[L]$. Therefore, the duration of a packet transmission, $T = L/R$, is also a random variable exponentially distributed, with parameter $\mu = 1/T = R/L$.

Finally, we assume that in case of collision, the affected nodes are able to capture the packet received with a higher energy level.

3.3 Spatially Distributed CSMA Networks

Using CSMA/CA, the operation of multiple nodes is coupled if they are inside the carrier sense range of the other, and use the same channel. This happens because as soon as they detect a transmission from the other node, they stop their backoff timer and wait until the channel becomes free to restart it again.

We refer to single-hop networks if all nodes are inside the data communication range of all the other nodes (i.e., any node can transmit packets to the desired destination directly). Otherwise, packets directed to destinations that are outside the data communication range of the transmitter have to be forwarded by intermediary nodes towards it. In this case, we have a multi-hop network. Note that in case of multi-hop networks, nodes that can not communicate directly can also interact between them due to the larger carrier sense range compared with the data communication range, which may cause an undesirable performance loss.

Finally, nodes from two independent networks can also interact if they operate in the same band and are inside the carrier sense range of each other. In this case, we have a coexistence problem, since both networks see their performance negatively affected.

3.4 Implications

Previous assumptions and considerations have the following implications:

- **Collision-free operation between any two nodes that can hear each other:** Given the assumptions of a continuous random backoff and the negligible propagation delay, the probability of packet collisions between two nodes that can hear each other is negligible.
- **Collisions with hidden nodes and capture effect:** Since the carrier sense range is assumed to be at least two times larger than the data communication range, all nodes that are able to transmit data packets to a target node are able to listen any on-going transmission directed to it and therefore, they can defer their backoff countdown accordingly. However, we consider that the capture effect allows a given receiver to decode the packet directed to it in case of a collision between hidden nodes. Collisions of that nature can happen when transmissions of nodes outside each other's carrier sense range overlap and one of the intended receivers is located inside the intersection of those transmitters' carrier sense ranges.

4   Continuous Time Markov Network Models

In this section we introduce the Continuous Time Markov Network model, which is a stylized Markovian model of N nodes sharing a wireless medium.

4.1   Markovian Model: The State Space and Transitions

Define Ω as the collection of all feasible *network states*, i.e. all subsets of the N nodes that can transmit simultaneously, and let $S_t \in \Omega$ be the network state at time t. We allow for heterogeneous backoff and transmitting rates, i.e. we assume that at node i the backoff rate is $\lambda_i = E[B_i]^{-1}$ and the transmitting rate is $\mu_i = E[T_i]^{-1} = R_i/E[L_i]$. Then, the transition rates between two network states $s, s' \in \Omega$ are

$$q(s, s') = \begin{cases} \lambda_i & \text{if } s' = s \cup \{i\} \in \Omega, \\ \mu_i & \text{if } s' = s \setminus \{i\}, \\ 0 & \text{otherwise.} \end{cases} \tag{1}$$

4.2   Detailed Balanced and Product-Form Stationary Distribution

The process $(S_t)_{t \geq 0}$ has been proven to be a time-reversible continuous-time Markov process in [10]. Therefore detailed balance applies and the stationary distribution $\{\pi_s\}_{s \in \Omega}$ can be expressed as in a product-form. Indeed, the detailed balanced relation for two adjacent feasible network states, s and $s \cup \{i\} \in \Omega$, is

$$\frac{\pi_s}{\pi_{s \cup \{i\}}} = \frac{\lambda_i}{\mu_i} = \frac{E[B_i]}{E[T_i]}. \tag{2}$$

For conciseness, we denote $\theta_i := \lambda_i/\mu_i$. Relation (2) gives that for any $s \in \Omega$

$$\pi_s = \pi_\emptyset \cdot \prod_{i \in s} \theta_i, \tag{3}$$

which, along with the normalizing condition $\sum_{s \in \Omega} \pi_s = 1$, implies that

$$\pi_\emptyset = \frac{1}{\sum_{s \in \Omega} \prod_{i \in s} \theta_i} \quad \text{and} \quad \pi_s = \frac{\prod_{i \in s} \theta_i}{\sum_{s \in \Omega} \prod_{i \in s} \theta_i}, \quad s \in \Omega. \tag{4}$$

Since the process $(S_t)_{t \geq 0}$ is irreducible and positive recurrent, it follows from classical Markov process results that the stationary distribution π_s for $s \in \Omega$ is equal to the long-run fraction of time the system spends in the network state s.

Let x_i be the throughput of node i, which is computed as follows:

$$x_i = \frac{E[L_i]}{E[T_i]} \left(\sum_{s \in \Omega : i \in s} \pi_s \right). \tag{5}$$

4.3 Insensitivity

It turns out that for the considered model the stationary distribution π (and thus any analytic performance measure linked to it, such as the throughput) is insensitive to the distributions of backoff countdowns and transmission times, in the sense that it depends on these only through the ratios θ_i of their means. The proof of the insensitivity result can be found in [8,11]. The insensitivity property is crucial since the actual behaviour of a network may not be in accordance with backoff and transmission times exponentially distributed.

5 Scenarios

We consider three different scenarios to illustrate that CTMN are a suitable tool to model the interactions between different nodes using CSMA/CA to share the medium. In detail, the considered scenarios are:

- Vehicular Ad-Hoc networks.
- Power Line Communication networks.
- Multiple overlapping WLANs supporting channel bonding.

All the throughput values plotted in this book chapter have been obtained analytically (i.e., from (5)). In case the reader is interested in the accuracy of the model compared with simulation and experimental results, please refer to the papers included in the Related Work section (Sect. 2).

5.1 Vehicular Networks

Vehicular networks, where vehicles communicate between them, as well as with APs (called Road Service Units, RSUs), are one of the most challenging scenarios for achieving an efficient communication due to the high mobility and rapid topology changes. A general overview of the applications and main challenges of vehicular networks can be found in [12].

Description of the Scenario. Overtaking on rural roads often becomes dangerous when oncoming traffic is detected by the driver too late or its speed is underestimated. Recently proposed cooperative overtaking assistance systems, which are based on Vehicular Ad hoc NETworks (VANETs), rely on real-time video transmission. In this case, a video stream captured by a camera installed at the windshield of a vehicle is compressed and broadcast to any vehicles driving behind it, where it is displayed to the driver. Further details regarding this scenario can be found in [13].

An example of this scenario formed by two groups of cars is depicted in Fig. 2. The first group formed by cars A, B and C moves from the left to the right, and the second group, formed by cars D and E, moves in the opposite direction. In detail, car A sends data to car B, car B sends data to car C, and car D sends data to car E. Note that cars C and E do not transmit packets. In this case, we can consider that the exchanged data corresponds to a video stream generated by the platoon's leading car. To illustrate the effect of mobility on the network performance, two different positions of the cars are considered. The first position represents the case where both group of cars are approaching each other. The second position represents the case where the two group of cars are side by side.

Model. In Figs. 3(a) and (b), we show the CTMNs that capture the feasible states of the vehicular networks depicted in Fig. 2(a) (position 1) and Fig. 2(b) (position 2), respectively.

Considering first the case in which the cars are in position 1, at the equilibrium, the mean fraction of time each state is active (i.e., the stationary distribution) is given by:

$$\pi_0 = \frac{1}{1 + \theta_A + \theta_B + \theta_D + \theta_B\theta_D} \qquad \pi_A = \frac{\theta_A}{1 + \theta_A + \theta_B + \theta_D + \theta_B\theta_D}$$

$$\pi_B = \frac{\theta_B}{1 + \theta_A + \theta_B + \theta_D + \theta_B\theta_D} \qquad \pi_D = \frac{\theta_D}{1 + \theta_A + \theta_B + \theta_D + \theta_B\theta_D}$$

$$\pi_{BD} = \frac{\theta_B\theta_D}{1 + \theta_A + \theta_B + \theta_D + \theta_B\theta_D}$$

with $\theta_A = \lambda_A E[T_A]$, $\theta_B = \lambda_B E[T_B]$, and $\theta_D = \lambda_D E[T_D]$.

However, since all cars have the same λ and μ parameters, we have that $\theta = \lambda/\mu$. Then,

$$\pi_0 = \frac{1}{1 + 3\theta + \theta^2} \qquad \pi_A = \frac{\theta}{1 + 3\theta + \theta^2} \qquad \pi_B = \frac{\theta}{1 + 3\theta + \theta^2}$$

$$\pi_D = \frac{\theta}{1 + 3\theta + \theta^2} \qquad \pi_{BD} = \frac{\theta^2}{1 + 3\theta + \theta^2}$$

Finally, the throughput achieved by each car is given by:

$$x_A = \frac{E[L_A]}{E[T_A]} (\pi_A) \qquad x_B = \frac{E[L_B]}{E[T_B]} (\pi_B + \pi_{BD}) \qquad x_D = \frac{E[L_D]}{E[T_D]} (\pi_D + \pi_{BD})$$

As it can be seen, the throughput achieved by cars B and D is higher than the throughput achieved by car A. This situation might harm the quality of the video sent by car A, causing packet losses due to buffer overflow.

Similarly, when cars are in position 2, all of them are in the coverage area of the others. Then, the mean fraction of time each state is active is given by:

$$\pi_0 = \frac{1}{1 + 3\theta} \qquad \pi_A = \frac{\theta}{1 + 3\theta} \qquad \pi_B = \frac{\theta}{1 + 3\theta} \qquad \pi_D = \frac{\theta}{1 + 3\theta}$$

which results in the same throughput for each car:

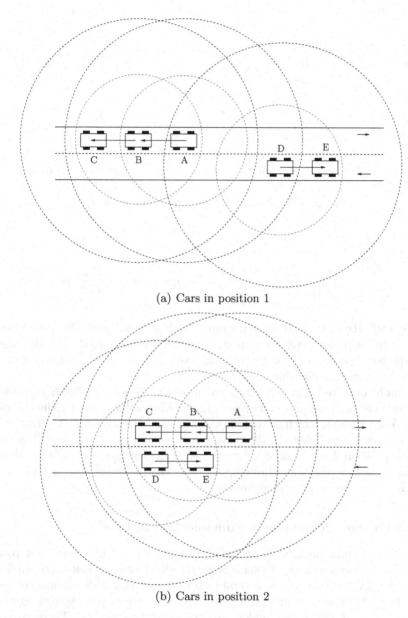

(a) Cars in position 1

(b) Cars in position 2

Fig. 2. Two group of cars moving in opposite directions are approaching. In this scenario, the leading car is transmitting a video flow to the cars following it.

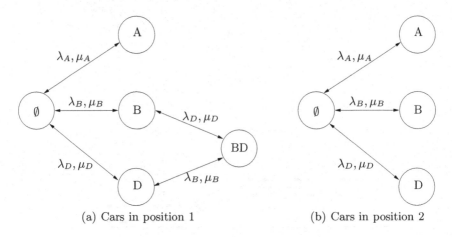

(a) Cars in position 1   (b) Cars in position 2

Fig. 3. Markov network for the vehicular scenario.

$$x_A = \frac{E[L_A]}{E[T_A]}\pi_A \qquad x_B = \frac{E[L_B]}{E[T_B]}\pi_B \qquad x_D = \frac{E[L_D]}{E[T_D]}\pi_D$$

Numerical Results and Discussion. In Fig. 4, we plot the throughput achieved by each car versus the expected backoff duration, $E[B]$. For all nodes, the expected duration of a packet transmission is $E[T] = 3$ ms, and the average packet size is $E[L] = 8000$ bits.

It can be observed that, when cars are in position 1, for very low $E[B]$ values, car A suffers from complete starvation. Higher $E[B]$ values increase the chances for car A to transmit, which increases its throughput. However, the throughput of car A will be always below the throughput achieved by cars B and D. When cars move to position 2, since all of them are inside the coverage area of the others, all vehicles achieve the same throughput. This example shows how mobility may severely affect the network performance.

5.2   Multi-hop Power Line Communication Networks

Power Line Communication (PLC) networks are formed by devices interconnected using electrical wires. Despite being classified as wired instead of wireless networks, PLC networking has several factors in common with wireless connectivity. PLC channels, as well as in wireless networks, are affected by propagation impairments and effects like hidden and exposed terminals [14]. These characteristics make the use of traditional medium access protocols for wired networks not suitable to PLC. In contrast, current PLC standards, such as Homeplug [15] and IEEE 1901 [16], use a CSMA/CA approach very similar in nature to that defined in IEEE 802.11 Distributed Coordination Function (DCF).

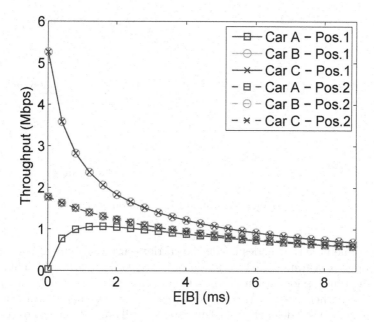

Fig. 4. Throughput achieved by each car.

The use of PLC devices is expected to grow in the years to come due to the recent availability of affordable and off-the-self devices. However, further research on higher than the physical layer needs to be carried out to fully demonstrate the capabilities and limitations of this technology. For instance, the evaluation of multi-hop PLC networks is still an open research area that imposes several challenges. The analytical framework presented here allows us to give a step further in this evaluation. Observe that, due to propagation impairments, multi-hop communication may be needed in certain PLC topologies, where the path between two communication pairs makes a direct communication not viable. That is the case of long electrical wires used in grids but also the case of large or signal-propagation-challenging buildings.

Description of the Scenario. Consider the multi-hop power line network depicted in Fig. 5, where effective connectivity (not actual wiring) and carrier sense ranges are depicted. This scenario is representative of a large building where nodes equipped with PLC modules connected to the mains run data-intensive applications. It also applies to other deployments, such as outdoors video surveillance with devices connected to urban furniture with access to the electrical grid, such as lampposts. In both cases, we assume nodes are not able to reach the central unit (point at which the data is processed, stored or sent to a server in the cloud) directly. In contrast, nodes must send their traffic sequentially using the other nodes in the chain as relays.

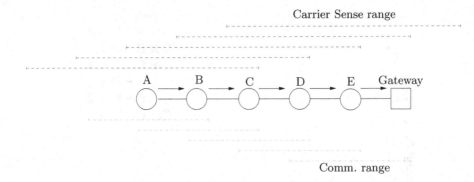

Fig. 5. Multihop PLC scenario.

We assume here that nodes inside the carrier sense range are able to decode the delimiter of a frame [15,16] but do not receive data correctly. Thus, they defer their transmissions when overhearing one and two-hop neighboring nodes. For instance, when node C transmits, all the other four nodes will sense the channel busy and will defer their backoff. Node C will only be allowed to transmit when all the other four nodes are idle, which, as we will see, severely affects its performance. On the contrary, nodes A and D can transmit simultaneously. The same applies for nodes A and E, as well as B and E.

We do not consider here sophisticated features of the standard that can influence the results, such as aggregation, frame bursting, contention free channel access, arbitration and flow control [15,16].

Model. The feasible states of the considered PLC network can be represented using the CTMN shown in Fig. 6, where each state represents a group of nodes that are active simultaneously. For instance, state A means that only node A is transmitting, while state AD means that both nodes A and D are simultaneously transmitting. As we can see, the state space of the CTMN is affected by both the network topology and the carrier sense range.

At the equilibrium, the mean fraction of time each state is active is given by:

$$\pi_\emptyset = \frac{1}{1 + \theta_A + \theta_B + \theta_C + \theta_D + \theta_E + \theta_A\theta_D + \theta_A\theta_E + \theta_B\theta_E}$$

$$\pi_A = \frac{\theta_A}{1 + \theta_A + \theta_B + \theta_C + \theta_D + \theta_E + \theta_A\theta_D + \theta_A\theta_E + \theta_B\theta_E}$$

$$\pi_B = \frac{\theta_B}{1 + \theta_A + \theta_B + \theta_C + \theta_D + \theta_E + \theta_A\theta_D + \theta_A\theta_E + \theta_B\theta_E}$$

$$\pi_C = \frac{\theta_C}{1 + \theta_A + \theta_B + \theta_C + \theta_D + \theta_E + \theta_A\theta_D + \theta_A\theta_E + \theta_B\theta_E}$$

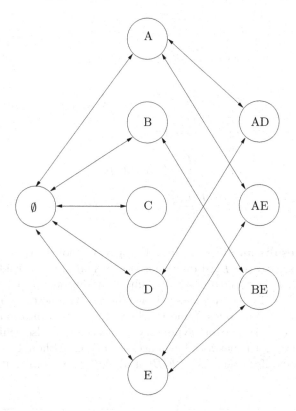

Fig. 6. CTMN representing the PLC scenario. We have not represented the transition rates for the sake of simplicity of illustration.

$$\pi_D = \frac{\theta_D}{1 + \theta_A + \theta_B + \theta_C + \theta_D + \theta_E + \theta_A\theta_D + \theta_A\theta_E + \theta_B\theta_E}$$

$$\pi_E = \frac{\theta_E}{1 + \theta_A + \theta_B + \theta_C + \theta_D + \theta_E + \theta_A\theta_D + \theta_A\theta_E + \theta_B\theta_E}$$

$$\pi_{AD} = \frac{\theta_A\theta_D}{1 + \theta_A + \theta_B + \theta_C + \theta_D + \theta_E + \theta_A\theta_D + \theta_A\theta_E + \theta_B\theta_E}$$

$$\pi_{AE} = \frac{\theta_A\theta_E}{1 + \theta_A + \theta_B + \theta_C + \theta_D + \theta_E + \theta_A\theta_D + \theta_A\theta_E + \theta_B\theta_E}$$

$$\pi_{BE} = \frac{\theta_B\theta_E}{1 + \theta_A + \theta_B + \theta_C + \theta_D + \theta_E + \theta_A\theta_D + \theta_A\theta_E + \theta_B\theta_E},$$

with $\theta_A = \lambda_A E[T_A]$, $\theta_B = \lambda_B E[T_B]$, $\theta_C = \lambda_C E[T_C]$, $\theta_D = \lambda_D E[T_D]$, and $\theta_E = \lambda_E E[T_E]$.

From the stationary distribution, we can obtain the throughput achieved by each node:

$$x_A = \frac{E[L_A]}{E[T_A]} \left(\pi_A + \pi_{AD} + \pi_{AE} \right)$$

$$x_B = \frac{E[L_B]}{E[T_B]} \left(\pi_B + \pi_{BD} \right)$$

$$x_C = \frac{E[L_C]}{E[T_C]} \left(\pi_C \right)$$

$$x_D = \frac{E[L_D]}{E[T_D]} \left(\pi_D + \pi_{AD} \right)$$

$$x_E = \frac{E[L_E]}{E[T_E]} \left(\pi_E + \pi_{AE} + \pi_{BE} \right)$$

Numerical Results and Discussion. In Fig. 7, we plot the throughput of each node with respect to the $E[B]$ duration. For all nodes, the considered average packet size is $E[L] = 12000$ bits, that results in an average packet transmission duration of $E[T] = 1359.02$ μs using Homeplug 1.0 parameters [15].

We can observe that nodes A and E achieve the same saturation throughput. As expected, due to the network symmetry, nodes B and D also achieve the same throughput. Clearly, the network bottleneck is node C. Although not completely solving the unfair effect, increasing $E[B]$ at all nodes ameliorates its magnitude.

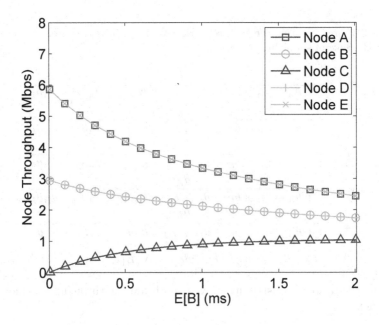

Fig. 7. Throughput achieved by each PLC node.

5.3   Channel Bonding in WLANs

Multimedia communications between multimedia devices, such as smart TVs, high definition video and music players, file storage servers, tablets, and laptops is one of the scenarios targeted by next generation WLANs. One of the strategies that can be used to satisfy the performance requirements of those applications in WLANs is channel bonding, which simply consists on the use of wider channels. The use of wider channels in WLANs has been considered recently in the IEEE 802.11n amendment [17] and further expanded in the IEEE 802.11ac amendment [18]. A wider channel is obtained by grouping several 20 MHz basic channels.

While the use of wider channels allows faster packet transmissions [19], it also increases the chances to overlap with other WLANs. Therefore, it is not obvious whether the resulting performance is improved compared to the single channel case.

Description of the Scenario. In Fig. 8, we show a scenario with 5 co-located WLANs. As it is shown in Fig. 9, WLANs A and B use a single basic channel, WLAN C uses two basic channels, WLAN D uses 4 basic channels and WLAN E uses 8 basic channels. We consider that increasing the channel width c times reduces the transmission time of a packet by the same factor c, i.e., the mean transmission time of a packet using c basic channels is $E[T_i]/c$, with $E[T_i]$ the transmission time when a single channel is used. In other words, we are not considering the performance loss caused by headers and control frames that are duplicated in every basic channel.

Model. In Fig. 10, we show the CTMN that captures the feasible states that represent the dynamics of the group of co-located WLANs shown in Fig. 8. Note that two WLANs overlap if they share at least one single channel and, therefore, they cannot be active simultaneously.

At the equilibrium, the mean fraction of time each state is active is given by:

$$\pi_\emptyset = \frac{1}{\phi} \qquad \pi_A = \frac{\theta_A}{\phi} \qquad \pi_B = \frac{\theta_B}{\phi} \qquad \pi_C = \frac{\theta_C}{\phi} \qquad \pi_D = \frac{\theta_D}{\phi} \qquad \pi_E = \frac{\theta_E}{\phi}$$

$$\pi_{AB} = \frac{\theta_A\theta_B}{\phi} \qquad \pi_{AC} = \frac{\theta_A\theta_C}{\phi} \qquad \pi_{BC} = \frac{\theta_B\theta_C}{\phi} \qquad \pi_{BD} = \frac{\theta_B\theta_D}{\phi}$$

$$\pi_{CD} = \frac{\theta_C\theta_D}{\phi} \qquad \pi_{ABC} = \frac{\theta_A\theta_B\theta_C}{\phi} \qquad \pi_{BCD} = \frac{\theta_B\theta_C\theta_D}{\phi},$$

with $\theta_A = \lambda_A E[T_A]$, $\theta_B = \lambda_B E[T_B]$, $\theta_C = \lambda_C E[T_C]/2$, $\theta_D = \lambda_D E[T_D]/4$, $\theta_E = \lambda_E E[T_E]/8$, and $\phi = 1 + \theta_A + \theta_B + \theta_C + \theta_D + \theta_E + \theta_A\theta_B + \theta_A\theta_C + \theta_B\theta_C + \theta_B\theta_D + \theta_C\theta_D + \theta_A\theta_B\theta_C + \theta_B\theta_C\theta_D$.

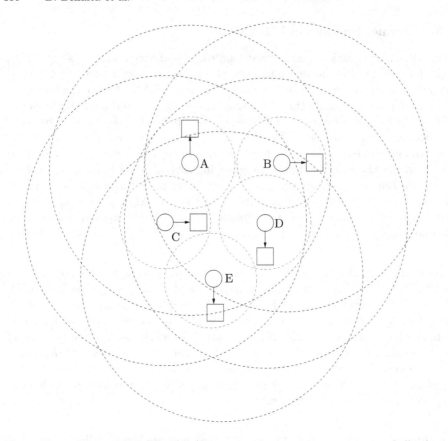

Fig. 8. Five co-located WLANs. All APs are inside the carrier sense area of all others. The channels used by each AP are shown in Fig. 9.

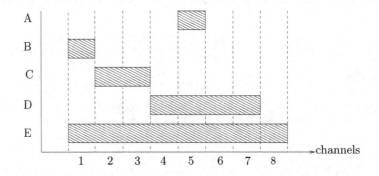

Fig. 9. Channels allocated to each WLAN.

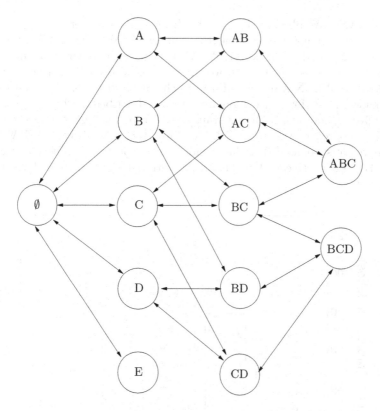

Fig. 10. CTMN that represents the multiple overlapping WLANs scenario. We have not represented the transition rates for the sake of simplicity of illustration.

We can obtain the mean throughput of WLAN i by multiplying the total time each WLAN is active by the WLAN bitrate, $\frac{E[L_i]}{E[T_i]/c}$, i.e.,

$$x_A = (\pi_A + \pi_{AB} + \pi_{AC} + \pi_{ABC}) \frac{E[L_A]}{E[T_A]}$$

$$x_B = (\pi_B + \pi_{AB} + \pi_{BC} + \pi_{BD} + \pi_{ABC} + \pi_{BCD}) \frac{E[L_B]}{E[T_B]}$$

$$x_C = (\pi_C + \pi_{AC} + \pi_{BC} + \pi_{CD} + \pi_{ABC} + \pi_{BCD}) \frac{E[L_C]}{E[T_C]/2}$$

$$x_D = (\pi_D + \pi_{BD} + \pi_{CD} + \pi_{BCD}) \frac{E[L_D]}{E[T_D]/4}$$

$$x_E = (\pi_E) \frac{E[L_E]}{E[T_E]/8}$$

Numerical Results and Discussion. In Fig. 11, we plot the throughput achieved by each WLAN when $E[T] = 0.1$ ms, $E[B] = 50\,\mu$s, and $E[L] = 12000$ bits for all WLANs. We observe that WLAN B achieves a higher throughput than WLAN A since it has less contenders. Similarly to WLAN B, WLAN C only contends with WLAN E. However, WLAN C achieves a higher throughput than WLAN B, since it uses a channel two times wider. WLAN D achieves the same throughput as WLAN A in spite of using a channel four times wider. This situation is known as performance anomaly, and was described in [20] for the case in which different nodes use different transmission rates. WLAN E uses the widest channel compared to the other WLANs. However, it is also the WLAN with more contenders, some of them independent of the others. This situation causes WLAN E to be inactive for long periods, resulting in the WLAN with the lowest throughput.

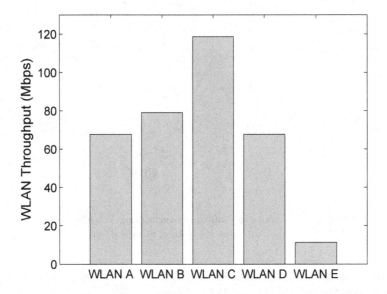

Fig. 11. Throughput achieved by each WLAN.

6   Summary

In this book chapter we have shown that Continuous Time Markov Networks can be applied to model CSMA/CA networks. To illustrate how this kind of models can be used, we have considered them to model three different toy scenarios: vehicular ad-hoc networks, PLC networks and multiple overlapping WLANs using channel bonding.

For each scenario, we have described the state space and the transitions between states by drawing its corresponding CTMN. Then, we have computed the stationary distribution of the Markov network and the per-node throughput. After that, we have evaluated the network performance, focusing on describing how the different nodes interact due to the use of CSMA/CA.

References

1. Laufer, R., Kleinrock, L.: On the capacity of wireless CSMA/CA multihop networks. In: IEEE INFOCOM 2013 (2013)
2. Herzen, J., Merz, R., Thiran, P.: Distributed spectrum assignment for home WLANs. In: IEEE INFOCOM 2013 (2013)
3. Boorstyn, R., Kershenbaum, A., Maglaris, B., Sahin, V.: Throughput analysis in multihop CSMA packet radio networks. IEEE Trans. Commun. 35(3), 267–274 (1987)
4. Wang, X., Kar, K.: Throughput modelling and fairness issues in CSMA/CA based ad-hoc networks. In: IEEE INFOCOM 2005, vol. 1, pp. 23–34. IEEE (2005)
5. Durvy, M., Thiran, P.: A packing approach to compare slotted and non-slotted medium access control. In: IEEE INFOCOM 2006 (2006)
6. Nardelli, B., Knightly, E.W.: Closed-form throughput expressions for CSMA networks with collisions and hidden terminals. In: IEEE INFOCOM 2012, pp. 2309–2317. IEEE (2012)
7. Bianchi, G.: Performance analysis of the IEEE 802.11 distributed coordination function. IEEE J. Sel. Areas Commun. 18(3), 535–547 (2000)
8. Liew, S.C., Kai, C.H., Leung, H.C., Wong, P.: Back-of-the-envelope computation of throughput distributions in CSMA wireless networks. IEEE Trans. Mob. Comput. 9(9), 1319–1331 (2010)
9. Bellalta, B., Belyaev, E., Jonsson, M., Vinel, A.: Performance evaluation of IEEE 802.11 p-enabled vehicular video surveillance system. IEEE Commun. Lett. 18(4), 708–711 (2014)
10. Kelly, F.P.: Reversibility and Stochastic Networks. Wiley, New York (1979)
11. van de Ven, P.M., Borst, S.C., Van Leeuwaarden, J.S.H., Proutière, A.: Insensitivity and stability of random-access networks. Perform. Eval. 67(11), 1230–1242 (2010)
12. Hartenstein, H., Laberteaux, K.P.: A tutorial survey on vehicular ad hoc networks. IEEE Commun. Mag. 46(6), 164–171 (2008)
13. Vinel, A., Belyaev, E., Egiazarian, K., Koucheryavy, Y.: An overtaking assistance system based on joint beaconing and real-time video transmission. IEEE Trans. Veh. Technol. 61(5), 2319–2329 (2012)
14. Ferreira, H.C., Lampe, L., Newbury, J., Swart, T.G.: Power Line Communications. Wiley, New York (2010)
15. Homeplug Powerline Alliance. Homeplug 1.0 Specification (2001)
16. IEEE Std 1901: Standard for Broadband over Power Line Networks: Medium Access Control and Physical Layer Specifications. ANSI/IEEE Std 1901 (2010)
17. IEEE P802.11n-2009: Draft Standard for Wireless LAN Medium Access Control (MAC) and Physical Layer (PHY): Enhancements for High Throughput (2009)
18. IEEE WG11ac: Draft Standard for Wireless LAN Medium Access Control (MAC) and Physical Layer (PHY) specifications Amendment 5: Enhancements for Very High Throughput for Operation in Bands below 6 GHz (2014)
19. Liao, R., Bellalta, B., Barcelo, J., Valls, V., Oliver, M.: Performance analysis of IEEE 802.11ac wireless backhaul networks in saturated conditions. EURASIP J. Wirel. Commun. Netw. 2013(226), 2013 (2013)
20. Heusse, M., Rousseau, F., Berger-Sabbatel, G., Duda, A.: Performance anomaly of 802.11b. In: INFOCOM 2003. Twenty-Second Annual Joint Conference of the IEEE Computer and Communications. IEEE Societies, vol. 2, pp. 836–843. IEEE (2003)

Approaches, Schemes, Mechanisms and Protocols

Energy-Awareness in Multihop Routing

Antonio Oliveira-Jr[1]([✉]) and Rute Sofia[2]

[1] University Federal of Goiás - UFG, Goiânia, Brazil
antoniojr@ufg.br
[2] COPELABS, University Lusófona, Lisbon, Portugal
rute.sofia@ulusofona.pt

Abstract. Recent advances in wireless technology lead to the possibility to explore new Internet connectivity models derived from the willingness of the end-user to share some Internet services. These networking architectures, known as *User-centric Networks*, introduce the Internet end-user as an active network controller, as part of the devices used in user-centric networking are devices carried and controlled by Internet end-users. The devices that are owned by end-users are portable, have limited storage as well as are limited in terms of battery capacity. Due to this, user-centric networks exhibit topological variability as the network dynamics follow a human tendency related with the willingness to share resources. In such context it is relevant to consider that routing approaches require robustness in regards to the limited energy capability of the devices. This is the topic addressed in this chapter, namely, how to keep current multihop routing approaches and yet provide them with features that make the network lifetime increase, based on energy-awareness concepts. The chapter covers notions and concepts concerning multihop routing energy-awareness; shows how to develop and how to apply energy-awareness in the most popular multihop routing protocols, providing also input concerning performance evaluation, as well as realistic specification that can be used in operational scenarios, showing that the proposed approaches are fully backward compatible with current solutions.

Keywords: Multihop routing · Energy-efficiency · User-centric networks

1 Introduction

Nowadays, the highly nomadic lifestyle that Internet users experience, the stronger entanglement between society and technology and advances in wireless technology such as *Software Defined Radio (SDR)* and *Wireless Fidelity (Wi-Fi)*, gave rise to new types of portable devices and connectivity models, e.g., *User-centric Networks (UCN)* [26,29]. Examples of such environments can be a network formed on-the-fly after a disaster of some nature, or even a municipality network where end-user devices share Internet access, e.g. FON [10].

In contrast to traditional Internet routing scenarios (be it based on wireless or wired technologies), these new user-centric scenarios pose different forwarding

© Springer International Publishing Switzerland 2014
I. Ganchev et al. (Eds.): Wireless Networking for Moving Objects, LNCS 8611, pp. 137–156, 2014.
DOI: 10.1007/978-3-319-10834-6_8

and routing challenges, due to their underlying assumptions, namely: (i) end-user devices may behave as networking nodes; (ii) nodes have a highly nomadic behavior; (iii) data is exchanged based on individual user interests and expectations; (iv) control and management requires decentralized and distributed solutions.

These UCN networking architectures rely on the interconnection of end-user equipment as a way to extend capillarity. Moreover, these networks rely on the development of Internet connectivity based on end-user, portable devices, thus considering heterogeneous nodes (in terms of energy consumption, for instance) and the topology exhibits high variability as nodes tend to disappear and appear in the network, based on their carriers interests and behavior. Such devices are, however, limited in terms of battery. Yet, in terms of routing, these environments rely on the most popular approaches for wireless networks, which do not consider energy-efficiency as a parameter related with *Quality of Service (QoS)* or *Quality of Experience (QoE)*.

As user-centric wireless environments rely on traditional multihop routing approaches, it is essential to consider ways to extend such routing with more robustness in terms of energy-awareness, with the motivation to increase network lifetime as a way to counter back the topological variability that is due to part of the devices being carried and/or controlled by the Internet end-user. In such context this chapter is dedicated to a debate on ways to improve energy-awareness in multihop routing.

The chapter is organized as follows. Section 2 provides notions and terminologies required to understand the different dimensions of energy-awareness in networking, in particular in wireless networks. Section 3 explains how to address energy-awareness while keeping backward compatibility with current shortest-path routing approaches. It also proposes a new set of routing metrics which provide nodes with an energy-aware ranking based on existing notions such as energy consumption models, energy capacity of a node, as well as residual energy of a node [13].

In terms of performance, Sect. 4 discusses and validates energy-aware routing metrics which can be applied to any available routing protocol. Such metrics have been validated in the context of the *Ad-Hoc on-demand Distance Vector (AODV)* protocol [21] and of the *Optimized Link State Routing (OLSR)* protocol [6], and the performance evaluation shows that the metrics significantly improve network lifetime, without incurring significant penalties in terms of network operation.

The chapter also contemplates Sect. 5 dedicated to an analysis concerning implementation aspects namely a routing architecture specification for energy-aware metrics which is an Internet Draft to the ROLL working group [15]. We conclude in Sect. 6, providing guidelines for future research in the context of energy-awareness in multihop routing.

2   Background

With the advent of Web 2.0 and the rise, both in variety and in coverage, of wireless technologies and user-friendly devices, there is a change in terms of Internet user behavior: the user is becoming more than simple consumer of services, to have roles where he/she shares or even provides networking services. Sofia and Mendes [26] describe new user-centric communication models, in which the user is not only a consumer but also a provider of communication opportunities (user empowerment) and alerts to the need to consider user-centric communications as part of an Internet of the future. This chapter considers the models with a specific focus on user-centric routing. Since most of the users are currently connected by means of wireless links, it is important to investigate algorithms and metrics to increase reliability and performance over multiple paths dynamic wireless networks: (i) multi-path due to wireless diversity; (ii) dynamic due to users' behavior.

In what concerns multihop routing, the most popular approaches such as AODV and OLSR have been engineered to sustain better QoS but not dynamic node movement. A line of work has addressed this need based on the definition of metrics that make a network more robust by taking into consideration link duration. Chama et al. [3] provide an extensive analysis on parameters capable of tracking a few aspects of mobility in routing protocols as a way to derive metrics that can be applied to multihop routing approaches, to make them more sensitive to node movement and hence, reduce the need for path recomputation.

A relevant aspect addressed in related literature concerns the capability to allow the network to expand based on heterogeneous and portable devices. These are often carried and transported by humans. In regards to reducing the energy consumption in mobile devices, there have been efforts in physical and data link layers as well as in the network layer related to the routing protocol as has been detailed by Oliveira Junior et al. [13]. Most of the related proposals consider energy-efficiency from an engineering perspective, i.e. extensions of the existing on-demand and link-state routing make modifications in the protocols to devise energy-awareness.

One of the major assumptions in UCN and for which routing has to be prepared is the intermittent characteristic of wireless connectivity. This inter-mittent behavior may occur in sparse networks such as in small villages, rural areas, or disaster areas, as well as in dense urban networks. In the latter case, intermittent connectivity may be due to wireless interference. Ad-hoc routing protocols such as AODV and OLSR assume that a complete path always exist between a source and a destination, and try to discover minimum cost paths. This means that such protocols are useful for networks with low to medium dynamics. While in UCNs the movement of nodes follows their owners behavior - human movement patterns -, behavior that may lead to situations where some end-to-end paths may not be temporarily suitable for communication. A family of algorithms (e.g. epidemic, gossip, greedy) tries to make use of user mobility to route information in loose connected graphs, as the ones provided by end-users. The primary focus of this family of algorithms is to increase the likelihood of finding paths, using only information about spontaneous local connectivity. However, such algorithms are agnostic to the status of the network in terms of connectivity (potential contacts), storage and queuing capability of nodes and bandwidth capability of links. Their final goal is only to increase the probability that a message is really delivered to its destination. A more realistic scenario for user-provided networks is the one in which: (i) most of the nodes have resource constraints, and (ii) local connectivity may also be predictable or scheduled (e.g. connectivity provided every day while driving to work). However, routing solutions for these UCN communication scenarios have received little attention to date. The needed investigation should analyze the trade-off between delivery probability and resource usage: for instance, distributing messages to a few or large number of nodes will increase the probability of delivering a message to its destination, but in return, more resources will be used.

2.1   Energy-Efficiency in Multihop Routing

Multi-hop routing has been extensively analyzed and optimized in terms of resource management, but in terms of energy efficiency there is a lack of a thorough analysis in wireless environments. On the other hand, there is considerable related work in the fields of energy efficiency and energy awareness for sensor networks. Even though it is relevant to consider the results achieved in such networks, there are specific requirements of UCNs which make energy awareness and efficiency problems that are not trivial to be solved. Firstly, UCN nodes are heterogeneous in terms of resources such as battery capacity. Secondly, such nodes exhibit frequent movement and are also expected to frequently join and leave a network.

Routing in UCNs can be adjusted to be energy-aware. In our work we have considered organic ways to make multi-hop routing more flexible, namely, the inclusion of energy-aware routing metrics in current multihop solutions.

Single-source shortest-path routing is the basis for today's Internet routing, independently of the type of technology. Routing is here defined as a process of computation of one or several possible paths in a network of nodes between a specific source and one or several destinations. Such paths serve the purpose to allow information transmission between source(s) and destination(s) in an optimal way, according to pre-defined optimality criteria. Routing can therefore be seen as a control plane process with the following components: topology discovery, path computation, path selection and storage, and topology maintenance. Routing components belong to the control plane. Data forwarding belongs to the data plane.

The objective of single-source shortest-path computation approaches is to find the shortest path from a single source vertex to all other vertices in a graph. For the specific case of single-source shortest-path routing in Internet, there are currently two main family of algorithms applied: the Dijkstra algorithm and distributed Bellman-Ford algorithm. Both Dijkstra and Bellman-Ford compute solutions to single-source shortest-path problem, and both use the technique of relaxation. The Bellman-Ford can solve with some edges with negative weight, Dijkstra is only positive weight, however if there is a negative cycle there is no shortest path. The running time of Dijkstra, even in simplest implementation, is better than Bellman-Ford. The distributed Dijkstra has been widely used in routing protocols, being its protocol formulation the Link State (LS) family.

Bellman-Ford is also widely implemented, being its protocol counter part the Distance Vector (DV) family. In the Internet and specially addressing IP, the most solution are either based in DV and LS family.

Multihop ad hoc routing protocols can be classified in two groups: reactive and proactive protocols. Reactive protocols find a route on demand by flooding the network with route request packets. The main disadvantages of such algorithms are: (i) high latency time in route finding; (ii) excessive flooding can lead to network clogging. Proactive protocols maintain a fresh list of destinations and their routes by periodically distributing routing tables throughout the network. The main disadvantages of such algorithms are: (i) respective amount of data for maintenance; (ii) slow reaction on restructuring and failures.

2.2 Energy-Aware Routing Metrics

Specifically attempting to make multihop routing more flexible, several authors have explored new metrics having in mind different types of optimization, e.g. reduction of energy spent across a path, on the global network. We overview the prior-art for the last years and we find out that there are few work specifically on pure energy-aware routing metrics, i.e., which consider only energy or battery parameters to design a metric. Our work focus on pure energy-aware routing metric.

Within this context, to minimize the energy consumed using transmission power as metric, the *Minimum Total Transmission Power Routing (MTPR)* approach [4], was developed to minimize the total transmission energy consumption of nodes in an acquired route, for ad-hoc scenarios where nodes are static and attempt to optimize the network lifetime. We can refer as a minimum energy route. MTPR prefers routes with more hops having short transmission ranges to those with fewer hops but having long transmission ranges and increases end-to-end delay. Since MTPR does not consider the remaining energy of nodes, it may not succeed in extending the lifetime of each node. MTPR still considers a shortest path routing, homogeneous nodes in network and mainly makes decisions of routing (choose a path) under the perspective of the sender's node, i.e. using the transmission power (Tx Power) of the node.

Addressing energy conservation, considering the remaining battery capacity the *Maximum Residual Energy Routing with Reverse Energy Cost (MREP)* proposal [32] attempts to keep residual energy at a maximum after a packet is sent. Their approach is applicable when delay is a lesser concern than global network lifetime and has as main performance parameter energy conservation.

Attempting to understand optimal properties that multihop routing should globally consider, C. K. Toh provides a relevant overview [27] of different routing properties to consider, being one of them efficient utilization of battery capacity. In this work, the author also addresses the performance of power-efficiency in ad-hoc mobile networks by analyzing four approaches which have as common goal to select an optimal path, being the optimum the minimization of the total power required on the network (across all nodes) and also the maximization of the lifetime of all nodes in the network. The author analyzes MTPR against the

Minimum Battery Cost Routing (MBCR) and the *Min-Max Battery Cost Routing (MMBCR)* [25] approaches. The author shows that the three approaches fall short in terms of guarantees that the minimum total transmission power paths will be selected under all circumstances. Hence, as workaround the author proposes a *Conditional Max-Min Battery Capacity Routing (CMMBCR)* which considers battery capacity as a route selection metric. When all nodes in some possible routes have remaining battery capacity above a threshold, a route with minimum total transmission energy is chosen among these routes. The CMM-BCR does not guarantee that the nodes with high residual energy will survive without energy breakage even when heavy traffic is passing through the node.

A more relevant metric to consider assuming that scenarios may involve heterogeneous nodes (in terms of battery) is the *Drain Rate (DR)* of a node [19]. DR is a metric that measures the energy dissipation rate (speed of energy consumption) in a given node. Each node monitors its energy consumption caused by the transmission, reception, and overhearing activities (in number of bits) and computes the energy drain rate. This metric is then used to predict the lifetime of nodes according to the current traffic conditions. Combined with the value of residual energy, the authors derived the *Minimum Drain Rate (MDR)* approach, which extends both node battery life as well as the connections lifetime by evenly distributing energy expenditure across all nodes. As a follow-up of this work, the authors propose the *Conditional Minimum Drain Rate (CMDR)* [19] which adds up to the previous work the minimization of the total transmission energy consumed per packet.

The most recent work on this topic in which the IETF WG ROLL recently proposed as standard is the RFC 6551 [30] which describes a set of link and node routing metrics and constraints, from which the node energy issue is one of them, being suitable for improving routing protocols for *Low Power and Lossy Networks (LLNs)*. In this context, Karkazis et al. [18] design a set of primary and composite metrics for RPL protocol which a energy-aware metric is one of them. The energy metric is expressed as the ratio between the maximum initial energy and the current energy value of a node, i.e., the remaining energy percentage. Still in this context, the authors of [17] have discussed the energy-based routing metric to apply in RPL. They have used the node residual energy estimation on a scale of 255 (full) to 0 (empty) in order to represent the node energy level. For path computation, a cost as the minimum node energy level captures the energy-based path weight.

Moreover, the metrics are mostly used as node selection metric and incorporated into the specific protocol operation.

3   Energy-Awareness in User-Centric Networks

UCNs integrate the end-user connected to the Internet by means of a variety of broadband access technologies, which the final segment is provided by a number of short-range technologies, among which Wi-Fi is a solution [1,29]. UCNs can also be seen as a subset of LLNs [8]. In such environments, the majority of devices are multimedia capable with strong limitations in terms of energy capabilities.

Hence, energy efficiency is a key aspect since wireless enabled mobile devices are heterogeneous in terms of battery capacity and energy consumption. By devising routing metrics to assist multihop routing protocols in becoming more efficient without adding too much operational complexity, one is improving the overall notion of energy aware networks.

Multihop routing solutions available today can be extended to integrate features that increase their flexibility concerning route selection, to counter back the topological variability that is increasing due to the application of myriads of wireless moving objects, in spontaneous deployments. Hence, the idea behind our work is to consider energy-aware routing metrics that can provide stability to current routing approaches, being such stability defined as improvement of the network lifetime and at the same time ensuring at least the same network performance.

3.1   Power Consumption Models

Concerning the source node perspective, there are three main modes of energy expenditure. A node is in *Transmit mode* when transmitting information. Hence, *Transmit Power (Tx Power)* for a node corresponds to the amount of energy (in Watts) spent when the node transmits a unit (bit) of information. A node is in *Receive mode* if it is receiving data. Hence, *Reception Power (Rx Power)* for a node corresponds to the amount of energy (in Watts) spent when the node receives a unit (bit) of information. Particularly for the case of 802.11, there are two additional states a node may be at. When not receiving or transmitting, the node is still listening to the shared medium (overhearing) and is said to be in *Idle mode*. When the node is not overhearing, then it is said to be in *Sleep mode*. In this mode, no communication is possible but there is still a low-power consumption. The way a node spends energy is based on an energy consumption model, which dictates how much energy (how many units) are spent for each mode per unit of data (transmitted, received, overheard).

Power consumption values are usually provided in the respective Network Interface Card (NIC) manuals or available on manufacturer websites. There are some recents work on power consumption measurements either for laptops and smartphones such as [24,31]. Table 1 shows some power consumption values of actual NICs with multimode (802.11 a/b/g/n) support provided by the vendors. We highlight that the most used Wi-Fi chipset for smartphone is the Broadcom BCM 4329, which is used in several popular smartphones from manufacturers like Samsung, Apple, HTC, Motorola and Google Nexus S.

An energy consumption model refers to the energy consumed by a node. In our work we have considered the model provided by Feeney and Nilson [9] which presents a general model for per packet energy consumption, i.e., energy spent by a node when it sends, receives, or discards a packet. The model considers the energy cost associated with each packet from a single node perspective and can be described using the linear Eq. 1:

$$Energy = m * size + b \tag{1}$$

Table 1. Power consumption of NICs for multimode IEEE 802.11(a/b/g/n) standards.

Device (NIC)	Power (mW)			
	Transmit	Receive	Idle	Sleep
Intel Wi-Fi Link 5300 801.11n (MIMO 3 antennas)	2100	1600	1450	100
Intel Wi-Fi Link 5300 801.11n (MIMO 2 antennas)	1990	1270	1130	100
Intel Wi-Fi Link 5300 801.11n (1 antenna)	1280	940	820	100
Intel PROset/Wireless Wi-Fi Link 4965AGN	1450	850	800	60
Cisco Aironet Wireless PCI Adapter AIR-PI21AG-E-K9	1828	1049	669	20
D-Link Wireless G PCI Adapter DWA-510	1485	858	786	49
Agilent Current Drain Analysis WLAN Network Card Test	1188	1138	1108	70
Sparklan 802.11n draft Mini-PCI Module WMIR- 215GN	1221	990	627	unspecified
PCIe mini card wireless LAN module WMPCIE- V01-R20	2013	1112	730	unspecified
Broadcom BCM4329 802.11a/b/g/n	1240	810	697	unspecified

where m and b are linear coefficients that must be experimentally derived and that vary depending on the type of operation, and where size is measured in bits.

However, a recent work [11] provides an experimental investigation of the per-frame energy consumption in IEEE 802.11 devices. The authors also proposes a new energy consumption model claiming that traditional models either neglect or amortize energy costs component in a fixed baseline cost. This model can be analyzed for considerations in future work. Gomez and Riggio [12] recently have been worked in power consumption measurements and energy savings for IEEE 802.11 standard.

3.2   Novel Energy-Aware Multihop Routing Metrics

Based on the notion that wireless capable nodes are heterogeneous in terms of energy capacity we have discussed and validated several metrics, summarizing the most relevant ones in this section [13]. Initially, we have proposed heuristics which consider an energy-awareness ranking of node based on idle times, which a node provides a ranking in terms of the node robustness to optimize the node lifetime as well as the global network lifetime. Then, a second heuristic we have considered the impact of node degree history for ranking the node to extend the lifetime.

Energy-Awareness Node Ranking (ENR). Based on the notion that in UCNs nodes are heterogeneous in terms of energy capacity ENR explores the fact that nodes that have been in idle mode for the majority of their lifetime, and that still exhibit a good estimate for their future energy level are the most adequate candidates to constitute a shortest-path.

In ENR we estimate how much of its lifetime has node i been in idle mode, to then provide an estimate towards the node's future energy expenditure, as this will for sure impact the node's lifetime. Such periods are the ones that are expensive to i in terms of energy. Hence, we consider the total period in idle time, t_{idle} over the full lifetime expected for a specific node, which is given by the elapsed time period T with the estimated lifetime of the node, as provided in Eq. 2. The estimated lifetime $C(i)$ provided by Garcia-Luna-Aceves et al. [19] have considered the ratio between residual energy and drain rate which can capture the heterogeneous energy capability of nodes.

$$ENR(i) = \frac{T - t_{idle}}{T \times C(i)} \tag{2}$$

ENR is therefore a node weight which provides a ranking in terms of the node robustness, from an energy perspective, and having as goal to optimize the network lifetime. The smaller $ENR(i)$ is, the more likelihood a node has to be part of a path.

Energy-Awareness Father-Son (EFS). Based on ENR, we consider in this work the *Energy-awareness Father-Son (EFS)* metric, which considers a composition of the ENRs of both a father and successor nodes, as specified in Eq. 3.

$$EFS(i, j) = ENR(i) \times ENR(j) \tag{3}$$

EFS provides a ranking which we believe is useful to assist the routing algorithm to converge quickly in particular in multipath environments, as the selection on which successor to consider shall be made up from, by the father node. The goal is, similarly to ENR, to improve the network lifetime without disrupting the overall network operation. Hence, the smaller $EFS(i, j)$ is, the more likelihood a link has to become part of a path.

The time instant when the route is selected could not better represent the right behavior of the metric in that time. Due to those characteristics of the metric, which can oscillate when the instant in time to select the path, it is adequate to consider that the metrics to be applied should integrate some history concerning prior behavior. To prevent adding too much status, one possibility is to consider a formula based on an *Exponential Moving Average*, providing more weight to the most recent events, as provided via Eqs. 4 and 5, where the coefficient α represents the degree of weighting, which we are using 0.3 in order to gives 70 percent of priority to the new calculated values.

$$iENR(i) = (1 - \alpha) \times iENR(i)_t + \alpha \times iENR(i)_{t-1} \tag{4}$$

$$iEFS(i, j) = (1 - \alpha) \times iEFS(i, j)_t + \alpha \times iEFS(i, j)_{t-1} \tag{5}$$

The coefficient α represents the degree of weighting, which has been tested exhaustively under different conditions [16].

The line of thought considered in the development of our energy-aware metrics is that the principle of shortest-path computation must be kept. Instead of hop-count, a metric that can provide an energy expenditure cost to a node is considered.

4   Performance Aspects

The sets of metrics described in Sect. 3, as well as variations, have been validated via discrete event simulations in the context of both AODV and OLSR. Operationally, these two protocols have a very different behavior, and applying global metrics to them independently of the protocol behavior is not trivial. However, from an energy-aware perspective, it is possible to do so, by considering that both families rely on shortest-path computation.

We also have evaluated the metrics with history against the ENR, EFS and hop count approaches. We have considered a study [2] of how mobile users interact with batteries to define the energy parameters. Our motivation was to ensure that validation is as realistic as possible.

We have considered the UM-OLSR implementation for NS-2 provided by [23] and default AODV modules. These modules have been changed to reflect the required changes detailed in next sections, being the code publicly available here [14].

4.1   Performance Metrics

The results analyze the benefits in terms of *network lifetime*. We define network lifetime as the time period since a topology becomes active up to the moment it becomes disconnected, from the perspective of destination nodes. In other words, such time period is counted since the topology becomes active, until a destination cannot be reached by any of the available sources in the topology.

Even though we analyze benefits in terms of network lifetime, we also want to understand the impact of the metrics on the overall network performance. For that, we consider additional aspects depending on the employed case: (i) *average end-to-end delay*, the time a packet takes between source and destination, comprising propagation and queuing delay. The end-to-end delay is computed per destination and then averaged across all destinations; (ii) *average throughput*, the average number of bytes reaching destination nodes, measured in Kbps. The results presented correspond to the average throughput in the network, which is computed first per destination and then averaged across all destinations in the network; (iii) *average packet loss*, the percentage of packets that does not reach the destination. Average packet loss corresponds to the number of packets dropped between source and destination, averaged across all of the destinations. To generate sound statistical results we relied on the Akaroa2 tool. All results have been computed within a 95 % confidence interval.

4.2   Implementation Aspects

We have used the reserved field of the control messages to include the energy-aware cost and then use it to determine the shortest path instead of hop count as in both AODV and OLSR (here referenced as *AODV-native* and *OLSR-native*). We have called *AODV-ENR* and *OLSR-ENR* the protocols running the ENR

Table 2. Scenario parameters.

Scenario	I	II
Area	600m x 600m	2587m x 2347m
Number of nodes	25	20
Movement	static	human behavior
Node speed	—	1 m/s
Simulation time	1000 sec	24 h
Energy parameters	heterogeneous	heterogeneous
Traffic model	Poisson (VBR)	Poisson (VBR)
Average packet size	512 bytes	512 bytes
Sending rate	128 Kbps	128 Kbps
Number of flows	4, 8 and 12	4, 8 and 12

metric, and for the EFS metric, we referenced them as *AODV-EFS* and *OLSR-EFS*. For the improved metrics, we have called *AODV-iENR* and *OLSR-iENR* the protocols running the improved iENR metric, and for the improved iEFS metric, we referenced them as *AODV-iEFS* and *OLSR-iEFS*. All approaches exchange HELLO messages every two seconds.

We have implemented the energy consumption model provided by [9] on the networking nodes which consider the energy expenditure of the transmission, reception, and idle modes.

4.3 Experimental Environment

We have considered the NS-2.34 default physical layer parameters with TwoRay-Ground propagation model. The scenarios are Wi-Fi based autoedited with 802.11 g parameters.

We have then considered two scenarios. The first scenario is a controlled random topology, where we consider the parameters described in Table 2 (Scenario I). The second scenario considered is derived from real data traces collected in North Carolina State University (NCSU) [22], where the parameters have been set as provided in Table 2 (Scenario II), from the traces. The NCSU comprises human mobility trace data of students enrolled on the computer science department who share common interests.

The rationale for those scenarios, as previously described, is to understand the behavior of the proposed metrics considering a controlled random topologies in different square area (i.e. dense and sparse scenarios), and a traces based topology as an example of user-centric environment closest to reality as possible.

There are some studies on how mobile users interact with batteries such as described in [2,7]. The main goal is to understand how users deal with limited battery lifetime on mobile devices according to the human habits.

Banerjee et al. [2] have conducted a systematic user study on battery use and recharge behavior on both laptop computers and mobile smartphones. This study has concluded that (i) most users recharges their devices when the battery has a large percentage of energy left, (ii) most recharges are driven by user context such as location, (iii) recharges usually occur when the battery level is much higher than an empty battery, and (iv) there are significant variations among users patterns and mobile systems.

We have followed the Banerjee et al. findings to define the energy parameters of mobile devices. The rationale for this choice is to better represent the wireless heterogeneous user-centric environment across different scenarios based on previously studies.

As study suggest, there are significant differences between laptop and mobile phone charging patterns. Laptop users tend to use a larger portion of their energy and they encounter low battery scenarios more commonly than mobile phone users. Hence, we have divided all nodes into two groups, in order to represent for instance the mobile smartphones and laptops.

4.4   Network Lifetime

All of the nodes of the described topologies have been set with initial energy levels picked up randomly but, for group 1 considering circa of 50 % of nodes having more than 70 % of energy level, and for group 2 considering circa of 50 % of nodes having between 20 % and 70 % of energy level. In order to represent the behavior of users shutdown the device and/or the battery is empty, we have also randomly picked up on and off periods of nodes, but ensuring that circa 15 %–30 % of nodes go down and then come up after 20 %–30 % of simulation time. The on and off periods repeats after 70 %–80 % of simulation time. The line of thought considered was to create a more real scenario, where there is more variability in terms of devices, energy levels, recharging, energy consumption (due to traffic fluctuation), and also due to path availability.

Figures 1 and 2 show the average network lifetime for the different approaches regarding scenario I and II. Concerning scenario I (Figs. 1(a) and 2(a)), we show results for the metrics applied to both AODV and OLSR routing protocols. Consistently, and independently of the number of flows, both iENR and iEFS result

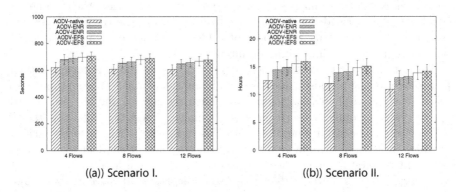

((a)) Scenario I.   ((b)) Scenario II.

Fig. 1. Network Lifetime for AODV.

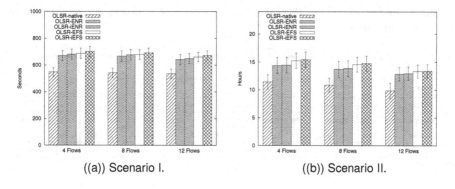

((a)) Scenario I.   ((b)) Scenario II.

Fig. 2. Network Lifetime for OLSR.

Table 3. Network lifetime improvement.

	Against native hop count approaches						Against ENR and EFS metrics					
Scenario	I			II			I			II		
Flows	4	8	12	4	8	12	4	8	12	4	8	12
OLSR-iENR	26.4%	26.9%	23.3%	29.3%	29.3%	33.2%	3.9%	3.8%	3.3%	3.5%	3.1%	3.0%
OLSR-iEFS	30.2%	29.7%	27.6%	38.4%	37.9%	37.6%	4.3%	5.2%	3.9%	5.0%	4.8%	4.3%
AODV-iENR	13.3%	11.0%	10.5%	19.5%	20.1%	22.8%	3.6%	3.5%	3.6%	4.0%	3.8%	3.7%
AODV-iEFS	15.9%	16.4%	13.7%	28.6%	27.8%	30.6%	3.4%	3.6%	3.5%	4.4%	4.1%	4.0%

in a slight better performance than ENR and EFS, in what concerns network lifetime. However, all metrics outperforms the native hop count approaches around 15 % for AODV and around 30 % for the OLSR. When looking at Scenario II (Figs. 1(b) and 2(b)), despite the change of network lifetime unit (seconds to hours), the results still hold, thus corroborating that the improved iENR and iEFS metrics result in significant benefits in what concerns network lifetime.

To better understand the magnitude of the improvement, Table 3 shows the relative improvement of network lifetime, which the improved iENR and iEFS metrics archive 3 %–5 % of gain comparing to ENR and EFS metrics. We believe this is due to the stable computed values by the metrics using history selecting a robust path.

Independently of the results, a slight improved of iENR and iEFS can be considered since it does not requires additional implementation aspects.

4.5 End-to-end Delay, Throughput and Packet Loss

As our main goal is to extend network lifetime without penalizing the network operation, Table 4 provides the relative diference of the iENR and iEFS metrics for the different approaches considering the average end-to-end delay, throughput and packet loss.

Table 4. *End-to-end delay, throughput* and *packet loss* improvement against native hop count approaches.

Metric	End-to-end delay improvement						Throughput improvement						Packet loss improvement					
Scenario	I			II			I			II			I			II		
Flows	4	8	12	4	8	12	4	8	12	4	8	12	4	8	12	4	8	12
OLSR-IENR	-23.0%	-17.5%	-7.0%	-24.9%	-10.1%	-14.7%	0.7%	-1.9%	0.2%	0%	-0.1%	0%	0.9%	-1.2%	0%	-1.3%	0%	0.1%
OLSR-IEFS	-14.5%	-8.5%	-5.2%	-19.7%	-7.2%	-10.3%	1.0%	0.9%	0.3%	0%	-0.1%	0%	1.7%	-1.0%	-0.5%	-1.0%	-0.1%	0.4%
AODV-IENR	5.0%	4.9%	1.0%	9.1%	2.6%	2.8%	1.5%	3.7%	6.8%	2.9%	7.5%	2.6%	2.5%	6.9%	6.1%	12.3%	3.3%	1.6%
AODV-IEFS	5.5%	6.2%	2.7%	10.6%	3.9%	3.5%	3.1%	4.6%	9.1%	4.0%	9.8%	6.4%	14.5%	9.7%	8.2%	13.9%	3.9%	4.1%

In scenario I, the end-to-end delay, even though low across all scenarios experimented, increases (as expected) for higher traffic load. Moreover, as in previous performance evaluations, while for AODV, iENR and iEFS result consistently in a lower end-to-end delay, with OLSR, the metrics achieve a slightly higher end-to-end delay.

The throughput results for different number of flows for scenario I and II is that when the number of flows increases, the load in the network seems to decrease. This is due to the higher packet loss (refer results on packet loss) - congested network. In what concerns AODV results, iENR and iEFS slightly improve throughput across all scenarios in comparison to ENR and EFS metrics which we believe due the stability of the improved metrics considering history. For OLSR, the improved metrics slightly improve the ENR and EFS metrics performance. As mentioned, the intention of the metrics were to provide a more robust path selection in order to improve network lifetime, without jeopardizing the overall network operation.

These results show that the metrics are at least as stable as the native versions of the protocols tested, and for AODV, they in fact indirectly improve the network operation.

The packet loss results show our iENR and iEFS metrics slightly improving packet loss comparing to all approaches, which means our improved metrics selects more robust paths when considering history.

5   Operational Aspects

The most popular multihop routing protocols stem from two distinct routing families: *link-state*, and *distance-vector* routing. Out of such families, the most popular protocols in use today are AODV (actually working progress AODVv2 [20]) and OLSR (actually working progress OLSRv2 [5]).

In this section we are going to explain main differences concerning these two protocols, as the intent is to assess whether or not we can truly provide metrics that can be applied to any multihop routing approach - the ones mentioned, and others arising now, or in the future. The purpose of any multihop routing protocol is to dynamically find paths to reach a destination and to select the best path, where best is connoted to the notion of *shortest path*.

In link state routing the nodes diffuse (depth-first search) a set of their link-state information throughout the whole network. Such packets would contain the identity of the source node, its neighbors, and the cost of routing to them. After the initial network discovery process, all nodes converge to have a perspective of the global topology, at the expense of a higher signaling. Distance vector routing is based on Bellman-Ford shortest path search algorithm. Nodes therefore keep status concerning destination cost, and next hop towards a destination. Every node periodically broadcasts and kept status concerning found destinations to neighbors.

Operationally, as explained, these two families of protocols have a very different behavior, and applying global metrics to them independently of the protocol behavior is not trivial. However, from an energy-aware perspective, it is possible to do so, by considering that both families rely on shortest-path computation.

Hence, the line of thought considered in the development of our energy-aware metrics is that the principle of shortest-path computation must be kept. Instead of hop-count, a metric that can provide an energy expenditure cost to a node is considered. The main caveat related with this change is that in order to keep accuracy, one must ensure that the protocol synchronizes path status adequately. This implies considering either a time-window mechanism, or updates to a node's cost each time a change occurs. These are regular techniques, where it is essential to find an adequate commitment between accuracy and low overhead due to the required signaling.

5.1   Specification Aspects for Distance-Vector Multihop Routing Approaches

To analyze the behavior of the proposed metrics in distance-vector approaches we have considered AODV. This section describes the operational procedures we have considered so far, to ensure that the protocol can cope with the new metrics.

AODV is a distance-vector protocol that works on-demand determining a route to a destination only when a node wants to send a packet to that destination. Routes are maintained as long as there is active traffic to the specific destination. Sequence numbers ensure the freshness of routes and are a way to mitigate transient loops and of avoiding counting-to-infinity. AODV nodes use four types of messages to communicate among each other. In the route discovery process are used *Route Request (RREQ)* and *Route Reply (RREP)* messages. Moreover, *Route Error (RERR)* messages are used for route maintenance; HEL-LOs are used to keep status concerning links (between neighbors).

The AODV protocol uses a hop count as metric to determine the shortest path between source and destination nodes. The routing information is only exchanged between directly connected neighbors. In order to accommodate our metrics, we have used the reserved field of the control messages to include the energy-aware cost and then use it to determine the shortest path instead of hop count as in native approach. For the node-based perspective, i.e., ENR metric, the protocol uses the node cost to compute the path. For the successor-based perspective, i.e., EFS metric, we have used the HELLO control messages to exchange the node cost and then define a binding cost between two nodes to compute the shortest path. The node cost sent from a node to its neighbors which its neighbors will have this information in advance to improve robustness.

5.2   Specification Aspects for Link-State Approaches

For the case of link-state we have considered OLSR. As a proactive link-state protocol, OLSR relies on flooding techniques to assist in a quick synchronization of the global topology perspective. OLSR is, however, optimized to the wireless media by relying on HELLO exchange which is capable of performing a 2-hop neighbor information discovery and then performing a distributed election of a set of *Multipoint Relay (MPR)* nodes. MPRs assist in decreasing control traffic overhead, since only those nodes are allowed to broadcast topology changes. Nodes use the topology information to compute next hop paths regarding to all nodes in the network by using shortest path hop count metric.

We also have used the reserved field of the control messages to accommodate our metrics allowing a node to send to its neighbors its energy level information. Based on that information, each node can have the perception of the energy level to the link towards the neighbors nodes. In order to allow OLSR to cope with the new metrics, we had to change the MPR selection mechanism. Instead of considering a selection based on shortest-path with a hop-count metric, we consider a selection based on our metrics. For that, when there are more than one 1-hop neighbors covering the same number of uncovered 2-hop neighbors, the one with the better energy cost to the current node is selected as MPR.

5.3   Applicability Guidelines for the RPL Approach

In order to use the metrics described in this chapter on the Routing Protocol for Low-Power and Lossy Networks (RPL) [28], no changes or adaptation to the protocol are needed. By separating the packet processing and forwarding processes from the routing path selection, RPL provides a very flexible way of using and incorporating different metrics.

RPL operates upon the concept of Destination-Oriented Directed Acyclic Graph (DODAG), where routes are calculated from all nodes to a single destination in the topology (root node). Each node in the topology has a Rank, that is basically a value that represents its distance to the topology root.

According to specific LLN applications, such routes are calculated in order to achieve different objectives that may be desired (e.g. minimize delay, maximize throughput, minimize energy usage), so different Objective Functions (OF) may be defined. An OF defines how routing metrics, constraints and related functions are used, in order to define the route between the nodes towards a single destination in the topology. That is, an OF, in conjunction with routing metrics and constraints, allows for the selection of a DODAG to join (if there is more than one), and a number of peers in that DODAG as parents (that is, an ordered list of parents). The OF is also responsible to compute the Rank of the node.

```
0                       1
0 1 2 3 4 5 6 7 8 9 0 1 2 3 4 5 6
+-+-+-+-+-+-+-+-+-+-+-+-+-+-+-+-+
| Flags |I| T |E|   Energy Cost  |
+-+-+-+-+-+-+-+-+-+-+-+-+-+-+-+-+
```

Fig. 3. Node Energy object structure

The RFC6551 [30] defines a very flexible mechanism for the advertisement of routing metrics and constraints used by RPL, even though no OF is presented. A high degree of flexibility is offered by that mechanism, and a set of routing metrics and constraints are also described in the document.

Impact on < object>. In order to use the metrics described in this document, the Node Energy object (NE), as defined in RFC6551, can be used without the need for any changes or adaptation. Figure 3 shows the NE structure is composed by a set of flags (8 bits), and an 8-bits field (E_E) used for carrying the value of the estimated energy.

To use the NE object with the metrics described in this document, the value of ENR or EFS metrics should be placed in the E_E field, and the flag 'E' (Estimation) should be set, indicating that a value for the estimated energy is provided in the E_E field. The other flags of the NE should be filled as defined in the standard.

6   Conclusions and Future Work

Energy efficiency is a key aspect to consider in multihop routing environments where devices are in movement, as part of such devices are today quite limited in terms of energy capability. The line of thought followed in this chapter is that in order to allow end-to-end routing on the Internet to adequate work in future Internet architectures, it is required to consider new metrics that incorporate properties that allow nodes to choose other-than-shortest-path solutions, while at the same time ensuring backward compatibility with the current solutions. We advocate that the principle of shortest-path computation must be kept. However, instead of relying on hop-count, a metric that can provide an energy expenditure cost to a node should be considered as a potential parameter of QoS, aligned with other network parameters, such as throughput.

A conclusion to draw is that the metrics proposed in Sect. 3 and validated in Sect. 4 have shown good improvements in terms of network lifetime. Such improvements were possible without adding any significant overhead be it to a node or network operation, as described in the different IETF specifications proposed in Sect. 5.

In terms of the behavior of EFS vs. ENR there seems to be an improvement in particular when scenarios have larger distances, and when the network load is higher. This implies that EFS seems to provide more robustness when scenarios have more variability (e.g. more nodes moving, and several successors at disposal). In terms of network lifetime and for the scenarios evaluated, ENR results in a small improvement. The greater advantage of applying EFS instead of ENR seems to relate with an improvement in throughput and a significant improvement concerning packet loss. Our belief for this gain relates to the fact that EFS allows nodes to react quicker to energy changes on a path - resulting paths will be more robust earlier in time, assuming that nodes have a reasonable out-degree (several successors available).

Thinking on real implementation, we have discussing the impact of energy awareness and operational aspects of the link-state and distance-vector routing families. Then, we have described and discussed the routing architecture specification for energy awareness submitted to the IETF working group ROLL [15]. The specification can be applied in any available multihop routing protocols, such as AODV, OLSR and RPL.

Acknowledgments. We thank all of the elements involved in the following projects: UCR, User-centric Routing (http://copelabs.ulusofona.pt/~ucr, 2010–2013), which involved COPELABS and University of Coimbra, Portugal; the European ULOOP - User-centric Wireless Local Loop (http://uloop.eu) project, scientifically coordinated by COPELABS, managed by Alcatel-Lucent BellLabs France, and including a total of 11 partners. We also thank Fundação Ciência e Tecnologia (FCT) scholarship SFRH/ BD/44005/2008 and the Cost Action WiNeMo - IC0906. We also thank to Fundação de Amparo a Pesquisa do Estado de Goiás (FAPEG).

References

1. Aldini, A., Bogliolo, A.: User-centric Networking - Future Perspectives. Lecture Notes in Social Networking. Springer, New York (2014)
2. Banerjee, N., Rahmati, A., Corner, M.D., Rollins, S., Zhong, L.: Users and batteries: interactions and adaptive energy management in mobile systems. In: Krumm, J., Abowd, G.D., Seneviratne, A., Strang, T. (eds.) UbiComp 2007. LNCS, vol. 4717, pp. 217–234. Springer, Heidelberg (2007)
3. Chama, N., Sofia, R.: A discussion on developing multihop routing metrics sensitive to node mobility. J. Commun. **6**, 56–57 (2011)
4. Chang, J.H., Tassiulas, L.: Energy conserving routing in wireless ad-hoc networks. In: Proceedings of Nineteenth Annual Joint Conference of the IEEE Computer and Communications Societies (INFOCOM 2000), vol. 1, pp. 22–31. IEEE (2000)
5. Clausen, T., Dearlove, C., Jacquet, P., Herberg, U.: The optimized link state routing protocol version 2. draft-ietf-manet-olsrv2-19 (Work in progress) (2013)
6. Clausen, T., Jacquet, P.: Optimized link state routing protocol (OLSR). RFC 3626, Internet Engineering Task Force (2003)
7. Dhir, A., Kaur, P., Jere, N., Albidewi, I.: Understanding mobile phone battery - human interaction for developing world a perspective of feature phone users in africa. In: 2012 2nd Baltic Congress on Future Internet Communications (BCFIC), pp. 127–134 (2012)
8. Dohler, M., Watteyne, T., Winter, T., Barthel, D.: Routing requirements for urban low-power and lossy networks. RFC 5548, IETF (2009)

9. Feeney, L., Nilsson, M.: Investigating the energy consumption of a wireless network interface in an ad hoc networking environment. In: INFOCOM 2001 - Proceedings of Twentieth Annual Joint Conference of the IEEE Computer and Communications Societies, vol. 3, pp. 1548–1557. IEEE (2001)

10. FON: Wifi community. http://www.fon.com

11. Garcia-Saavedra, A., Serrano, P., Banchs, A., Bianchi, G.: Energy consumption anatomy of 802.11 devices and its implication on modeling and design. In: Proceedings of the 8th International Conference on Emerging Networking Experiments and Technologies (CoNEXT 2012), pp. 169–180. ACM, New York (2012)

12. Gomez, K.M., Sengul, C., Bayer, N., Riggio, R., Rasheed, T., Miorandi, D.: Achilles and the tortoise: Power consumption in IEEE 802.11n and IEEE 802.11g networks. In: IEEE Online Conference on Green Communications. IEEE (2013)

13. Oliveira Jr., A., Sofia, R., Costa, A.: Energy-awareness in multihop routing. In: 2012 IFIP Wireless Days (WD), pp. 1–6 (2012)

14. Oliveira Jr., A.: Energy-aware metrics for multihop routing, ns2 module. COPE-SITI-SW-13-06 (2013). http://copelabs.ulusofona.pt/scicommons/index. php/publications/show/573

15. Junior, A., Sofia, R.: Energy-awareness metrics global applicability guidelines. IETF Internet Draft, draft-ajunior-roll-energy-awareness-01 (working in progress) (2014). http://datatracker.ietf.org/doc/draft-ajunior-roll-energy-awareness/

16. Junior, A., Sofia, R.: User-centric routing. Thesis Proposal, 2nd Doctoral MAP-i Symposium, Faculty of Science, Department of Computer Science, Porto University (2009)

17. Kamgueu, P.O., Nataf, E., Djotio Ndié, T., Festor, O.: Energy-based routing metric for RPL. Rapport de recherche RR-8208, INRIA (2013). http://hal.inria.fr/ hal-00779519

18. Karkazis, P., Leligou, H., Sarakis, L., Zahariadis, T., Trakadas, P., Velivassaki, T., Capsalis, C.: Design of primary and composite routing metrics for rpl-compliant wireless sensor networks. In: 2012 International Conference on Telecommunications and Multimedia (TEMU), pp. 13–18 (2012)

19. Kim, D., Garcia-Luna-Aceves, J.J., Obraczka, K., Cano, J.C., Manzoni, P.: Routing mechanisms for mobile ad hoc networks based on the energy drain rate. IEEE Trans. Mobile Comput. **2**(2), 161–173 (2003)

20. Perkins, C.E., Ratliff, S., Dowdell, J.: Dynamic MANET On-demand (AODVv2) Routing. draft-ietf-manet-aodvv2-03 (working in progress) (2014)

21. Perkins, C.E., Belding-Royer, E.M., Das, S.R.: Ad hoc on-demand distance vector (aodv)routing. RFC Experimental 3561, Internet Engineering Task Force (2003)

22. Rhee, I., Shin, M., Hong, S., Lee, K., Kim, S., Chong, S.: CRAWDAD data set ncsu/mobilitymodels (v. 2009–07-23) (2009). http://crawdad.cs.dartmouth.edu/ ncsu/mobilitymodels

23. Ros, F.J.: UM-OLSR. http://masimum.dif.um.es/?Software:UM-OLSR

24. Serrano, P., De La Oliva, A., Patras, P., Mancuso, V., Banchs, A.: Greening wireless communications: status and future directions. Comput. Commun. **35**(14), 1651–1661 (2012)

25. Singh, S., Woo, M., Raghavendra, C.S.: Power-aware routing in mobile ad hoc networks. In: MobiCom 1998: Proceedings of the 4th Annual ACM/IEEE International Conference on Mobile Computing and Networking, pp. 181–190. ACM, New York (1998)

26. Sofia, R., Mendes, P.: User-provided networks: consumer as provider. IEEE Commun. Mag. Feature Topic Consum. Commun. Netw. Gaming Entertain. **46**(12), 86–91 (2008)

27. Toh, C.K.: Maximum battery life routing to support ubiquitous mobile computing in wireless ad hoc networks. IEEE Commun. Mag. **39**(6), 138–147 (2001)
28. Winter, T., Thubert, P., Brandt, A., Hui, J., Kelsey, R., Levis, P., Pister, K., Struik, R., Vasseur, J., Alexander, R.: RPL: IPv6 routing protocol for low-power and lossy networks. RFC 6550, IETF (2012)
29. ULOOP: User-centric Wireless Local-Loop. European IST FP7 Project X, grant number 257418) (2010–2013). http://uloop.eu
30. Vasseur, J., Kim, M., Pister, K., Dejean, N., Barthel, D.: Routing metrics used for path calculation in low-power and lossy networks. RFC 6551, IETF (2012)
31. Warty, N., Sheshadri, R.K., Zheng, W., Koutsonikolas, D.: A first look at 802.11n power consumption in smartphones. In: Proceedings of the First ACM International Workshop on Practical Issues and Applications in Next Generation Wireless Networks, PINGEN 2012, pp. 27–32. ACM, New York (2012)
32. Xie, Q., Lea, C.T., Golin, M., Fleischer, R.: Maximum residual energy routing with reverse energy cost. In: GLOBECOM 2003- IEEE Global Telecommunications Conference, vol. 1, pp. 564–569 (2003)

An Overview of Energy Consumption in IEEE 802.11 Access Networks

Vitor Bernardo[1]([✉]), Marilia Curado[1], and Torsten Braun[2]

[1] Center for Informatics and Systems, University of Coimbra, Coimbra, Portugal
{vmbern,marilia}@dei.uc.pt
[2] Institute of Computer Science and Applied Mathematics,
University of Bern, Bern, Switzerland
braun@iam.unibe.ch

Abstract. Nowadays users are expecting to have some type of Internet access, independently of the place where they are. This is indeed supported by the fact that wireless access networks are becoming available almost everywhere through different types of service providers. In this context, new applications have emerged with demanding requirements from the network, but also from the end-user device capabilities. Energy is the most prominent limitation of end user satisfaction within the anytime and anywhere connectivity paradigm. Since IEEE 802.11 is one of the most widely used wireless access technologies, this work provides insights on the study of its energy consumption properties, laying the grounds for further improvements towards enhanced battery lifetime. Experimental energy assessment results demonstrate the efficacy of power saving mechanisms and the relevance of wireless devices' state management.

Keywords: Energy · Wireless · IEEE 802.11 · Power saving · Testbed · Methodology

1 Introduction

The deployment of Next Generation Networks (NGN) [1] comprehends a considerable number of wireless devices moving with different speeds, patterns and communicating through various radio interfaces. The NGN heterogeneity together with the fast deployment of all the applications of cloud computing [2] and the usage of many applications as a service, bring many of the common optimization problems (e.g., handover) to the application level, where the network interface energy consumption can be one of the key decision factors. As a result, the energy consumption becomes an important end-user experience parameter, since end-users aim to maximize the device battery life [3].

Concerning the relationship between wireless access networks and energy consumption, although numerous efforts have been done to create low power radio technologies (e.g., IEEE 802.15.4 and ZigBee), IEEE 802.11 [4] stands out within the context of wireless access communications. With the proliferation of

© Springer International Publishing Switzerland 2014
I. Ganchev et al. (Eds.): Wireless Networking for Moving Objects, LNCS 8611, pp. 157–176, 2014.
DOI: 10.1007/978-3-319-10834-6_9

IEEE 802.11 ready devices, ranging from sensors to mobile phones or laptops, this technology emerges also as a strong candidate to support the upcoming Internet of Things (IoT) [5].

This chapter introduces the key energy saving protocols defined in the IEEE 802.11 standard and discusses the most relevant energy aware optimization solutions found in the literature. Additionally, an empirical and flexible energy consumption methodology [6] to be used within any USB network interface is discussed, and an experimental investigation using the mentioned methodology, in a real wireless testbed, is conducted. The obtained results show that considerable energy savings can be achieved with a proper management of the IEEE 802.11 most deployed power saving algorithm (i.e., the Power Save Mode).

The remainder of this chapter is structured as follows. Section 2 presents the standard power saving mechanisms defined in IEEE 802.11 and the most relevant related work concerning power saving optimization. A methodology to measure energy consumption in real environments is introduced in Sect. 3, followed by an experimental investigation on IEEE 802.11 energy consumption in Sect. 4. Finally, Sect. 5 presents the main conclusions and contributions of the chapter.

2   Related Work on Energy Consumption

This section introduces the standard power saving techniques defined in the IEEE 802.11 standard in Subsect. 2.1, followed by the discussion of the related work on power saving optimization in Subsect. 2.2.

2.1   IEEE 802.11 Power Saving

The IEEE 802.11 standard [4] defines a power management mode that allows the station (STA) to turn off both transmitter and receiver capabilities in order to save energy. The power management operations are distinct in infrastructure and ad-hoc modes. This work will discuss power management operations in the infrastructure mode, since it is the most widely used. The IEEE 802.11 power saving procedure was originally defined by IEEE 802.11-1997 and it is generically named Power Save Mode (PSM) (or Power Save Polling). Later, the IEEE 802.11e [7] introduced, together with many Quality of Service (QoS) related enhancements, two additional power save mechanisms, the unscheduled and the scheduled Automatic Power Save Delivery (APSD). More recently, IEEE 802.11n [8] also announced two contributions to the power save schemes, namely the Spatial Multiplexing (SM) Power Save and the Power Save Multi-Poll (PSMP) techniques. A brief description of these techniques will be performed in the next subsections.

Power Save Mode (PSM). In the Power Save Mode, the STA is able to stay disconnected from the network for a certain period. The STA must inform the AP about the current power management mode by defining the corresponding power management bits in the control frames. When the power saving is enabled for a certain STA, the AP buffers all the packets to that station. If the AP has packets buffered to a certain STA, it will send this information via the traffic indication map (TIM) within the Beacon frames. In PSM, a STA must wake-up regularly to receive the TIM information present in Beacon frames. Listening must be performed every N beacons, where $N \geq 1$. This period is named Listen Interval. By performing this action a STA, which does not have any data buffered on the AP, will be required to awake up recurrently, resulting in unnecessary energy consumption.

To receive the buffered frames in the AP, the STA must send back a Power Save Poll (PS-Poll) frame. When receiving a PS-Poll frame from a STA, the AP can acknowledge it first or send the queued data directly. In the first time, the AP sends only one frame to the STA and sets the "More Data" bit in the frame. When a STA receives a frame with the "More Data" information bit enabled, it must send back a PS-Poll to the AP.

The PSM usage allows the AP to buffer the packets to a certain STA when in sleep mode, however it does not have any mechanism to buffer packets from the STA to the AP. As a result, when an application wants to send a packet to the core network, it will not be queued and the sleep mode will be immediately interrupted.

Automatic Power Save Delivery (APSD). IEEE 802.11e introduces the QoS paradigm in the standard by defining two distinct QoS prioritization schemes, a distributed one defined by the Enhanced Distributed Channel Access (EDCA) channel access mode, and a centralized one defined by the Hybrid Coordination Function Controlled Channel Access (HCCA). Aligned with the QoS prioritization modes, a novel power save mode entitled Automatic Power Save Delivery (APSD) was specified. APSD introduces a concept named Service Period (SP), which is a time reserved for a certain STA to exchange data with the AP. With the employment of the SP concept, the STAs do not need to contend the channel, which results in less energy consumption.

The APSD can work in two distinct modes: scheduled (S-APSD) and unscheduled (U-APSD). The S-APSD is a centralized approach and can use both EDCA and HCCA as access policy, while U-APSD is a distributed method, which uses EDCA. The key point in the U-APSD design is the usage of the STA uplink frames as triggers to deliver the buffered data in the AP while the STA is sleeping. By employing such design, the STA has full control on the awake moment, as this instant does not need to be previously negotiated with the AP. Additionally, the STA does not need to listen regularly for the AP beacons. The U-APSD usage is specially indicated for bidirectional scenarios, but alternative schedule techniques might be used to trigger the AP buffered data. The AP can be triggered by receiving either a QoS Data frame or a QoS null frame (equivalent to the PS-Poll frame in the legacy PSM). For instance, an STA without uplink traffic to be transmitted to the network can use the QoS null frame to enquire the AP about remaining buffered frames.

The EDCA channel access method defines four Access Categories (AC), namely AC_VO, AC_VI, AC_BE and AC_BK, which represent voice, video, best effort and background applications, respectively. Each access category can be configured individually regarding buffered data triggering, which enables additional control concerning the STA energy management capabilities.

In the S-APSD centralized scheme the AP schedules the instants when each STA using S-APSD should awake-up to receive data. Both HCCA and EDCA can be used as channel access methods, nonetheless the implementation of the first is not mandatory in the standard. Additional information regarding APSD can be found in the literature [9].

Spatial Multiplexing (SM) Power Save. Spatial Multiplexing (SM) Power Save was introduced in IEEE 802.11n considering the energy demands usually associated with MIMO techniques, as the operation with multiple antennas in multiple channel requires extra power. The SM Power Save allows the STA to disconnect all but one of its radio frequency (RF) chains. The SM Power Save mode can operate into two distinct modes: static and dynamic.

When operating in the static mode, the IEEE 802.11 ready STA must disconnect all but one radio frequency (RF) chain, being comparable to a legacy IEEE 802.11g STA. The AP is notified that the STA will be operating in the static SM power save mode, requiring the AP to send only a single spatial stream to the client, until the client informs about the availability of additional RF chains. With the dynamic mode, the STA also keeps only one active RF chain, but in this mode the STA can promptly activate additionally RF chains when receiving a frame.

Power Save Multi-Poll. IEEE 802.11n also introduced another power save mechanism entitled Power Save Multi-Poll (PSMP). The PSMP aims to solve the issues related with channel contention needed in the ASPD method described above. In the ASDP, the STAs are required to send a PS-Poll frame (i.e., QoS null frame) to the AP in order to collect its buffered packets. The contention generated by these actions might be critical for network performance if many STA are requesting the buffered packets, resulting in lower channel efficiency.

In PSMP, the AP can schedule data transmission according to the application QoS constraints, namely delay and bandwidth. The AP will specify the scheduling for a certain STA downlink and uplink traffic in the beacon frames, allowing the STA to awake up only when it is able to transmit data. Although the PSMP mechanism can reduce contention of the polling mechanism and improve the channel efficiency, it is not as energy efficient as the U-ASPD, since the STA must awake up periodically to receive the schedule information contained in the beacons sent by the AP [10].

2.2   Power Save Mode Optimizations

When analyzing the state of the art concerning energy saving mechanisms for IEEE 802.11, there are several occasions to consider cooperation between energy aware mechanisms at lower (e.g. MAC layer aggregation) and upper layers. As an example, the cooperation between frame aggregation and the native power save mechanisms in the IEEE 802.11 standard, namely Power Save Mode (PSM) or Unscheduled Automatic Power Save Delivery (U-APSD), still is at an early research stage.

Trying to overcome this gap, Camps-Mur et al. [11] have studied the impact of IEEE 802.11 MAC layer aggregation on both PSM and U-APSD schemes. In practice, the main difference between the PSM and the U-APSD is related with the proactivity implemented in the U-APSD scheme. Unlike PSM, where only the Access Point (AP) is able to inform the station about pending packets, in the U-APSD the station can itself ask the AP for new downlink messages pending in the AP's queue. A complete discussion regarding the power saving features introduced in IEEE 802.11e is performed in [12].

Apart from the energy consumption study, Camps-Mur et al. work also focus on the IEEE 802.11 QoS mechanisms, aiming to study the employment of energy consumption optimization techniques while keeping the Quality of Service. As a result, two QoS sensitive applications (voice and video) were used together with two non-QoS sensitive applications (web browsing and FTP). The tested conditions encompass four different scenarios: IEEE 802.11 PSM (without aggregation), IEEE 802.11 PSM + ZFA (Zero Delay Frame Aggregation), U-APSD and U-APSD + ZFA. When analyzing the QoS sensitive applications without using aggregation, it is clear that U-APSD outperforms PSM. The main reason pointed by the authors is the smaller signaling overhead (e.g., polling or RTS/CTS handshake messages) generated by U-APSD. In PSM the polling is only performed by the AP to all the stations. As a result, all the stations aim to access to the medium immediately after receiving the polling information, resulting in a higher collision probability. If aggregation is used, due to decreasing signaling messages, IEEE 802.11 PSM achieves better results than U-APSD. The non-QoS sensitive applications have the same behavior as the QoS sensitive ones. The main reason for this performance, according to the authors' conclusions, is the channel efficiency improvement that is achieved in both cases. Nonetheless, a detailed investigation about the energy efficiency and the network delay introduced in both scenarios was not presented.

Namboodiri and Gao [13] proposed an algorithm, named GreenCall, centered on the U-APSD capabilities, aiming to conserve energy during VoIP calls. The algorithm goal is to minimize the energy consumption, while keeping VoIP quality within a certain acceptable level. In practice, GreenCall tries to increase the time spent by the network interface in the sleep state. Besides an exhaustive theoretical analysis, the proposal was also validated through real testbed assessment and trace-driven simulations. The empirical study encompasses real energy consumption equipment and Linux based end-user devices equipped with IEEE 802.11n interfaces (able to support the U-APSD power save scheme). As highlighted by the authors, a key point resulting from the performed empirical evaluation is that the increasing the delay does not necessarily represent substantial energy savings. However, the GreenCall algorithm achieved energy savings of 80 % for almost all the scenarios, while U-APSD can itself save around 40 % on the device energy consumption. Moreover, taking into account the typical voice call time during a day, a mobile device utilizing the GreeCall proposal can reduce device's overall energy consumption by around 20 %.

Lorchat et Noel [14] have proposed to use frame aggregation to save energy. The main motivation for the work was the possibility to send small packets together, which can bring considerable energy savings, since the Ethernet MTU is 1500 bytes and the IEEE 802.11b/g MTU is 2272 bytes (and up to 7935 bytes in IEEE 802.11n), the employment of aggregation techniques can be useful. The implementation of the proposed aggregation scheme, similar to the A-MSDU approach in the IEEE 802.11n standard, shows energy-efficient benefits when using the proposed frame aggregation technique, but also highlights some costs. The work discusses possible energy costs of extra CPU and memory needed to perform the aggregation. The authors argue that frame aggregation employment must take into account the current bit error rate in the channel, because retransmission might have higher energy cost than transmitting each single frame. However, aggregation can also bring some benefits for error-prone scenarios, since the number of frames being sent is lower and, as a result, the number of medium collisions will tend to be lower.

Lin et al. [15] studied the new A-MPDU aggregation mechanism of the IEEE 802.11n standard, aiming at proposing an optimal frame size adaptation algorithm. There is a clear tradeoff between throughput and delay performance when employing aggregation. The attained results show the positive impact in both throughput and delay when using the developed adaptive frame aggregation algorithm compared with fixed and random aggregation sizes. Moreover, the simulation outcomes also underline the strong correlation between the bit error rate and the optimal aggregation size. Other enhanced A-MSDU frame aggregation schemes for IEEE 802.11n was proposed by Saif et al. [16], aiming at reducing the aggregation headers originally proposed in the standard. The new aggregation scheme, called mA-MSDU, uses as main motivation the need to introduce an additional new header for each subframe sent when using the standard A-MSDU. Considering the presented results, the suggested dynamic selection of the aggregation method has some advantages when compared with the single usage of A-MSDU or A-MPDU, even employing dynamic aggregation size.

According to Palit et al. [17] the feasibility of employing packet aggregation is strongly related with the scenario and/or application. In order to understand the typical packet distribution in a smartphone data communication, the authors have analyzed the mobile device traffic. The main observations are that around 50 % of the packets have a size lower than 100 bytes and 40 % have an inter-arrival time of 0.5 ms or less. These conditions enable a good opportunity to do packet aggregation. Using this motivation, the authors have studied the impact of packet aggregation in the smartphones' energy consumption. The proposed aggregation scheme uses a buffering/queue system in the access point (AP) together with the Power Save Mode (PSM) on the client side. By default the last IEEE 802.11 standards (e.g. IEEE 802.11n) already defined a buffer at the access point, where all the packets destined to a mobile station in sleep mode are buffered and sent later. The proposed packet aggregation mechanism was named Low Energy Data-packet Aggregation Scheme (LEDAS). LEDAS receives packets from the different applications through the Logical Link Control (LLC) sub-layer and performs aggregation. For each packet, four additional bytes are used to ensure the correct packet de-aggregation. Although this is a simple aggregation mechanism, it has the advantage of being fully compliant with the IEEE 802.11 standard and with all other TCP/IP compliant transmission protocols (i.e., the solution is not dependent on the access technology). When employing the LEDAS module, the energy savings are between 40 and 60 %, but there is a huge increase in the mean packet delay. Moreover, the study does not take into account the possible bad conditions (e.g., collisions) in the access channel, which can disturb even more the delay.

3   A Flexible Methodology to Measure Energy Consumption in Real Environments

This section describes a flexible methodology to measure energy consumption in real environments. Subsection 3.1 introduces the methodology and explains the underlying designed options, followed by a discussion and comparison with the most relevant work regarding energy assessment in testbeds in Subsect. 3.2.

3.1   Methodology

This energy measurement methodology, proposed in [6], was designed to fulfill a set of requirements concerning the assessment of energy consumption in real system equipment, as follows:

- *Testbed measurement:* it is important to perform testbed assessments in order to accurately measure the energy impact in real life systems;
- *High precision measurements:* to guarantee a good accuracy of testbed energy measurements it is vital to use a hardware capable to support multiple samples per second, since energy in small devices (i.e., network interface) tends to have slight variations over time;
- *Independent network interface assessment:* it is essential to limit the measurements solely to the network interface, which allows a proper investigation of the impact of a certain action in the wireless interface energy demands;
- *Technology states evaluation:* it is crucial to enable the possibility to study the different states used in the each network technology, since their correct management might lead to considerable energy savings.

Figure 1 depicts the energy testbed setup, designed to accomplish the defined prerequisites.

Apart from the "End-User Device", the energy measurement setup encompasses a "Controller Machine" and a high-precision "Digital Multimeter".

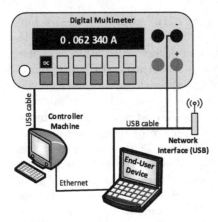

(a) Energy measurement diagram   (b) Digital multimeter usage

Fig. 1. Energy measurement setup (Adapted from [6])

The multimeter is a Rigol DM3061, which supports sampling rate of 50.000 samples/second. Since this unit implements the Universal Serial Bus Test and Measurement Class Specification (USBTMC) standard interface and is compliant with the Standard Commands for Programmable Instruments (SCPI) commands (IEEE 488.2 [18]), it is possible to control the multimeter with a standard machine. The "Controller Machine" works as management unit, being responsible to initiate, stop, and collect all the energy related data. This unit can also be connected to the "End-user Device" via Ethernet, enabling a fast and reliable point to control the application level experiments.

The usage of an external USB network interface, ensures the possibility to accurately measure the energy consumed by the network card only, as desired. Moreover, this approach allows the described methodology to be used within any USB network card, namely IEEE 802.11, Bluetooth, or 4G Long Term Evolution (LTE).

As the energy measurements will be done by collecting the current values only, the USB cable was intercepted in the common-collector voltage (VCC) cable (i.e., +5 VDC), as shown in Fig. 1b. Nevertheless, others in literature [19, 20] highlight as a main issue concerning the energy measurement in testbeds, the need to provide a stable continuous voltage to the system. In the preliminary tests performed, the USB network interface was directly connected to the "End-User Device" and the impact on the voltage drawn was noticeable. To overcome this limitation, the USB network interface was connected to an external AC powered USB HUB (not illustrated in the figure), able to give continuous stable power to the USB network card. The analysis performed concerning voltage drawn when employing the external USB HUB has shown voltage drops always lower than 1 % of the total employed voltage, which is negligible in the overall system analysis.

3.2   Related Work on Energy Consumption Measurement

The research question regarding energy-efficient communication is strongly related to the hardware energy consumption itself, which has a significant impact in the overall results and various studies in the literature addressed the problem by measuring total energy consumption of the end-user device. Although these techniques can be a feasible approach to analyze these systems when compared with the challenge to perform accurate theoretical models for simulation, they do not measure accurately the energy consumed only by the network interface.

Balasubramanian et al. [21] have studied energy consumption in mobile phones with multiple network interfaces, where the main goal was to evaluate the energy-efficiency of 3G, GSM and IEEE 802.11. Their main contribution is the development of a protocol that reduces energy consumption of applications by scheduling the transmission, named TailEnder. Wang and Manner [19] used an Android based phone, and tested energy consumption using Enhanced Data rates for GSM Evolution (EDGE), High Speed Packet Access (HSPA) and IEEE 802.11 wireless technologies. The impact of packet size and packet rate were addressed in the study, but only the total energy consumed by the device was measured, which is a clear drawback when trying to optimize network protocols or applications. Additionally, the study was done using only a specific phone model, which does not exclude the possibility of direct impact of the phone board implementation on the measured energy values.

Rice and Hay [20] proposed a methodology to measure energy consumption of mobile phones IEEE 802.11 interface, by replacing the battery with a personalized plastic battery holder, which allows an accurate measurement within the phone real energy circuit. To avoid the rapid energy consumption changes caused by the high-frequency components of the mobile phones, the measurement system employs a high-precision resistor. While this work is able to measure accurately the mobile phone energy consumption behavior, it is not able to perform an accurate evaluation of the IEEE 802.11 impact on the energy consumed by the mobile phone, since the energy measurements report to the overall mobile phone energy consumption.

The presented methodology enables a flexible energy consumption assessment technique, which can be employed on all USB network interfaces, but also with mobile phones or other devices. As a high-precision equipment was employed, this methodology can also be used to study and improve network or MAC layer level protocols, aiming at saving energy in the IEEE 802.11 interface. Additionally, it can also help to fill the existing gap regarding the testbed experimental evaluation of new wireless access networks, such as the IEEE 802.11ac or 4G Long Term Evolution technology.

4   Investigating Energy Consumption in Wireless Access Networks

This section describes experimental investigations concerning the energy consumption of wireless access networks, using IEEE 802.11 as case study. Nevertheless, as already described in Sect. 3, this methodology can be employed with any USB network card.

The main objective of this assessment is to show how to perform an empirical energy assessment in a real wireless access network. Additionally, by using the presented energy evaluation methodology, a twofold investigation is performed. First, the impact of wireless states management in the network interface energy consumption is discussed, followed by some insights concerning relationship between application design and its energy demands.

4.1   IEEE 802.11 Access Network Testbed and Scenarios

This subsection presents the University of Coimbra IEEE 802.11 testbed. The testbed is composed by a IEEE 802.11n access point, the Cisco Linksys E4200, and by two distinct USB network interfaces: the Cisco Linksys AE1000 dual-band (2.4 GHz and 5 GHz) and the Linksys TP-LINK WN-721n single-band (2.4 GHz). As the energy measurement testbed is fully independent of the employed network interface, it will be possible to use any other USB network interface. The Cisco Linksys E4200 access point is dual-band (2.4 GHz and 5 GHz) and supports Multiple-Input and Multiple-Output (MIMO) 3x3 (6 internal antennas).

Figure 2 depicts the testbed architecture, which encompasses the previously described *Access Network*, and a *Core Network* responsible to manage all the network services and servers.

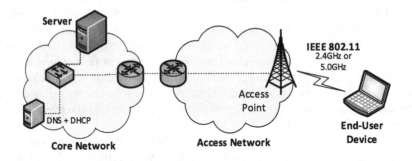

Fig. 2. IEEE 802.11 testbed architecture

The "End-User Device" employed in this setup was an Asus EEE 1001PX-H netbook (CPU: Intel Atom N450 1.66 GHz; RAM: 2 Gb), while the "Server" entity, in the *Core Network*, was running in a HP ProLiant DL320 G5p server (CPU: Intel Xeon X3210 2.16 GHz; RAM: 4 Gb). Both "End-User Device" and "Server" were running Debian 7 with kernel 3.2.0-4, respectively, the 32 and the 64 bits versions. The traffic referred as "receiving" has "Server" as source and "End-User Device" as destination, while the "transmitting" represents the traffic sent from the "End-User Device" to the "Server".

The results presented in the next subsections were obtained using the methodology presented in Sect. 3, and include 20 runs for each test setup with a confidence interval of 95 %. The tests were done in three distinct wireless access scenarios, as depicted in Table 1.

Table 1. Experimental evaluation scenarios

Name	Description
NetworkCard-A 2.4GHz	Tests performed using in the Linksys TP-LINK WN-721n in the 2.4 GHz frequency (the only supported)
NetworkCard-B 2.4GHz	Tests with the Cisco Linksys AE1000 dual-band network card, using the 2.4 GHz frequency
NetworkCard-B 5.0GHz	Tests employing the Cisco Linksys AE1000 dual-band, using the 5.0 GHz frequency

Each test performed has a total duration of 80 s, whereas the first and the last 10 s of the experiment were not considered, in order to avoid the impact of the energy consumed by the User Datagram Protocol (UDP) socket establishment and release procedures. As a result, all the energy results presented only consider the energy consumed during the 60 s.

4.2   Investigating Energy Consumption of IEEE 802.11 States

This section discusses the impact of each state of the network interface's overall energy consumption. The IEEE 802.11 relevant PHY layer states, which might have impact on the network card energy consumption, are defined as follows:

- **Disconnected/Init:** network interface is disconnected from the network, i.e. the radio is switched-off;
- **Idle:** network interface is associated with the access point, but no data is being transferred;
- **Sleep:** network interface is in a *doze state*. In this state it is not possible to send or receive IP traffic, but the station remains associated with the network. This state was studied by enabling the IEEE 802.11 Power Save Mode, discussed in Sect. 2.1;
- **Transmitting (TX):** network interface is sending IP traffic to the network;
- **Receiving (RX):** network interface is receiving IP traffic from the network.

The described IEEE 802.11 states transitions diagram is illustrated in Fig. 3.

Figure 4 shows the average power (in milliwatt) used by the three scenarios defined (see Table 1) in *DISCONNECTED*, *IDLE* and *SLEEP* states. As energy consumption of *TX* and *RX* states is affected by the traffic configuration and pattern, these states will be further discussed.

When comparing the network cards tested, it can be observed that the *NetworkCard-A 2.4GHz* average power in the *DISCONNECTED* state is higher

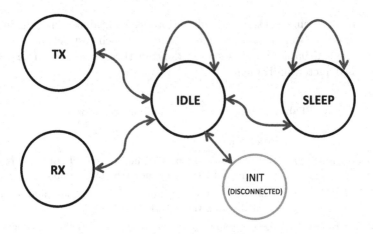

Fig. 3. Simplified IEEE 802.11 states diagram

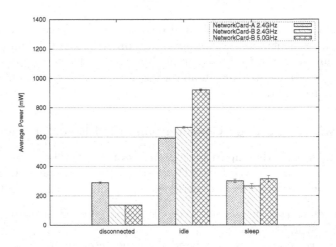

Fig. 4. Average power in disconnected, idle and sleep states

than both *NetworkCard-B 2.4GHz* and *NetworkCard-B 5.0GHz*. The average power in this state is the same for *NetworkCard-B 2.4GHz* and *NetworkCard-B 5.0GHz*, since it is the same USB network card.

In *IDLE* state the behavior is slightly different. The *NetworkCard-B 5.0GHz* needs more energy to support this state, when compared with the other two scenarios. While the *NetworkCard-A 2.4GHz* spends roughly twice more energy in *IDLE* state when compared with *DISCONNECTED* state, the *NetworkCard-B 2.4GHz* and *NetworkCard-A 5.0GHz* need, respectively, about 5 and 7 times more energy.

This behavior is mainly related with the network interface internal design. In this particular case study, it might be related with the supported MIMO type, since *NetworkCard-A* only supports 1x1:1 MIMO (1 internal antenna) and *NetworkCard-B* can benefit from the usage of 2x2:2 MIMO (2 internal antennas). Others in literature have shown the MIMO impact on the energy consumption [22].

Comparing with the *IDLE* state, the *SLEEP* state usage is able to achieve energy savings of around 50 %, 60 % and 65 %, respectively, for *NetworkCard-A 2.4 GHz*, *NetworkCard-B 2.4 GHz* and *NetworkCard-B 5.0 GHz* scenarios.

Although, due to the internal components design, there might be absolute power consumption differences in similar states, one can observe that the power consumption trend among the three depicted states is similar for all the scenarios. This standard energy consumption behavior is extremely relevant, since there are clear energy benefits in keeping the interface as long as possible in the *SLEEP* state, as highlighted during the related work discussion in Sect. 2.

4.3   Investigating the Power Saving Effectiveness

This subsection has two goals. First, it aims at showing the impact of IEEE 802.11 Power Save Mode usage in a real scenario. Second, it explores power consumption during state transition, introduced in the previous subsection, by establishing a set of actions aiming at forcing the most common transitions.

The transition between states depends on the actual network state at IP level. Therefore, a sequence of actions has been defined to study those transitions. Table 2 shows the defined action sequences, including the possible states and the start/end time (in seconds) for each action.

Table 2. Action sequence for testing states transitions

#	Possible states	Action	Time	
			Start	End
1	*DISCONNECTED*	Wait for 4 s	0	0
2	*IDLE, TX, RX*	Connect to the network	4	*
3	*IDLE, SLEEP*	Wait for 10 s	4	14
4	*TX, RX*	Ping "Server" during 10 s	14	24
5	*IDLE, SLEEP*	Wait for 5 s	24	29
6	*IDLE, TX, RX*	Disconnect from the network	29	*
7	*DISCONNECTED*	-	29	35

*Action includes connecting or disconnecting times, which might be slightly variable

Figure 5 depicts the power (in milliwatt) over time (seconds) for the *NetworkCard-A 2.4 GHz* scenario, with the IEEE 802.11 Power Save Mode disabled, during the execution of the previous presented sequence. As *NetworkCard-B 2.4 GHz* and *NetworkCard-B 5.0 GHz* scenarios have similar behavior, only this scenario will be illustrated. To allow enough precision to depict all the small power fluctuations, this study was performed with a rate of 50.000 samples per second. However, due to the very small power fluctuations captured, the usage of a smoothing technique to depict the values was required. As a result, the power values presented in the following figures are using a moving average of 1000 samples.

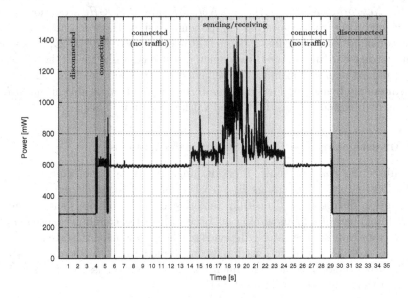

Fig. 5. *NetworkCard-A 2.4GHz* states transition with power saving disabled

The relationship between the network card interface state and the power consumption is clearly visible. When connecting to the network ($time = 4$ s, from now on $t = time$) the power consumption has some fluctuations, mainly because there is information being sent and received from the network. The power consumption becomes stable since no traffic has to be sent or received ($t \geq 5.5$ s and $t \leq 14$ s). During this period, the network card is in the *IDLE* state. Since power saving mode is disabled in this scenario, it not possible to change to the *SLEEP* state.

The power cost of sending and receiving IP traffic ($t \geq 14$ s and $t \leq 24$ s) is evidently outlined. Here, the power fluctuations are bigger since the usage of the Internet Control Message Protocol (ICMP) (using the *ping* tool) enables bidirectional traffic in the channel, and several state transitions turn up in short time intervals.

When the traffic transmission ends ($t = 24$ s) the network card backs into *IDLE* state, until it disconnects again from the network after 5 s ($t = 29$ s).

Figure 6 also shows the power (in milliwatt) over time (seconds) for the same sequence and scenario (*NetworkCard-A 2.4GHz*), but with the IEEE 802.11 Power Save Mode enabled.

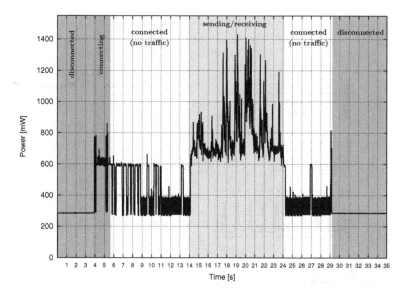

Fig. 6. *NetworkCard-A 2.4 GHz* states transition with power saving enabled

The power consumption behavior is very similar to the one showed in the case where power saving mode is disabled, unless when there is no IP traffic to be sent or received. In this case, the system implementation of IEEE 802.11 Power Save Mode allows the network interface to change the state from *IDLE* to *SLEEP*. Such state changes have a direct impact in power consumption, as depicted in the lower power consumed in both ($t \geq 5.5$ s and $t \leq 14$ s) and ($t \geq 24$ s and $t \leq 29$ s) intervals.

Even though this representation gives a good overview of the power consumption behavior over time, it is not able to show the fast power fluctuations captured by the used high precision measurement technique. Therefore, it is important to look in the available data with more detail.

Figure 7 zooms four key actions of the data depicted in Fig. 6, namely the network connection, the starting of data transmission/reception, the ending of transmission/reception, and the disconnection from the network.

Figure 7a depicts the connecting phase, starting in ($t = 4$ s). The higher power needed by the network interface to enter and setup the wireless network can be observed. The power consumption increasing of almost 2 times when changing from *SLEEP* to *RX* and/or *TX* state is illustrated in Fig. 7b. Figure 7c shows the end of transmission/reception and illustrates power consumption reduction when IP transmission is finished ($t = 24$ s).

Unlike in the *DISCONNECTED* state, when a network interface is in the *SLEEP* state, power fluctuations occur regularly. The regular power fluctuations in *SLEEP* state are caused by the IEEE 802.11 Power Save Mode (PSM) protocol design (see Sect. 2.1). When operating in PSM, the device needs to regularly wake up for receiving the *Beacon Frames*, which allow the device to be informed of

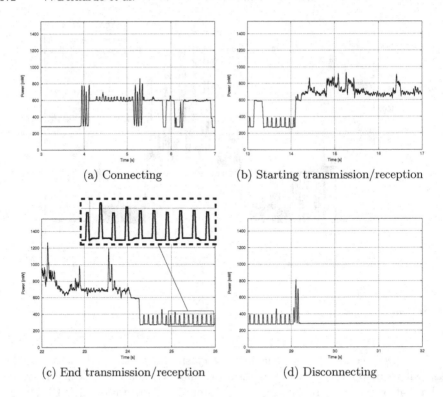

(a) Connecting

(b) Starting transmission/reception

(c) End transmission/reception

(d) Disconnecting

Fig. 7. Detailed state transitions when employing *NetworkCard-A 2.4 GHz* with power saving enabled

pending data at the Access Point. Such fact produces the power consumption behavior depicted in Fig. 7c zoom box (red dashed). This zoom box in the subfigure represents 1 s of duration, and 10 power peaks related with *Beacon Frames* reception can be observed. As the beacon interval in the used Access Point is configured to 100 ms, there will be 10 beacons to be received each second, as depicted.

Figure 7d illustrates the network disconnecting phase, starting in $(t = 29\,s)$. The higher power consumption requested upon disconnecting is mainly related with the extra power needed to change to such state, but also to send disconnecting information to the network (e.g., releasing IP address). Again, in the $(t \geq 26\,s$ and $t \leq 27\,s)$ interval, the *Beacon Frames* reception impact on power consumption in the *SLEEP* state can be perceived.

The possibility to investigate the states' energy consumption with this detail creates a good asset to employ this methodology in the validation of novel energy-aware protocols or applications.

4.4   Investigating the Packet Size Impact

This subsection investigates the packet size impact on the energy consumption. The tests were done employing Constant Bit Rate (CBR) with a fixed sending of 100 packets per second. As explained before, each test has a total duration of 80 s, but the first and the last 10 s of each experiment were not considered aiming to avoid the impact of upper layer protocol establishment and release procedures in the energy consumption.

Figure 8 shows the energy consumption in Joule (y-axis) needed to transfer 6000 packets (i.e., 100 packet per seconds during 60 s). The studied packet sizes range from 64 byte to 1400 byte (value near the Maximum Transmission Unit (MTU) for Ethernet), as depicted on the x-axis. Additionally, each scenario was also tested independently in *RX* and *TX* states.

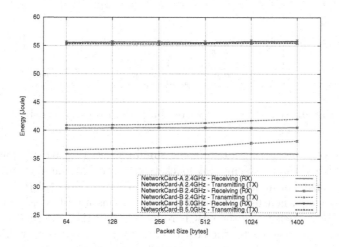

Fig. 8. Energy consumption with distinct packet sizes

The obtained results for *NetworkCard-A 2.4GHz* and *NetworkCard-B 2.4GHz* scenarios show a non negligible energy consumption difference between the energy needed to transfer the same amount of information in the *TX* and the *RX* states. Nonetheless, the same relationship can not be verified for the *NetworkCard-B 5.0GHz* case. In this later scenario, the energy consumption to send and receive the total 6000 packets is similar in the *TX* and *RX* states. Yet, by analyzing the error bars in this scenario, it is possible to notice a higher uncertainly in the *NetworkCard-B 5.0GHz* scenario when compared with the others.

Apart from the performance comparison between the distinct network cards, it is also important to assess the impact of packet size in the energy consumption. Such study is commonly performed by analyzing the energy cost per bit transmitted [23].

Figure 9 depicts average energy cost per bit transmitted/received in milliJoule (y-axis) for the tested packet sizes using the *NetworkCard-A 2.4 GHz* scenario. Again, as the other scenarios have similar related behavior only this one will be depicted.

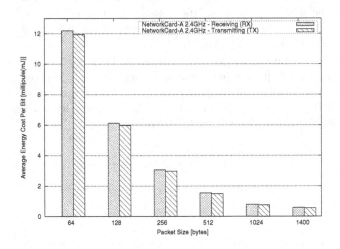

Fig. 9. Average energy cost per bit with distinct packet sizes

The cost of transmitting a byte using small packets (e.g. 64 byte packet size) is clearly higher than transmitting packets near the Maximum Transmission Unit (MTU) size. For instance, in the depicted *NetworkCard-A 2.4 GHz* scenario, each bit received when using 64 byte packet size has a cost of 12.19 mJ, while using a 128 byte packet size the cost is roughly a half (i.e., 6.12 mJ). Moreover, using packets with 1400 byte, the cost of each byte received is only 0.58 mJ. As expected, according to the values presented in Fig. 8, the energy consumption per bit when transmitting (TX) and receiving (RX) the data is very low (around 0.04 mJ).

By analyzing these results, the importance of the packet size on the energy consumption becomes clear. For instance, the typical small packet size applications like Voice Over IP (VoIP) are potential energy demanding applications, whereas the bulk data transfer applications should be more energy efficient, since typically larger packets are used. Concerning the importance of the aggregation others in literature, e.g., [14], have studied the benefits of employing aggregation techniques.

5   Conclusions

Energy efficiency in wireless access networks plays an important role in the end-user quality expectations. The mostly deployed wireless access network standard, IEEE 802.11, has introduced several power saving optimization mechanisms aiming to maximize the end-users devices' battery lifetime. Furthermore, others in literature have proposed optimizations to the standard mechanisms, ranging from generic MAC layer optimizations to the ones fully dependent on the application. This chapter has introduced both the standard mechanisms and the most relevant related work concerning power saving mode optimization in IEEE 802.11 networks.

Additionally, a technology independent and flexible empirical methodology to assess energy consumption in all USB network cards has been presented. The experimental investigation conducted using the mentioned methodology in a real IEEE 802.11 testbed highlighted the energy benefits of using power saving modes correctly. By observing the attained results, it was possible to conclude that the correct management of the wireless states might lead to energy savings up to 65 %. The gathered data also depicted the application level designed impact on the energy consumption, namely by adjusting the packet size or using aggregation techniques.

Acknowledgments. This work was partially supported by the COST framework, under Action IC0906 (WiNeMO), as well as by the iCIS project (CENTRO-07-ST24-FEDER-002003), co-financed by QREN, in the scope of the Mais Centro Program and European Union's FEDER. The first author was also supported by the Portuguese National Foundation for Science and Technology (FCT) through a Doctoral Grant (SFRH/BD/66181/2009).

References

1. Lee, C., Knight, D.: Realization of the next-generation network. IEEE Commun. Mag. **43**(10), 34–41 (2005)
2. Jamshidi, P., Ahmad, A., Pahl, C.: Cloud migration research: a systematic review. IEEE Trans. Cloud Comput. **1**(2), 142–157 (2013)
3. Chen, Y., Zhang, S., Xu, S., Li, G.: Fundamental trade-offs on green wireless networks. IEEE Commun. Mag. **49**(6), 30–37 (2011)
4. IEEE: Ieee std 802.11-2012 (revision of ieee std 802.11-2007). IEEE, pp. 1–2793 (2012)
5. Tozlu, S., Senel, M., Mao, W., Keshavarzian, A.: Wi-fi enabled sensors for internet of things: a practical approach. IEEE Commun. Mag. **50**(6), 134–143 (2012)
6. Bernardo, V., Curado, M., Staub, T., Braun, T.: Towards energy consumption measurement in a cloud computing wireless testbed. In: 2011 1st International Symposium on Network Cloud Computing and Applications (NCCA), pp. 91–98 (2011)
7. IEEE: Ieee std 802.11e-2005 (amendment to ieee std 802.11, 1999 edition (reaff 2003). IEEE, 0_1-189 (2005)
8. IEEE: Ieee std 802.11n-2009 (amendment to ieee std 802.11-2007 as amended by ieee std 802.11k-2008, ieee std 802.11r-2008, ieee std 802.11y-2008, and ieee std 802.11w-2009). IEEE, pp. 1–565, October 2009
9. Prez-Costa, X., Camps-Mur, D., Vidal, A.: On distributed power saving mechanisms of wireless lans 802.11e u-apsd vs 802.11 power save mode. Comput. Netw. **51**(9), 2326–2344 (2007)
10. CISCO: 802.11n: The next generation of wirelessperformance. White paper, CISCO (2011)

11. Camps-Mur, D., Gomony, M.D., PéRez-Costa, X., Sallent-Ribes, S.: Leveraging 802.11n frame aggregation to enhance qos and power consumption in wi-fi networks. Comput. Netw. **56**(12), 2896–2911 (2012)
12. Perez-Costa, X., Camps-Mur, D.: Ieee 802.11e qos and power saving features overview and analysis of combined performance [accepted from open call]. IEEE Wirel. Commun. **17**(4), 88–96 (2010)
13. Namboodiri, V., Gao, L.: Energy-efficient voip over wireless lans. IEEE Trans. Mob. Comput. **9**(4), 566–581 (2010)
14. Lorchat, J., Noel, T.: Energy saving in ieee 802.11 communications using frame aggregation. In: 2003 GLOBECOM '03 Global Telecommunications Conference, IEEE. vol. 3, pp. 1296–1300, December 2003
15. Lin, Y., Wong, V.: Wsn01-1: frame aggregation and optimal frame size adaptation for ieee 802.11n wlans. In: 2006 GLOBECOM '06 Global Telecommunications Conference, IEEE, pp. 1–6 November 2006
16. Saif, A., Othman, M., Subramaniam, S., Hamid, N.: An enhanced a-msdu frame aggregation scheme for 802.11n wireless networks. Wirel. Pers. Commun. **66**(4), 683–706 (2012)
17. Palit, R., Naik, K., Singh, A.: Impact of packet aggregation on energy consumption in smartphones. In: 2011 7th International Conference on Wireless Communications and Mobile Computing (IWCMC), pp. 589–594, July 2011
18. IEEE: Standard digital interface for programmable instrumentation - part 2: codes, formats, protocols and common commands (adoption of (ieee std 488.2-1992). IEC 60488–2 First edition 2004–05; IEEE 488.2, pp. 1–261 (2004)
19. Wang, L., Manner, J.: Energy consumption analysis of wlan, 2g and 3g interfaces. In: 2010 IEEE/ACM International Conference on Green Computing and Communications (GreenCom), Cyber, Physical and Social Computing (CPSCom), pp. 300–307, December 2010
20. Rice, A., Hay, S.: Measuring mobile phone energy consumption for 802.11 wireless networking. Pervasive Mob. Comput. **6**, 593–606 (2010)
21. Balasubramanian, N., Balasubramanian, A., Venkataramani, A.: Energy consumption in mobile phones: a measurement study and implications for network applications. In: Proceedings of the 9th ACM SIGCOMM Conference on Internet Measurement, IMC '09, New York, NY, USA, ACM, pp. 280–293 (2009)
22. Li, G., Xu, Z., Xiong, C., Yang, C., Zhang, S., Chen, Y., Xu, S.: Energy-efficient wireless communications: tutorial, survey, and open issues. IEEE Wirel. Commun. **18**(6), 28–35 (2011)
23. INFSO-ICT-247733 EARTH (Editors: Jose Alonso-Rubio, Pter Fazekas, Per Skillermark, Wieslawa Wajda): Most Suitable Efficiency Metrics And Utility Functions. INFSO-ICT-247733 EARTH - Delivery D2.4, pp. 1–55 (2012)

Resource Management and Cell Planning in LTE Systems

Giovanni Giambene[1]([✉]), Tara Ali Yahiya[2], Van Anh Le[1], Krzysztof Grochla[3], and Konrad Połys[3]

[1] University of Siena, Via Roma, 56, 53100 Siena, Italy
giambene@unisi.it
[2] Laboratoire de Recherche En Informatique, University of Paris-Sud, Orsay, France
[3] Institute of Theoretical and Applied Informatics of PAS, Baltycka 5, 44-100 Gliwice, Poland

Abstract. Future 4G cellular systems will address the need for capacity increase for the support of diverse services. It is therefore of fundamental importance to design innovative 4G cellular systems able to support the increase in the traffic demand. This Chapter deals with LTE systems and the design of a new reuse scheme, called *Soft Frequency Reuse* (SFR), that is able to increase the cell capacity that is studied, considering the impact of different scheduling schemes and of different user mobility patterns. A consistent SFR scenario has been implemented in both Ns-3 and OMNeT++ environments. An analytical approach is proposed to evaluate the cell capacity with SFR that has been validated by means of Ns-3 simulations. Finally, OMNeT++ simulations have permitted to highlight the significant impact of the scheduling scheme and user mobility on cell capacity; different mobility patterns have been taken into account.

Keywords: LTE · Cell planning · Soft frequency reuse

1 Introduction

Digital information and data traffic are experiencing an exponential worldwide growth that represents a challenge to be addressed by network planners [1]. In this scenario, mobile communications will play a major role because broadband wireless connections have surpassed wired ones since 2011. This is the scenario that future 5G systems will have to deal with. *Long Term Evolution* (LTE) is popularly known as a 4G technology and can be considered as the technology of choice for most existing *Third Generation Partnership Project* (3GPP) and 3GPP2 mobile operators, since it will provide economy of scale and an efficient use of the radio spectrum [2]. LTE, whose radio access is called *Evolved UMTS Terrestrial Radio Access Network* (E-UTRAN), is expected to substantially improve end-user throughput, cell capacity and reduce user plane latency, bringing significantly-improved user experience with full mobility support. With the emergence of the *Internet Protocol* (IP) as the protocol of choice

I. Ganchev et al. (Eds.): Wireless Networking for Moving Objects, LNCS 8611, pp. 177–197, 2014.
DOI: 10.1007/978-3-319-10834-6_10

for carrying all traffic types, LTE is expected to provide support for IP-based traffic with end-to-end *Quality of Service* (QoS) [3].

In the LTE architecture, E-UTRAN consists of a single node, i.e., the *eNode B* (eNB) that interfaces with the *User Equipment* (UE). The protocol architecture of the LTE air interface can be separated between control and user planes. In the user plane, the application creates data packets that are processed by protocols such as TCP, UDP and IP; instead, in the control plane, the *Radio Resource Control* (RRC) protocol generates the signalling messages (radio resource management, admission control, enforcement of QoS negotiated, ciphering/deciphering of user and control plane data, compression/decompression of downlink/uplink user plane packet headers, etc.) that are exchanged between eNB and UE. In both cases, the information is processed by the *Packet Data Convergence Protocol* (PDCP), the *Radio Link Control* (RLC) protocol, and the *Medium Access Control* (MAC) protocol, before being passed to the physical layer (PHY) for transmissions. IP packet segmentation is performed at the RLC layer.

The aim of this Chapter is to analyse a special frequency reuse scheme proposed for LTE and called *Soft Frequency Reuse* (SFR). The interest is to study SFR with both analysis and simulations in order to determine the configuration that permits us to maximize cell capacity. This work represents a significant improvement with respect to the study carried out in [3], where we have adopted a less accurate modelling of SFR and where we have not conducted a simulation study to validate the analysis proposed. We expect that the present work can help network planners when designing 4G LTE systems based on SFR.

1.1 LTE Key Features and Radio Resources

LTE supports both *Time Division Duplexing* (TDD) and *Frequency Division Duplexing* (FDD). Both TDD and FDD are widely deployed and the decision about which duplexing format to adopt depends on the particular application. This Chapter is devoted to the FDD case.

OFDMA is used in downlink in order to obtain robustness against multipath interference and high affinity to advanced techniques such as frequency domain channel-dependent scheduling and *Multiple-Input Multiple-Output* (MIMO) antenna systems. Instead, *Single Carrier-Frequency Division Multiple Access* (SC-FDMA) is used in uplink in order to have a low *Peak-to-Average Power Ratio* (PAPR), user orthogonality in the frequency domain, and multi-antenna application. OFDMA divides the total stream into multiple sub-streams with lower data-rates. Each sub-stream is then mapped to an individual data sub-carrier that is modulated using QPSK, 16QAM, or 64QAM with different coding rate combinations. LTE uses bandwidths from 1.25, 2.5, 5.0, 10.0 to 20.0 MHz.

A *sub-channel* (i.e., a group of 12 sub-carriers) is the smallest logical allocation unit in the frequency domain; the *slot* (i.e., a group of 6–7 *symbols*) is the smallest allocation unit in the time domain. The LTE OFDMA frame structure can be considered like a grid, where a 10 ms radio frame is composed of ten 1 ms sub-frames (twenty 0.5 ms slots). The sub-frame time is also called *Transmission Time Interval* (TTI). The signal transmitted in each slot is described by a resource grid of sub-carriers and available OFDM symbols. A *Physical Resource Block* (PRB) consists of one sub-channel for one slot of duration in time. Resource allocation to UEs is updated on a TTI basis. Then, PRBs are grouped into transport blocks that use the same *Modulation and Coding Scheme* (MCS). Table 1 describes the different modulation and coding combinations supported by LTE and indexed according to the *Channel Quality Indicator* (CQI) [4].

The *Signal-to-Interference and Noise* (SINR) thresholds for the AWGN case have been determined for the different MCSs with the corresponding efficiency η_i according to the following model and related formulas that have also been used to perform simulations in Ns-3 [5] and OMNeT++ [6]:

$$\eta_i = \log_2\left(1 + \frac{SINR_i}{\Gamma}\right) \quad \Rightarrow \quad SINR_i = 10\log_{10}\left[\Gamma\left(2^{\eta_i} - 1\right)\right] \text{ in dB} \qquad (1)$$

where $\Gamma = -\frac{2}{3}\ln\left(5 \times BER\right)$ and BER $= 0.00005$ and where the efficiency of the i-th MCS η_i can be determined on the basis of the data in Table 1 according to the following formula:

$$\eta_i = r_i\log_2\left(M_i\right) \quad \Rightarrow \quad 2^{\eta_i} = M_i^{r_i} \qquad (2)$$

For different channel conditions, $SINR_i$ conversions are adopted by introducing the concept of *Effective SINR* (ESINR). This is equivalent to take some margins on the SINR threshold values of the AWGN case.

LTE provides both *Hybrid ARQ* (H-ARQ) at PHY layer and ARQ at layer 2, supported by the RLC protocol. H-ARQ is a technique, combining *Forward Error Correction* (FEC) and *Automatic Repeat Request* (ARQ) methods, in which unsuccessful previous attempts are saved and used jointly with FEC retransmissions [7]. When the receiver fails to decode a transport block, it sends a *Negative-Acknowledgment* (NACK) to the transmitter, but it keeps bits from the failed attempt for future use. When the transmitter receives the NACK or a certain time elapses without any feedback, it retransmits new data to recover the missing transport block. LTE utilizes an *Incremental Redundancy* (IR) H-ARQ scheme with 1/3 turbo encoder (FEC code) and CRC for transport block error detection. IR entails to progressively send parity packets in each subsequent transmission. The receiver H-ARQ process performs a soft combination of the bits from the previous failed attempt with the currently-received retransmission. This permits to minimize the number of retransmissions. The maximum number of H-ARQ retransmissions is 3. The H-ARQ round trip time is 8 TTI. Each H-ARQ process is of the *Stop-And-Wait* (SAW) type. Multiple H-ARQ processes run in parallel to keep up the transmission of transport blocks, while the receiver is decoding already-received transport blocks. This method allows the continuous use of the transmission resources. As for the ARQ process operated at RLC layer, in the case of an error in a packet received at this layer, a packet retransmission is requested. The H-ARQ *Block Error Rate* (BLER) of a transport block is of the order of 10^{-1} after the first transmission, while the residual error rate of the packet delivered by H-ARQ to the RLC layer is of the order of 10^{-3} [8].

Table 1. Characteristics of the different transmission modes and SINR thresholds for AWGN channel conditions with *Single Input Single Output* (SISO) antenna scheme.

CQI_i	Modulations	Code rate r_i	Modulation size, M_i	SINR thresholds, $SINR_i$ (AWGN)
1	QPSK	78/1024	4	−2.1054
2	QPSK	120/1024	4	−0.1083
3	QPSK	193/1024	4	2.1776
4	QPSK	308/1024	4	4.5647
5	QPSK	449/1024	4	6.6514
6	QPSK	602/1024	4	8.4275
7	16QAM	378/1024	16	9.9379
8	16QAM	490/1024	16	11.8495
9	16QAM	616/1024	16	13.7624
10	64QAM	466/1024	64	14.9370
11	64QAM	567/1024	64	16.9703
12	64QAM	666/1024	64	18.8734
13	64QAM	772/1024	64	20.8506
14	64QAM	873/1024	64	22.6980
15	64QAM	948/1024	64	24.0546

1.2   Evolution Towards LTE-A

LTE systems have an increasing diffusion everywhere. The interest now is on gradually shifting towards a further LTE evolution, referred to as *LTE-Advanced* (LTE-A) [9]. This evolution will include significant improvements in terms of performance and capacity as compared to current LTE deployments.

The link performance of current cellular systems such as LTE is already quite close to the Shannon limit. From a pure link-budget perspective, the very high data-rates targeted by LTE-A require a higher SINR than that typically experienced in wide-area cellular networks. Although some link improvements are possible (e.g., using additional bandwidth or increasing the MCS efficiency), it is necessary to find approaches for improving the SINR level, such as allowing a denser infrastructure at reasonable costs. In particular, 3GPP LTE-A has proposed to use *Heterogeneous Network* (HetNet) deployments to improve system capacity and to provide a better coverage at hot spots [10]. The objective of HetNets is the improvement of the overall capacity as well as a cost-effective and green radio solution by deploying additional network nodes (i.e., eNBs) within the local area, such as low-power micro-/pico- network nodes, *Home-Evolved Node Bs* (HeNBs)/*Closed Subscriber Group* (CSG) cells, femto-cells, and relay nodes. Low-power micro-nodes and high-power macro-nodes can be maintained under the management of the same operator and share the same frequency bands. In this case, joint radio resource and interference management are needed to avoid too high interference for low-power nodes. In some other cases, low- and high- power nodes can use discontinuous bands of an operator (carrier aggregation) so that mutual interference is avoided. Macro network nodes with large *Radio Frequency* (RF) coverage areas are deployed in a planned way for blanket coverage of urban, suburban, and rural areas. Instead, local nodes with small RF coverage areas aim to complement the macro network nodes for coverage extension or throughput enhancement. Moreover, global coverage can be provided by satellites (macrocells) according to an integrated system concept.

Another important innovation considered for LTE-A is the adoption of MIMO antenna solutions that are already used in LTE and will play an even more important role in LTE-A. Both Spatial Diversity MIMO and Spatial Multiplexing MIMO are supported by LTE-A. Moreover, 8×8 MIMO is adopted in downlink and 4×4 MIMO is envisaged for uplink transmissions. The selection of the type of MIMO depends on the channel quality: for situations with low SINR, it is better to use Spatial Diversity MIMO; instead, Spatial Multiplexing MIMO should be adopted in the presence of high SINR values.

2 Frequency Reuse Schemes

An important cell planning technique is to reuse the same frequency bands among sufficiently-separated cells so that the mutual interference among cells using the same frequency is negligible. There are several frequency reuse schemes that are characterized by different *Inter-Cell Interference* (ICI) levels, as detailed below.

2.1 Survey of Frequency Reuse Schemes

In a multi-cell network scenario employing frequency reuse across different cells, ICI occurs when neighbouring cells use the same frequency bands. The most severe form of ICI typically occurs on or near the edge of a cell. *ICI Coordination* (ICIC) techniques, whereby UEs in a cell are allocated with frequency resources that are orthogonal to all or to a part of the interfering UEs in adjacent cells, are needed to reduce ICI effects especially at cell borders. As such, various frequency reuse schemes have been proposed. The most straightforward approach is the so-called fixed frequency reuse scheme, whereby the whole bandwidth is divided into K non-overlapping parts that are assigned to K neighbouring cells. This frequency planning scheme allows to control ICI at the cost of a reduced spectral efficiency. A basic scheme is adopting a hexagonal cellular layout with $K = 3$.

A more refined frequency reuse scheme is *Fractional Frequency Reuse* (FFR), where different sets of sub-channels are allocated to the UEs in the cell-edge area of adjacent cells in order to control the ICI levels and where all spectrum can be used by UEs in the central part of the cell. All sub-channels are transmitted with the same power level. Different FFR variants are available, depending on the differentiation on the portions of bandwidth used in the cell centre and at cell edge. SFR is an enhancement of FFR in that there is a differentiation in the transmission power for cell-centre UEs with respect to cell-edge UEs in order to reduce ICI at cell edge [11].

2.2   Soft Frequency Reuse

With SFR, UEs within each cell are divided into two groups (i.e., cell-centre UEs and cell-edge UEs), depending on the distance from the eNB. Cell-edge UEs are restricted to the reserved cell-edge bandwidth; instead, cell-centre UEs have exclusive access to the cell-centre bandwidth and can also have access to the cell-edge bandwidth, but with a lower priority than cell-edge UEs. Usually, the cell-edge bandwidth in one cell/sector is fixed to $1/K$-th of the whole bandwidth with the aim of ensuring that adjacent cells/sectors can allocate non-overlapping frequency bands to their cell-edge UEs [12,13]. K is called *Frequency Reuse Factor* (FRF). FRF of 1 is very attractive, but entails high ICI levels, thus impacting on the traffic capacity of a cell. FRF of 1 could be adopted only for those UEs closer to the eNB, let us say within a distance ρ_0. Instead, the external part of the cell should adopt a higher FRF level, denoted by K. This solution is implemented by the SFR scheme, as proposed by 3GPP LTE, where typically $K = 3$ [13]. Hence, $1/K$-th of the whole bandwidth BW is used in the external part of the cell, where packets are transmitted by the eNB with power level P_{Te} per sub-channel. Instead, the central part of the cell can even use the whole bandwidth BW, but with a lower transmission power P_{Tc} per sub-channel. Let us denote:

$$\rho_0 = \mu R_c \quad \text{and} \quad P_{Te} = \omega P_{Tc} \tag{3}$$

where $\mu \in (0, 1]$ denotes the normalized cell-centre radius (R_c is the maximum cell range for which we will use the same value as that of the classical frequency reuse K) and where $\omega > 1$ represents the border-to-centre power ratio. Of course P_{Te} and P_{Tc} depend on the transmission power available at the eNB (downlink case).

The reuse of resources with SFR and $K = 3$ is shown in Fig. 1, where the central part of the cell has a different colour to represent the fact that a full-frequency reuse can be adopted in that part of the cell. This figure also shows reference distances D_1, D_2, and R_c.

Considering a uniform UE distribution in the cell (circular cell with radius R_c) and adopting a *Round Robin* (RR) service discipline, the probability (or the percentage of time) that the eNB is transmitting to cell-centre UEs, β, is obtained as:

$$\beta = \frac{\pi \rho_0^2}{\pi R_c^2} = \left(\frac{\rho_0}{R_c}\right)^2 = \mu^2. \tag{4}$$

If a TTI is fully devoted to cell-centre UEs, the whole capacity BW is available to these UEs. Otherwise, if a TTI is used to allocate resources to both cell-centre UEs and cell-edge UEs, the capacity available to cell-centre UEs is $(K-1)BW/K$; instead, the capacity available for cell-edge UEs is BW/K. We refer here to this second case.

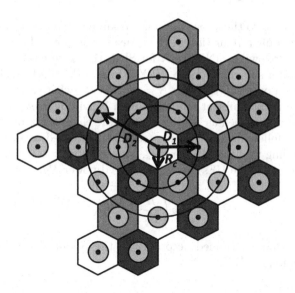

Fig. 1. System layout and frequency planning for the SFR scheme with $K = 3$.

Before concluding this Section, let us consider the implications of HetNets on cell planning with SFR; we can note that there might be strong interference for UEs in the areas where macro-cells are close to pico-cells. For instance, we can have a UE connected to a macro-cell and near a pico-cell. In this case, this UE will suffer from interference coming from the pico-cell [14]. To mitigate the interference, the macro-cell can assign a specific set of sub-channels to this UE, while we block this set of sub-channels in the pico-cell, by setting the power level in the pico-cell to 0 (or to a very small value) for this set of sub-channels. This technique is similar to what we have done so far with SFR, differentiating the sub-channels used in the cells as well as the power levels depending on the UE distance. This method entails some throughput reduction for pico-cells, but given the small numbers of UEs connected to them, this problem can be negligible. The main cell planning issue here is to define the criteria according to which there is the need to use pico-cells.

3   Capacity Evaluation with SFR and Optimization

Let S denote the total number of sub-channels in the whole bandwidth BW; S also corresponds to the number of PRBs per TTI divided by 2. Let T denote the number of sub-channels available at the edge of the cell. We consider the constraint that the total transmission power at the eNB on the whole bandwidth BW is equal to P_T. This entails the following condition to characterize P_{Tc} and P_{Te} expressing the fact that the sum of the transmission power on all sub-channels at the eNB is equal to P_T [13]:

$$P_T = \omega T P_{Tc} + (S - T) P_{Tc} \quad \Rightarrow \quad P_{Tc} = \frac{P_T}{\omega T + S - T} \tag{5}$$

Hence, according to the above formula (5) an increase in the cell-edge transmission power entails a reduction in the transmission power for cell-centre sub-channels. In the following SINR study for SFR, the noise level N is referred to the bandwidth of a sub-channel (i.e., BW/S) since the SINR itself is the ratio of powers received on a sub-channel: $N = kT_0 BW/S$, where k is the Boltzmann constant and T_0 is the ambient temperature in Kelvin degrees.

The useful signal as well as interfering ones are characterized by power levels according to the following law, relating (sub-channel-based) transmission power P_{Tx} (corresponding to either P_{Tc} or P_{Te}, respectively for transmissions to cell-centre UEs or to cell-edge UEs) and the received power P_R:

$$P_R = \varphi \left(\frac{R}{R_c}\right)^{-\nu} P_{TX} \qquad (6)$$

where φ and ν are determined according to the *Stanford University Interim* (SUI) model as follows [15]:

$$\varphi = \begin{cases} \left(\frac{R_0}{R_c}\right)^\gamma \left(\frac{\lambda}{4\pi R_0'}\right)^2 10^{\frac{-[s+X_f+X_h+L_T+L_R]+G_T+G_R}{10}}, & if \ \frac{R}{R_c} > \frac{R_0'}{R_c} \\ \left(\frac{\lambda}{4\pi R_c}\right)^2 10^{\frac{-[s+L_T+L_R]+G_T+G_R}{10}}, & if \ \frac{R}{R_c} \le \frac{R_0'}{R_c} \end{cases}$$

$$\nu = \begin{cases} \gamma, & if \ \frac{R}{R_c} > \frac{R_0'}{R_c} \\ 2, & if \ \frac{R}{R_c} \le \frac{R_0'}{R_c} \end{cases}$$

(7)

where $X_f = 6 \times \log_{10}(f \ [\text{GHz}]/2)$ is a correction factor for frequencies above $2 \, \text{GHz}$ (here, $f = 2.1 \, \text{GHz}$), $X_h = -d \times \log_{10}(h_{UE}/2)$ is a correction factor for the receiver antenna height (here, $h_{UE} = 1.5 \, \text{m}$ is the UE antenna height), s represents a shadowing term (either a normal random variable in dB or a 95-th percentile term to take some planning margins), R_0 is a nominal reference distance of 100 m, and where the path loss exponent γ (depending on the propagation environment), α and R_0' (a threshold distance for a change in the path loss slope) are detailed in [3,15].

Let φ^* denote the value of φ for $R > R_0'$. In this study, we use a fixed value for s (margin). The consideration of a normal distribution for s in dB (so that SINR becomes a random variable) is left to a future study. In the derivation of SINR, we consider the ratio of the transmission powers on groups of sub-carriers (a sub-channel); of course, we have to consider the same number of sub-carriers at numerator and denominator. As for R_c, we use the maximum cell range achievable by the classical reuse scheme with the same K value and the same link budget conditions (antenna, path loss, etc.) and referring to the most protected MCS level #1 with $SINR_1$, as shown in Table 1. This is an arbitrary choice, since also different R_c values could be considered. Basically, this choice allows to plan the cell range with no or small outage probability at cell border.

Please note that we could even consider other propagation models for the SFR study (e.g., the Hata model), but these aspects are beyond the scope of the present Chapter.

With SFR, we study the ICI level and then SINR by differentiating two cases: cell-centre UEs and cell-edge UEs. We limit the consideration of interfering signals to the first two tiers of adjacent cells with respect to a central reference cell (eNB). Moreover, as a first approximation, we denote by D_1 and D_2 the distances of a reference UE from the interfering eNBs of the first and second tier of adjacent cells, respectively. These distances are approximated as the distances between the eNB of our reference UE and the eNBs of the interfering cells: $D_1 = \sqrt{3}R_c$ and $D_2 = \sqrt{3K}R_c$.

For cell-centre UEs (referring to the white reference cell at the centre of Fig. 1), there are interfering transmissions in both the first and the second tiers of adjacent cells. As for the first tier, the interference power with level I_{c1} is the result of 3 interfering transmissions to cell-centre UEs with transmission power P_{T_c} per sub-channel (gray and darkest adjacent cells) and 3 interfering transmissions to cell-edge UEs with transmission power P_{T_e} per sub-channel (gray and darkest adjacent cells).

$$I_{c1} = 3\varphi^* \left(\frac{D_1}{R_c}\right)^{-\gamma} P_{Tc} + 3\varphi^* \left(\frac{D_1}{R_c}\right)^{-\gamma} P_{Te} \tag{8}$$

As for the second tier, the interference power with level I_{c2} is the result of 9 interfering transmissions to cell-centre UEs with transmission power P_{T_c} per sub-channel (white, gray, and darkest cells) and 3 interfering transmissions to cell-edge UEs with transmission power P_{T_e} per sub-channel (gray and darkest cells).

$$I_{c2} = 9\varphi^* \left(\frac{D_2}{R_c}\right)^{-\gamma} P_{Tc} + 3\varphi^* \left(\frac{D_2}{R_c}\right)^{-\gamma} P_{Te} \tag{9}$$

In conclusion, we have:

$$I_c = I_{c1} + I_{c2} \tag{10}$$

For cell-edge UEs, we adopt the same approach to determine the interference coming from the first and the second tiers of adjacent cells. As for the first tier, the interference power with level I_{e1} is the result of 3 interfering transmissions to cell-centre UEs with transmission power P_{Tc} per sub-channel (gray adjacent cells) and 3 interfering transmissions to cell-centre UEs with transmission power P_{T_c} per sub-channel (the darkest adjacent cells).

$$I_{e1} = 6\varphi^* \left(\frac{D_1}{R_c}\right)^{-\gamma} P_{Tc} \tag{11}$$

As for the second tier, the interference power with level I_{e2} is the result of 6 interfering transmissions to cell-edge UEs with transmission power P_{T_e} per sub-channel (white cells) and 6 interfering transmissions to cell-centre UEs with transmission power P_{T_c} per sub-channel (gray and darkest cells).

$$I_{e2} = 6\varphi^* \left(\frac{D_2}{R_c}\right)^{-\gamma} P_{Te} + 6\varphi^* \left(\frac{D_2}{R_c}\right)^{-\gamma} P_{Tc} \tag{12}$$

In conclusion, we have:

$$I_e = I_{e1} + I_{e2} \tag{13}$$

We consider that interfering signals always travel a distance greater than R_0' so that they are characterized by $\varphi = \varphi^*$ and $\nu = \gamma$. In order to derive the SINR for cell-centre UEs, $SINR_c$, we consider that our reference UE is at a distance $R \leq \rho_0$ from its eNB, that $P_{TX} \equiv P_{Tc}$ and that the power received is according to (6). Instead, in order to express the SINR for cell-edge UEs, $SINR_e$, we consider that our reference UE is at a distance $R > \rho_0$ from its eNB and $P_{TX} \equiv P_{Te}$. Then, SINR as a function of the distance R of the UE from its eNB is determined by $SINR_c$ in (14) for $R \leq \rho_0$ and by $SINR_e$ in (15) for $R > \rho_0$ according to the formulas below where ν and φ also depend on R/R_c:

$$SINR_c \left(\frac{R}{R_c}, \mu, \omega, P_{Tc}\right) = \frac{\left(\frac{R}{R_c}\right)^{-\nu}}{\frac{3\varphi^*}{\varphi}\left[(1+\omega)(\sqrt{3})^{-\gamma} + (3+\omega)(\sqrt{3K})^{-\gamma}\right] + \frac{N}{\varphi P_{Tc}}} \tag{14}$$

$$SINR_e \left(\frac{R}{R_c}, \mu, \omega, P_{Tc}\right) = \frac{\left(\frac{R}{R_c}\right)^{-\nu}}{\frac{6\varphi^*}{\varphi}\left[\frac{1}{\omega}(\sqrt{3})^{-\gamma} + (1+\frac{1}{\omega})(\sqrt{3K})^{-\gamma}\right] + \frac{N}{\varphi\omega P_{Tc}}} \tag{15}$$

SINR behaviours for different μ and ω values are shown in Fig. 2 for $P_T = 37\,$dBm, $BW = 5\,$MHz and 'intermediate' propagation conditions [15]. From this graph, we can see that the SINR curve has a discontinuity at $R = \rho_0$ due to the change in the conditions for interference, transmission power, and available bandwidth.

This approach to determine SINR could be easily adapted to model cell sectorisation. In this case, we should reduce the number of interfering cells and add the antenna gain to the link budget. Further details on cell sectorisation are beyond the scope of the present work. However, we believe that the following SFR optimization approach is also valid for a sectorised scenario.

The aim of the following study is to present traffic engineering implications for planning the LTE coverage with SFR so that the rough approximation of circularly-shaped cells (radius R_c) is acceptable. We assume that the UEs serviced by an eNB are uniformly distributed in the cell. Hence, the number of UEs receiving transmissions according to a certain MCS (or the corresponding CQI) is proportional to the area within the cell that is covered by that MCS mode.

If SINR does not monotonically decrease with the distance, as in our SFR case, the same CQI_i value can be adopted in two disjoint rings: one for distances lower than ρ_0 and another for distances greater than ρ_0. Let A_{ci} denote the area of the ring in the cell-centre zone where mode CQI_i is used. Moreover, let A_{ei} denote the area of the ring in the cell-edge zone where mode CQI_i is used. Areas A_{ci} and A_{ei} are disjoint. The total area where the transmission mode

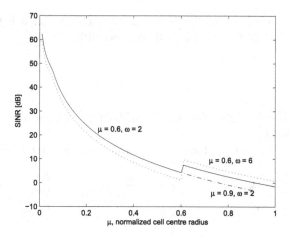

Fig. 2. Examples of SINR behaviour.

corresponding to CQI_i is used is $A_i = A_{ci} + A_{ei}$. This area can be formally characterized by the radii fulfilling the following condition:

$$SINR_i \leq SINR\left(\frac{R}{R_c}, \mu, \omega, P_{Tc}\right) < SINR_{i+1}. \tag{16}$$

Area A_{ci} is limited by radii $R_{c,i}$ and $R_{c,i+1}$ so that $0 \leq R_{c,i+1} \leq R_{c,i} \leq \rho_0$. Moreover, A_{ei} is limited by radii $R_{e,i}$ and $R_{e,i+1}$ so that $\rho_0 \leq R_{e,i+1} \leq R_{e,i} \leq R_c$. In these conditions, $R_{c,i}$ is obtained by solving $SINR_c = SINR_i$ using the $SINR_c$ expression in (14). In case of no solution in the range $0 - \rho_0$ for this SINR condition, we take the limiting value 0 or ρ_0 for $R_{c,i}$, depending on the fact that the threshold value $SINR_i$ is too high or too low for the $SINR_c$ values for cell-centre UEs. If $SINR_1$ is too high, we have outage in the cell centre. Moreover, $R_{e,i}$ is obtained by solving $SINR_e = SINR_i$ using the $SINR_e$ expression in (15). In case of no solution in the range $\rho_0 - R_c$ for this SINR condition, we take the limiting value ρ_0 or R_c for $R_{e,i}$, depending on the fact that the threshold value $SINR_i$ is too high or too low for the $SINR_e$ values for cell-edge UEs. If $SINR_1$ is too high, we have outage at the cell border.

Let Ω_{ci} denote the probability that mode CQI_i is used for cell-centre UEs and Ω_{ei} the probability that mode CQI_i is used for cell-edge UEs. These probabilities are obtained as:

$$\Omega_{ci} = \frac{A_{ci}}{\pi R_c^2} \quad \text{and} \quad \Omega_{ei} = \frac{A_{ei}}{\pi R_c^2} \quad \text{for } i = 1, \ldots, 15 \tag{17}$$

Note that probabilities Ω_{ci} and Ω_{ei} above are normalized on the whole cell area and not on the area of the part (cell-centre or cell-edge) they refer to. We consider Ω_{ci} for $i = 0$ to represent the outage probability in the cell-centre area (i.e., outage occurs in the cell-centre area if the condition $SINR_c < SINR_1$ is fulfilled) and we consider Ω_{ei} for $i = 0$ to represent the outage probability in the cell-edge area (i.e., outage occurs in the cell-edge area if the condition $SINR_e < SINR_1$ is fulfilled). The following condition is met:

$$\sum_{i=1}^{15} (\Omega_{ci} + \Omega_{ei}) \leq 1 \tag{18}$$

where equality is valid only when there is no outage. The overall outage probability is given by $\Omega_{c_0} + \Omega_{e_0}$.

Probabilities Ω_{ci} and Ω_{ei} for $i = 1, \ldots, 15$ can be derived as shown below:

$$\Omega_{ci} (SINR_i, SINR_{i+1}, \mu, \omega, K, P_{T_c}) = \frac{\pi R_{c,i}^2 - \pi R_{c,i+1}^2}{\pi R_c^2} = \left(\frac{R_{c,i}}{R_c}\right)^2 - \left(\frac{R_{c,i+1}}{R_c}\right)^2$$
$$\Omega_{ei} (SINR_i, SINR_{i+1}, \mu, \omega, K, P_{T_c}) = \frac{\pi R_{e,i}^2 - \pi R_{e,i+1}^2}{\pi R_c^2} = \left(\frac{R_{e,i}}{R_c}\right)^2 - \left(\frac{R_{e,i+1}}{R_c}\right)^2$$
$$\tag{19}$$

The dependence of probabilities Ω_{ci} and Ω_{ei} on P_{Tc} (or equivalently P_T) is negligible. These probabilities are used below to express the mean PHY-layer capacity of a cell.

The cell capacity with a certain CQI_i is obtained under the scheduling assumption that all PRBs of a TTI are transmitted with the same modulation and coding scheme of that CQI_i and this is possible because we consider that the system is fully loaded both in its central area and in its edge area. We consider the gross cell capacity, including the capacity spent for control channels. Moreover, we differentiate between cell-centre capacity C_{ci} and cell-edge capacity C_{ei}, since the available bandwidth BW is divided between cell-centre and cell-edge parts according to the coefficients $(K-1)/K$ and $1/K$. We have:

$$C_{ci} = 12 \times 7 \times \eta_i \times \frac{(K-1) \times N_{PRB}(BW)}{K \times TTI}$$
$$C_{ei} = 12 \times 7 \times \eta_i \times \frac{N_{PRB}(BW)}{K \times TTI} \tag{20}$$

where $TTI = 1$ ms and $N_{PRB}(BW)$ is the number of PRBs per TTI, considering the whole available bandwidth, BW [3].

We obtain the average PHY-layer capacity of a cell, C, by summing the capacities C_{ci} and C_{ei} weighted by the probabilities of using CQI_i in the cell centre or in the cell edge:

$$C (\mu, \omega, BW, K, P_{Tc}) = \sum_{i=1}^{15} \{C_{ci} \times \Omega_{ci} + C_{ei} \times \Omega_{ei}\} =$$
$$= \sum_{i=1}^{15} \{\eta_i [(K-1) \, \Omega_{ci} + \Omega_{ei}]\} \frac{12 \times 7 \times N_{PRB}(BW)}{K \times TTI} \tag{21}$$

Note that the dependence on thresholds $SINR_i$ has been omitted in the notation of the mean cell capacity C. We can use (21) to select the values of μ and ω that maximize the cell capacity. Figure 3 shows the behaviour of the capacity C as a function of μ and ω for $P_T = 37$ dBm, $BW = 5$ MHz, 'intermediate' propagation conditions, and AWGN channel, according to the SINR thresholds in Table 1. Note that if there is outage in the cell for a given configuration of μ and ω, we have considered in the following graphs a cell capacity equal to zero (even if the actual cell capacity is not zero) in order to make it evident that some configurations of μ and ω correspond to outage conditions. Hence, in Fig. 3 the darkest area corresponds to outage configurations in the cell of radius R_c; these configurations are not good for cell planning purposes. The graph in Fig. 3 shows that the PHY-layer cell capacity C has an optimal configuration (maximum) for μ around 0.8 and ω around 1.6. The results in Fig. 3 are quite insensitive to variations of P_T (only the cell range changes).

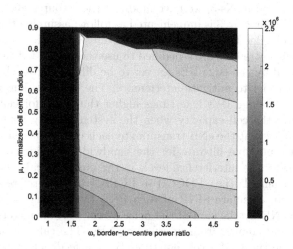

Fig. 3. PHY-layer capacity as a function of μ and ω in the AWGN channel case. The side bar maps the gray scale to the capacity in bit/s.

Similar results to those in Fig. 3 could be achieved considering MAC-layer capacity including the effects of H-ARQ retransmissions.

4   Simulation Results

In this Section, we present simulation results to analyse the capacity of LTE with SFR. The following system configuration has been adopted for all simulations:

- SUI propagation model for an intermediate scenario
- System bandwidth $BW = 5\,\mathrm{MHz}$
- Omni-directional antennas at both eNBs and UEs
- eNB transmission power $P_T = 37\,\mathrm{dBm}$
- Uniform UE distribution in the cells
- Cell range R_c equal to 1666 m (AWGN channel), the reference value of the classical frequency reuse with $K = 3$
- Cellular hexagonal layout with a reference central cell (eNB) and 18 adjacent cells (1st and 2nd tiers of cells)
- Shadowing margin $s = 15.8\,\mathrm{dB}$

– SFR with cell-edge reuse factor $K = 3$
– In order to simplify the model, we have assumed that all sub-carriers (sub-channels) experience the same SINR conditions.
– SINR thresholds are used for the different CQIs according to Table 1.

4.1   Model Validation with the Ns-3 Simulator of LTE

The Ns-3 environment already supports an LTE simulator [5]. In order to get the SFR scheme included in Ns-3, we have modified the resource allocator module. In particular, SFR for $K = 3$ is implemented as follow: assuming that the system is fully loaded, cell-edge UEs are allowed to use only $1/3$ of the whole bandwidth BW, instead cell-centre UEs are scheduled to use the rest $2/3$ of the bandwidth. The channels used by cell-edge UEs are set to be different from those of the six adjacent cells in order to mitigate interference. The transmission power for one sub-channel for cell-edge UEs is ω times higher than that for cell-centre UEs. In order to study the cell capacity when the system is fully loaded (downlink traffic), we consider that the eNB transmits to each UE in the cell a UDP traffic at the maximum possible bit-rate for the bandwidth considered; this is done in order to consider the interference levels in the most critical conditions. Each eNB uses pilot channels (i.e., PDCCH + PCFIC) to send reference signals to UEs that, in turn, calculate SINR of each PRB by dividing the power of the signal from the eNB by the sum of the noise power plus all powers received on the same PRB and coming from interfering eNBs. The calculation of SINR is used to determine the CQI level sent to eNB by a feedback signal. The MCS of each sub-channel corresponds to the CQI level of that sub-channel. In our study, all sub-channels used by a UE have the same CQI value. Referring to the simulation area of 19 cells, we consider UEs randomly placed in the cells and we categorize them as in the cell-centre area or in the cell-edge one depending on the distance from their eNB. Then, we measure the SINR for each UE in the central cell and determine the corresponding cell capacity as the average of the capacity provided to the UEs in the different parts of this cell.

The graph in Fig. 4 shows the comparison between the SINR behaviour from the analysis in Sect. 3 and that obtained from Ns-3 simulations in the AWGN channel case. We can note that the agreement is quite good and that there is a slight difference when approaching cell borders due to the approximations in the analysis on the derivation of the distance of interferers.

The following graph in Fig. 5 shows the capacity (net capacity without control channels) obtained from Ns-3 simulations for different combinations of ω and μ, assuming an RR scheduler that is consistent with the assumptions made in Sect. 2. These results have been obtained considering fixed users and outage conditions. These results show that the optimal configuration is quite close to that predicted by the theoretical approach in Sect. 3; some small differences are due to following issues: (i) the rough granularity (steps of 0.1 for both μ and ω) adopted for performing simulations; (ii) the inclusion of the control channels capacity in the total capacity in the analysis (control channels roughly entail a 14 % capacity overhead).

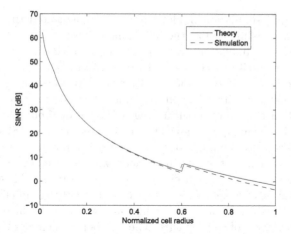

Fig. 4. SINR behaviours from Ns-3 simulations and the theory in the AWGN channel case for $\omega = 2$ and $\mu = 0.6$.

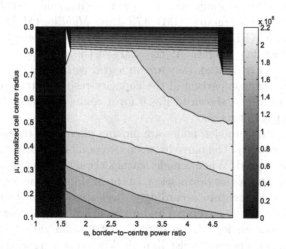

Fig. 5. Capacity with SFR from simulations for AWGN channel and different values of the normalized cell-centre radius μ and border-to-centre power ratio ω.

4.2   Impact of Mobility on SFR Cell Capacity

Client (UE) mobility heavily influences the performance of wireless networks. In the analysis carried out in the previous part of this Chapter, we have assumed that clients are uniformly distributed in the cell and that clients' locations do not change. This is not the case of the real world, where clients move while they exchange traffic through the LTE network. The distribution of client positions within the area covered by the cell influences its capacity, because clients close to the eNB can communicate using more effective MCS levels. In this Section, we evaluate the impact of mobility on cell capacity with SFR via simulations.

An OMNeT++ [6] simulation model has been implemented that supports all the characteristics highlighted at the beginning of Sect. 4.

The OMNeT++ simulation area consists of 19 eNBs located as shown in Fig. 1. Only the capacity of the central cell was analyzed. It is assumed that all clients request best effort traffic and that the RR scheduler is adopted. We consider the whole capacity of a cell, also including control channels capacity. The cell capacity is calculated as the average of the throughput offered to all UEs within range. The throughput of a UE was calculated using the SUI propagation model (as in Sect. 3), assuming a total transmission power $P_T = 37\,$dBm and $BW = 5\,$MHz. The calculation of cell capacity was repeated every 100 ms of the simulation time to evaluate how it changes in response to the changing locations of network nodes (it corresponds on average to 0.5 m change in client location). The simulation time has been set to 10 days and we have obtained both average and standard deviation of cell capacity. The number of clients of the cell was set to 100. These clients were roaming within the area covered by the eNB according to a mobility model as detailed below.

Four different client mobility models have been implemented: *Random Waypoint* (RW) [16], *Gauss-Markov* (GM) [17], *Mass Mobility* (MM) [18], and *Real Life Mobility Model* (RLMM) [19]. The mean speed of a client has been set to 18 km/h in all mobility models. At the start of the simulation, all clients are uniformly spatially distributed: they are on a grid with equal distances of 100 m from each other. The comparison of the capacity results obtained with the different mobility models is shown in Fig. 6 for a configuration with $\mu = 0.8$ and $\omega = 1.6$, as selected in Sect. 3.

In the RW mobility model, nodes are moving directly to the next randomly-chosen point (waypoint). The move between two points is according to a straight line with constant speed. When a node reaches the next point, it waits for some time and then chooses a new destination. In the MM model, nodes have a certain mass and apply a momentum accordingly. Nodes move in a straight line for a certain time interval (5 s on average) and make a turn with an angle randomized around the previous angle, using a normal distribution with an average of 30 degrees. Node speed is normally distributed. When a node reaches the boundary of the simulated area, it reflects off the wall according to the same angle. The lower rate of changes in the movement makes cell capacity changes much smaller on a short time scale, but the correlation of the movement may cause quite high changes in the total cell throughput. RLMM simulates the changes of human behaviour in relation to weekly and daily cycles. The day is divided into periods during which human movement patterns are very different, like for instance the 8 h working time or the 8 h sleeping time (when the client does not move) and the travel time from the work place to home (when the client intensively moves between two points on the simulated area). The simulations have shown that these patterns very heavily influence the mean cell capacity: it is almost constant during nighttimes (when clients do not change the location and have constant modulation) and rapidly changes during the periods of heavy commuting to and from work. The GM mobility model assumes that mobile nodes have an initial speed and direction, and takes this into consideration to compute the values for the next step. Thus, the movement is much more smoothed, but the traveled distances are higher than in other models, so that capacity has a higher variation.

Comparing the results of the different mobility patterns we can notice that the average cell capacity is similar for GM and MM models, but the RW model gives much higher average cell capacity. In any case, all mobility models yield higher cell capacity values than those considered in Sect. 3, because all mobility models tend to distribute the clients close to the cell centre; this phenomenon is emphasized in the case of the RW mobility model [20]. The standard deviation of the cell capacity changes significantly from model to model. From the RLMM model we can see that the changes in human movement characteristics during day and night make the variance of cell capacity much higher than one could anticipate from simpler mobility models, because there are long periods with constant capacity (nigh time and working time), as can be seen in Fig. 8 in the next Sub-section.

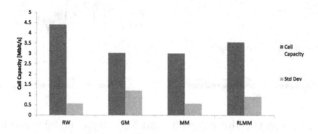

Fig. 6. Average and standard deviation of cell capacity for RW, GM, MM, and RLMM mobility models for normalized cell-centre radius $\mu = 0.8$ and border-to-centre power ratio $\omega = 1.6$.

4.3   Simulation Study of SFR Under Different Scheduling Policies

In the previous analysis, we have assumed that the transmission time (amount of PRBs) is allocated evenly among all mobile clients, as in the case of the RR scheduling algorithm. However, in addition to the RR scheduler, we consider the *Proportional Fair* (PF) scheduler [21]. With RR, every client UE is scheduled for equal times allocated without taking the channel quality into account. This entails the allocation of the same amount of PRBs to every client, assuming that there are always data available for transmissions. Depending on the MCS level used by each client, the transmission rate may be very different from client to client. With PF, each data flow is assigned with a data rate or a scheduling priority (depending on the implementation) that is inversely proportional to its anticipated resource consumption. PF ensures that every client can transmit the same amount of data, regardless of the channel quality. The goal is to guarantee fairness among flows. PF is a scheduling option well suited to non-real time traffic.

To evaluate how cell capacity is influenced by the scheduler, we have implemented both RR and PF schedulers within the OMNeT++ model [22] in the

SFR scenario. The simulations have been executed according to the parameters shown at the beginning of Sect. 4. In the following Figs. 7 and 8, the cell capacity has been compared between the two scheduling algorithms, considering the four mobility models under investigation. We can note that the PF scheduler heavily decreases the total cell capacity. This is caused by more PRBs allocated to serve clients with lower MCS levels to maintain the fairness of throughput provided by the eNB to its clients. The PF scheduler also decreases the amplitude of capacity changes. This can be seen in particular for the RLLM mobility model, since the cell capacity with PF is much steadier than that with the RR scheduler.

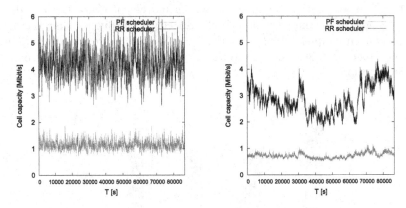

Fig. 7. Cell capacity in time for RW (left) and MM (right) mobility models with RR scheduler (black) or PF scheduler (grey) for SFR with normalized cell-centre radius $\mu = 0.8$ and border-to-centre power ratio $\omega = 1.6$ for 24 h of simulation time.

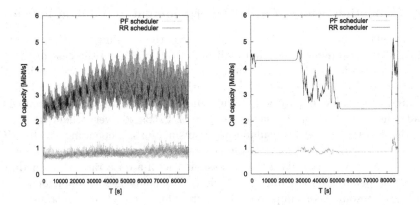

Fig. 8. Cell capacity in time for GM (left) and RLMM (right) mobility models with RR scheduler (black) or PF scheduler (grey) for SFR with normalized cell-centre radius $\mu = 0.8$ and border-to-centre power ratio $\omega = 1.6$ for 24 h of simulation time.

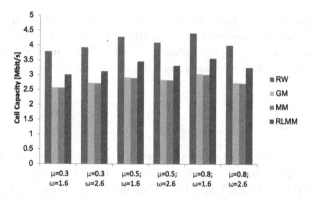

Fig. 9. Average cell capacity for RR scheduler with different mobility models and different SFR parameters.

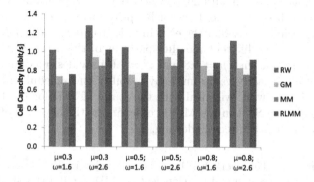

Fig. 10. Average cell capacity for PF scheduler with different mobility models and different SFR parameters.

The mobility models may distribute the users in the cell in different ways (especially in terms of the closeness to the eNB) [20], what creates different average capacity values and different optimization conditions for μ and ω with respect to those considered in Sect. 3. Thus, we have carried out simulations to evaluate the cell capacity in configurations where μ and ω are around the optimized point, as identified in the previous Section: $\mu = 0.8$ and $\omega = 1.6$. In particular, we have considered 6 points distributed in the μ - ω plane near the optimal point: that is μ between 0.3 and 0.8 and ω between 1.6 and 2.6. Results are shown in Figs. 9 and 10 for RR and PF schedulers, respectively. We can note that the results in Fig. 9 show that the optimum point is for $\mu = 0.8$ and $\omega = 1.6$, and this is consistent with the results of the analysis in Sect. 3 (Fig. 3) and those of the Ns-3 simulations in Subsect. 4.1 (Fig. 5). Instead, the results in Fig. 10 provide a different optimum point, because the PF scheduler is adopted; nevertheless, the configuration with $\mu = 0.8$ and $\omega = 1.6$ still provides a high capacity close to the maximum in this case. In Figs. 9 and 10, there are quite large differences in cell capacity between RW and the other mobility models, because the RW mobility model tends to concentrate (more than the other mobility models) the users close to the cell centre. As already explained, this effect that is present in all mobility models [20,23] justifies the difference in capacity between the analysis in Sect. 3 and the simulation results shown in Subsects. 4.2 and 4.3.

5   Conclusions

In this Chapter, we have presented a framework to analyse the capacity of multi-cellular LTE systems based on soft frequency reuse. A system model has been proposed in order to characterize the SINR depending on two SFR important parameters, such as the normalized cell-centre radius μ and the border-to-centre power ratio ω. An optimization of these parameters has been carried out by means of analysis, Ns-3 simulations, and OMNeT++ simulations. We have also shown that the cell capacity and the SFR optimization are also influenced by the scheduling technique used at the eNB in order to manage the different traffic flows as well as by the different mobility patterns of the users. We have shown that the configuration with $\mu = 0.8$ and $\omega = 1.6$ provides maximum (or close-to-maximum) cell capacity values in many mobility and scheduling conditions.

A possible future work will deal with the study of SFR for the HetNet scenario, with modelling SFR in the MIMO case, and with the study of the effects of the lognormally-distributed shadowing.

Acknowledgments. This work has been in part supported by a grant of Polish National Center for Research and Development no. LIDER/10/194/L-3/11.

References

1. Cisco White Paper: Cisco Visual Networking Index: Global Mobile Data Traffic Forecast Update, 2013–2018, 5 February 2014
2. Ali-Yahiya, T.: LTE and Its Performance. Springer, New York (2011)
3. Giambene, G., Ali-Yahiya, T.: LTE planning for soft frequency reuse. In: Proceedings of Wireless Days 2013, Valencia, Spain, 13–15 November 2013
4. 3GPP: E-UTRA Multiplexing and Channel Coding, TS 36.212, Release 12 (2013)
5. LTE simulator for Ns-3. http://lena.cttc.es/manual/lte-design.html#H-ARQ
6. Varga, A., Hornig, R.: An overview of the OMNeT++ simulation environment. In: Proceedings of the 1st International Conference on Simulation Tools and Techniques for Communications, Networks and Systems and Workshops (Simutools'08), Belgium (2008)
7. 3GPP: Medium Access Control (MAC) Protocol Specification, TS 36.321 V12.0.0 (2013-12)
8. Park, H.-S., Lee, J.-Y., Kim, B.-C.: TCP performance degradation of in-sequence delivery in LTE link layer. Int. J. Adv. Sci. Technol. **37**, 27–36 (2011)
9. Ghosh, A., Ratasuk, R., Mondal, B., Mangalvedhe, N., Thomas, T.: LTE-advanced: next-generation wireless broadband technology. IEEE Wireless Commun. **17**(3), 10–22 (2010)

10. Hu, R.Q., Qian, Y., Kota, S., Giambene, G.: HetNets - a new paradigm for increasing cellular capacity and coverage [Guest Editorial]. IEEE Wireless Commun. **18**(3), 8–9 (2011). (Special issue)

11. Yu, Y.: Network planning for transparent mode IEEE 802.16j relay-based network. Ph.D. thesis, University College Dublin, Ireland (2010)

12. Novlan, T.D., Ganti, R.K., Ghosh, A., Andrews, J.G.: Analytical evaluation of fractional frequency reuse for OFDMA cellular networks. IEEE Trans. Wireless Commun. **10**(12), 4294–4305 (2011)

13. Xie, Z., Walke, B.: Enhanced fractional frequency reuse to increase capacity of OFDMA systems. In: Proceedings of the 3rd International Conference on New Technologies, Mobility and Security (NTMS 2009), Cairo, Egypt (2009)

14. Kosta, C., Hunt, B., Quddus, A.U., Tafazolli, R.: On interference avoidance through inter-cell interference coordination (ICIC) based on OFDMA mobile systems. IEEE Commun. Surv. Tutorials **15**(3), 973–994 (2013)

15. Erceg, V., Greenstein, L.J., Tjandra, S.Y., Parkoff, S.R., Gupta, A., Kulic, B., Julius, A.A., Bianchi, R.: An empirically-based path loss model for wireless channels in suburban environments. IEEE J. Sel. Areas Commun. **17**(7), 1205–1211 (1999)

16. Hyytia, E., Virtamo, J.: Random waypoint mobility model in cellular networks. Wireless Netw. **13**, 177–188 (2007)

17. Ariyakhajorn, J., et al.: A comparative study of random waypoint and Gauss Markov mobility models in performance evaluation of MANET. In: Proceedings of the International Symposium on Communication and Information Technologies, ISCIT-06 (2006)

18. Perkins, C.E., Wang, K.: Optimized smooth handoffs in mobile IP. In: Proceedings of the Fourth IEEE Symposium on Computers and Communications (ISCC '99) (1999)

19. Gorawski, M., Grochla, K.: The real-life mobility model: RLMM. In: Proceedings of the Second International Conference on Future Generation Communication Technologies, London (2013)

20. Bettstetter, C., Wagner, C.: The spatial node distribution of the random waypoint mobility model. In: Proceedings of the WMAN Conference, Ulm, pp. 41–58 (2002)

21. Kwan, R., Leung, C., Zhang, J.: Proportional fair multiuser scheduling in LTE. IEEE Sign. Process. Lett. **16**(6), 461–464 (2009)

22. Varga, A.: The OMNeT++ discrete event simulation system. In: Proceedings of the European Simulation Multiconference (ESM2001), Prague, Czech Republic (2001)

23. Mousavi, M.S., et al.: Mobisim: a framework for simulation of mobility models in mobile ad-hoc networks. In: Proceedings of the Wireless and Mobile Computing, Networking and Communications Conference 2007 (WiMOB 2007) (2007)

Improving Video QoE in Unmanned Aerial Vehicles Using an Adaptive FEC Mechanism

Roger Immich[1]([✉]), Eduardo Cerqueira[2], and Marilia Curado[1]

[1] Department of Informatics Engineering, University of Coimbra,
Pinhal de Marrocos, 3030-290 Coimbra, Portugal
{immich,marilia}@dei.uc.pt
[2] Institute of Technology, Federal University of Para,
Av. Augusto Correa, 01, Belém, Para 66.075-110, Brazil
cerqueira@ufpa.br

Abstract. Unmanned aerial vehicles (UAV) are rising in popularity together with video applications for both military and civilian use. Because of that, it is necessary to address a set of challenges related to the device movement, scarce resources as well as high error rates, making evident the need for an adaptive mechanism to strengthen video transmissions. Adaptive Forward Error Correction (FEC) techniques are known to be suitable to enhance the Quality of Experience (QoE) of video transmitted over error-prone wireless networks with high mobility. This book chapter proposes an adaptive video-aware FEC mechanism that uses motion vectors details to improve real-time UAV video transmissions, providing both higher user experience and better usage of resources. The benefits and drawbacks of the proposed mechanism along with the related work are analysed and put up for test through simulations and evaluated using QoE metrics.

Keywords: Motion Vectors (MV) · Forward Error Correction (FEC) · Video-aware FEC · Fuzzy logic · QoE · Unequal Error Protection (UEP)

1 Introduction

The rapid growth of both, autonomous and nonautonomous unmanned aerial vehicles (UAV) [1], with the objective of video surveillance, exploitation, and reconnaissance is evident in the last years. The deployment of these vehicles is no longer exclusive of military and special operation applications, as the civilian use of small UAVs has also increased due to ease operation, robust, and cost-effective wireless networking technologies, such as 4G LTE. These devices can be helpful in a variety of situations. For example, in traffic surveillance, public parades, festivals, sports events, in short, at any event that brings together a large amount of people [2,3], the use of UAVs can be preferred over fixed video cameras due to

---

R. Immich, E. Cerqueira – CNPq Fellow, Brazil.

I. Ganchev et al. (Eds.): Wireless Networking for Moving Objects, LNCS 8611, pp. 198–216, 2014.
DOI: 10.1007/978-3-319-10834-6_11

their mobility and low cost operation in comparison to manned systems. Other applications are to cover large areas with no previous infrastructure, in natural disaster sites, rescue missions [4], as well as monitoring and inspecting critical infrastructures, such as power plants, long pipelines, large industrial areas, railways, harbours.

The benefits of UAV with video-capability are clear, however, even with proper equipment, robust data integration and visualization tools, poor-quality video streaming can compromise the usability of the system. These video streams are watched by humans, and a good quality is essential to, for example, identify faces, damaged power lines or pipes, as well as track conditions. However, it is known that real-time video transmission over wireless networks with Quality of Experience (QoE) support brings new challenges. It needs a steady and continuous flow of packets, which can be affected by a number of factors. First of all, these networks tend to have poor connectivity quality [5]. In addition, the channel conditions can quickly fluctuate over time owing to the high mobility of the nodes and terrain structures, as well as other wireless communication issues like noise, multipath fading, and channel interference [6]. Another challenge is to fairly use the available bandwidth [7]. It is critical to make an efficient use of resources preventing the induction of network congestion and high packet loss rate. This is especially important in resource-consuming services like video transmission. Furthermore, the video quality as perceived by the users is also important, a good clean image will help to identify persons, objects, and places, while providing a better chance to act accordingly in each case.

The quality of live video streams, in terms of QoE [8], is the overall acceptability of end-users and is related to, but differs from the extensively studied concept Quality of Service (QoS). Generally speaking, QoE quantifies the video quality according to the user perception and these characteristics must be taken into consideration in networking adaptation mechanisms. This need is even more evident in dynamic wireless environments with high error rates, such as, in UAV video streams. The optimized distribution of live video streams with QoE support is one of the main challenges in highly dynamic wireless environments. Choosing the proper adaptive redundancy control mechanism with QoE and network-awareness is decisive for an efficient use of resources, while increasing the video quality as perceived by end users.

Several factors can affect the video QoE. These factors are not restricted to network parameters as aforementioned, but also to the video characteristics, such as codec type, bitrate, the length of the Group of Pictures (GoP), as well as the video content, such as the degree of details and motion intensity [9]. Because of that, an adaptive redundancy control mechanism is required to improve the video quality in high dynamic and error-prone wireless networks, especially involving mobile nodes. A good way to quantify the motion intensity in a certain video portion (e.g., a frame or GoP) is to use the Motion Vectors (MV) in it. MV are a key part of the video compression, where they are used to store the changes from adjacent frames. This means that the changes can be related to the next frame or both previous and next frames. By using the information held by the MV, it is possible to quantify the motion intensity. Since each video sequence has its own characteristics in terms of motion and complexity levels, the adaptive redundancy control mechanism must recognize them and perform the protection in accordance with their importance. To do that, an Unequal Error Protection (UEP) scheme is desired to shield the most important information providing better QoE.

Through the use of an adaptive protection mechanism it is possible to protect the most important data, improving the video transmission and attaining both high video quality and low network overhead. To this end, Forward Error Correction (FEC) techniques have been used successfully in real-time video transmission services [10]. FEC enhances the video transmission by sending redundant data along with the original data set. Because of that, when a data loss occurs, the original data can be reconstructed using the redundant information [11]. However, the wireless resources are limited and often unfairly distributed. In order to overcome these problems and to allow multiple simultaneous transmissions, an adaptive cross-layer FEC-based mechanism is required. This mechanism should also be UEP- and QoE-aware to decrease the redundant information, while increasing the human perception. This is feasible by adjusting the amount of redundancy based on the content relevance from the QoE perspective, giving more protection to the most important data.

This book chapter describes a cross-layer adaptive video-aware mechanism that uses motion vectors details, FEC, and Fuzzy logic to improve the resilience of UAV (uavFEC) video transmission with both UEP and QoE-awareness. Even though some video-aware FEC-based mechanisms are found in the literature, as detailed in the related work, they tend to consume unnecessary bandwidth by sending QoE-unaware information. To address this issue, the uavFEC dynamically configures itself, using fuzzy logic, to send redundant information of only the most important data, improving the human experience when watching live video flows, while providing users and authorities (e.g., firefighters and paramedics) with a high perception of videos and allowing them to reduce human reaction times.

Fuzzy logic has been used in several video related mechanisms, such as to detect video shot boundaries in content-based video applications [12], to perform congestion control of real-time video stream in wireless networks [13], and also to perform a dynamic bandwidth and buffer allocation on multimedia traffic [14], as well as for QoE estimation of audio and video transmissions [15]. However, to the best of our knowledge, there is no proposal of an adaptive mechanism using fuzzy logic to handle in an abstract way the concepts of motion vectors to enhance QoE in highly dynamic and error-prone wireless networks. The uavFEC also uses the fuzzification process to cope with a number of video characteristics in order to find the specific degree of membership which corresponds the motion intensity of each video sequence. In doing that, it is possible to assign an optimal amount of redundant data only to QoE-sensitive data. This means that only the more sensitive video information will have an adjustable amount of redundant data, therefore ensuring a high video quality and downsizing the resource usage.

These are important features in highly dynamic networks that can be only achievable through the adoption of an adaptive mechanism. Another important advantage is the energy savings that are achieved by sending less redundant information, thus using less power. The proposed solution was assessed using real video sequences from small UAVs and objective QoE metrics.

The remainder of this book chapter is structured as follows. The related work is shown in Sect. 2. Section 3 describes uavFEC and its evaluation is presented in Sect. 4. Conclusions and future work are summarized in Sect. 5.

2   Related Work

Several mechanisms have been proposed to improve the video quality over wireless networks, however, to the best of our knowledge, there is no proposal of an adaptive video-aware mechanism to enhance the video transmission of UAVs. One of these proposals is the Adaptive Cross-Layer FEC (ACFEC) that uses a packet-level error correction [16]. It adopts a MAC layer loss counter, which is increased on each loss, and it is used to determine the amount of FEC redundancy. In doing so, when the wireless connections are good, the counter will held a small number, producing less redundant traffic. Nevertheless, a network overhead assessment was not conducted, proving difficult to determine the efficiency of the proposal. Additionally, the video characteristics are not considered, which are known to have a direct influence on the video resilience to packet loss and QoE.

Another approach uses a retransmission-based adaptive source-channel rate control [17]. This allows to track in real-time the decoder buffer occupancy and channel state, making possible to use the best redundancy amount. Despite the authors claim that it improved the QoE for end-users, no actual QoE metrics were used, they relay only on QoE prediction using packet loss information. Another point is that it does not measure the network overhead caused by the proposed scheme.

An alternative mechanism defines a dynamic FEC block length, which can be adjusted according with both, the number of continuous losses and the packet loss rate to improve video transmissions [18]. This approach only takes into consideration the network parameters, leaving out information about QoE and video characteristics which are very important in the adaptation scheme to define a correct amount of redundancy.

Another solution is the Cross-Layer Mapping Unequal Error Protection (CLM-UEP) [19]. This mechanism provides a tailored amount of redundancy based on the frame type and packet loss rate. However, this approach does not deal with important video characteristics, such as the frame position within the GoP and, especially, the motion intensity. As aforementioned, these video characteristics have a substantial influence in order to find the more appropriate amount of redundancy, consequently saving important device and network resources.

3 Adaptive Video-Aware Fuzzy Logic Mechanism

Considering the open issues aforementioned, in particular the lack of QoE- and video-aware proposals which include clear indicators of motion intensity, such as the motion vectors (MV), and the network state, this work proposes and evaluates a cross-layer adaptive video-aware FEC mechanism (uavFEC) based on MV and fuzzy logic. The primary goal is to enhance the video transmission of small UAV. This solution is an improvement of our previous work [20] and the main enhancements are described next.

Figure 1 depicts the overall operation of our mechanism. The video is captured, packetized, and delivered to uavFEC. After that, our mechanism will gather information about the video characteristics, such as the distance pointed by the motion vectors, frame type, GoP length, and relative position of P-Frames. These information are obtained through cross-layer techniques and loaded on the fuzzy interface engine to compute a suitable redundancy amount. Another important feature of uavFEC is the use of the network status to improve even further the amount of redundancy, allowing to enhance the video quality without adding unnecessary network overhead.

In order to conceive the uavFEC, first of all, a knowledge database needs to be created through exploratory analysis using hierarchical clustering. This database stores information about the relation between several video characteristics and their impact on the quality of the videos. Further details can be found in [20]. The combined use of this knowledge database and human expertise allows the definition of several fuzzy rules and sets. The offline process needs to be executed only once. Following this analysis, the information is loaded in the fuzzy interface engine and can be used in the real-time decision making process. This is an

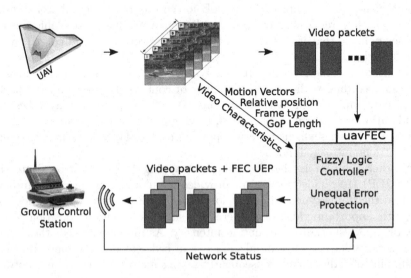

Fig. 1. uavFEC

important step, since the real-time mechanism can be faster and more accurate, as fewer variables need to be handled.

uavFEC also uses the network state as one of the inputs to the adaptive mechanism. This information is jointly employed with the GoP length, motion vectors distance, frame type, and the relative position, to determine a suitable amount of redundancy. After that, using an improved UEP technique, a proper amount of redundancy will be added, sparing resources while increasing the video quality. A detailed description of the adaptive mechanism is presented below.

The use of fuzzy logic in the proposed mechanism allows it to be more comprehensive and dynamic, because it can take into consideration a larger number of video and network details and still be fast enough to operate in real-time schemes as expected in a highly dynamic UAV network. Additionally, fuzzy logic can be considered a problem-solving methodology that aims to define what the system should do rather than attempting to fully understand its operation. It adopts a simple approach to provide definitive conclusions relying on imprecise, ambiguous, or vague information.

In order to use fuzzy logic it is necessary to define several components, such as rules, sets, and membership functions. The rules define how the system behaves. The fuzzy sets, in contrast to classical sets that an element either belongs or does not belong to, are capable to have a degree of membership. At last, the membership functions are designed to represent the significance of each element in the fuzzy set.

The process of designing the fuzzy logic components that will be used in the uavFEC mechanism enfolds a series of exploratory analysis to define the behaviour and value of each one of them. The first step is to quantify the motion intensity. In order to do that, an exploratory analysis using hierarchical clustering with Euclidean distance was conducted. This is a statistical method of partitioning data into groups that are as homogeneous as possible. Motion vectors (MV) data is used to create these clusters. The idea of MV was obtained from classical mechanics and their vector-oriented model of motion. This model describes the movement of objects as simply as the sequence of small translations on a plane. To produce a large data base, the MV of several UAVs video sequences were extracted. Then, through Euclidean distance, it was computed how far each vector is pointing and summed together with all others in the same frame. This was used instead of just counting the MV, because one frame can have a lot of vectors pointing to a close distance where another frame can have less vectors, but pointing much farther away, thus presenting higher motion intensity. Figure 2 depicts an example. At frame #21 the UAV is turning right, thus, it is possible to see that the MV are longer than in frame #34, when the UAV finished the turn and starts hovering. The Euclidean distance sums of all MV in these frames are 109300 and 14117, for frame #21 and #34 respectively. However, the total number of MV in each frame is 4959 (frame #21) and 4963 (frame #34). This means that, even tough frame #34 has more MV, they are describing less motion than those stored at frame #21, more precisely, they are 7.74 times smaller.

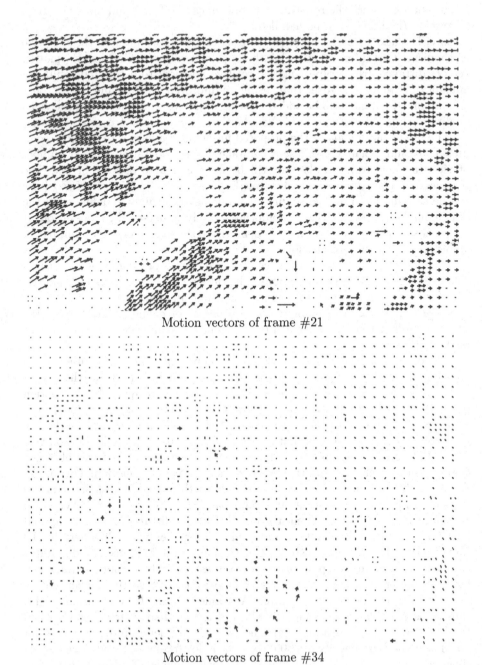

Motion vectors of frame #21

Motion vectors of frame #34

Fig. 2. Motion vector comparative

```
fl::InputLVar* Motion = new fl::InputLVar("MotionIntensity");
 Motion->addTerm(new fl::ShoulderTerm("LOW", 10000, 30000, true));
 Motion->addTerm(new fl::TriangularTerm("MEDIUM", 21000, 80000));
 Motion->addTerm(new fl::ShoulderTerm("HIGH", 60000, 130000, true));
 engine.addInputLVar(Motion);
```

Fig. 3. Motion intensity input set

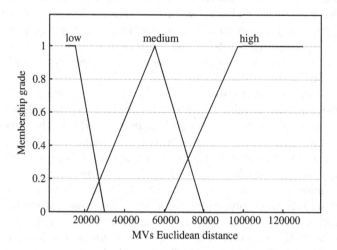

Fig. 4. Motion intensity membership function

```
fl::InputLVar* PLR = new fl::InputLVar("PacketLossRate");
 PLR->addTerm(new fl::TriangularTerm("LOW", 0, 15));
 PLR->addTerm(new fl::TriangularTerm("MEDIUM", 5, 30));
 PLR->addTerm(new fl::TriangularTerm("HIGH", 20, 100));
 engine.addInputLVar(PLR);
```

Fig. 5. Packet loss rate input set

With the distance described by all MV in all frames, the sets must be defined. To do that, the frames were clustered together according to the motion intensity. Based on the linkage distance between the clusters, the motion intensity was divided into three clusters, namely "small", "medium", and "high", as presented in Fig. 3.

After defining the sets, it is necessary to set up the membership functions. This definition is a complex and problem-dependent task. Because of that, it is preferable to use piecewise linear functions (formed by straight-line sections), because they are simple and more efficient with respect to computability and resource requirements. Figure 4 shows the graphical representation of our membership functions.

After delineating the motion intensity, the packet loss rate set must be defined. The aim of this activity is to quantify the packet loss rate against the video quality in terms of QoE. In other words, a loss rate of 10 % can be considered low in our approach, however, it might be unacceptable in other applications, such as a voice over IP call. To define this set, a number of network simulations with several packet loss rates as well as a broad collection of UAV video sequences were carried out, as shown in the Fig. 5. On average, the video quality was considered good when the network losses were between 0 % and 10 %. Between 5 % and 20 %, a tolerable video quality was perceived, but over 15 % the quality quickly decreased, soon becoming unacceptable. Because of that, three categories were defined, namely "low", "medium", and "high", as shown in Fig. 6.

Another stage is to delineate the redundancy set. The main goal of this set is to establish the output value which will be used to add the redundancy. Here again a combination of experiments and human knowledge in the field were used to specify what could be considered a "small", "medium", and "large" amount of redundancy. The values obtained and the graphical representations of the membership functions are displayed in Figs. 7 and 8, respectively.

After defining all the fuzzy sets, the IF-THEN structure must be created. This is a straightforward procedure, because if the transmitted video has low levels of motion activity (according to the motion vectors) and the packet loss rate is low as well, then the uavFEC will attribute also a low redundancy. The same procedure is valid for "medium" and "high" motion activities and packet loss rate as depicted in Fig. 9.

After defining the rules and sets, they need to be loaded in the Fuzzy Logic Controller (FLC). This activity has to be performed just once, during the system setup period (bootstrap). After the FLC definition, it will calculate the degree of membership of each input information, resulting in a precise amount of redundancy on-the-fly.

This is important because video transmission is delay-sensitive, meaning that if a frame is received after its decode deadline it cannot be displayed. Moreover, unlike neural networks or genetic algorithms, FLC does not need a period of online training or convergence, making it a proper tool for real-time control. Additionally, the calculations can be very simple, especially when triangular or trapezoidal membership functions are adopted [21], and even further reduce to a simple operation through fuzzy control surface.

4   Performance Evaluation and Results

The main goal of the uavFEC mechanism is to improve the perceived video quality without adding unnecessary network overhead, thus saving resources. The evaluation experiments were carried out by using the Network Simulator 3 (NS-3). The evaluation scenario is composed of up to four UAVs, equipped with a 4G LTE radio at 800 MHz. These UAVs can be operated in autonomous or nonautonomous mode. In a surveillance scenario, for example, it is possible to have

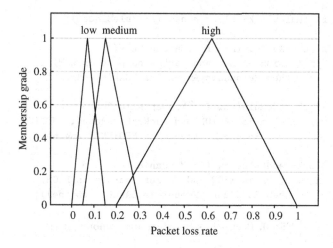

Fig. 6. Packet loss membership function

```
fl::OutputLVar* Redundancy = new fl::OutputLVar("RedundancyAmount");
  Redundancy->addTerm(new fl::ShoulderTerm("SMALL", 0.55, 0.70, true));
  Redundancy->addTerm(new fl::TriangularTerm("MEDIUM", 0.60, 0.80));
  Redundancy->addTerm(new fl::TriangularTerm("LARGE", 0.75, 1));
engine.addOutputLVar(Redundancy);
```

Fig. 7. Motion activity output set

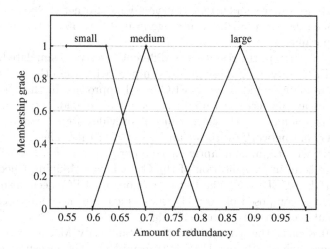

Fig. 8. Redundancy amount membership function

a human operating the UAV. This allows to have an instantly change of direction and speed during the pursuit of a suspect. Because of that, the mobility model was defined as random waypoint [22]. All UAVs are in line-of-sight and

```
fl::RuleBlock* block = new fl::RuleBlock();

block->addRule(new fl::MamdaniRule("
    if (Motion is LOW and PacketLossRate is LOW)
        then RedundancyAmount is SMALL", engine));

block->addRule(new fl::MamdaniRule("
    if (Motion is MEDIUM and PacketLossRate is MEDIUM)
        then RedundancyAmount is MEDIUM", engine));

block->addRule(new fl::MamdaniRule("
    if (Motion is HIGH and PacketLossRate is HIGH)
        then RedundancyAmount is LARGE", engine));
```

Fig. 9. Packet loss × redundancy amount rules

communicate directly with an ad-hoc connection to ground control station which was equipped with a portable base station and antenna. A set of twenty real UAV video sequences in high definition (720p), GoP length of 19:2, and H.264 codec were used. Due to the ad-hoc communication and the high definition videos, the flying range is limited to a radius of 900 m from the base station. A Frame-Copy error concealment method is active, this means that lost frames are replaced by the last good one received. The Packet Loss Rate (PLR) varies according to the movement of the UAVs, namely distance from the portable base station and velocity, and also due to concurrent transmissions of others UAVs. Because the aforementioned details, the PLR can range from 0 % to 45 %. Table 1 shows the simulation parameters.

In order to compare the results, five different cases were simulated. The first is without FEC, serving as baseline to compare with the others. The second case is a non-adaptive video-aware FEC-based approach. In this case, only I- and P-Frames are protected with equal amount of redundancy, which was set to 65 %. This amount was chosen because it provides a good tradeoff between video quality and network overhead under several PLRs. The next case is our previous work with a simple adaptive unequal error protection (ViewFEC) [20]. Another case is an implementation of the Cross-Layer Mapping Unequal Error Protection (CLM-UEP) [19]. The last case is our uavFEC mechanism. The set up simulation is composed of 20 real UAVs video sequences and 5 cases, each one was simulated 30 times with each video.

Figure 10 depicts the average Structural Similarity Metric (SSIM) for all video sequences when only one UAV is transmitting. The measurement of this metric is fairly simple, however, it is consistent with the human visual system, given good results [23]. In the SSIM, values closer to one indicate a better video quality. As expected, when the UAV is far away from the ground control station there is a decline in the video quality. In the baseline case, without FEC, a sharp decline in the video quality after 400 m is perceived. Conversely, the UAVs using a FEC-based mechanism are able to sustain a better video quality longer,

Table 1. Simulation parameters

Parameters	Value
Display size	1280×720
Display aspect ratio	16:9
Frame rate mode	Constant
Frame rate	29.970 fps
GoP	19:2
Codec	H.264
Container	MP4
Propagation model	FriisPropagationLossModel
UAV velocity	45–65 km/h (28–40 mph)
LTE Frequency band	800 MHz
LTE Mode	FDD
LTE Bandwidth	5 MHz
eNodeB Operating Power	22 dBm
Antenna Gain	16 dBi

and it is only noticeable after 500 m for case 2, and after 700 m for cases 3–5. Almost the same behaviour is shown in Fig. 11 which demonstrates the results for 2 UAVs transmitting simultaneously. One clear difference between these two scenarios is the increase in the standard deviation on the baseline case. This can be explained by the natural resiliency of some videos to packet loss due to different video characteristics. Video sequences with low motion intensity are more resilient to loss, and generally have better results in the QoE-aware assessment. On the other hand, videos with high motion intensity tend to have poor results.

As the number of video sequence flows begins to increase, the quality of the transmitted video starts to decrease sooner than before. Figures 12 and 13 depict this tendency. In the first two scenarios (with one and two UAVs), the uavFEC managed to keep the SSIM above 0.7 up to 700 m (other approaches only up to 600 m). However, with three and four UAVs, the uavFEC was able to maintain the SSIM over 0.7 only up to 600 m, after that, there is a sharp decline in the video quality in all of the assessed mechanisms. This can be attributed to a more congested network due to several transmissions together with the distance from the ground control station.

Figure 14 depicts the comparison of uavFEC and the related work (CLM-UEP) [19]. The graph shows the average percentage of QoE improvement against the amount of redundancy added by the mechanisms in all scenarios (from 1 to 4 UAVs). A positive percentage means that our mechanism had better QoE results than CLM-UEP. In all four scenarios, uavFEC presented a slight better video quality until 600 m, more precisely, on average between 0.59 % and 5.00 % better. The real advantage of uavFEC is noticeable after the 700 m, when it enhances

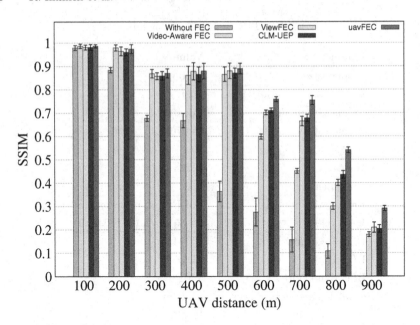

Fig. 10. SSIM QoE for all scenarios with one UAV

even further the video quality. The uavFEC was able to achieve improvements, on average, between 11.59 % and 28.52 % better than CLM-UEP. Taking this into consideration, it is clear that our mechanism performs better in higher distance, where the PLR is also higher. This gives uavFEC the capability to operate in wide coverage areas.

It is also shown by Fig. 14 the comparison of the amount of redundancy added by both, CLM-UEP and uavFEC. A negative percentage means that our mechanism adds less redundancy than CLM-UEP. In all four scenarios, uavFEC added less redundancy until 600 m, which was around 3.75 % and 15.12 % less on average, and still managed to transmit the videos with higher QoE. This means that the uavFEC was able to improve the video quality and at same time save resources. After 700 m, our mechanism begins to increase the redundancy. This happens because the uavFEC was developed to enhance the video quality over higher distances, which make the networks more susceptible to errors. Considering this, the mechanism will have to increase the protection of the most important video data, adding more overhead. For example, at 700 m our mechanism added on average 4.49 % more redundancy, and at 900 m added 10.19 %. Increasing the redundancy is an expected response of our mechanism to further improve the video quality, which can be confirmed through the QoE assessment in the same figure. In summary, the uavFEC provides a good tradeoff between video quality and network overhead.

A further analysis of Fig. 14 shows that up to 500 m both mechanisms had similar QoE results, with uavFEC having a modest higher video quality. The

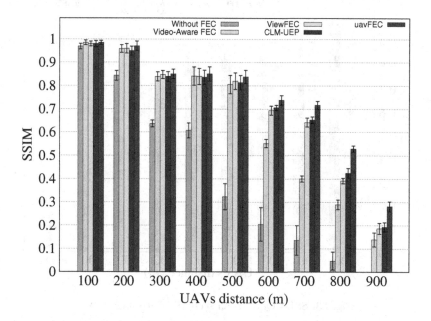

Fig. 11. SSIM QoE for all scenarios with two UAVs

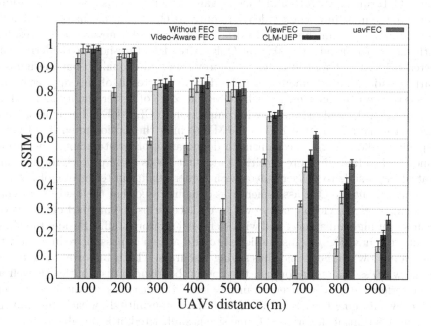

Fig. 12. SSIM QoE for all scenarios with three UAVs

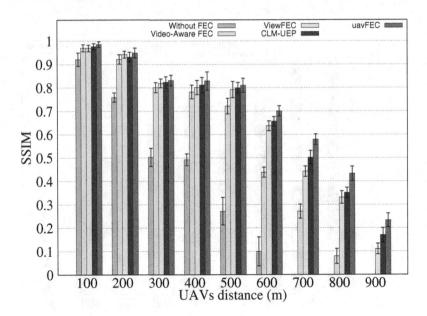

Fig. 13. SSIM QoE for all scenarios with four UAVs

major difference was the considerable smaller network overhead, this means that uavFEC, through its QoE- and Video-aware techniques, was able to add redundancy to the most important video data only. At 600 m, our mechanism still adds less redundancy than the related work, but it is already showing better results, with an improvement of 5.00 % on QoE. After this threshold, considering the increasing distance and in order to improve the video quality, our mechanism starts to add a larger amount of redundancy. The result of this approach, are videos transmitted on average with more than 28 % of better quality and adding no more than 11 % of redundancy in comparison to CLM-UEP. The main advantage of the uavFEC is that it uses the MV to infer the motion intensity of video sequences, allowing the mechanism to define an appropriate amount of redundancy and to find the more sensitive data that needs more protection. In doing that, it is possible to deliver videos with higher quality in terms of QoE.

Throughout the QoE assessment was demonstrated that the uavFEC mechanism enhances the video quality over several scenarios, having particularly good results over higher distances and with increased network traffic. Besides the video quality, the uavFEC was also designed to add as less as possible redundancy, to maintain a low overhead and thus saving resources. This is important due to the scarce wireless channel resources, the uneven bandwidth distribution as well as the interference by concurrent transmissions. The network overhead was computed by summing the size of all video frames transmitted by each mechanism. This means that, if the original frame size is subtracted, it is possible to find the specific amount of redundancy added only by the approaches. Two mechanisms assessed are non-adaptive, video-aware FEC and ViewFEC, and because of that

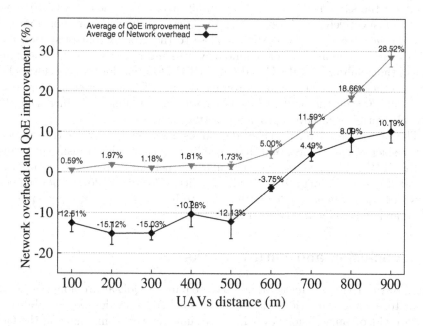

Fig. 14. QoE and Redundancy against UAV distance

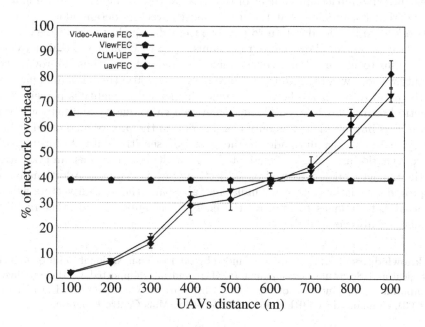

Fig. 15. Network overhead for all scenarios

they have the same network overhead in all distances, which was 65.10 % and 38.90 %, respectively, as shown in Fig. 15. These mechanisms are not appropriate because even when the UAVs are close to the ground control station they add a considerable amount of redundancy, wasting resources. The same figure depicts the results for uavFEC and CLM-UEP. Both mechanisms perform close to each other up to 600 m, but in average the uavFEC has lower network overhead. Over 600 m, the uavFEC starts to add more redundancy, increasing the network overhead, however, providing better video quality.

The uavFEC mechanism achieved good results making the video transmission more resilient to packet loss and thus, enabling a longer video transmission range for the UAVs. The results are particularly beneficial in higher distance with several UAVs, providing a better video quality of live video flows, allowing end-users such as, civilians and/or authorities, to have a high quality perception of videos and thus reducing reaction times.

5   Conclusion and Future Works

The growth of video delivery over UAVs requires a QoE-aware adaptive mechanism to enhance the video quality. The uavFEC provides the capability to improve video transmissions over high dynamic networks, maximizing the QoE without adding unnecessary network overhead. In doing that, it allows better use of the wireless resources for video delivery, especially over long-range transmissions. The impact and benefit of the uavFEC were demonstrated using a set of experiments, proving that the use of motion vectors details along with the network state is a good option to improve the video quality level in UAVs.

The experiments show that our mechanism (uavFEC) achieved a higher video quality up to 600 m adding considerable less redundancy, thus improving the quality without wasting resources. Conversely, over 700 m there is a mild increase in the network overhead, however, a much higher video quality is perceived. In practical terms, this is a good tradeoff between video quality and network overhead. This improvement was only possible due to the precise amount of redundancy that our mechanism adds to the most QoE sensitive data. As future work, more scenarios are going to be adopted, e.g., multi-hop networks, an evaluation of the impact of delay, as well as subjective QoE assessment. Additionally, an improved correlation between simulation values and the motion vectors will be addressed, techniques to improve the energy consumption and other mobility models are also going to be used.

Acknowledgment. This work was funded by the Brazilian National Counsel of Technological and Scientific Development (CNPq) and also supported by the Intelligent Computing in the Internet of Services (iCIS) project (CENTRO-07-ST24-FEDER-002003), co-financed by QREN, in the scope of the Mais Centro Program.

References

1. Kumar, R., Sawhney, H., Samarasekera, S., Hsu, S., Tao, H., Guo, Y., Hanna, K., Pope, A., Wildes, R., Hirvonen, D., et al.: Aerial video surveillance and exploitation. Proc. IEEE **89**(10), 1518–1539 (2001)
2. Puri, A.: A survey of unmanned aerial vehicles (UAV) for traffic surveillance. Department of Computer Science and Engineering, University of South Florida (2005)
3. Bekmezci, İ., Sahingoz, O.K., Temel, Ş.: Flying ad-hoc networks (FANETs): a survey. Ad Hoc Netw. **11**(3), 1254–1270 (2013)
4. Bernard, M., Kondak, K., Maza, I., Ollero, A.: Autonomous transportation and deployment with aerial robots for search and rescue missions. J. Field Robot. **28**(6), 914–931 (2011)
5. Frew, E., Brown, T.: Networking issues for small unmanned aircraft systems. J. Intell. Rob. Syst. **54**(1–3), 21–37 (2009). http://dx.doi.org/10.1007/s10846-008-9253-2
6. Lindeberg, M., Kristiansen, S., Plagemann, T., Goebel, V.: Challenges and techniques for video streaming over mobile ad hoc networks. Multimedia Syst. **17**, 51–82 (2011)
7. Liu, T., Liao, W.: Interference-aware QoS routing for multi-rate multi-radio multi-channel IEEE 802.11 wireless mesh networks. IEEE Trans. Wireless Commun. **8**(1), 166–175 (2009)
8. Piamrat, K., Viho, C., Bonnin, J.-M., Ksentini, A.: Quality of experience measurements for video streaming over wireless networks. In: Third International Conference on Information Technology: New Generations, pp. 1184–1189 (2009)
9. Yuan, Y., Cockburn, B., Sikora, T., Mandal, M.: A GoP based FEC technique for packet based video streaming. In: Proceedings of the 10th WSEAS International Conference on Communications, ICCOM'06, pp. 187–192 (2006)
10. Nafaa, A., Taleb, T., Murphy, L.: Forward error correction strategies for media streaming over wireless networks. IEEE Commun. Mag. **46**(1), 72–79 (2008)
11. Lee, J.-W., Chen, C.-L., Horng, M.-F., Kuo, Y.-H.: An efficient adaptive FEC algorithm for short-term quality control in wireless networks. In: Advanced Communication Technology (ICACT), pp. 1124–1129, February 2011
12. Fang, H., Jiang, J., Feng, Y.: A fuzzy logic approach for detection of video shot boundaries. Pattern Recognit. **39**(11), 2092–2100 (2006). http://www.sciencedirect.com/science/article/pii/S0031320306002093
13. Fleury, M., Jammeh, E., Razavi, R., Ghanbari, M.: Resource-aware fuzzy logic control of video streaming over IP and wireless networks. In: Hassanien, A.-E., Abawajy, J.H., Abraham, A., Hagras, H. (eds.) Pervasive Computing. Computer Communications and Networks, pp. 47–75. Springer, London (2010)
14. Fauzi, F., Yang, D.: Fuzzy logic for bandwidth allocator applies on IP multimedia traffic. In: International Conference of Information and Communication Technology (ICoICT), pp. 416–421 (2013)
15. Pitas, C., Charilas, D., Panagopoulos, A., Constantinou, P.: Adaptive neuro-fuzzy inference models for speech and video quality prediction in real-world mobile communication networks. IEEE Wirel. Commun. **20**(3), 80–88 (2013)
16. Han, L., Park, S., Kang, S.-S., In, H.P.: An adaptive FEC mechanism using cross-layer approach to enhance quality of video transmission over 802.11 WLANs. In: TIIS, pp. 341–357 (2010)

17. Hassan, M., Landolsi, T.: A retransmission-based scheme for video streaming over wireless channels. Wirel. Commun. Mob. Comput. **10**, 511–521 (2010)
18. Tsai, M.-F., Chilamkurti, N.K., Zeadally, S., Vinel, A.: Concurrent multipath transmission combining forward error correction and path interleaving for video streaming. Comput. Commun. **34**, 1125–1136 (2011)
19. Lin, C.-H., Wang, Y.-C., Shieh, C.-K., Hwang, W.-S.: An unequal error protection mechanism for video streaming over IEEE 802.11e WLANs. Comput. Netw. **56**(11), 2590–2599 (2012)
20. Immich, R., Cerqueira, E., Curado, M.: Cross-layer FEC-based mechanism for packet loss resilient video transmission. In: Biersack, E., Callegari, C., Matijasevic, M. (eds.) Data Traffic Monitoring and Analysis. LNCS, vol. 7754, pp. 320–336. Springer, Heidelberg (2013)
21. Pedrycz, W.: Why triangular membership functions? Fuzzy Sets Syst. **64**(1), 21–30 (1994). http://www.sciencedirect.com/science/article/pii/0165011494900035
22. Bouachir, O., Garcia, F., Larrieu, N., Gayraud, T.: Ad hoc network QoS architecture for cooperative unmanned aerial vehicles (UAVs). In: Wireless Days, pp. 1–4. IEEE (2013)
23. Wang, Z., Bovik, A.C., Sheikh, H.R., Simoncelli, E.P.: Image quality assessment: from error visibility to structural similarity. IEEE Trans. Image Process. **13**(4), 600–612 (2004)

M2M Aspects of WiNeMO

Group Communication in Machine-to-Machine Environments

André Riker[✉], Marilia Curado, and Edmundo Monteiro

Centre for Informatics and Systems of the University of Coimbra,
Coimbra, Portugal
{ariker,marilia,edmundo}@dei.uc.pt

Abstract. M2M systems bring new horizons to the current concept of smart environments, since M2M enables a new set of services and applications. One of the main M2M features is the large number of resource-constrained devices that usually perform collective communication. This characteristic requires the design of network solutions that support the Data Aggregation (DA) of groups of Low Duty Cycling (LDC) devices. If LDC and DA are not designed jointly, the intermittent periods caused by Low Duty Cycling make the execution of Data Aggregation impracticable or with low performance. To address this problem, this book chapter describes the Group Communication Architecture for M2M Environments (GoCAME). This architecture enables the joint execution of DA and LDC, taking into account two-way latency tolerance, and multiple data-types. GoCAME also assures the concurrent execution of data requests, managing groups of nodes to provide the best strategy to reply to each data request.

Keywords: Group communication · Machine-to-Machine · M2M · Low Duty Cycling · Data aggregation · Concurrent data request

1 Introduction

The current computing environments composed of small devices and low-cost communication technologies have driven to the concept of Machine-to-Machine (M2M). M2M can be defined as the technology that is able to provide remote control for a large number of devices with little or no human intervention [1]. Although there are no restrictions in terms of communication and types of devices, most recent M2M scenarios involve wireless, low power and low-cost devices [2]. In addition, most of these devices are equipped with sensors or actuators, or with both.

The numerous applications of M2M will greatly benefit society and industry, since deploying multiple sensors in a monitoring system is no longer cost prohibitive. In smart metering scenarios, applications aim to monitor and control equipment involved in the production and distribution of utilities (e.g. energy, heat, gas and water) [3]. In the M2M automotive scenario, vehicles will be able

© Springer International Publishing Switzerland 2014
I. Ganchev et al. (Eds.): Wireless Networking for Moving Objects, LNCS 8611, pp. 219–238, 2014.
DOI: 10.1007/978-3-319-10834-6_12

to make contact with other vehicles and/or external entities, by informing their geographic location, speed and mechanical reports. Healthcare applications will enable data to be obtained about the condition of the body (e.g. blood pressure, body temperature, heart rate, weight and body location) via body sensors. In the city monitoring scenario, many private and public services are integrated to enable the supply of new resources, manage current services (e.g. public transport information and traffic control) and implement services (e.g. police operations in strategic locations). Finally, in the track of objects scenarios, applications provide a comprehensive view of the state of assets.

M2M applications and scenarios result in new types of traffic. Currently, the usual Internet traffic is characterized by human accessing information and Human-to-Human (H2H) communications. The H2H Internet services, such as, web-browsing, file downloading and web-mail, are characterized by large blocks of data. On the other hand, the M2M traffic is characterized by having a wide variation of traffic characteristics [4]. It is important to notice that the M2M communication involves two-way (forward and backward) communication, and each direction has distinct latency requirements to be satisfied. In addition, each M2M application communicates more than a single data-type.

The M2M data traffic is delivered to many entities, called Data-Consumer Entities (DCE). The DCE use a service platform (middleware) to request data from M2M devices. The middleware layer promotes the necessary interoperability between many stakeholders, and reduces the costs with software development. With the aid of the middleware service layer, several DCE can request data from the M2M devices, concurrently. Each data request has a group formation criteria (e.g. geographic location, data-type and list of devices ID). Then, the responses for the data requests are produced by the groups of M2M devices that satisfy the criteria.

Maximize the network lifetime is one of the biggest challenges of M2M, since most M2M devices have constrained energy resources. Hence, the long-term operation of M2M systems can only be assured by having mechanisms able to maximize the network lifetime. To achieve this, the nodes must run Low Duty Cycling (LDC) mechanisms, turning off (sleep) the radio transceiver periodically [5], and Data Aggregation (DA) mechanisms, extracting the data redundancies along the route through summary functions [6]. Both, DA and LDC are mechanisms that are necessary to reduce the energy consumption of M2M communication.

However, most of the LDC solutions are designed to perform data gathering without DA, since due to the intermittent periods of connectivity caused by LDC, it is a complex task to execute DA and LDC mechanisms concurrently. Besides, M2M platform brings new challenges to the M2M communication, as for example, to support multiple and concurrent data requests generated by the DCE. Other important requirements to be fulfilled by DA and LDC solutions are multiple data types and two-way communication latency. Therefore, the traditional solutions of DA and LDC fail to fulfill these requirements, since most of the solutions of DA and LDC are not jointly designed, addressing the problem independently and not assuring the integration of the parts. Only a few studies in the literature consider the factors related to the simultaneous execution of LDC and DA mechanisms. Those that lead to the integration of both mechanisms are not designed for M2M communication, since they do not take into account the existence of multiples data-types, neither promote communication satisfying two-way communication, nor support concurrent data requests.

This chapter describes the suitable solutions to support group communication in M2M environments, especially for applications requiring the periodic communication of energy-constrained and wireless devices. To address the challenges of this context, this work proposes an Group Communication Architecture for M2M Environments (GoCAME), which enables the joint operation of DA and LDC in M2M environments. The remainder of this chapter is structured as follows. The M2M network architecture is shown in Sect. 2. Section 3 describes the state of the art and Sect. 4 introduces GoCAME. The comparison with state of art solutions is presented in Sect. 5 and the conclusion is presented in Sect. 6.

2   M2M Network Architecture

The combination of wired and wireless network technologies may result in several variants of network architectures able to provide communication for the M2M systems. By integrating network technologies, some solutions ([7] and [8]) have shown the M2M network architecture as a Heterogeneous Hierarchical Architecture (HHA).

As can be observed in Fig. 1, the lower layer is the M2M Capillary Network, which is formed of M2M Devices and M2M Gateways. These devices can be connected on Bluetooth [9] and Zigbee [10], which run on the 2.4 GHz band. In addition, the M2M capillary Network can also be connected via WiMedia [11] technology, which runs on the Ultra-Wideband.

The M2M Devices are devices designed to maintain low costs per unit, allowing the deployment of large number of units. In addition, the hardware capabilities of the M2M Devices are restricted in terms of Central Unit Processing (CPU), battery autonomy and memory. This limited hardware capacity imposes severe restrictions on the functionalities carried out by M2M Devices. In general, they send short data reports and display messages or perform some simple operation (e.g. regulation or switches off/on). In contrast with the M2M Devices, most of the M2M Gateways generally have a constant energy supply and robust hardware.

The M2M Access Network Layer is the communication system that provides Internet connection (Core Networks) to the M2M Gateways. Examples of M2M Access Network technologies are: Ethernet, Wi-Fi [12], Asymmetric Digital Subscriber Line (ADSL), Long Term Evolution (LTE) and Worldwide Interoperability for Microwave Access (WiMAX).

By means of M2M Gateways, the HHA reduces the number of machines that are directly connected, as well as the traffic load and the number of subscribers over the Access Network Layer. The M2M Gateway nodes must forward the data from the M2M Devices to the Access Network Layer and vice-versa, by

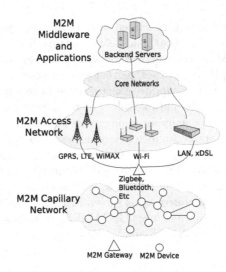

Fig. 1. Network Architecture of M2M Communication.

supporting connections between both layers [2]. For instance, when an external node needs to contact an M2M Device that is attached to a M2M Gateway, this external node must first contact the appropriate M2M Gateway, and then, the M2M Gateway is able to establish a connection with the particular M2M Device. This means that the M2M Gateway can act as a proxy, by providing a service of remote access [2].

The M2M Middleware and Application layers are at the top of the HHA. These layers are the destination of the information collected by the nodes. The M2M Middleware and Application Layer are usually hosted in the Backend Servers and equipped with powerful hardware resources that are able to process a large number of transactions [13]. The M2M communication depends on several interfaces between various parties, stakeholders, business logic networking and the roles of M2M partners [14]. Most of these factors are open and have still not been completely defined. Thus, the HHA is a tentative design for an appropriate M2M Architecture, since it is susceptible to alterations.

After reviewing the main concepts of the M2M architecture, the next section studies the solutions that extend the network lifetime of M2M devices, which communicate in group.

3   State-of-the-Art

Two prominent approaches that address the maximization of network lifetime of groups are Data Aggregation and Low Duty Cycling. While DA mechanisms are data centric approaches, LDC mechanisms are designed to provide the appropriated synchronization between senders and receivers. More details about these approaches are given below.

3.1 Data Aggregation

Data Aggregation is the approach that summarizes a set of data readings, by exploiting the spatio-temporal correlations to reduce the amount of data. Certainly, high levels of correlation are present if there is a large number of nodes sensing the same particular environment and/or phenomenon. During the process of data gathering, the more quickly the redundancies are eliminated, the lower will be the amount of resources wasted on redundancies. Hence, DA must be executed along the path, inspecting the packets and performing processing functions (also called aggregation functions).

The application interests are the key to determine the behavior of the DA mechanism. According to the application interests, the DA mechanisms should adapt the aggregation functions by applying a specific aggregation function or using multiple aggregation functions simultaneously. Some aggregation functions are:

- **Elimination of Duplication:** Due to some factors (e.g. proximity, static sensor target behavior), a set of devices can produce equal data readings. Therefore, eliminating duplicated data readings is a useful aggregation function for applications that are concerned with sensing targets with static characteristics or in scenarios with a high density of sensors [15]. On both occasions, the occurrence of duplicated data readings is more likely to occur.
- **Merger:** The header suppression aggregation function avoids header repetition, by combining multiple payloads into a single message. It is a simple means of reducing the amount of data, since it does not change the data readings. It can be used in application scenarios requiring a high degree of accuracy. This aggregation function can be applied to a wide range of application domains and in a large set of network technologies [16]. Header suppression provides great benefits to M2M applications that have small message payload, since they spend a great deal of resources on header transmission.
- **Statistical:** The use of statistical aggregation functions (e.g. Count, Minimum, Maximum, Sum and Average) is very common for applications. This is because some applications are satisfied with data reporting computed by statistical operations instead of data reporting composed of every individual sensor reading. This aggregation function has a great potential to reduce the amount of data while showing the tendency of the overall data readings [17].

Besides the aggregation function, the second important aspect of the DA is the aggregation structure, which determines the aggregation points along the path [18]. The traditional routing approaches forward data along the shortest path (with respect to some specified metric). However, when there is a need to maximize the performance of the aggregation function and minimize energy expenditure, information must be routed on the basis of their content to improve the aggregation performance [6].

The third important aspect of DA is the aggregation timeout, which determines how long each aggregation point should delay the communication to receive more neighboring data. The aggregation timeout is generally solved by scheduler approaches that compute the timings of communication of each node in the network.

Based on Fasolo et al. [6] and Rajagopalan and Varshney [19], a taxonomy of Data Aggregation was conceived (depicted in Fig. 2). From a general standpoint, DA approaches can be classified as Scheduler and Structure proposals. The Scheduler proposals are the approaches that aim to optimize transmission times and the aggregation timeout. In contrast, the Structure proposals are the approaches that compute the paths to optimize the DA performance.

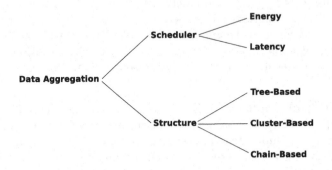

Fig. 2. Taxonomy of DA approaches (adapted from [6] and [19]).

Structure. The Structure proposals can be divided into Cluster-Based, Chain-Based and Tree-Based. It should be noted that in the context of these approaches, the final destination of the aggregated data is the sink node. The Cluster-Based approach divides the nodes into clusters and selects a node to be the cluster head. The cluster head is responsible for collecting the data from the cluster members and executing the aggregation function.

The Low-Energy Adaptive Clustering Hierarchy (LEACH) [20] proposal is one of the most popular Cluster-Based proposals. LEACH selects a new cluster head periodically, and assumes that every node is capable of being a cluster head. When a cluster head is elected, it broadcasts a message to all the other nodes. All the cluster members that receive multiple advertisements must select a cluster head. This selection is based on the signal strength and LEACH assumes that the cluster heads are able to transmit directly to the sink node.

Another Cluster-Based proposal is Hybrid Energy-Efficient Distributed clustering approach (HEED) [21], which selects the cluster heads based on the residual energy combined with a parameter that measures the node proximity with its neighbors.

The Clustered Diffusion with Dynamic Data Aggregation (CLUDDA) [22] solution is based on interest messages, which are query messages created by the sink node. In CLUDDA the aggregation points are dynamically selected, depending on the query.

Although Cluster-based and Tree-Based solutions are hierarchical approaches, they have differences. Generally, in Cluster-Based, the cluster head is the main aggregation point, creating a 3-depth aggregation structure (non-cluster, cluster heads and sink). In Tree-Based solutions, there are several aggregation points, creating an N-depth aggregation structure.

Tiny AGgregation (TAG) [15] is a Tree-Based solution that follows the tree construction phase. This uses queries to inform the type of aggregation function, as well as the aggregation timeout of each aggregation point. After the query dissemination, TAG assumes that all nodes have the relevant information to transmit periodically. The DA timeout of each aggregation point is computed by dividing the Data Reporting period by the maximum depth of the tree.

The Chain-Based approaches compute the spanning tree in a different way from the Tree-Based approaches. Chain-Based approaches arrange the nodes in a linear chain, creating a 1-breadth aggregation structure. PEGASIS [23] is one of the most popular examples of a Chain-Based approach. In carrying out chain construction, PEGASIS uses the greedy algorithm, which initiates the chain construction by means of the farthest node from the sink and updates the structure so that it includes the closest neighbor as a successor on the chain. An alternative to the greedy algorithm is a centralized solution, in which the sink node computes the chain.

Scheduler. Another class of Data Aggregation solution, called Scheduler, addresses the latency problem caused by the execution of Data Aggregation. In DA, there is a tradeoff involving energy and latency. This tradeoff is related to the fact that as more time the aggregation point waits, more it aggregates data and improves the throughput efficiency, reducing the energy consumption. However, when the aggregation point holds data before forwarding, it adds latency to the end-to-end communication.

The objective of Scheduler solutions is to find for a particular DA structure a scheduler that minimizes the latency and the energy consumption. So, the Scheduler solutions coordinate the activities of the nodes along the time to achieve the best balancing strategy of latency and energy. The DA Scheduler solutions can be designed as either centralized or distributed. The centralized solutions have the problem of low performance in the case of the network dynamics (e.g. node mobility, failure and topology changes).

Huang et al. [24] propose a scheduling algorithm for DA strucutures that has the latency bound of $23R + \Delta - 18$, where Δ is the maximum node degree and R is the network radius. However, this solution is not collision-free, which adds latency and energy consumption. Chen et al. [25] proposes a scheduling solution that is collision-free, but has a larger latency bound $(\Delta - 1)R$. In addition, both approaches are centralized solutions, which require the sink node to compute the scheduler. The scheduler solution proposed by Yu et al. [26] is computed in a distributed fashion, and has a latency bound of $24D + 6\Delta + 16$, where D is the network diameter and Δ is the maximum node degree.

The solution proposed by Joo et al. [27] assumes the existence of an aggregation tree and proposes a centralized scheduler. In contrast, Xu et al. [28] propose a distributed solution for constructing the aggregation tree and finding an aggregation scheduler. Ghosh et al. [29] explore multi-channels to improve the latency of data collection.

3.2 Low Duty Cycling

Low Duty Cycling improves the network lifetime by maintaining the devices as long as possible with the radio transceivers turned off. This approach aims to switch off the radio (sleep mode) as soon as there is no data to send/receive, and to switch it on as soon as news packets need to be transmitted or received (active mode). The change of the device mode is, usually, referred as Duty-Cycling, which can be defined as the fraction of time that devices are active during their lifetime [5].

As an example, the LDC mechanisms can improve the network lifetime from 40 to 65 months, which means they are granted two additional years of lifetime [30]. According to the data sheet of Chipcon CC1100 radio [31], a node consumes on average $15\,\mu A$ to sniff the channel once every second, while the same node consumes $15\,mA$ for the reception or transmission of packets at data rates of $250\,Kbps$. The length of the sniffing period is normally in the order of hundreds of μs to ms.

The simplest case of an LDC operation is when it is assumed that every LDC device has at least one always-on neighbor. In these scenarios, the LDC operation is simple because in any moment the LDC device can turn on its radio and establish communication with the always-on neighbor. However, LDC is more complex in multi-hop networks, since it has to coordinate the time when the nodes are active, by allowing the neighbor devices to be active at the same time, allowing the nodes to communicate data. Therefore, independently of the network topology, the LDC solution has to maintain the appropriate path connectivity between the nodes.

Figure 3 shows the taxonomy of LDC approaches (adapted from [32]). The Low Duty Cycling can be classified as Topology Control, Sleep protocols and MAC protocols with Low Duty Cycling.

Topology Control Solutions. Topology Control solutions use topology information to dynamically determine the minimum number of active nodes. By drawing on the information used by these solutions, it is possible to further divide the topology control solutions in Location-Driven and Connectivity-Driven approaches, which use the node's position and connectivity, respectively.

The main Location-Driven proposal is Geographic Adaptive Fidelity (GAF) [33]. In GAF, the network is divided into small virtual grids. This division must satisfy the following condition: there must be a link that connects all the nodes from the adjacent virtual grids. In each virtual grid, just one node needs to be active at a time. However, the network must have a high density of nodes to

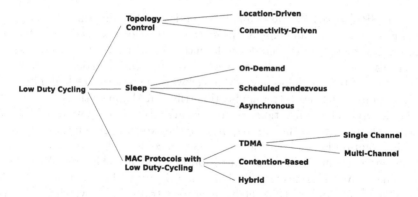

Fig. 3. Taxonomy of LDC approaches (adapted from [32]).

satisfy this condition, otherwise the nodes will not sleep. Feng et al. [34] improve the GAF, by taking into account the node mobility and the transmission range.

The main Connectivity-Driven proposals are Span [35] and Adaptive Self-Configuring sEnsor Networks Topologies (ASCENT [36]). Span selects coordinators to be always-on and perform multi-hop communication. The other nodes stay in sleeping mode and periodically check the coordinator. Span adopts the following rule to select the coordinator: if there is no connectivity path between two non-coordinator neighbors, one of these neighbors must become a coordinator. Periodically, the coordinators check if it can stop being a coordinator, which occurs if there is a connectivity path with each pair of its neighbors.

The ASCENT solution proposes the existence of passive and active nodes. The passive nodes do not forward packets or exchange routing control information. The main task of passive nodes is to monitor the network status. On the other hand, the active nodes forward data and routing information. Initially, only some of the nodes in the network are active. When the data loss reaches an unacceptable level, the active nodes broadcast a 'help' message, requesting the passive nodes to become active nodes. This process continues until the data loss reaches an acceptable level.

Sleep Solutions. Sleep protocols are solutions implemented on top of the MAC protocol (e.g. at the network or application layer). These solutions can be divided into the following: On-Demand, Scheduled Rendezvous and Asynchronous approaches [37]. On-Demand solutions (e.g. STEM [38] and [39]) use two radios, the low-energy radio remains turned on and it is used to send signaling, waking up the nodes when a device wants to communicate with other. The data transmission is performed via a high-rate radio, which has higher power consumption.

The Scheduled Rendezvous solution schedules a time slot for a sub-group of nodes to wake up at the same time. Each sub-group wakes up and remains in active mode during a time interval. The simplest solution is the Fully Synchronized

Pattern (FSP) [40], which wakes up all the nodes at the same time. In the evolution of FSP, Keshavarzian et al. [30] propose the creation of a tree and determine an active time for each node that depends on the position in the tree. Keshavarzian et al. shows LDC solutions that optimize the communication in only one-way (forward direction) have high latency in the backward direction. The high latency of these solutions is impractical for applications (like M2M applications) that require communication in both directions. So, Keshavarzian et al. compute the active and sleep periods to minimize the time required for the two-way communications. However, this solution is not free from collisions, since nodes in the same tree level wake up and transmit at the same time. Contrasting with [30], Green Wave Sleep Scheduling (GWSS) [41] avoids collisions and it is inspired by coordinated traffic lights. GWSS provides a LDC scheduler for light traffic loads, which is free from collisions and has optimum latency. However, this solution is not designed for two-way communication.

Asynchronous approaches compute the wake up times of each node, and ensure that neighbors always have overlapped active intervals within a certain number of cycles. This approach was introduced by Tseng et al. [42] for IEEE 802.11 single-hop Ad Hoc Networks, but Stinson [43] improves this solution for multi-hop communication. Furthermore, the solution given by Kim et al. [44] proposes an asynchronous LDC mechanism that maintains multiple candidate next-hop nodes and selects the one which first wakes up.

MAC Protocols with Low Duty Cycling. Some LDC solutions have been implemented coupled with MAC and PHY protocols. These solutions can be divided into Time Division Multiple Access (TDMA)-Based and Contention-Based. The TDMA-Based solutions assign time slots to each node, to define when the nodes should wake up. As each node transmits in a particular time slot, it solves the problem of collisions. TRAMA [45] is one of the most relevant TDMA proposals. TRAMA executes a distributed election algorithm periodically to select one transmitter within each two-hop neighbor. During a pre-defined time interval the nodes change information in order to know the network topology [46].

Another TDMA-based solution is given by Fu et al. [47]. This is designed to support M2M data traffic composed of multiple-data types. This feature is important for the LDC design because each data-type has different latency and timings requirements, so the scheduler should be aware about these requirements to coordinate the transmissions appropriately. However, the TDMA sleep scheduling proposed is designed for single-hop communication.

The drawbacks of TDMA-based solutions include its high synchronization and low performance in low traffic and large-scale conditions. Thus the proposed TDMA-based solution given by Ma et al. [48] is designed to improve the performance of the TDMA scheduler in case there is a low data-rate. In addition, it minimizes the state transitions, collisions and period of idle listening.

All the TDMA-based solutions presented so far use single-channel. Multi-Channel TDMA approaches explore the capability of nodes to tune the transceiver in multiple channels. Using different channels, two devices can transmit data in nearby areas at the same time [49]. On this basis, some approaches explore Multi-Channels capability to improve the LDC. Y-MAC [50] is proposed to schedule the times the transmissions will occur and assigns a channel for each transmission. Although Y-MAC is a TDMA protocol, there is a broadcast and unicast period. Every node wakes up in the broadcast period, when the occupied time slots are informed to the nodes. Y-MAC only assigns time slots to the receiver. If multiple senders want to transmit data to the same receiver, they will content for the medium. The loser contender changes its channel and waits for the receiver notification.

The Contention-Based MAC solutions incorporate a random element that enables the nodes to wake up at the packet arrival times or in accordance with random setting timers. The Contention-Based solutions operate in a fully distributed manner, which requires a contention algorithm to avoid collisions [51]. Sensor-MAC (S-MAC) is one of the most important MAC protocols designed for LDC operation. The S-MAC operation allows the nodes to choose their own LDC schedule based on the schedule information broadcasted by their neighbors. The device may execute a single or several LDC schedules, and the LDC schedules may be created either by the device itself or by a neighbor device. The LDC schedules are broadcasted, via SYNC messages, during a synchronization period. The information provided by the SYNC messages enables the devices to maintain a schedule table, which contains the LDC schedule of every known neighbor. If a node listens to the wireless medium and does not hear a LDC schedule from another neighbor, it creates its own LDC schedule, and announces it using the SYNC message. In case the node listens to a new neighbor schedule, the node follows the new schedule.

The S-MAC defines the basis for many other Contention-Based MAC protocols, such as T-MAC [52] and B-MAC [53]. S-MAC, T-MAC and B-MAC protocols use RTS (Ready-to-Send) and CTS (Clear-to-Send) messages to avoid collisions. The RTS message is used to alert a node that there is a sender intending to transmit data. If the receiver node receives the RTS message without collision, it responds the RTS with a CTS message. Other nodes that overhear the RTS/CTS messages should know that the period the wireless medium will be used, so they should not try to use it until the transmission is finished. Thus, the RTS/CTS messages reduce the number of collisions and avoid long periods of traffic overhearing.

In general Contention-Based MAC protocols are robust, scalable and adapting more easily to traffic conditions than the TDMA approaches. However, owing to the collisions and contention, the TDMA solutions have lower energy consumption than the Contention-Based approaches [32].

Finally, the hybrid approaches have a dual behavior: when the level of contention is low, they adopt a Contention-Based approach, and when the level of contention is high, they adopt a TDMA approach. An example of a hybrid solution is Z-MAC [54].

4 Group Communication Architecture for M2M Environments (GoCAME)

GoCAME is an M2M architecture designed to enable low power group communication and to allow multiples Data-Consumer Entities (DCE) execute different and concurrent actions (e.g. actuations and data requests) on groups of M2M devices. To achieve low power group communication, GoCAME uses Data Aggregation and Low Duty Cycling jointly. Both mechanisms prolong network lifetime, since DA reduces the necessary period of transmission and reception of data (applying aggregation functions), and LDC reduces the idle listening, collisions and state changes.

4.1 Layers, Messages and Tasks

GoCAME is composed by three layers, named M2M applications (M2M App), M2M middleware (M2M Midd) and M2M Capillary networks (M2M CN). Each of these layers provides services for the layer above. On the top of the architecture, Data-Consumer Entities interact with the M2M App layer, producing data requests (containing interests and criteria) and commands. The M2M Midd layer processes the data requests finding the group of nodes to response the data request or to execute the commands. Finally, in the M2M CN, the joint DA and LDC mechanism finds the best DA and LDC settings to communicate the data reporting of existing groups. In this context, the best setting means satisfy the application and maximize the network lifetime.

Figure 4 shows GoCAME operation. The interaction messages and the tasks are depicted by Labels 1, 3, 7 and 9, and 2, 4, 5 and 8, respectively. These interactions and tasks were conceived in accordance to the ETSI standards [55]. A detailed description about each label presented in Fig. 4 is given below:

1. **Data Request Messages:** The M2M applications send data requests or actuation commands to the middleware. Listing 1 presents an example of a Data Request, which defines a frequency of communication, a delay tolerance, an aggregation function and a Location-based criteria for group formation. Recall that other aggregation functions (e.g. Min, Count and Avg) and group formation criteria (e.g. set of nodes ID, nodes with particular types of sensors or actuators, level of energy) can be used.
2. **Middleware Group Manager Component (MGMC):** The middleware receives the data requests and selects a group of devices that should provide data reporting or execute the commands. This middleware component supports the creation and deletion of groups, controlling to which group(s) a particular M2M device belongs and providing an identification to each group. The MGMC is an internal middleware component defined in ETSI standards as *Network Reachability, Addressing and Repository.* The MGMC maintains an repository with information about every node in the M2M CN, including the node ID, types of data, types of power resource, the geographic position (if available), hardware features, mobility and the history of two-way latency.

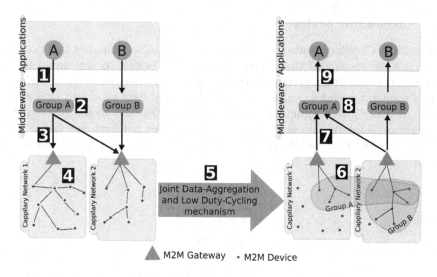

Fig. 4. Joint DA and LDC mechanism for M2M communication.

To create, edit or delete an group on the M2M Capillary Networks, the MGMC uses the information stored in this repository, which is refreshed periodically;

3. **Group Control Messages:** The middleware contacts the M2M Gateways which have any nodes in their domain belonging in the selected group;
4. **Messages Delivery:** The M2M gateways inform the devices about the data requests or commands;
5. **Joint Data Aggregation and Low Duty Cycling Mechanism:** To reply to the data requests, the joint DA and LDC mechanism updates the aggregation structure, the aggregation function and the wake up scheduling;
6. **Aggregated Data from M2M groups:** M2M devices provide the in-network aggregation of each group;
7. **Group Data Reporting:** The M2M Gateways send the aggregated data reporting to the middleware;
8. **Aggregation of Group Data Reporting:** The middleware aggregates the data reporting from different capillary networks;
9. **Data Reply:** The M2M applications receive the relevant data reporting.

Listing 1. Data Request Message Example

```
 1 <DataRequest>
 2         <id> A </id>
 3         <Frequency> 1 </Frequency>
 4         <DelayTolerance> 0.5 </DelayTolerance>
 5         <AggFunction> Max </AggFunction>
 6         <GroupCriteria>
 7             <LocationLat> 40.20 </LocationLat>
 8             <LocationLon> -8.42 </LocationLon>
 9             <Range> 100 </Range>
10         </GroupCriteria>
11 </DataRequest>
```

4.2   Cooperator Nodes

In the M2M Capillary Networks, nodes can belong to a group, but it is possible (during some moments) that some nodes do not belong to any group (Non-Members). In addition to this, both (members and non-members nodes) can act as cooperator nodes, which are nodes that relay data produced by another node. As every group communicates their aggregated data to the gateway, the cooperator nodes are necessary in case a group does not have any inside path to the gateway. To illustrate this idea, Fig. 5 shows the cooperator nodes of a group j.

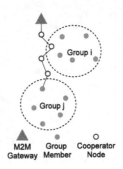

Fig. 5. Cooperator nodes.

This collaboration represents additional energy consumption for the cooperator nodes, but in scenarios with multiple gateways the cooperator can alternate, achieving fair cooperation.

4.3   Creation and Maintenance of Groups

Figure 6 shows the sequence diagram of creation of new groups. As can be observed, the applications send data requests to the MGMC, specifying the data request parameters, such as: period of data reporting (e.g. 15 s), function (e.g. max, min, count and average), delay tolerance (e.g. 1.5 and 2 s) and criteria of group formation. The MGMC selects the group of nodes based on the data request parameters and knowing the available information about the nodes (e.g. type of data, topology and mobility). After the group is computed and stored, the MGMC sends a *CreateScheduling* message to the M2M gateways of the new group.

After the reception of the *CreateScheduling* message, the joint mechanism computes the group aggregation structure, finding the set of nodes (called aggregation points) that will execute data aggregation. In addition, the joint mechanism selects, if necessary, the set of coorperator nodes. Knowing the aggregation points and the cooperator nodes, the mechanism computes the scheduling of

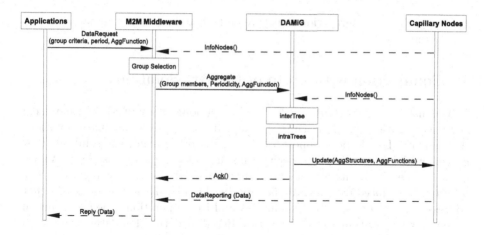

Fig. 6. Creation of new groups.

involved nodes, assigning the states (sleep, listening, transmit and receive) that should be executed in each time slot of the scheduling.

The groups remains until the group members need to be changed (e.g. update settings, join, leave, delete group). The events that cause change in the groups are: topology, data request criteria, DA parameters changes and conflicting data requests. The first is related to the nodes and the environment. The second and third are associated to the application interest and the fourth is related with the interests of concurrent DCE.

Figure 7 depicts the sequence diagram of the aggregation structure and scheduling maintenance. In case the MGMC detects any of the aforementioned events requiring changes, the MGMC sends the *GroupEdition* to the joint mechanism the nodes that should leave or join a particular group, or the new DA parameters. After reception of this message, the joint mechanism computes, if

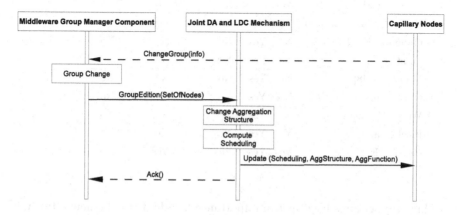

Fig. 7. Maintenance of the aggregation structure and scheduling.

234 A. Riker et al.

necessary, the new aggregation structure and scheduling, or just updates the DA parameters.

5 Comparison with State of the Art Solutions

Table 1 lists the main solutions designed to prolong the network lifetime using Data Aggregation and Low Duty Cycling. It can be seen that most solutions that support DA do not support LDC. On the other hand, the solutions that implement Low Duty Cycling mechanisms are not designed to use Data Aggregation, since the paths are not computed to maximize the aggregation. The solutions introduced by Wu et al. [56] and Incel et al. [57] are the few works that address most of the aspects of a joint DA and LDC operation. The first solution proposes an algorithm to create a Tree-Based structure for data aggregation and computes a scheduler for the aggregation tree. The scheduler minimizes the active-sleep transitions and the energy spend on idle listening. However, it does not consider the existence of multiple data-types, or study how the proposed solution affects two-way communication and it does not use multi-channels to improve the communication. The second solution computes the aggregation tree, the sleep scheduler and the transmission scheduler, using multi-channel. This solution also does not consider multiple data types and two-way communication.

Table 1. Comparison with state of the art solutions.

Works	DA	LDC	Multiple data-types	Two-way latency	Concurrent data requests
Yu et al. [26]	- -	No	No	No	No
Joo et al. [27]	Yes	No	No	No	No
Xu et al. [28]	Yes	No	No	No	No
Ghosh et al. [29]	Yes	No	No	No	No
Keshavarzian et al. [30]	No	Yes	No	Yes	No
Guha et al. [41]	No	Yes	No	No	No
Fu et al. [47]	No	Yes	Yes	No	No
Ma et al. [48]	No	Yes	No	No	No
Kim et al. [50]	No	Yes	No	No	No
Wu et al. [56]	No	Yes	Yes	No	No
Incel et al. [57]	Yes	Yes	No	No	No
GoCAME	Yes	Yes	Yes	Yes	Yes

Three key features have special importance for M2M environments: two-way communication, multiple data-types and concurrent data gathering from M2M groups. With regard to two-way latency, only Keshavarzian et al. [30] optimize the LDC for two-way communication, avoiding high latency in backward direction. Although an LDC for two-way communication demands more energy than an LDC for one-way communication, it is necessary to assure acceptable levels of delays for communication in backward direction (e.g. commands and update information).

Regarding the aspect of the multiple data-types composing the network traffic, only the work [47] supports this feature. Furthermore, none of the works are designed to support concurrent data gathering from M2M groups. This is because the current solutions assume that there will be only one data request begin executed on the network and the data requests, usually, involves the data communication of the whole capillary network. This assumption is unrealistic in M2M environments where there are multiple Data-Consumer Entities interested on the M2M data and in large scenarios, where the data requests do not demand the communication of all nodes but only a group of nodes.

6   Conclusion

In the M2M era, new forms of communication are possible and new services and applications will be available. By exploring the extensive number of services and the wide range of scenarios, an immense market potential has emerged for the M2M networks, including transportation, utilities, security, retails services and healthcare. Low constrained devices produce most part of the M2M applications data, which requires efficient use of energy. Besides, in the M2M environments, DCE dynamically produces concurrent data requests demanding the communication of particular groups of nodes.

Data Aggregation and Low Duty Cycling are key mechanisms to save energy resources. They reduce the amount of data communicated and the time the wireless transceiver is turned on. However, without a joint design, these mechanisms can be incompatible, resulting in low performance. The state of art shows that most of the LDC solutions assume the existence of an aggregation structure, but do not provide the appropriate connectivity to it. On the other hand, most of the DA solutions do not minimize the collisions, the state transitions and idle listening and they are not design to two-way communication. Few solutions enable DA and LDC to be executed simultaneously. The works that integrate both mechanisms do not take into account important M2M requirements, such as: two-way latency, multiple data-types and simultaneous groups communication.

To fill this gap, this work proposes the GoCAME which is an M2M architecture designed to enable group communication with low power consumption for M2M environments. GoCAME allows the execution of concurrent data requests and commands. Besides, the proposed architecture enables the joint execution of LDC and DA for two-way communication as well as in scenarios involving multiple data-types. Hence, compared with other solutions designed to prolong the network lifetime, GoCAME shows better design for the aspects related to the group communication in M2M environments.

Acknowledgments. This work was partially funded by the iCIS project, under the grant CENTRO-07-ST24-FEDER-002003; and CAPES/CNPq (Brazil) through the Ciencia sem Fronteiras Program/2013.

References

1. Booysen, M., Gilmore, J., Zeadally, S., Van Rooyen, G.: Machine-to-machine (m2m) communications in vehicular networks. Article, Korea Society of Internet Information (KSII) (2012)
2. Zhang, Y., Yu, R., Xie, S., Yao, W., Xiao, Y., Guizani, M.: Home m2m networks: architectures, standards, and qos improvement. IEEE Commun. Mag. **49**(4), 44–52 (2011)
3. Hassan, R., Radman, G.: Survey on smart grid. In: Proceedings of the IEEE SoutheastCon 2010 (SoutheastCon), pp. 210–213. IEEE (2010)
4. Lioumpas, A., Alexiou, A., Anton-Haro, C., Navaratnam, P.: Expanding lte for devices: requirements, deployment phases and target scenarios. In: 11th European Wireless Conference 2011 - Sustainable Wireless Technologies (European Wireless), pp. 1–6, April 2011
5. Hao, J., Zhang, B., Mouftah, H.T.: Routing protocols for duty cycled wireless sensor networks: a survey. IEEE Commun. Mag. **50**(12), 116–123 (2012)
6. Fasolo, E., Rossi, M., Widmer, J., Zorzi, M.: In-network aggregation techniques for wireless sensor networks: a survey. IEEE Wirel. Commun. **14**(2), 70–87 (2007)
7. Zhang, J., Shan, L., Hu, H., Yang, Y.: Mobile cellular networks and wireless sensor networks: toward convergence. IEEE Commun. Mag. **50**(3), 164–169 (2012)
8. Tekbiyik, N., Uysal-Biyikoglu, E.: Energy efficient wireless unicast routing alternatives for machine-to-machine networks. J. Netw. Comput. Appl. **34**(5), 1587–1614 (2011)
9. Bluetooth, S.: Bluetooth specification version 1.1 (2001). http://www.bluetooth.com
10. Alliance, Z.: Zigbee specification. Document 053474r06, Version 1 (2006)
11. Alliance, W.: Wimedia logical link control protocol. WLP Specification Approved Draft 1 (2007)
12. Alliance, W.: Wi-fi standards (2007)
13. Matoba, K., Abiru, K., Ishihara, T.: Service oriented network architecture for scalable m2m and sensor network services. In: 2011 15th International Conference on Intelligence in Next Generation Networks (ICIN), pp. 35–40, October 2011
14. Jumira, O., Wolhuter, R.: Value chain scenarios for m2m ecosystem. In: 2011 IEEE GLOBECOM Workshops (GC Wkshps), pp. 410–415, December 2011
15. Madden, S., Franklin, M.J., Hellerstein, J.M., Hong, W.: Tag: a tiny aggregation service for ad-hoc sensor networks. ACM SIGOPS Oper. Syst. Rev. **36**(SI), 131–146 (2002)
16. Tsitsipis, D., Dima, S., Kritikakou, A., Panagiotou, C., Koubias, S.: Data merge: a data aggregation technique for wireless sensor networks. In: 2011 IEEE 16th Conference on Emerging Technologies & Factory Automation (ETFA), pp. 1–4. IEEE (2011)
17. AbdelSalam, H.S., Rizvi, S.R., Olariu, S.: Energy-aware task assignment and data aggregation protocols in wireless sensor networks. In: 6th IEEE Consumer Communications and Networking Conference, CCNC 2009, pp. 1–5. IEEE (2009)

18. Manjhi, A., Nath, S., Gibbons, P.B.: Tributaries and deltas: efficient and robust aggregation in sensor network streams. In: Proceedings of the 2005 ACM SIGMOD International Conference on Management of Data, pp. 287–298. ACM (2005)
19. Rajagopalan, R., Varshney, P.K.: Data aggregation techniques in sensor networks: a survey. IEEE Commun. Surv. & Tutor. **8**, 48–63 (2006)
20. Handy, M., Haase, M., Timmermann, D.: Low energy adaptive clustering hierarchy with deterministic cluster-head selection. In: 4th International Workshop on Mobile and Wireless Communications Network, pp. 368–372. IEEE (2002)
21. Younis, O., Fahmy, S.: Heed: a hybrid, energy-efficient, distributed clustering approach for ad hoc sensor networks. IEEE Trans. Mob. Comput. **3**(4), 366–379 (2004)
22. Chatterjea, S., Havinga, P.: A dynamic data aggregation scheme for wireless sensor networks (2003)
23. Lindsey, S., Raghavendra, C., Sivalingam, K.M.: Data gathering algorithms in sensor networks using energy metrics. IEEE Trans. Parallel Distrib. Syst. **13**(9), 924–935 (2002)
24. Huang, S.H., Wan, P.J., Vu, C.T., Li, Y., Yao, F.: Nearly constant approximation for data aggregation scheduling in wireless sensor networks. In: 26th IEEE International Conference on Computer Communications, INFOCOM 2007, pp. 366–372. IEEE (2007)
25. Chen, X., Hu, X., Zhu, J.: Minimum data aggregation time problem in wireless sensor networks. In: Jia, X., Wu, J., He, Y. (eds.) MSN 2005. LNCS, vol. 3794, pp. 133–142. Springer, Heidelberg (2005)
26. Yu, B., Li, J., Li, Y.: Distributed data aggregation scheduling in wireless sensor networks. In: IEEE, INFOCOM 2009, pp. 2159–2167. IEEE (2009)
27. Joo, C., Choi, J.G., Shroff, N.B.: Delay performance of scheduling with data aggregation in wireless sensor networks. In: 2010 Proceedings IEEE INFOCOM, pp. 1–9. IEEE (2010)
28. Xu, X., Li, X.Y., Mao, X., Tang, S., Wang, S.: A delay-efficient algorithm for data aggregation in multihop wireless sensor networks. IEEE Trans. Parallel Distrib. Syst. **22**(1), 163 (2011)
29. Ghosh, A., Incel, Ö.D., Kumar, V., Krishnamachari, B.: Multichannel scheduling and spanning trees: throughput-delay tradeoff for fast data collection in sensor networks. IEEE/ACM Trans. Netw. (TON) **19**(6), 1731–1744 (2011)
30. Keshavarzian, A., Lee, H., Venkatraman, L.: Wakeup scheduling in wireless sensor networks. In: Proceedings of the 7th ACM International Symposium on Mobile Ad Hoc Networking and Computing, pp. 322–333. ACM (2006)
31. Instruments, T.: Cc1100 data sheet (2003)
32. Anastasi, G., Conti, M., Di Francesco, M., Passarella, A.: Energy conservation in wireless sensor networks: a survey. Ad Hoc Netw. **7**(3), 537–568 (2009)
33. Xu, Y., Heidemann, J., Estrin, D.: Geography-informed energy conservation for ad hoc routing. In: Proceedings of the 7th Annual International Conference on Mobile Computing and Networking, pp. 70–84. ACM (2001)
34. Feng, W., Alshaer, H., Elmirghani, J.: Green information and communication technology: energy efficiency in a motorway model. IET Commun. **4**(7), 850–860 (2010)
35. Chen, B., Jamieson, K., Balakrishnan, H., Morris, R.: Span: an energy-efficient coordination algorithm for topology maintenance in ad hoc wireless networks. Wirel. Netw. **8**(5), 481–494 (2002)
36. Cerpa, A., Estrin, D.: Ascent: adaptive self-configuring sensor networks topologies. IEEE Trans. Mob. Comput. **3**(3), 272–285 (2004)
37. Armstrong, T.: Wake-up based power management in multi-hop wireless networks. Term Survey Paper, University of Toronto (2005)

38. Schurgers, C., Tsiatsis, V., Srivastava, M.B.: Stem: topology management for energy efficient sensor networks. In: IEEE Aerospace Conference Proceedings, vol. 3, p. 3-1099. IEEE (2002)

39. Gu, L., Stankovic, J.A.: Radio-triggered wake-up for wireless sensor networks. Real-Time Syst. **29**(2–3), 157–182 (2005)

40. Kijewski-Correa, T., Haenggi, M., Antsaklis, P.: Wireless sensor networks for structural health monitoring: a multi-scale approach. In: ASCE Structures 2006 Congress (2006)

41. Guha, S., Basu, P.B., Chau, C.K., Gibbens, R.: Green wave sleep scheduling: optimizing latency and throughput in duty cycling wireless networks. IEEE J. Sel. Areas Commun. **29**(8), 1595–1604 (2011)

42. Tseng, Y.C., Hsu, C.S., Hsieh, T.Y.: Power-saving protocols for IEEE 802.11-based multi-hop ad hoc networks. Comput. Netw. **43**(3), 317–337 (2003)

43. Stinson, D.R.: Combinatorial Designs: Construction and Analysis. Springer, New York (2004)

44. Kim, J., Lin, X., Shroff, N.B.: Optimal anycast technique for delay-sensitive energy-constrained asynchronous sensor networks. IEEE/ACM Trans. Netw. (TON) **19**(2), 484–497 (2011)

45. Rajendran, V., Obraczka, K., Garcia-Luna-Aceves, J.J.: Energy-efficient, collision-free medium access control for wireless sensor networks. Wirel. Netw. **12**(1), 63–78 (2006)

46. Demirkol, I., Ersoy, C., Alagoz, F.: Mac protocols for wireless sensor networks: a survey. IEEE Commun. Mag. **44**(4), 115–121 (2006)

47. Fu, H.L., Chen, H.C., Lin, P., Fang, Y.: Energy-efficient reporting mechanisms for multi-type real-time monitoring in machine-to-machine communications networks. In: 2012 Proceedings IEEE INFOCOM, pp. 136–144. IEEE (2012)

48. Ma, J., Lou, W., Wu, Y., Li, X.Y., Chen, G.: Energy efficient tdma sleep scheduling in wireless sensor networks. In: IEEE INFOCOM 2009, pp. 630–638. IEEE (2009)

49. Incel, O.D.: A survey on multi-channel communication in wireless sensor networks. Comput. Netw. **55**(13), 3081–3099 (2011)

50. Kim, Y., Shin, H., Cha, H.: Y-mac: An energy-efficient multi-channel mac protocol for dense wireless sensor networks. In: Proceedings of the 7th International Conference on Information Processing in Sensor Networks, pp. 53–63. IEEE Computer Society (2008)

51. Karl, H., Willig, A.: Protocols and Architectures for Wireless Sensor Networks. Wiley.com (2007)

52. Van Dam, T., Langendoen, K.: An adaptive energy-efficient mac protocol for wireless sensor networks. In: Proceedings of the 1st International Conference on Embedded Networked Sensor Systems, pp. 171–180. ACM (2003)

53. Polastre, J., Hill, J., Culler, D.: Versatile low power media access for wireless sensor networks. In: Proceedings of the 2nd International Conference on Embedded Networked Sensor Systems, pp. 95–107. ACM (2004)

54. Rhee, I., Warrier, A., Aia, M., Min, J., Sichitiu, M.L.: Z-mac: a hybrid mac for wireless sensor networks. IEEE/ACM Trans. Netw. (TON) **16**(3), 511–524 (2008)

55. ETSI, T.: Functional architecture. ETSI TS 102.169 Machine-to-Machine communications (2010)

56. Wu, Y., Li, X.Y., Liu, Y., Lou, W.: Energy-efficient wake-up scheduling for data collection and aggregation. IEEE Trans. Parallel Distrib. Syst. **21**(2), 275–287 (2010)

57. Incel, O.D., van Hoesel, L., Jansen, P., Havinga, P.: Mc-lmac: a multi-channel mac protocol for wireless sensor networks. Ad Hoc Netw. **9**(1), 73–94 (2011)

Simulation Based Studies
of Machine-to-Machine Communications

Evgeny Osipov[1(✉)], Laurynas Riliskis[1], Timo Lehikoinen[2],
Jukka Kämäräinen[2], and Marko Pellinen[2]

[1] Luleå University of Technology, Luleå, Sweden
{Evgeny.Osipov,Laurynas.Riliskis}@ltu.se
[2] VTT Technical Research Centre of Finland, Espoo, Finland
{timo.lehikoinen,jukka.kamarainen,
marko.pellinen}@vtt.fi

Abstract. Simulations are essential for understanding complex systems such as
Cyber Physical Systems. The creation of reliable multi-disciplinary simulation
tools that can be used to support the entire development process has been
identified as a major scientific goal in several research roadmaps and agendas for
the coming 15 years. This chapter presents two showcases, which highlight the
necessity of trustworthy simulation tools, especially in the case of machine-to-
machine communications. First the performance of UWB radio technology in
context of vehicle automation is evaluated. Second the experiences from performing the entire cycle of protocol development for machine-to-machine
communications are presented. The two presented showcases support a conclusion that a successful simulation platform should have a user-friendly simulation framework and models that support virtualization. This will enable the
incorporation of simulations into day-to-day engineering practice and thereby
shrink the gap between the real and the virtual developing environments.

Keywords: Machine-to-machine · Simulations · UWB · WSN · Symphony

1 Introduction

The developers' experiences with the design, development, and deployment of low
layer protocols for time-critical machine-to-machine (m2m) applications could be far
from being pleasant. The number of man-hours required to develop and tailor these
protocols to the specific hardware used in these applications greatly exceeded all
expectations. One factor that made this task particularly laborious and challenging was
the common occurrence of false positives in simulations performed using existing tools.
While simulations conducted using these tools were useful for addressing logical and
design-related challenges, they did not provide information that would have made it
possible to anticipate any of the issues discussed above. Moreover, it was found that the
effectiveness and performance of the system was strongly dependent on the operating
system used in the low-end devices.

Modeling, analysis, and simulation are essential for understanding complex systems such as Cyber Physical Systems. The creation of reliable multi-disciplinary

© Springer International Publishing Switzerland 2014
I. Ganchev et al. (Eds.): Wireless Networking for Moving Objects, LNCS 8611, pp. 239–254, 2014.
DOI: 10.1007/978-3-319-10834-6_13

simulation tools that can be used to support the entire development process has been identified as a major scientific goal in several research roadmaps and agendas for the coming 15 years.

For example, "A roadmap for US robotics" [1] states that "dynamic simulation technology will be used daily throughout the engineering life-cycle (e.g., research and development, marketing, concept study, detailed design, testing, operation, product updating, problem solving, maintenance, operator training)". Similarly, the European Roadmap for Industrial Process Automation [2] identifies an "Open Simulator Platform" as a prioritized ideal concept and states that it will be necessary "to optimize the efficiency of simulation-based development through full interoperability between simulation tools over the complete development process".

It is envisioned that the simulation platform will be model-based with the ability to handle many model sources and to act as an integration platform for their virtual deployment. A simulation platform of this sort could function as an enabler by allowing the same platform to be used at every stage of the developmental process, from the first proof of concept study to the provision of aftermarket support. The availability of a distributed and open simulation platform could also lead to the creation of new services based on (or in) a simulator platform.

"Machine-to-machine" (m2m) is a broad term referring to technologies that allow both wireless and wired systems to communicate with other devices of the same type. In the case of the large-scale cellular networks this type of systems is defined under term *machine type communications* [8]. It is projected that devices such as smart meters, smart appliances would exchange data over a number of architectures involving cellular data networks as a broadband carrier.

In this chapter we focus on the last leg of the machine-to-machine hierarchy – the local scale communications between devices over low-power wireless links. While a vast pool of result was collected in the area of wireless sensor networks over past decade, yet this technology has not yet emerged on the market. One of the major reasons for this is the absence of tools for accurate simulation based studies and analysis, which would shorten the path from the ide to market.

This chapter presents two simulation-based studies. The first study investigates the "old-new" radio technology – Ultra Wide Band (UWB) – in machine-to-machine applications. While UWB radio was developed long time ago, in the context of low-power wireless sensor networks its usage is still new. While the first low-power UWB chips are becoming available from the vendors, the major experimental environment is still simulations. The first part of the chapter (Sect. 2) aims at investigating the major performance characteristics of the UWB-enabled sensor network. The section presents the details of the experimental methodology as well as reports on the major findings.

The second study focuses on a different radio technology the standard IEEE 802.15.4a – based. The purpose of this study is *not to* evaluate the limits of the particular technology, but rather to demonstrate the pitfalls, which the developers of the machine-to-machine functionality may encounter while designing, implementing and analysing real systems. Without contradicting to the results presented in Sect. 2, Sect. 3 argues that most of the commonly used simulators do not capture the internal processes in m2 m nodes. As such the realism of the simulation-based studies using such simulators is rather low. In many cases even though, the high-level system performance can be predicted using standard simulation facilities, it is hard to project their results on micro-time scale and therefore arguing about time-critical applications. At the end of Sect. 3 a novel open-source simulation framework, named Symphony, is presented as a possible solution for bridging the gap between the simulation and the real-world deployment.

2 Using UWB Technology in Machine-to-Machine Communications

Ultra Wide Band (UWB) technology has been researched already for over 20 years. In this section we discuss especially Impulse Radio UWB (IR-UWB) with is basically created by driving a very short pulse into an antenna circuit. Unfortunately real life is not so easy; generating a useful UWB transmission is far more complex as described above.

The UWB we discuss in this chapter is standardized in IEEE 802.15.4 (2011). The older version (2006) of this specification together with the addendum IEEE 802.15.4a (2007) was combined to this, new version. UWB in this standardized version was several years very expensive to implement because of the lack of chip-sets implementing it. There are some pioneers that have been working several years to develop a chip to enable implementing of UWB in mass-production equipment. Not before than 2013 the first commercial UWB chip is finally brought into production by an Irish company, DecaWave Ltd.

In the development of UWB chips the main focus seem to have been in ranging (positioning) and this is probably the most interesting feature of UWB. The wide bandwidth (>500 MHz) makes it possible to transmit very fast rising/sinking edges and thus measure flying time, it is distance, of pulses accurately. But UWB is extremely practical in data transmission, too. UWB can transmit data relatively fast, at least compared to other short distance radio technologies. It is energy efficient, it does not disturb existing, traditional radio transmissions and it is immune to the disturbances of these.

The goal of this study is to evaluate the effects on the overall capacity of a network of sensor nodes by utilizing UWB technology in Physical layer (PHY). The simulation demonstrated that just utilizing UWB PHY increases the capacity of simulated network substantially. Packet delay was reduced and the overall speed of data transfer increased even when using standard Medium Access Control (MAC) and Network layers (NWK). With small modifications to MAC the capacity was further increased. With a modified MAC utilizing UWB PHY we could indeed create a sensor network that can satisfy strict real-time constraints of machine-to-machine communications in the context of vehicle automation.

2.1 Modelling of a Wireless Sensor Network

Simulation was used to study the applicability of standardised technologies in the demanding real-time wireless sensor network in vehicles. Vehicle or working machine sets quite tight requirements for the wireless technology (and to the wired technology, too) to be utilised. The main requirements are reliability (achievable with redundancy) and demand for real-time data transmission. Real-time means in this context the time during which we have to deliver required data packets from a sensor to the control system in every case. If the required packets are not delivered inside this critical time-frame, the control system must go to a safe-mode thus ending the operation active. A thumb rule for this is as reliable data transmission as using wired networks.

This study satisfies two requirements: (a) to keep the critical time between 10 and 50 ms and (b) to achieve reliability comparable to that achieved by using wired networks.

The simulation was carried out in three steps. The first step was to use Zigbee network. In the second step, the standard Zigbee PHY was replaced by the UWB radio of IEEE 802.15.4 which increased the data transmission speed remarkably. The standard PHY offered only 250 kb/s as UWB offered speeds 110 kb/s, 850 kb/s, 6.81 Mb/s and 27 Mb/s. We used only 6.81 Mb/s in our simulation. MAC was modified according to IEEE 802.15.4. The third step was to modify used MAC's to be able to better take advantage of the speed of UWB radio.

The main subject of the simulation was to focus on reliability and delays in real-time networks. The requirement of working machines is mostly a deterministic connectivity. It means that every sensor and appliance in the network has in all cases its own moment of time for receiving and sending. Simulation tries to find out the maximal throughput of all combined MAC/PHY. The network configurations used in simulation are somewhat simplified and thus not directly applicable to practical networks.

2.2   Model Used in Simulation

Simulations were done using a model of IEEE 802.15.4 (2003) [3] developed for OPNET Modeller. The model simulates all devices of a Zigbee network, but we limited our work to a simple star network topology. As we developed the used model to contain modifications for IEEE 802.15.4 UWB, the biggest changes we made were done to MAC layer. The only change in the PHY layer model was transmission speed, which was changed to 6.81 Mb/s.

In simulation we concentrated on the performance on MAC and Network layers we neither simulated signal propagation in PHY nor did we simulate Bit Error Rate (BER), external disturbances etc. In these simulations, all sent data packets were also received so data packets are not lost because of external interference or multipath propagation.

Simulation was used to model a network using only one channel. We put as much load on this single channel as possible to investigate the applicability of a standard MAC to a real-time data transfer in machine environment. Simulation was used in star topology network. The network has only one coordinator and seven devices except on the third simulation (with nonstandard, modified MAC) were we used ten devices.

Data transfer modelled was a simple one, where the sensors sent data frames to the coordinator. Coordinator sent beacon-messages to synchronise sensors and Acknowledge-messages (ACK) to acknowledge successful receiving of data frames. This arrangement made it easier to analyse results and to compare various technologies simulated.

In the simulations the receiver always acknowledged the sender with and ACK packet. ACK is sent automatically in PHY, if this functionality is activated. IEEE 802.15.4 standard limits re-sending to maximal seven. We used standard setting for re-sending, three. This means that if sender does not receive an ACK after third re-sending, the packet will be abandoned. Table 1 contains parameters of MAC and Network layers, which were used in the simulation. The differences between used models can be easily found. Some parameters used for Application layers (APL) are presented as well. These parameters define the size and interval of Guaranteed Time Slot (GTS) and Carrier Sense Multiple Access (CSMA) frames used in sensors. Each sensor sends a 32 bits long data packet to the coordinator using the same interval. The interval is swept from 1 to 100 ms. These data packets were built according to Zigbee standard. Thus even though the payload was only 32 bits, the actual length of MAC Service Data Unit (MSDU) is 200 bits.

Personal Area Network (PAN) coordinator is responsible of synchronising the network. It uses beacon messages for this purpose. The network was simulated in beacon mode making it possible to utilise GTS during Contention Free Period (CFP) thus enabling each device to send a data packet without competition as would be the case in non-beacon mode (Carrier Sense Multiple Access With Collision Detection, CSMA/CA.

The size of the superframe is controlled in IEEE 802.15.4 using Superframe Order (SO) and Beacon Order (BE) parameters. A superframe according IEEE 802.15.4 has always 16 timeslots. Maximum number of GTS is seven in any superframe. The first timeslot is reserved for the beacon message sent by coordinator or router. SO defines the length of the superframe. The value of 1 sets the length of the superframe to 30,72 ms. Time for one timeslot can be calculated using Eq. 1.

$$timeslotDuration = aBaseSlotDuration \times 2^{SO} \qquad (1)$$

In our simulation of a standard IEEE 802.15.4 network both BO and SO were set to two leading to a superframe length of 61,44 ms. It was not possible to use a shorter frame, because we wanted to use GTS packets. In simulating a standard IEEE 802.15.4 network BO and SO were set to one leading to a superframe length of 30,72 ms. Simulating the non-standard network SO and BO were set to one, too. But the lengths of superframe and timeslots were shorter because of aBaseSlotDuration parameter was set to 30 and Symboltime was reduced from standard 16 microseconds to 10 µs. PHY layer enables the transmission and reception of PHY Protocol Data Unit (PPDU) by using the physical radio channel. PPDU consists of three basic components: Synchronising Header (SHR), Physical Header (PHR) and a variable length payload (PHY Payload). The data frame of 802.15.4 is maximum 127 bytes long. IEEE 802.15.4 (UWB) offers several bitrates to select from: 110 kilobits/second, 850 kb/s, 6.81 Mb/s and 27.24 Mb/s. Thereto UWB technology allows usage of variable lengths of SHR and PHR and even various bitrates for sending them.

Real life applications introduce numerous delays caused by the hardware and software, which are not taken into account on the simulation model. On practical level, the packets received through PHY are processed on various layers above the PHY (i.e. MAC, Network and Application). Thus the time for processing the data on these

Table 1. Parameters used in simulations.

		802.15.4	802.15.4a	Nonstandard
SUPERFRAME PARAMETERS	BEACON ORDER (BO)	2	1	1
	SUPERFRAME ORDER (SO)	2	1	1
	SUPERFRAME DURATION	61,44 ms	30,72 ms	9,60 ms
	BEACON INTERVAL	61,44 ms	30,72 ms	9,60 ms
	TIME SLOT DURATION	3,84 ms	1,92 ms	0,60 ms
	FINAL CAP SLOT NUMBER	8	8	5
	FINAL GTS SLOT NUMBER	7	7	10
CSMA PARAMETERS	MAXIMUM BACKOFF NUMBER	5	5	5
	MINIMUM BACKOFF EXPONENT	1	1	1
	MAXIMUM BACKOFF EXPONENT	5	5	5
CSMA traffic parameters	Packet interval	100–5 ms	100–1 ms	100–1 ms
	Packet size	32 bit	32 bit	32 bit
	Acknowledgement	yes	yes	yes
GTS traffic parameters	Packet interval	100–5 ms	100–1 ms	100–1 ms
	Packet size	32 bit	32 bit	32 bit
	Acknowledgment	yes	yes	yes
NETWORK LAYER	Maximum child routers	2	2	2
	Maximum children nodes	20	20	20
MAC layer constant	aBaseSlotDuration	60	60	30
	aMinCAPLength	440 symbols	120 symbols	120 symbols
	aUnitBackoffPeriod	20 symbols	20 symbols	10 symbols
	aNumSuperframeSlots	16	16	16
	Symboltime	16 µs	16 µs	10 µs
	Max GTS slot number	7	7	14
	macAckWaitDurationTime	864 µs	110 us	105 µs
	aMinLIFSPeriodTime	640 µs	39,74 µs	39,74 µs
	aMinSIFSPeriodTime	192 µs	11,92 µs	11,92 µs
PHY	Data rate	250 kb/s	6,81 Mb/s	6,81 Mb/s

higher layers, and the communication between the layers, causes delays depending on the hardware and efficiency of the software used.

The only delays this simulation model takes into account are the Inter Frame Space (IFS) and the time used for waiting for the ACK message (macAckWaitDuration).

These delays were used on the first two simulations as they are specified in the standard, but on the third simulation (with nonstandard, modified MAC) the time for waiting the ACK message was reduced to 105 μs.

2.3   Results of Simulations

First we compare the time required for data packets in simulated models. From this data we get values for many parameters controlling MAC layer. To get data through in real-time, we try to set BO and SO of superframe as small as possible. But to enable GTS data transfer a single timeslot has to be longer than the total time required to send a data packet, i.e. SHR + PHR + PPDU + + ACK. Using IEEE 802.15.4 gave a GTS Tx of 2176 microseconds, with BO and SO set to two. IEEE 802.15.4 UWB gave a GTS Tx of only 267 μs because of the faster bitrate used. Thereto the total time of an ACK message was remarkably shorter. One aspect that shortens the total time required to transmit a data packet is the shorter time required for IFS, too. According to IEEE 802.15.4 UWB IFS is calculated using the length of preamble symbol (993,6 ns) which is roughly a 16th part of the symbol time specified in IEEE 802.15.4 (16 μs).

In our simulation each sensor created a CSMA and a GTS data packet using a pre-set interval. We began with an interval of 100 ms leading to a total duration of 30 s for the simulation. For shorter intervals the total duration of the simulation was reduced so that with an interval of 1 ms the total duration of the simulation was 5 s.

Figure 1 illustrates the amount of successfully transmitted data packets with different transmission intervals. The graph displays the amount of data packets successfully sent from the Application Layer of sensors to the Application Layer of the coordinator using selected channel. In the simulation each sensor acts as a sender and the coordinator acts as a receiver. The graph clearly shows the superiority of UWB technology in data transmission. The non-standard MAC (Standard_out_GTS) transmits the times the amount of data packets as standard IEEE 802.15.4 both utilising GTS data transfer. Using the standard IEEE 802.15.4 UWB gave almost the same transmit speed utilising GTS data transfer. With CSMA the differences are not so large, but UWB still clearly defeats the older technology. Please remark that CSMA starts to loose data packets already with an interval of 50 ms.

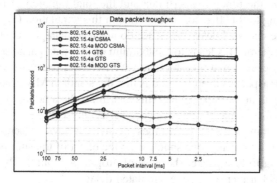

Fig. 1. The amount of successfully transmitted of data packets.

We deliberately simulated various technologies at their extreme limits with a real-time data transfer a continuous data stream which leads to unreliable operation of standard CSMA technology. This is clearly illustrated in Fig. 2. In IEEE 802.15.4 CSMA we start losing data packets already when interval is 75 ms. Using IEEE 802.15.4a functions well with an interval of 75 ms, but shortening interval to 25 ms causes this technology to lose already 20 % from data packets. Using GTS data transfer IEEE 802.15.4a UWB is capable to transmit data even with an interval of 5 ms, even when we used ten devices. Going below this value reduces the reliability of data transmission drastically.

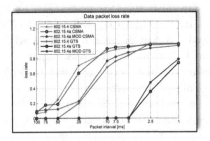

Fig. 2. The reliability of packet transfer.

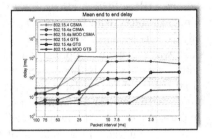

Fig. 3. The total delay of data transfer.

One interesting objective was to modify the standard MAC to reduce delay. This was implemented by shortening the length of superframe and timeslot. Superframe was shortened from 30.72 to 9.60 ms and the length of a single timeslot was reduced from 1.92 to 0.60 ms respectively. This time, 0.60 ms, was still enough for IEEE 802.15.4 UWB to send two GTS data packets using ACK. Without ACK it was possible to send even 3 data packets thus enabling us to achieve an update rate (interval) of 3 ms.

The benefit of modifying the standard MAC of IEEE 802.15.4 can clearly be seen in Fig. 3, that illustrates the total delay of data transfer (the time from APL of device generates a data packet to the time APL of coordinator receives the packet). Using modified MAC (Standard_out_GTS) the average transmit delay of GTS packets is 5 ms using an interval of 5 ms or more. Using standard IEEE 802.15.4a MAC (802.15.4a_GTS) the average delay of GTS packets is 15 ms. The delay caused in MAC is maximum the time of superframe and the total duration of transmitting data packets, so totalling to 9 600 + 262 = 9 862 ms in this simulation (Standard_out_GTS MAC). This is the maximal delay, when we do not feed data packets from APL faster than we can send them. This leads to a maximum of 400 data packets/second using an interval of 5 ms, because one timeslot can carry two data packets using ACK.

One important aspect to keep in mind is that the standard MAC has a maximum of seven GTS timeslots in the superframe. This fact limits the amount of sensors utilising GTS data transfer to a maximum of seven. In the third phase we simulated (standard_out) a superframe with ten GTS timeslots and ten devices (sensors). When analysing the graph of total delay, one should note the effect of transmit buffer to the total delay when starting to lose packets because of drop of reliability. This can be seen in the graph as a sudden increase of the simulated delay.

3 Practical Considerations in the Design of Communications Protocols for Wireless Sensor Networks: The Need for Bridging the Gap Between Simulations and Reality

This section describes the experiences gained and lessons learned during the design of a Medium Access Control (MAC) protocol for time-critical mission sensor networks that was developed for use with two projects: WSAN4CIP [4] and iRoad [5]. The protocol was designed and implemented for use in two different scenarios. In both cases, custom hardware platforms were developed to fulfill the specific requirements of the two projects. Both platforms were ported to enable the use of the same operating system. It was, therefore, initially assumed that it would be possible to use the developed protocol in both target scenarios without requiring any modification other than the specification of appropriate parameter values. However, this did not prove true. The two systems used different hardware, and the differences in the associated driver implementations significantly prolonged the development process. It was ultimately necessary to create platform-specific modifications of the protocols because the performance specifications for the components provided in their datasheets were inconsistent with their performance in real nodes.

Selected parts of the protocol's full specification that are relevant in the context of this dissertation are presented below. Detailed information on the work is provided in [6]. The key changes that were made to the protocol specification and its implementation are highlighted. The discussion on the problems encountered while developing the protocol motivates the need for more advanced simulation framework, which closely resembles the processes happening in real hardware. The section is concluded by overviewing the main operations of Symphony a simulation framework, which was developed to bridge the exiting gap.

3.1 The Protocol

While the details of the protocol's operation are presented in [6]. Here we summarize its main features as illustrated in Fig. 4. To facilitate further discussion, it is assumed that the nodes share a pre-deployed secret and their clocks are synchronized with one-second precision.[1] This initialization is performed off-line at a centralized point before the nodes are deployed. When the protocol is active, all nodes re-synchronize with substantially increased precision during the bootstrap phase. The protocol is designed for use with low-power radio transceivers that have 16 available radio channels (8 of which are orthogonal). Each node is equipped with one radio interface and is pre-configured with a unique identifier.

The FDMA and TDMA schedules are constructed independently and probabilistically in each node. Consequently, the schedules in one node may partially overlap with those of other nodes within two hops. The schedules are established at the

---

[1] Experience gained through designing, benchmarking and deploying the protocol suggests that this assumption is unlikely to hold in reality. However, it is used deliberately in the text until the deployment issues are discussed.

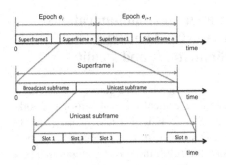 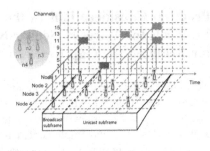

a: Epochs, superframes, subframes and slots.   b: MAC operations in the time and frequency domains.

Fig. 4. Overview of HMAC operations.

beginning of each epoch by computing a cryptographic hash function $f1 = Hash(e; ID_s; ID_d) mod N$. To compute the transmission schedule, a data block is constructed which includes the epoch number, e, and identifiers of the source and destination nodes (ID_s, and ID_d, respectively). The resulting hash value is mapped to either a channel number, $CH \in [1;N_{ch}]$, or a slot number, $S \in [1;N_{slots}]$, depending on the purpose for which it was computed, by taking *hash mod N*. The broadcast channel is computed similarly, using the function $R_{BCAST} = Hash(e; 0xFF) mod N_{ch}$. In the time domain, the broadcast communications always occur at the beginning of the superframe. Figure 4 illustrates the separation of the concurrent transmissions in the frequency and the time domains.

3.2   On the Implementation of the Proposed MAC Protocol

The MAC protocol was implemented on two different hardware platforms. The initial development and debugging was performed on the Mulle[2] platform.

3.3   Scheduler Phases and Frames

The core of the HMAC implementation is a scheduler that executes the phases of the protocol described below at the appropriate times. Essentially, the scheduler is a state machine and uses the hardware-independent *Alarm* component of TinyOS to schedule the timing of the different phases. Once the alarm is set, the Alarm component waits for the relevant timer to expire and then executes the *Alarm.fired()* event. It is vital for the Alarm component to be accurate and consistent on all nodes because it affects the performance of many parts of the system.

The timing of every operational phase of HMAC has a profound impact on the protocol's overall functionality. During the initial stages of the protocol's implementation, it became apparent that the time delays caused by switching between different

---

[2] Mulle Platform. Documentation is available at http://www.eistec.se.

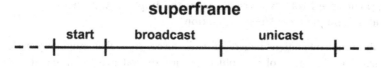

Fig. 5. Structure of the superframe.

states of the transceiver, computing channel and slot numbers, and performing other operating system tasks introduced an unacceptable shift in the protocol's timeline. An additional start frame was therefore added into the superframe to compensate for these delays, as shown in Fig. 5. The start subframe is used to perform tasks such as switching to the *current* broadcast channel, scheduling a packet for transmission, and calculating the channel and time slot numbers. The benefit of the extra subframe is that it can be used to perform additional computationally heavy operations such as encryption and signing without affecting the protocol's functionality.

When an alarm is triggered, the operations of the current phase are executed and the hardware clock is configured for the next phase. Table 2 shows measured overhead values for retrieving the current time and setting the alarm. Table 3 shows the execution times for the different phases of HMAC.

Table 2. Execution times for the *Alarm* functions.

Alarm functions	Execution time (μs)
start	100
getNow	15

Table 3. Execution times for different phases of the HMAC protocol.

State of HMAC	Execution time (μs$)
Start	100
Broadcast send	440
Unicast idle	130
Unicast active	10
Unicast send	570
Unicast receive	90

After having profiled the execution time for the different states of the MAC protocol and the Alarm functions, a timing precision of a few microseconds was achieved. It was thus possible to maintain the variation in superframe length within a range of 1 microsecond. Due to the inaccuracy of the timing operations and the non-deterministic behaviour of the hardware, the length of the unicast slots was extended; as currently implemented, their duration in debugging mode is twice that originally specified.

3.4 Performance Problems Arising from the Implementation and Techniques for Their Mitigation

During the implementation phase, it was discovered that imposing strict time requirements on the protocol is problematic for several reasons. First, it is hard to achieve time synchronization between nodes. Second, the execution time for software components in TinyOS has a non-negligible impact on protocol operations. In addition, the time required for radio hardware operations must also be taken into account. For example, it can take between 200 µs and 800 µs to change channels in this system. For comparative purposes, setting a hardware alarm takes 90–120 µs. Interestingly, it has been observed that the time consumed by the transceiver's hardware operations is not deterministic; nodes from the same batch exhibited varying performance. Third, it was noted that the real time clocks on different nodes differed in their performance. Furthermore, even within a single node, the timing of alarm firing could vary by up to several hundreds of microseconds. The node's clock was built into the MCU, so its performance was sometimes degraded when the MCU was put to sleep.

3.5 On the Assessment of Hardware and Software Component Performance

In order to satisfy dependability requirements, the performance of the hardware platform and software components should be assessed experimentally *before* beginning the protocol design process. Different operations should be profiled on a multiple nodes in order to determine the timing range of the target hardware. It is important to note that the time profile of the hardware should be established while it is running the operating system that is to be used in the system of interest, since even a lightweight OS such as TinyOS has some computational overhead. Furthermore, in most cases, it is difficult or impossible to determine whether a given delay in a specific operation has its origin in hardware or in software. Ideally, a general purpose test suite should be developed in order to establish a profile of the target hardware platform when running the chosen operating system. Profiling should be done on several different nodes in order to accurately estimate the variation in performance that should be expected.

3.6 Symphony: A Framework for Accurate and Holistic Wireless Sensor Network Simulation

The overall purpose of Symphony is to provide a holistic framework in which the development of software for m2 m nodes and simulations of its functionality can be performed in a single integrated development environment. In brief, when using Symphony, a m2 m developer always has access to a real implementation of their application in an OS that is used in m2 m hardware such as TinyOS,[3] FreeRTOS[4]

---

[3] See http://www.tinyos.net for more information.

[4] See http://www.freertos.org for more information.

or Contiki.[5] Symphony uses virtualization and hardware modeling techniques that allow the developer to work on a real node while also smoothly integrating the real implementation of the application with a general purpose network simulator that enables extensive testing of its distributed functionality in a controlled and repeatable manner. Technically, Symphony consists of four operating and programming scopes: a software scope, a hardware scope, a data feed scope, and an orchestration and communication scope. Figure 6 shows Symphony's high-level architecture.

The software scope deals with the mapping of function calls to the underlying hardware scope. The level of abstraction is configurable, and the scheduler of the underlying WSN OS is preserved. The hardware scope consists of a clock and a series of models for hardware components such as radio devices and sensors. These hardware models ensure that the application code is executed on a device-specific time scale. The data feed scope contains mechanisms for either actively or passively feeding data to the relevant software handlers or specific sensor nodes. The orchestration scope is implemented on top of the general-purpose network simulator ns-3. It is responsible for integrating all of the other scopes with the sophisticated communication models and ns-3 event scheduling engine to create a holistic simulation environment.

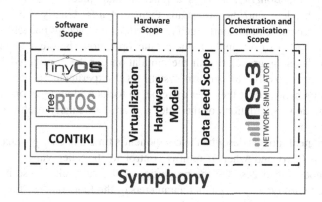

Fig. 6. A high-level architectural overview of Symphony.

All of Symphony's operational scopes are parameterized using a single XML configuration file. Symphony thus bridges the gap between simulated and real WSN software. It has numerous features that make it a unique development environment. Specifically, it:

1. Enables the user to experiment with the code base that would be used in a real deployment;
2. Preserves the execution model of the underlying operating system;
3. Accounts for the effects of hardware-induced delays on the performance of distributed applications and protocols;
4. Enables experimentation with a range of clock skew models;

---

[5] See http://www.contiki-os.org for more information.

5. Enables experimentation with several different applications and different WSN operating systems within a single simulation;
6. Provides a customizable level of simulation detail, ranging from fine-grained firmware emulation to system-level experiments;
7. Allows the user to investigate performance-related phenomena across the entire sensory data path.

While the details of each operating scope are presented in [7] in this section we present common to all scopes modeling principles, which allows execution of simulations on different levels of abstraction.

In Symphony, nodes are simulated using a set of models that provide homogeneous descriptions of the behaviors of both hardware and software components in terms of execution times and energy consumption. Assume a sensor's software consists of three components, C1, C2, and C3, which implement functionality at different levels of granularity. C1 is the lowest level (i.e. hardware) component and may represent something like a radio device and the associated driver. It performs the primitive operations of sending and receiving bytes. The C2 component represents a higher level of functionality, such as a function that queues packets, inspects and modifies their headers, and then transmits them onwards. Finally, C3 represents the highest level software components, such as functions that accept packets, encrypt and decrypt them, and perform application-specific operations before transmitting them onwards. The level of granularity in the simulation can be configured by the user. For example, it is possible to perform system-level experiments using only application-level components, or, at the other extreme, to focus on low-level operations using driver-level models. Simulations of the latter sort are particularly useful for very fine-grained debugging.

The component models describe the component's time and energy behavior when it is called via a (call) and when it returns control to its caller via a (callback). The component models also describe the properties of the callback. These include information on the return type and the input parameters of the function. The time and energy values are determined by measuring the time required for the device of interest to perform a specific operation and the energy consumed when doing so. The acquisition of such measurements is referred to as profiling.

Profiling is typically performed as part of a systematic measurement campaign. The best way of determining the execution time and the energy consumption of a specific network component is to use external measuring equipment. It is anticipated that a library of profiles for different components and platforms will be assembled over time and made available to Symphony users.

Symphony offers a generic and OS-agnostic virtualization platform. Currently it is undergoing the preparation to an open source release. In the mean time the source code of the Symphony framework is freely available for downloading upon request to one of the first two authors of this chapter.

4 Summary

This chapter presents the authors' experiences with experimenting, designing, developing, deploying MAC layer protocols for time-critical machine-to-machine applications. The number of man-hours required to develop and tailor these protocols to the specific hardware used in these applications greatly exceeded all expectations. One factor that made this task particularly laborious and challenging was the common occurrence of false positives in simulations performed using existing tools. While simulations conducted using these tools were useful for addressing logical and design-related challenges, they did not provide information that would have made it possible to anticipate any of the issues discussed above. Moreover, it was found that the effectiveness and performance of the system was strongly dependent on the operating system used in the WSN nodes.

The lack of realism in current modeling and simulation tools is illustrated in Sect. 4. In contrast to the situation discussed in Sect. 2, simulation tools and theoretical models that should have been applicable to the task at hand were available in this case. However, the performance of the protocol that was ultimately developed did not match that predicted using these tools. The main lesson drawn from this project was that many existing models and simulation tools produce unrealistic results and that it is not possible to directly transfer code developed using typical simulation environments generated with existing tools into real nodes.

The main lesson learned from this study is that there is a need for simulation and virtualization techniques capable of handling node models that provide realistic performance metrics. The findings of this chapter find their reflection in simulation framework, named Symphony, tailored to the case of machine-to-machine communications. The framework's key feature is its ability to perform ultra-large scale holistic experiments on WSN functionality with millions of nodes using configurable levels of abstraction. The behavior observable using Symphony is very similar to the run-time behavior that developers would observe in reality. This is achieved via the virtualization of real-world operating systems and by using measurement-based hardware emulation and software component models.

References

1. Christensen, H., Batzinger, T., Bekris, K., Bohringer, K., Bordogna, J., Bradski, G., Brock, O., Burnstein, J., Fuhlbrigge, T., Eastman, R., et al.: A roadmap for us robotics: from internet to robotics, 2013 edition. Computing Community Consortium and Computing Research Association, Washington DC (US), [Online], March 2013. http://robotics-vo.us/sites/default/files/2013

2. Lingman, P.A., Gustafsson J., et al., European roadmap for industrial process automation 2013. ProcessIT.EU, [Online], May 2013. http://www.processit.eu/Content/Files/Roadmap

3. Open-Zb, 2011. IEEE 802.15.4 OPNET Simulation Model. http://www.open-zb.net

4. Wireless Sensor and Actuator Networks For Critical Infrastructure Protection. [Online], November 2009. http://www.wsan4cip.eu/

5. Birk, W., Osipov, E.: On the design of cooperative road infrastructure systems. ser. Research report / Luleå University of Technology, Gustafsson, T., Birk, W., Johansson, A., (eds.) System och interaktion. Luleå: Luleå tekniska universitet, p. 7, May 2008
6. Osipov, E., Riliskis, L.: On synthesis of dependable MAC protocol for two real-world WSN applications. In: 2011 Baltic Congress on Future Internet Communications (BCFIC Riga), pp. 41–49. IEEE, Feb 2011
7. Riliskis, L.: Methodologies and practical tools for realistic large scale simulations of wireless sensor networks. Ph.D. Thesis, Luleå University of Technology, Luleå, Sweden, [Online] (2014). http://pure.ltu.se/portal/files/89656576/Laurynas_Riliskis.pdf
8. System improvements for machine-type communications. Technical report 3GPP TR 23.888 V11.0.0

Communication and Security in Machine-to-Machine Systems

Iva Bojic[1]([☒]), Jorge Granjal[2], Edmundo Monteiro[2], Damjan Katusic[1],
Pavle Skocir[1], Mario Kusek[1], and Gordan Jezic[1]

[1] Faculty of Electrical Engineering and Computing,
University of Zagreb, Unska 3, 10000 Zagreb, Croatia
iva.bojic@fer.hr
[2] Department of Informatics Engineering,
University of Coimbra, Polo 2, 3030-290 Coimbra, Portugal

Abstract. Machine-to-Machine (M2M) systems and technologies currently constitute a hot topic in the field of Information and Communication Technology (ICT), and reflect an increasing need for technologies enabling applications in diverse areas, as well as interactions between continuously increasing numbers of connected devices. Important participants in making M2M systems widely used and applicable in numerous real-life scenarios are standardization organizations. They try to develop technical specifications that address the need for a common M2M service layer, which can be realized through various hardware and software implementations. This chapter presents current standards and architecture of M2M systems with the focus on communication and security issues, while also discussing current and future research efforts addressing important open issues. One of the main problems in the area is correlated with heterogeneous devices, which are using different technologies for communication. Because of communication technology diversity, research challenges are to uniquely identify devices, and to enable them to communicate securely. To tackle the former, previously proposed, a unique identifying scheme that enables device identification regardless of used technology is explained. Regarding the latter, we analyze how current standards and architecture of M2M systems define basic processes for secure connection establishment, and also discuss open issues, both in respect to aspects not covered by current standards and in relation to research proposals which may integrate with M2M systems in future versions of the standards.

Keywords: M2M · Communication identifiers · M2M security · 6LoWPAN security

1 Introduction

Abbreviation M2M has several different meanings: Mobile-to-Mobile, Machine-to-Machine, Machine-to-Man (or vice-versa), Machine-to-Mobile (or vice-versa) [1].

© Springer International Publishing Switzerland 2014
I. Ganchev et al. (Eds.): Wireless Networking for Moving Objects, LNCS 8611, pp. 255–281, 2014.
DOI: 10.1007/978-3-319-10834-6_14

In this chapter we will use it in the context of Machine-to-Machine communication. M2M communication is established between two or more entities without any need of direct human intervention [2,3]. Actors in such an environment include broad range of communication capable devices: computers, mobile phones, tablets, but also a variety of sensors, actuators, pieces of industrial and medical equipment, and countless other everyday devices [4,5]. Another important aspect of M2M communication, as it can be seen from its longer acronym M2(CN2)M that stands for Machine-to-(Communication-Network-to)-Machine [6], is the notion of the underlying communication network that allows bidirectional exchange of information between these devices. M2M systems find applications in different areas such as home and industry automation [7], connected consumer [8], smart metering [9], healthcare [10], smart traffic [11], and many others. Work done by Beecham Research is one of many attempts trying to systematize all application areas applicable to M2M systems paradigm [12]. Through this variety of possible uses, M2M communication helps to achieve the vision of connected things - Internet of Things (IoT) [13,14], a world where ubiquitous and intelligent applications contribute to a better and safer world.

The number of connected devices is rapidly growing. International Data Corporation predicts there will be 15 billion devices communicating over the network by the year 2015 [15], while Cisco Internet Business Solutions Group (IBSG) forecasts 25 billion devices connected to the Internet by 2015 and 50 billion by 2020 [16]. Machina Research white paper states that by 2022 there will be 18 billion M2M connections globally, up from approximately 2 billion today [17]. Ericsson claims that their vision of more than 50 billion connected devices by 2020 may seem a bit ambitious today, but with the right approach, it is within reach [5]. Due to this rapid growth, the concept of M2M communication is gaining more and more significance. Interoperability, between devices based on different access network technologies (e.g. mobile (2G/3G/4G), Wi-Fi, Bluetooth), using different platforms and data models is still very limited or non-existent [18]. The idea is to connect a plethora of different devices that communicate through different technologies and thus create a heterogeneous environment. In order to enable connection of heterogeneous devices, globally accepted standards have to be developed to achieve ubiquitous connectivity and security. In addition, service platforms that will be reusable across different application areas and will unify isolated vertical "silo" solutions, based on common device capabilities, have to be developed [6]. Apart from standardization, policy and government incentives are also necessary to speed up the maturity of M2M systems [19]. On one hand, governments allocate funds for the development of certain technologies which are thought to increase the quality of everyday life (e.g. smart metering in households). On the other, regulation incentives provide precise directions for the development of the sets of standards applicable within a certain country or a region.

Standardization efforts in the area of M2M communication are very strong. One of the most influential standardization organizations involved in creating common standards for M2M communication is the European Telecommunications

Standards Institute (ETSI) [20]. Recently it has joined six other standardization organizations from around the world in forming a global M2M initiative: oneM2M [21]. These organizations are: Association of Radio Industries and Businesses (ARIB) [22] and Telecommunication Technology Committee (TTC) [23] from Japan, Alliance for Telecommunications Industry Solutions (ATIS) [24] and Telecommunications Industry Association (TIA) [25] from the USA, China Communications Standards Association (CCSA) [26], and Telecommunications Technology Association (TTA) [27] from South Korea. The goal of oneM2M is to develop technical specifications which address the need for a common M2M service layer, which can be realized through various hardware and software implementations, to connect diverse M2M devices with M2M servers [21]. The oneM2M initiative has not published any standards yet, but this is planned for 2014. Such specifications relate to how M2M devices may be identified, how they communicate, and also with how such interactions and communication between M2M systems may be supported with security in place. The M2M system in a very simplified aspect, as will become clear in the following sections when current considerations regarding architecture standardization by ETSI will be presented, consists of M2M devices, M2M gateways, and M2M servers.

Apart from heterogeneity in types of M2M devices, M2M systems should also allow communication between different M2M entities (i.e. M2M devices, M2M gateways, or M2M servers), ignoring the differences in the network technologies, including the underlying used addressing mechanism. For example, in an Internet Protocol (IP) based network, the communication establishment between M2M entities should be possible when either static or dynamic IP addressing is used regardless of the use of public or private IP address space. Moreover, it is very important to emphasize that IP connectivity is not the only option, i.e. M2M devices can be connected using different M2M area networks (e.g. Zigbee, Bluetooth, M-BUS). Interactions with security technologies developed for such M2M area networks must also be considered. Therefore, a common identification scheme for different entities within M2M system has to be developed. In ETSI standards, the need for identification of a single M2M entity is addressed in [28]. Single M2M device can support several different communication technologies at once. Therefore, this identifier has to be independent of access networks that M2M devices use for communication. ETSI, among several other identifiers, recognizes pre-provisioned identifier used for the bootstrapping procedures of M2M devices, and in this chapter we will explain how it was proposed in [29] it should look like.

One of the main problems in any information system is security, and M2M systems are certainly no exception. With a huge market expected for M2M devices and networks, M2M systems need to be properly developed and deployed. We also realize that many of the applications envisioned for M2M will only be realizable if security is properly addressed from the start. Despite an urgent need for proper security mechanisms and procedures, various characteristics of M2M systems and applications may pose challenges to the design of appropriate security mechanisms. Among such difficulties we may identify the support of heterogeneous communication technologies and protocols, of autonomous communication between M2M devices, the limitations on hardware capabilities of many M2M sensing and actuating platforms, and expectations from users regarding security, in particular privacy and liability [30]. Although many lessons and technical solutions have been learned from research in areas such as mobile ad hoc networks [31,32] or wireless sensor networks [33], M2M systems may also require new approaches to security.

The employment of different wired and wireless communication technologies motivated by the usage of a common service platform determines the careful evaluation of the adopted cryptographic algorithms, or on the other hand the design of new ones. The support of autonomous communication requires also appropriate universal identification techniques, such as we discuss in this chapter. The characteristics and resource constraints of M2M systems also pose challenges to the design of appropriate security technologies that are able to deal with heterogeneous sensing and actuating M2M devices. Regarding expectations on security of the users of M2M systems and applications, privacy and liability appear as important factors, as users will require that systems allow the control of how much personal information is exposed, while on the other end certain applications will require that a certain degree of personal information is guaranteed to be available [34]. In the light of such challenges, this chapter analyses how security is addressed in the context of the M2M architecture defined by ETSI [28] that we describe in the next section. Given the significance of this architecture for the future of M2M communication and security technologies, this analysis sheds some light on how security is currently being addressed in the area of M2M.

This chapter is organized as follows. In Sect. 2, we give an overview of M2M high-level and functional architectures. Also, we provide a high level description of one of many possible sets of specific service capabilities (SCs) that will allow efficient deployment of M2M applications. Section 3 describes M2M communication scenarios with focus on identification, authorization, trust, and security. A brief overview of proposed pre-provisioned identifier that can uniquely identify M2M devices is given. Section 4 presents current research opportunities on communication and security in M2M systems, and discusses standardization challenges that will enable further development of M2M systems as they evolve and gradually replace proprietary technologies. Section 5 concludes the chapter.

2   M2M Architecture Defined by ETSI

ETSI's work regarding the M2M communication has been so far mostly focused on different use case scenarios (e.g. smart metering [9], eHealth [10], connected consumer [8], automotive applications [11], city automation [7]), M2M communication service requirements [35], its high-level and functional architecture [28], as well as defining M2M interfaces [36]. ETSI closely co-operates with other standardization organizations such as 3rd Generation Partnership Project (3GPP) [37], 3GPP2 [38], Open Mobile Alliance (OMA) [39], and Broadband Forum

(BBF) [40] in integration efforts of their respective technologies into M2M systems. Their work in the M2M architecture domain is twofold. First, they define a high-level architecture view that identifies all constituents of M2M systems, their roles, and relationships. Second, they also define a functional architecture view together with reference points between different entities in M2M systems, as well as M2M service capabilities, and common functions that are being shared among different applications.

2.1 High-Level Architecture

A high-level architecture of M2M system consists of a Device and Gateway Domain, and a Network Domain (c.f. Fig. 1) [28]. The device and gateway domain is composed of the following elements:

- **M2M Device** - runs **M2M Device Applications (DA)** using M2M Device Service Capabilities Layer (DSCL).
- **M2M Gateway** - runs **M2M Gateway Applications (GA)** using M2M Gateway Service Capabilities Layer (GSCL).
- **M2M Area Network** - provides connectivity based on Personal or Local Area Network technologies (e.g. Zigbee, Bluetooth) between M2M devices and M2M gateways. The case of device-to-device communication is out of the scope of ETSI's efforts (denoted in dashed line in Fig. 1).

The network domain is composed of the following elements:

- **M2M Access Network** - allows M2M devices and M2M gateways to communicate with the Core Network. It can be based on any of the following existing access network solutions: Digital Subscriber Line (DSL), satellite, GSM EDGE Radio Access Network (GERAN), Universal Terrestrial Radio Access Network (UTRAN), evolved UTRAN (eUTRAN), Wi-Fi (IEEE 802.11), and Worldwide Interoperability for Microwave Access (WiMAX), that can be optimized for M2M communication if needed.
- **M2M Core Network** - enables interconnection with other networks, provides IP connectivity or other connectivity options, service and control functions, and roaming. Similarly to access network, it can be based on varied existing core networking (CN) solutions (3GPP CN, ETSI Telecoms & Internet converged Services & Protocols for Advanced Networks (TISPAN) CN, and 3GPP2 CN) that ought to be optimized for specific M2M communication needs if necessary.
- **M2M Network Service Capabilities Layer (NSCL)** - provides M2M functions that are shared by different M2M applications.
- **M2M Applications** - run the service logic and use M2M service capabilities available via open interfaces.
- **M2M Network Management Functions** - consist of all the functions (e.g. provisioning, supervision, and fault management) required to manage access and core networks.

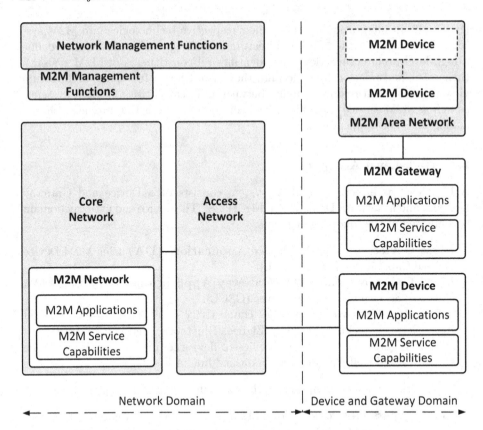

Fig. 1. High-level architecture of M2M system (adapted from [28])

– **M2M Management Functions** - consist of all the functions (e.g. M2M Service Bootstrap Function (MSBF)) used to facilitate the bootstrapping of permanent M2M service layer security credentials) required to manage M2M service capabilities in the network domain.

2.2 Functional Architecture

Each M2M domain has its own service capabilities layer (i.e. Network SCL, Gateway SCL, and Device SCL), which provides functions that are exposed on the mIa, dIa, mId, and mIm reference points [36] (c.f. Fig. 2). The **mIa** reference point enables a Network Application (NA) access to the M2M service capabilities in the network domain. It supports possibility for NA to register to the NSCL, to subscribe for notifications for specific events, with a proper authorization to read or write information in N/G/DSCLs, and to conduct device management actions. The **dIa** reference point enables a Device Application residing in a non-legacy M2M device an access to different M2M service capabilities in that same M2M device or in an M2M gateway. Furthermore, this reference point enables a Gateway Application residing in an M2M gateway to access the different M2M service capabilities in the same M2M gateway, and supports the ability of DA/GA to register to the GSCL or DA to register to the DSCL. Through this reference point, DA and GA should also be able with a proper authorization to read or write information in N/G/DSCLs. The **mId** reference point enables an M2M SCL residing in a non-legacy M2M device or M2M gateway to communicate with the M2M SCL in the network domain and vice versa. It supports the ability of G/DSCLs to register to the NSCL. It should also give support for information exchange between N/G/DSCLs, subscription to specific events, device management, and provide security related features. Finally, the **mIm** reference point extends the reachability of services offered over mId reference point. It is an inter-domain reference point, used for communication between NSCLs of different M2M service providers, that relies on public core network connectivity functions. Functionalities of all four reference points are in more details explained in [36].

One of main M2M standardization objectives is the development of functionalities that will allow efficient deployment for M2M applications. Service Capabilities are logical groupings of functions that can be shared by different applications. With standardized vertical interfaces (i.e. Application Programming Interfaces (APIs)) that allow applications to use service capabilities, and standardized horizontal interfaces between SCs on the service level, this objective is within a reach. The remainder of the section provides a high level description of one of many possible sets of specific SCs [28]. These service capabilities can be, with little differences, instantiated for each of the network or gateway and device domains (x in each of the below stands for either N for network, G for gateway, or D for device). The only exception is a Telco operator exposure that is specific for the network domain.

- **Application enablement (xAE)** - is the single contact point to M2M applications. It exposes functionalities implemented in each of the SCLs via a single reference point: mIa/dIa (depending on the SCL in question).
- **Generic communication (xGC)** - is the single point of contact for communication with each of the SCLs. This capability provides transport session establishment and teardown along with security key negotiation, encryption and integrity protection on data exchanged with the SCLs. Key material for the latter is derived upon secure session establishment.
- **Reachability, addressing, and repository (xRAR)** - provides a mapping between the name of an M2M entity or a group of M2M entities and its/their reachability status. It also manages subscriptions and notifications pertaining to events and allows creating, deleting, and listing of a group of M2M entities. It stores M2M application (NA/DA/GA) and SCL (DSCL, NSCL) data, and makes it available on request or based on subscriptions.
- **Communication selection (xCS)** - provides network selection, based on policies, when each of the available M2M entities can be reached through

several networks or several bearers. It also includes alternative network or communication service selection after a communication failure.

- **Remote entity management (xREM)** - acts as a remote management client to perform the device remote entity management functionalities (e.g. software and firmware upgrades, fault (FM), performance (PM), and configuration management (CM)) for the M2M entities. It supports several management protocols, such as OMA-DM [41] and BBF TR-069 [42].
- **Security (xSEC)** - supports M2M service bootstrap and key hierarchy for authentication and authorization procedures. It also initiates mutual authentication and key agreement, and is responsible for the storage and handling of M2M connection keys.
- **History and data retention (xHDR)** - is an optional capability deployed when required by policies. It archives relevant information referring to messages exchanged over the reference points and also internally to each of the SCLs based on policies.
- **Transaction management (xTM)** - is an optional capability that deals with transactions. Transaction is an operation that involves several atomic operations. This capability triggers a roll-back if any individual operation fails, aggregates the results of the individual operations, and commits the transaction when all individual operations have completed successfully.
- **Interworking proxy (xIP)** - is also an optional capability that enables interworking between non-ETSI compliant devices and the SCLs. It can be implemented either as an internal capability of DSCL/GSCL, or an application communicating via reference point dIa with DSCL/GSCL.
- **Compensation brokerage (xCB)** - is another optional capability deployed only when needed. It submits compensation tokens (i.e. electronic money) to requesting customers, bills the customer of compensation tokens after the validity of compensation tokens is verified, and finally refunds service providers for tokens acquired as compensation for services provided to customers.
- **Telco operator exposure (xTOE)** - enables interworking and using of core network services exposed by the network operator.

Regarding security, ETSI defines a set of functions and procedures to support security-related capabilities, with the main goal of supporting and providing fundamental security mechanisms and properties in the context of M2M systems, applications, and devices. Later in the chapter we analyze in greater detail such mechanisms, namely in the context of the various procedures defined for M2M communication establishment. For example, key negotiation, and encryption and integrity protection are supported in the context of the various communication between M2M entities, together with the required key bootstrap and negotiation functionalities. Cryptographic keys are used to support authentication and authorization of the M2M devices participating in a given M2M domain, in the context of the various procedures such as M2M device registration, management, and provisioning. As previously identified, the various security procedures are also visible in the context of the reference points defined for the architecture, particularly as regards to identification, authorization, registration, and interactions (reading or writing) with service capabilities layers.

3 Communication Establishment

ETSI distinguishes two types of **M2M devices**: those that implement ETSI M2M service capabilities (marks them as D), and those that do not (marks them as D'). Both types of devices are still considered ETSI compliant, and there are two ways how they can connect to the network domain: directly or indirectly (through **M2M gateway**) (c.f. Fig. 2). M2M gateway serves as a proxy for the network domain, which means that all the procedures mentioned in the previous section (registration, authentication, authorization, management, and provisioning) are performed through it. In the first case, M2M devices connect to the network domain via the **M2M access network**. In the second case, M2M devices connect to the M2M gateway using the **M2M area network**. To summarize, M2M devices can be connected to M2M network domain:

- directly through mId interface to NSCL (e.g. M2M device 1 (type D) in Fig. 2),
- indirectly through dIa interface to GSCL (e.g. M2M device 2 (type D') in Fig. 2),
- directly through dIa interface to NSCL (e.g. M2M device 3 (type D') in Fig. 2).

However, an M2M device may not support IP protocol for communication[1], in which case it is called a **legacy M2M device** and is marked as d. A legacy M2M device can be connected to M2M network domain:

- indirectly through Gateway Interworking Proxy (GIP) on M2M gateway (e.g. M2M device 4 in Fig. 2),
- indirectly through Device Interworking Proxy (DIP) on a non-legacy M2M device (type D) (e.g. M2M device 5 in Fig. 2),
- directly through Network Interworking Proxy (NIP) (e.g. M2M device 6 in Fig. 2).

M2M devices in both cases, if connected to IP network (e.g. Internet), communicate using IP protocol. In the first case (direct connectivity), an M2M device usually has a public IP address, while in the second case (indirect connectivity) it has a private one. The 3GPP standard *System Improvements for Machine-Type Communications* [43] analyses three possible addressing scenarios for communication between M2M server in the network domain and M2M device in the device and gateway domain. First scenario involves M2M server and M2M device both located in the IPv6 address space, in the second scenario M2M server is located in the public IPv4 address space and M2M device is located in the private IPv4 address space, and the third scenario involves both M2M server and M2M device located in the same private IPv4 address space. Using a taxonomy proposed in our previous work [44], we can classify aforementioned M2M

---

[1] If M2M device uses connectivity protocols such as ZigBee, Z-Wave, or Bluetooth that do not natively support IP.

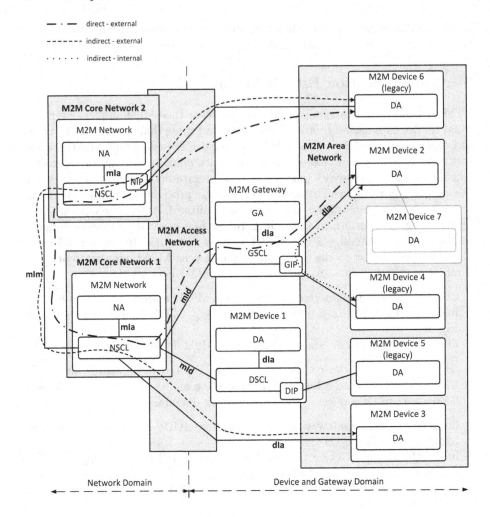

Fig. 2. Functional architecture of M2M system

communication types between two M2M devices into three categories. When both M2M devices are directly connected to a network domain via an M2M access network, then this type of communication can be classified as *direct* and *external*. In Fig. 2, an example would be communication between M2M device 6 and M2M device 3 (denoted in dashed line), as both are directly connected to an M2M access network. Furthermore, when one M2M device is connected directly to a network domain, while the other one is connected to an M2M gateway using an M2M area network, then this type of communication is *indirect* and *external*. Examples in Fig. 2 are M2M device 6 which is connected directly to M2M access network, and M2M device 2 which is connected indirectly through an M2M gateway (denoted in dot dashed line). Finally, when both devices are connected to an M2M gateway using an M2M area network, then this type of communication is classified as *indirect* and *internal*. In Fig. 2, an example of internal communication is between M2M devices 2 and 4 which are connected through an M2M gateway (denoted in dotted line). Figure 2 also features device 7 (denoted in transparent shade) which is an example of potential device-to-device communication with device 2. Such communication scenario is out of the scope of ETSI's standardization efforts and therefore is not featured in any of the analyses.

The process of communication establishment in M2M systems defined in [28] consists of the following six procedures: application registration, network bootstrap, network registration, M2M service bootstrap, M2M service connection, and SCL registration of D/GSCL with NSCL.

Application Registration procedure involves registration of an application (DA, GA, or NA) with local SCL. It allows interactions between local applications (i.e. those connected via the local SCL), while enabling M2M communication between applications connected on other SCLs requires involvement of several other procedures.

Network Bootstrap procedure defines initial configuration settings that allow an M2M device/gateway to connect and register to its access network, if it is based on fixed or mobile technologies. One example of these procedures is a bootstrap procedure from Universal Integrated Circuit Card (UICC).

Network Registration procedure consists of registration of an M2M device/ gateway with its access network, taking into account the characteristics of corresponding access network technologies. For example, registration of an M2M device in a 3GPP Network such as Universal Mobile Telecommunications System (UMTS) involves IP address assignment, mutual authentication as two sides agree on a set of security keys, authorization for using specific access network services, as well as initiation of potential accounting operations.

M2M Service Bootstrap procedure, together with M2M service connection procedure, defines basic prerequisites for the communication establishment and registration of an M2M D/GSCL with the NSCL. It involves, apart from the usual actors, the M2M Service Bootstrap Function and the M2M Authentication Server (MAS). Former facilitates the bootstrapping of permanent M2M Service Layer Security Credentials (**M2M Root Key**) between the M2M D/G/NSCL entities, as well as MAS, while the latter serves as a safe location for storage. If the M2M service credentials have been pre-provisioned (e.g. in UICC), the M2M service bootstrap procedure is not needed. Otherwise, it is conducted with or without the assistance of an associated access network layer.

M2M service connection procedure includes a mutual authentication of mId end points (D/GSCL and NSCL), an optional agreement on an **M2M Connection Key** derived from an M2M root key, as well as an optional establishment of a secure encrypted session via mId.

SCL Registration procedure, as its name suggests, is involved in a D/GSCL registration with NSCL. Successful completion of M2M service connection procedure between D/G/N M2M entities is a prerequisite for performing SCL registration. This procedure occurs either periodically or on demand. When this procedure is used periodically, the frequency of registration updates is decided by the M2M service provider. Successful registration, among others, results in an exchange of context information between D/GSCL and NSCL.

In other words, when a new M2M device enters the M2M system, it needs to establish an initial contact with a corresponding SCL and an access network, and then conduct all relevant credential creations and exchanges to establish a secure connection with its communication peer (e.g. M2M server in a network layer) within the M2M system. Only when this process is successfully completed, an M2M device is able to communicate with other entities in the M2M system (e.g. report measured sensor data to the server or update new version of software).

As for most security approaches, one fundamental security-related aspect of the ETSI M2M architecture [28] is how cryptographic keys are employed to support security mechanisms. The standard defines two types of keys, an M2M root key (Kmr) and an M2M connection key (Kmc). Kmr is used to support mutual authentication between the D/G M2M node and the M2M service provider, while a Kmc key is derived to protect communication in the context of the specific connection. Kmr must be set up for each specific D/G M2M node, in the context of a particular M2M service provider, for example during manufacturing or the deployment phase, and is also related to a particular M2M node identifier, as previously discussed. After successful authentication, Kmc is derived and delivered from the MAS to the M2M node where it is stored in a local secure environment domain (e.g. using UICC).

In general, security-sensitive functions and data (credentials and key material) shall be protected using a secure domain, which may be optionally integrity-protected using asymmetric cryptography for the provisioning and validation of trusted reference values. Integrity-validation extends to both devices and gateways, and allows verifying if a device is authorized to connect to the network, and enables validation of executable code on M2M devices, according to different security policies. Successful integrity validation may also be defined as a precondition for successful M2M service bootstrap, although we must note that all integrity-related steps are currently defined as optional in the ETSI M2M architecture [28]. Two further aspects deserve our attention in relation to how security keys are handled in this architecture. One is that, for M2M applications where the M2M service provider and access network provider have a trust relationship, access network credentials may be used to obtain the Kmr key, which consequently opens the door for the adoption of new authentication mechanisms designed at diverse layers of the network stack. The other is that the expiration of Kmc is left to particular policies from M2M service providers, which may constitute a problem if policies allow the same Kmc to be used to support symmetric encryption during unacceptably long periods of time.

3.1   Application Registration

Application Registration involves local registration of an M2M application with the local SCL, and the purpose of this procedure is to allow the M2M application to use M2M services offered by the local SCL. As a result, the local SCL obtains context information on the registered applications. Two applications registered to a common local SCL can communicate via that local SCL. For the purpose of an application-level authentication and encryption, application specific keys can be generated optionally as previously discussed, thus a Kmc obtained from the Kmr root key after mutual authentication may be used also to protect application registration. Application registration depends on other procedures and thus also on the security procedures described in the following phases of connection establishment, as we proceed to discuss.

3.2   Network Bootstrap & Network Registration

The purpose of network bootstrap is to configure an M2M device or gateway with the initial configuration data required to connect and register to the access network. Bootstrap can occur from a secured environment domain (e.g. UICC), resulting in the data required to perform access network registration. Alternatively, bootstrap can also employ an over-the-air mechanism to provision the access credentials (including key material) required for registration operations. As for network registration, it involves the registration of the M2M device/gateway with the access network, based on the corresponding access network standards. This may involve (mutual) authentication with the access network, with the two ends agreeing on a set of security keys to protect the access network session. Registration may also involve IP address assignment, authorization approval for using specific access network services, and the initiation of access network accounting operations. Both the network bootstrap and network registration specific procedures are currently defined to be out of scope of the current ETSI specification [28].

3.3   M2M Service Bootstrap & M2M Service Connection

In order to successfully complete procedures of the connection establishment process and establish communication, each M2M entity has to have a proper unique identifier, and eventually address based on the used communication technology so it can be reached by other M2M entities. ETSI proposes several identifiers which are used during M2M service bootstrap and M2M service connection procedures regarding successful connection setup in M2M systems [28]:

- **Pre-provisioned Identifier** - represents an ID and needs to be pre-provisioned by the M2M device/gateway manufacturer and is considered out of scope for this document.
- **M2M Node Identifier (M2M-Node-ID)** - represents globally unique logical representation of the M2M components in the M2M device, M2M gateway, or M2M network. Such components include one SCL, M2M service bootstrap function if any, and an M2M service connection function. On a global level, M2M-Node-ID uniquely identifies a particular M2M entity.

– **M2M Service Connection Identifier (M2M-Connection-ID)** - identifies an M2M service connection, which is instantiated upon M2M D/GSCL
getting authenticated and authorized by an NSCL for connectivity.

The creation of an M2M root key during the M2M service bootstrap procedure requires a pre-provisioned identifier that is typically assigned during the
manufacturing process of an M2M device. Figure 3 shows a simplified version of
the main activities that occur between M2M entities during either the service
bootstrap or service connection setup procedures. Identifiers that are associated
with M2M devices/gateways are considered inside the scope of current standards
[36], except for the pre-provisioned identifier. Therefore, in this chapter we will
present related work where it is explained how this identifier is formed in order
for it to be globally known and unique in the whole M2M system. We will also
discuss its format and its (dis)advantages.

In [29] authors propose how to construct a pre-provisioned identifier that can
uniquely identify an M2M device regardless of used communication technologies.
Namely, the same M2M device can establish communication using more than
one communication technology. However, sent data has to be associated with
the M2M device no matter which technology is used.

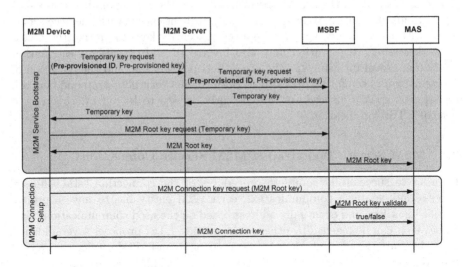

Fig. 3. Simplified view on the M2M connection establishment [29]

Because of all aforementioned, the identifier proposed in [29] is of a variable
length where its header denotes the list of communication technologies that some
M2M device supports, and bytes that follow after the header denote corresponding communication technologies identifiers/addresses (c.f. Fig. 4). The authors
specified the order of only the first four bits of the identifier header (i.e. Bluetooth on bit 0, Wi-Fi on bit 1, Wireless M-Bus on bit 2, and ZigBee on bit 3)

leaving out the meaning of the other bits[2]. If the value of the bit in the header is equal to zero, then it means that this M2M device does not support that communication technology. Opposite to that, if the value of the bit in the header is one, the M2M device supports the corresponding communication technology.

The last bit of every byte in the identifier header is reserved for denoting whether it is necessary to expand the header with other bytes. Namely, if the device supports communication technologies that are not specified within the first byte, then the last bit of the first byte has to be equal to one, otherwise it should be zero. Bytes that come after the identifier header consist of addresses of communication technologies that the M2M device supports. For communication technologies specified within the first four bits (e.g. Bluetooth, Wi-Fi, Wireless M-Bus, and ZigBee), those identifiers/addresses are of different lengths: six bytes for Bluetooth and Wi-Fi, less than a byte for Wireless M-Bus, and eight bytes for ZigBee.

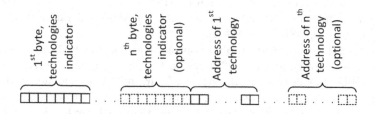

Fig. 4. Proposed identification scheme [29]

With this proposal, the identifier is tightly coupled with the hardware. In the proposed identification scheme, there must be at least one supported communication technology while the upper limit does not exist. This is one of its advantages, together with the fact that because of the variable length, it is no longer than it should be. However, on the other hand, the question is what if a communication module of some M2M device gets broken and has to be replaced with another one. Since every communication module has its unique identifier, the new module will not have the same identifier as the old one had. Consequently, the M2M device will change it. The advantage of this approach is that tampering with the device's communication can be detected. The disadvantage is that if the device is broken or malfunctioning and needs to be replaced by another device, the M2M system will detect that as a new device and some extra management effort will be needed to link the old identifier with the new one, thus preserving information about this change of the M2M device identifier. If the device identifier would be a layer-3 identifier, then this additional effort is not needed, but the start-up procedure needs to deal with that. Also, detecting the device tampering after defining the identifier will not be possible.

---

[2] The authors said that the order of other bits should be standardized by standardization organizations active in the field of M2M systems.

We may note that, if the M2M device credentials have been pre-provisioned (e.g. in UICC), in practice no M2M service bootstrap is needed. Otherwise, depending on relationship between the access network provider and the M2M service provider, the M2M service bootstrap may by either assisted or without assistance from the network layer.

In the former, the access network involves security operations, and access network security credentials may be used for service layer bootstrapping. In particular, the ETSI standard defines procedures for M2M service bootstrap assisted by various network access mechanisms, from which Kmr and (possibly) M2M node and SCL identifiers result and are provisioned to the MAS. Mechanisms are defined for the support of Generic Bootstrapping Architecture (GBA) capable M2M gateways and devices, for bootstrap based on Extensible Authentication Protocol (EAP) [45] using EAP for GSM Subscriber Identity Module (EAP-SIM) [46] or EAP method for UMTS Authentication and Key Agreement (EAP-AKA) [47] credentials and for EAP-based network access authentication, in which network access authentication is utilized for the generation of the Kmr key, which is applicable to networks using EAP-based mutual authentication and key agreement (e.g. Wi-Fi, WiMAX).

As for M2M service bootstrap without access network assistance, the access network layer only transports M2M traffic but does not provide any security for such traffic. In this context, the standard currently defines an access network independent M2M service bootstrap mechanism. This mechanism is aligned with the M2M architecture, ensures mutual authentication between the D/G M2M node and the M2M service bootstrap server with perfect forward and backward secrecy in respect to the negotiated Kmr root key. The mechanism supports authentication based on Identify-Based Authentication Key Exchange (IBAKE) [48], EAP, or TLS [49] to protect the exchanged authentication messages. For certificates-based M2M service bootstrap, bootstrap credentials shall include globally unique identifiers, and the device must also be configured with the information related to certificate validation in the context of a root trust anchor (Certification Authority, CA). Certificate validation also supports validation of certificates using certificate revocation lists (CRL) or the Online Certificate Status Protocol (OCSP) [50].

Permanent security credentials bootstrapped using the M2M service bootstrap procedures are stored in a safe location, M2M MAS. This server can be an Authentication, Authorization and Accounting (AAA) server. On the other end, security credentials established for D/G M2M nodes during the same procedure are stored in a secured environment domain at the node itself. The credentials negotiated in the context of the bootstrap procedure are used for mutual authentication and secure communication between the D/GSCL on the D/G M2M node and M2M service capability layer in the network (NSCL), as well as for authorization of access to specific M2M services, and related accounting/billing functionality.

The M2M service connection takes place between a D/G M2M node and the network domain of the M2M service provider, for which an M2M root key

(Kmr) has been established as previously discussed. The M2M service connection enables mutual authentication of the mId end points and key agreement, in the context of an M2M service connection session established between the two mId end points. This connection is optionally encrypted using a Kmc key agreed between both communicating parties, which enables the establishment of a secure session (encrypted communication) via mId. This includes the protection of subsequent SCL registration messages, as we describe next. Other than mutual authentication and M2M connection key agreement, M2M service connection also enables reporting of integrity validation security attributes for those M2M service providers that support integrity validation, and the optional establishment of secure sessions using encrypted communication over mId. After successful establishment of M2M service connection, SCL registration and subsequent M2M (secure) communication can take place. The architecture also defines a mechanism for the usage of TLS-PSK for establishing Kmc between a D/G M2M node and network M2M node with the assistance of MAS (similarly to EAP), with whom the D/G M2M node has already established Kmr. As for M2M service connection based on GBA, it applies to scenarios where the access network and M2M service providers have a trust relationship (also possibly being the same entity). GBA may thus also support mutual authentication and key agreement between the D/G M2M node and the network M2M node.

3.4 SCL Registration

The SCL Registration procedure enables a D/GSCL to register with an M2M service capability layer in the network (NSCL), in order to be able to use M2M services offered by the network. A pre-requisite for this registration is an M2M service connection that has been established by the M2M service connection procedure previously discussed, with all the related security requirements verified. After SCL registration, information exchanged between M2M devices, gateways, and the network may be protected with data origin authentication, integrity, replay protection, confidentiality, and privacy. The architecture defines three distinct ways the mId may be secured: via access network layer security, via channel security, or via object security. Access network layer security is viable if the underlying access network is already physically or cryptographically secured, and in this case a careful study must be conducted in order to properly align end-points at the access network layer with the M2M network layer. As for channel security, a secure communication channel may be established between the D/G M2M node and the network M2M node, to protect all the exchanged information. This channel can be established after the M2M service connection procedure takes place. Finally, an M2M implementation may also rely on object security by applying security at the protocol payload level. We may also note that more than one security approach may be combined in a given M2M deployment.

4   Research Opportunities and Standardization Challenges in M2M Systems

Regarding the previously discussed characteristics and functionalities of M2M systems, while also considering the ETSI M2M architecture, we are able to identify various open issues that may motivate future research and standardization efforts in M2M communication and security, as we proceed to discuss.

4.1   Research Opportunities: Communication and Identification

Current standards have proposed a hierarchical organization of entities in three layers: M2M servers, M2M gateways, and M2M devices, and they have defined M2M architecture only for those devices that support IP. In real-world systems these assumptions are not always true. Namely, IP protocol, in a way, may be too complex for small devices such as sensors due to their energy constraints. On the other end, one can also consider existing optimizations enabling IP for particular classes of sensing devices, such as with IPv6 over Low power Wireless Personal Area Networks (6LoWPAN) [51]. Moreover, many applications in distributed systems rely on flat, i.e. peer-to-peer architecture between devices that can communicate using different communication technologies (e.g. sensor networks, ad-hoc networks). There are two possible directions of how this problem could be solved. One possible solution is to achieve communication between devices without an M2M gateway regardless of communication technology, and other would be to modify current applications in such a way that they work even when devices do not communicate directly, but through an M2M gateway. Both approaches have their advantages and disadvantages that are discussed in the following sections.

Finally, in a wider context, research opportunities in M2M systems include achieving management functionalities. Namely, due to a huge number of interconnected and heterogeneous M2M entities, it is challenging to manage M2M systems. Some of the functionalities that need to be supported are: fault management, configuration management, and software upgrade, then mobility management, account management, and security management [52]. Fault management should support periodic, on demand and/or event driven reporting of faults that occurred in M2M systems. Configuration management and software upgrade should enable changing of M2M device states remotely (e.g. configuring M2M devices for reporting with specific parameters). Mobility management should provide support for both vertical and horizontal handoff, regardless of the used communication technology. Account management should include charging schemes for M2M service usage for both pre-paid and post-paid types. Finally, security management should provide end-to-end security.

Non-IP Based Protocols. Standards dominantly use IP based communication between M2M devices. The problem with IP based communication is that some

M2M devices (e.g. small sensors) are resource constrained, so they cannot implement Transmission Control Protocol/Internet Protocol (TCP/IP) stack (standards call them legacy devices). M2M gateways serve as proxies between M2M devices and the rest of the network, regardless of the communication technologies these devices support. Therefore, gateways implement interworking proxy functions (e.g. Gateway Interworking Proxy, GIP) that allow communication between IP and non-IP M2M devices by providing interfaces for otherwise incompatible protocol stacks. Each of the currently available M2M gateway implementations (e.g. Actility Cocoon [53], OpenMTC [54]) provides these functionalities, as it was initially conceived in ETSI standards [28], and are constantly developing new solutions. The second problem is that for some low level technologies there are no existing standards that provide TCP/IP stack over that technology. There are numerous initiatives that are trying to overcome this deficiency, so they are developing simplified IP stacks over existing low energy protocol suites, many of which are still in draft phase: Routing Over Low power and Lossy networks (ROLL) [55], 6LoWPAN [56], ZigBee over IP [57], Bluetooth Low Energy (BLE) over IP [58]. These initiatives are accompanied by the appropriate extensions on the application layer (e.g. Constrained Application Protocol (CoAP) [59] as a low energy replacement for Hypertext Transfer Protocol (HTTP)). In this setting main challenges are how to identify such devices and how to incorporate them into the existing standards. Pre-provision identifier proposed in [29] is an effort in that direction, because its variable header length supports any number of the existing communication technologies an M2M device can currently use (e.g. Bluetooth, ZigBee, Wireless M-Bus), but also provides room for future expansions to new communication technologies. It is important to emphasize that proposed identifier does not change anything in the original communication standard, because it only takes over the existing addressing/identification schemes and incorporates them in its fields.

Peer-to-Peer M2M Device Communication. Applications in distributed systems can be generally classified into two categories: *specific purpose* applications (e.g. collecting information about electricity consumption) and *general purpose* applications (e.g. identification of new M2M devices), where the specific purpose applications usually rely on services provided by the general purpose applications. Up till now, general purpose applications have been developed for homogeneous and peer-to-peer like distributed systems. Without a doubt, these applications will need to be adjusted according to M2M specificities. Namely, most of these applications rely on the fact that devices can communicate among themselves directly without gateways. However, this scenario is not covered in current M2M standards. Introducing this kind of communication brings different problems such as how to discover nearby M2M device (e.g. by broadcasting or by contacting gateway), how to define parameters of communication (e.g. protocols on top of lower layer communication), how to identify and achieve trust among different M2M devices without M2M gateways, etc. Moreover, a prerequisite of most of the applications is that devices are the same, but in M2M systems that is usually not the case. Consequently, applications need to be changed in such a way they would work in M2M systems where devices are diverse.

M2M Devices Always Accessible. In some cases M2M devices need to be always accessible from M2M gateway. If such M2M device (e.g. M2M device is smart meter measuring gas consumption at home) is powered by battery, then continuous energy consumption is unacceptable because battery needs to be charged or replaced in a short period, which is costly. In this setting, M2M devices usually go to sleep mode, sleep for some time, wake up, do the job, and go back to sleep mode. To be able to switch devices between sleep and operating modes, the information about its context which characterizes the situation of an entity, has to be stored somehow. One of the possible solutions is by using Rich Presence Information (RPI) which indicates the willingness or the ability of a user (or device in an M2M network) to communicate with other users (devices) in a communication network [60]. In this proposal, RPI is stored on an M2M gateway, and all negotiations are carried out by agents. Server Agent initiates communication with devices through M2M gateways. M2M gateway forwards requests only to those devices which are, according to RPI data, available. The problem is what if M2M gateway needs to communicate to that M2M device while it is in sleep mode. In that case, M2M gateway needs somehow to wake up the device from sleep mode. The research challenge is how to wake up the M2M device and that M2M device in sleep mode consumes as small amounts of energy as possible. There are also problems with security in such settings, as data obtained from sleeping devices (and possibly cached at the M2M gateway) should be properly authenticated and protected in regard to its confidentiality and integrity, among other security-related requirements.

4.2   Research Opportunities: Security and Privacy

The various challenges posed to the addressing of security in M2M may benefit from a paradigm shift in how the various security requirements are guaranteed. For example, scenarios without a security infrastructure in place (contrary to the previously analyzed ETSI M2M architecture) may consider classic security solutions side-by-side with new decentralized and distributed approaches. As in some scenarios M2M systems may be unable to derive definitive conclusions about the identity or intents of other devices, security mechanisms may need to consider compromises between the enforcement of definitive security controls and the acceptance of controlled risks [30].

Other aspects are trust and privacy, which may motivate the design of new security mechanisms and approaches. Distributed and autonomous trust management and verification mechanisms will be required to support autonomous M2M device-to-device identification and authorization [34]. M2M applications may also require the control of privacy and liability, as previously discussed. For some M2M applications (in the context of the IoT) the user will require to be able to control the amount of personal information exposed to third parties, for instance in maintaining privacy while exposing personal records in healthcare applications. On the other end, other M2M applications may require that some of that information is available in case of necessity, for instance with M2M vehicular applications in case of traffic accidents. Challenges also exist in the usage of M2M architectures such as the one from ETSI, side-by-side with emerging communication and security solutions.

Heterogeneity and Resource Constraints of M2M Systems. Given the limitations on the computational capabilities of many sensing and actuating platforms, security technologies must be developed to cope with heterogeneous devices, some of which may be very limited. In this context, further mechanisms are required to integrate such devices in M2M environments supported by architectures with the characteristics of the ETSI M2M architecture. For example, applications using passive Radio-Frequency IDentification (RFID) tags are unable to support security mechanisms requiring the exchange of many messages and communication with servers on a network domain. Lightweight solutions for symmetric and asymmetric cryptography [61,62], which have been proposed in recent years, provide a useful guidance in this context. The heterogeneity of sensing/actuating M2M devices may also be addressed by security approaches at higher layers of the protocol stack or at the middleware, in line with the approach previously discussed.

Identification, Authorization, and Trust. Identification and authorization of M2M devices in a dynamic and autonomous world will pose serious research challenges. Authentication mechanisms should work side-by-side with distributed trust management and verification mechanisms. Any two M2M devices should be able to build and verify a trust relationship with each other, and this problem is certainly more challenging in environments without a security infrastructure in place. Trust will be an important requirement for designing new identification and authentication systems for M2M. As authentication is related with identification, M2M systems will probably need to incorporate some type of secure identifier, tying information identifying the device or application with secret cryptographic material. Current proposals point to the usage of X.509-based certified secure identifiers, for example using IEEE 802.1AR [63], or on the other end of self-generated uncertified secure identifiers, also called cryptographically generated identifiers [64,65]. As M2M systems require that privacy is balanced against disclosure of information, new authentication mechanisms relying on appropriate secure identifiers and incorporating privacy-preserving mechanisms are required. This aspect may also be incorporated in new trust computation mechanisms, as the evaluation of the risk in accepting communication with a partially unknown device may also consider the level of privacy accepted for an M2M application.

As distributed and autonomous trust mechanisms will be required for M2M environments, trust must be established on an M2M device from the start. Local state control via secure boot (local trust validation) may be enforced for M2M devices, similarly to the mechanisms previously analyzed in the context of the ETSI M2M architecture. This secure boot may allow the establishment of a trusted environment providing a hardware security anchor and a root of trust, from which different models for trust computation may be adopted. In this context, the Trusted Computing Group (TCG) [66] has proposed autonomous and remote validation models. Autonomous validation (using for example smart cards storing authentication secrets) presents the problem of requiring costly in-field replacements of compromised devices. Remote validation presents problems related to scalability and complexity, regarding limitations of M2M devices.

A promising avenue for research in this field may be that of semiautonomous validation [34]. Semiautonomous validation combines local validation with remote validation, meaning that a device is able to validate trust for another device and communicate with a trusted third-party in situations of absolute necessity (in many environments such third party may not be available at all). Distributed semiautonomous trust verification mechanisms are therefore necessary for M2M environments. The previously described M2M architecture from ETSI also incorporates the usage of secured and trusted environment domains, controlled by the M2M service, as a cornerstone for the (secure) usage of security credentials on M2M devices and gateways.

Anonymity and Liability. As previously discussed, anonymity and liability are two interrelated security requirements for M2M applications. Such requirements are not only related with security, but they are also vital for the social acceptance of many applications envisioned for M2M. Anonymity is necessary as applications may only be accepted if the user is guaranteed to have a certain degree of protection of its personal (or other) information. Liability is a deeply related requirement, as other applications may require access to private information in case of necessity, for example for legal purposes. As anonymity will be required in M2M, research can target the applicability of light weighted formal anonymity models such as k-anonymity [67] to M2M environments. Possible alternative approaches are the development of mechanisms for data transformation and randomization. Intrusion detection will also be relevant for autonomous M2M environments. Autonomous and cooperative methods allowing the early detection of node compromises may be the path to follow in this domain [68].

4.3   Standardization Challenges

As previously discussed, standardization on communication and security mechanisms and architectures to support M2M environments are essential for the evolution of M2M as a fundamental cornerstone of the IoT. Thus, research and standardization must symbiotically address security as a fundamental enabling aspect of future M2M applications. Research challenges must consider the efforts of standardization on M2M, and technologies developed by standardization bodies need to address security from the start. Standardization is also important because M2M can replace proprietary technologies such as Supervisory Control

And Data Acquisition (SCADA) [69,70] in the future. Unlike SCADA, M2M devices are able to push data to a server and M2M also works with standardized technologies. Such factors will push towards the replacement of proprietary technologies with M2M solutions in the long term. This will open a huge market for M2M, but also many security and management challenges.

In the context of standardization, it is reasonable to expect that as the technology matures new opportunities and bridges between work being developed at different working groups may appear. For example, current efforts at the Internet Engineering Task Force (IETF) [71] include the work being developed at 6LoWPAN [51,72], Routing Over Low power and Lossy networks (ROLL) [55], and Constrained RESTful Environments (CoRE) [73] working groups. Work developed at these groups seeks to define a stack for the usage of Internet communication protocols on low-energy area networks, which qualify as M2M area networks in the context of the previously discussed ETSI M2M architecture. Considering the previously described security procedures and mechanisms defined in this architecture, one can investigate how security mechanisms being developed for 6LoWPAN-based communication protocol may fit in the ETSI M2M architecture described in this chapter. Possible approaches are mechanisms proposed to integrate security at the network layer [74] using 6LoWPAN communication technologies. This integration is also related with the evolution of sensing devices to adopt the usage of Representational state transfer (REST) web-services approaches, such as the IETF CoAP [59], which currently lacks security mechanisms. Also in the context of end-to-end communication between Internet and constrained M2M devices using CoAP-based REST communication, techniques have been proposed to support security in an efficient manner at the transport [75] and application layers [76]. Such mechanisms thus may provide the support for end-to-end or indirect (via an M2M gateway) communication with 6LoWPAN-based sensing devices, in the context of M2M systems enabled by architectures with the characteristics of the ETSI architecture.

Finally, we may refer that engineering and research challenges also reside in the design of new sensing platforms for M2M devices. A security co-processor may enable efficient cryptographic operations in low-end sensing and actuating platforms, and more complete hardware-based security solutions can also be used, such as the one currently proposed with Trustchip [77]. New platforms may be designed to allow efficient computation of security algorithms appropriate to M2M applications, and security-related data may be stored (as defined in the ETSI M2M architecture) using secure hardware modules with the characteristics of the Trusted Platform Module (TPM) proposed by the TCG [66] group. The usage of such a module allows the secure binding of the device identification and secret cryptographic information. As the usage of such hardware modules may not be economically feasible, research should address the design of alternative software secure-storage solutions and its impact on the overall security of M2M devices and applications.

In conclusion, various characteristics of M2M devices and applications will demand a new approach on how security and management is addressed.

The ubiquity and autonomous nature of many M2M applications will dictate that many security-related decisions are performed in the absence of a centralized and trusted security infrastructure. In other contexts, such an infrastructure may be available as defined by ETSI. Considering the autonomous nature that is expected for many M2M applications, aspects such as autonomous communication, privacy and liability (among others) will pose major challenges to engineering and research. Many of the required security mechanisms will operate autonomously and in a distributed fashion.

5   Concluding Remarks

As previously discussed, efforts from organizations such as ETSI, as well as from other organizations and researchers, are currently enabling architectures and communication technologies capable of supporting future complex M2M systems accommodating various application scenarios. M2M systems are primarily characterized by heterogeneity, i.e. their reliance on great variety of standardized communication technologies. Therefore, we propose a new pre-provisioned device identifier, transparent of the underlying communication technology. Nonetheless, there are still many open issues in the area of achieving end-to-end communication interoperability between various technologies, added by the fact that M2M systems integration into IoT environment will require further convergence on communication, data, and service levels. As in the current Internet architecture, security will remain of prime importance and will in fact represent a fundamental enabling factor of most of the current applications of M2M communication. In this chapter we have analyzed how communication establishment and security are addressed in the context of the ETSI M2M architecture [28], and also what are the main open issues that will require further efforts from both research and standardization. As we have observed, M2M architectures support valuable technologies and rules for the implementation of M2M systems, but in the context of the IoT we may expect that not all applications will be ruled by a single reference architecture. For example, applications may be unattended and M2M devices may require autonomous secure communication, and in this scenario a well-defined security infrastructure may be absent. Also in this context, important issues of security such as trust, privacy, and anonymity demand for immediate efforts from research and standardization bodies.

Acknowledgments. This work was supported by two projects: "Machine-to-Machine Communication challenges" funded by Ericsson Nikola Tesla, Croatia, and iCIS project (CENTRO-07-ST24-FEDER-002003), which is co-financed by QREN, in the scope of the Mais Centro Program and European Union's FEDER.

References

1. Galetic, V., Bojic, I., Kusek, M., Jezic, G., Desic, S., Huljenic, D.: Basic principles of Machine-to-Machine communication and its impact on telecommunications industry. In: Proceedings of the 34th International Convention MIPRO, 2011, pp. 89–94 (2011)
2. SingTel M2M. http://info.singtel.com/large-enterprise/about-m2m. Accessed 30 Mar 2014
3. 3GPP, TR 22.868 Study on Facilitating Machine-to-Machine Communication in 3GPP Systems (2008)
4. Watson, D.S., Piette, M.A., Sezgen, O., Motegi, N.: Machine-to-Machine (M2M) technology in demand responsive commercial buildings. In: Proceedings of the ACEEE Summer Study on Energy Efficiency in Buildings, 2004, pp. 1–14 (2004)
5. Emmerson, B.: M2M: the internet of 50 billion devices. Win-Win, pp. 19–22 (2010)
6. Boswarthick, D., Hersent, O., Elloumi, O.: M2M Communications: A Systems Approach. Wiley-Blackwell, New York (2012)
7. ETSI, TR 102 897 Use Cases of M2M Applications for City Automation (2012)
8. ETSI, TR 102 857 Use Cases of M2M Applications for Connected Consumer (2013)
9. ETSI, TR 102 691 Smart Metering Use Cases (2010)
10. ETSI, TR 102 732 Use Cases of M2M Applications for eHealth (2013)
11. ETSI, TR 102 898 Use Cases of Automotive Applications in M2M Capable Networks (2013)
12. M2M World of Connected Services - Beecham. www.m2m.com/docs/DOC-1221. Accessed 30 Mar 2014
13. Atzoria, L., Iera, A., Morabito, G.: The internet of things: a survey. Comput. Netw. 54(15), 2787–2805 (2010)
14. Miorandi, D., Sicari, S., Pellegrini, F.D., Chlamtac, I.: Internet of things: vision, applications and research challenges. Ad-hoc Netw. 10(7), 1497–1516 (2012)
15. Gantz, J.: The Embedded Internet: Methodology and Findings (2009)
16. Evans, D.: The Internet of Things: How the Next Evolution of the Internet Is Changing Everything (2011)
17. Hatton, M.: The Global M2M Market in 2013 (2013)
18. Zorzi, M., Gluhak, A., Lange, S., Bassi, A.: From today's INTRAnet of things to a future INTERnet of things: a wireless- and mobility-related view. IEEE Wirel. Commun. 17(6), 44–51 (2010)
19. Katusic, D., Weber, M., Bojic, I., Jezic, G., Kusek, M.: Market, standardization, and regulation development in Machine-to-Machine communications. In: Proceedings of the 20th International Conference on Software, Telecommunications and Computer Networks, 2012, pp. 1–7 (2012)
20. ETSI M2M. www.etsi.org/technologies-clusters/technologies/m2m. Accessed 30 Mar 2014
21. oneM2M. www.onem2m.org. Accessed 30 Mar 2014
22. Association of Radio Industries and Businesses. www.arib.or.jp/english. Accessed 30 Mar 2014
23. Telecommunication Technology Committee. www.ttc.or.jp/e. Accessed 30 Mar 2014
24. Alliance for Telecommunications Industry Solutions. www.atis.org. Accessed 30 Mar 2014
25. Telecommunications Industry Association. www.tiaonline.org. Accessed 30 Mar 2014

26. China Communications Standards Association. www.ccsa.org.cn/english. Accessed 30 Mar 2014
27. Telecommunications Technology Association. www.tta.or.kr/English. Accessed 30 Mar 2014
28. ETSI, TS 102 690 M2M Functional Architecture (2011)
29. Katusic, D., Skocir, P., Bojic, I., Kusek, M., Jezic, G., Desic, S., Huljenic, D.: Universal identification scheme in Machine-to-Machine systems. In: Proceedings of the 12th International Conference on Telecommunications, 2013, pp. 71–78 (2013)
30. Jiang, D., ShiWei, C.: A study of information security for M2M of IOT. In: Proceedings of the 3rd International Conference on Advanced Computer Theory and Engineering, 2010, pp. 576–579 (2010)
31. Djenouri, D., Khelladi, L., Badache, N.: A survey of security issues in mobile ad-hoc networks and sensor networks. IEEE Commun. Surv. Tutorials 7(4), 2–28 (2005)
32. Cho, J.-H., Swami, A., Chen, R.: A survey on trust management for mobile ad-hoc networks. IEEE Commun. Surv. Tutorials 13(4), 562–583 (2011)
33. Wang, Y., Attebury, G., Ramamurthy, B.: A survey of security issues in wireless sensor networks. IEEE Commun. Surv. Tutorials 8(2), 2–23 (2006)
34. Cha, I., Shah, Y., Schmidt, A.U., Leicher, A., Meyerstein, M.V.: Trust in M2M communication. IEEE Veh. Technol. Mag. 4(3), 69–75 (2009)
35. ETSI, TS 102 689 M2M Service Requirements (2010)
36. ETSI, TS 102 921 mIa, dIa and mId Interfaces (2012)
37. 3rd Generation Partnership Project. www.3gpp.org. Accessed 30 Mar 2014
38. 3rd Generation Partnership Project 2. www.3gpp2.org. Accessed 30 Mar 2014
39. Open Mobile Alliance. www.openmobilealliance.org. Accessed 30 Mar 2014
40. Broadband Forum. www.broadband-forum.org. Accessed 30 Mar 2014
41. Open Mobile Alliance, OMA Device Management Protocol (2008)
42. Broadband Forum, TR-069: CPE WAN Management Protocol (2011)
43. 3GPP, TR 23.888 System Improvements for Machine-Type Communications (2012)
44. Bojic, I., Jezic, G., Katusic, D., Desic, S., Kusek, M., Huljenic, D.: Communication in Machine-to-Machine environments. In: Proceedings of the 5th Balkan Conference in Informatics, 2012, pp. 283–286 (2012)
45. Aboba, B., Blunk, L., Vollbrecht, J., Carlson, J., Levkowetz, H.: Extensible Authentication Protocol (2004)
46. Haverinen, H., Salowey, J.: Extensible Authentication Protocol Method for Global System for Mobile Communications Subscriber Identity Modules (2006)
47. Arkko, J., Haverinen, H.: Extensible Authentication Protocol Method for 3rd Generation Authentication and Key Agreement (2006)
48. Cakulev, V., Sundaram, G., Broustis, I.: IBAKE: Identity-Based Authenticated Key Exchange (2012)
49. Dierks, T., Rescorla, E.: The Transport Layer Security Protocol Version 1.2 (2008)
50. Santesson, S., Myers, M., Ankney, R., Malpani, A., Galperin, S., Adams, C.: X.509 Internet Public Key Infrastructure Online Certificate Status Protocol (2013)
51. IPv6 over Low power WPAN. https://datatracker.ietf.org/wg/6lowpan. Accessed 30 Mar 2014
52. Pandey, S., Choi, M.-J., Kim, M.-S., Hong, J.: Towards management of Machine-to-Machine networks. In: Proceedings of the 13th Asia-Pacific Network Operations and Management Symposium, 2011, pp. 1–7 (2011)
53. Actility Cocoon. http://cocoon.actility.com. Accessed 30 Mar 2014
54. The OpenMTC Vision. www.open-mtc.org/index.html. Accessed 30 Mar 2014
55. Routing Over Low Power and Lossy Networks. http://datatracker.ietf.org/wg/roll/charter. Accessed 30 Mar 2014

56. Hui, J., Thubert, P.: Compression Format for IPv6 Datagrams over IEEE 802.15.4-Based Networks (2011)
57. ZigBee IP Specification Overview. www.zigbee.org/Specifications/ZigBeeIP/Overview.aspx. Accessed 30 Mar 2014
58. Nieminen, J., Savolainen, T., Isomaki, M., Patil, B., Shelby, Z., Gomez, C.: Transmission of IPv6 Packets over Bluetooth Low Energy (2013)
59. Shelby, Z., Hartke, K., Bormann, C.: Constrained Application Protocol (2013)
60. Kusek, M., Lovrek, I., Maracic, H.: Rich presence information in agent based Machine-to-Machine communication. In: Proceedings of the 17th International Conference in Knowledge Based and Intelligent Information and Engineering Systems, pp. 321–329 (2013)
61. Xiong, X., Wong, D.S., Deng, X.: TinyPairing: a fast and lightweight pairing-based cryptographic library for wireless sensor networks. In: Proceedings of the IEEE Wireless Communications and Networking Conference, 2010, pp. 1–6 (2010)
62. Delgado-Mohatar, O., Fúster-Sabater, A., Sierra, J.M.: A light-weight authentication scheme for wireless sensor networks. Ad-hoc Netw. 9(5), 727–735 (2011)
63. IEEE 802.1AR, Secure Device Identity. www.ieee802.org/1/pages/802.1ar.html. Accessed 30 Mar 2014
64. Moskowitz, R., Nikander, P., Jokela, P., Henderson, T.: Host Identity Protocol (2008)
65. Heer, T., Varjonen, S.: Host Identity Protocol Certificates (2011)
66. Trusted Computing Group. www.trustedcomputinggroup.org. Accessed 30 Mar 2014
67. Sweeney, L.: k-anonymity: a model for protecting privacy. Int. J. Uncertain. Fuzz. Knowl.-Based Syst. 10(5), 557–570 (2002)
68. Lu, R., Li, X., Liang, X., Shen, X., Lin, X.: GRS: the green, reliability, and security of emerging Machine-to-Machine communications. IEEE Commun. Mag. 49(4), 28–35 (2011)
69. Boyer, S.A.: SCADA: Supervisory Control and Data Acquisition. International Society of Automation, Raleigh (2009)
70. Igure, V.M., Laughter, S.A., Williams, R.D.: Security issues in SCADA networks. Comput. Secur. 25(7), 498–506 (2006)
71. Internet Engineering Task Force. www.ietf.org. Accessed 30 Mar 2014
72. Granjal, J., Sa Silva, J., Monteiro, E., Sa Silva, R., Boavida, F.: Why is IPSec a viable option for wireless sensor networks. In: Proceedings of the IEEE International Conference on Mobile Ad Hoc and Sensor Systems, 2008, pp. 802–807 (2008)
73. Constrained RESTful Environments. https://datatracker.ietf.org/wg/core. Accessed 30 Mar 2014
74. Granjal, J., Monteiro, E., Sa Silva, J.: Network-layer security for the internet of things using TinyOS and BLIP. Int. J. Commun. Syst. 1–14 (2012)
75. Granjal, J., Monteiro, E., Sa Silva, J.: End-to-end transport-layer security for internet-integrated sensing applications with mutual and delegated ECC public-key authentication. In: Proceedings of the IFIP Networking Conference, 2013, pp. 1–9 (2013)
76. Granjal, J., Monteiro, E., Sa Silva, J.: On the feasibility of secure application-layer communications on the web of things. In: Proceedings of the IEEE 37th Conference on Local Computer Networks, 2012, pp. 228–231 (2012)
77. Trust Chip Mobile Device Security. www.koolspan.com/trustchip. Accessed 30 Mar 2014

MHT-Based Mechanism for Certificate Revocation in VANETs

Jose L. Muñoz[1]([⊠]), Oscar Esparza[1], Carlos Gañán[1], Jorge Mata-Díaz[1],
Juanjo Alins[1], and Ivan Ganchev[2]

[1] Departament Enginyeria Telemàtica,
Universitat Politècnica de Catalunya, Barcelona, Spain
{jose.munoz,oscar.esparza,carlos.ganan,jmata,juanjo}@entel.upc.es
[2] Telecommunications Research Centre,
University of Limerick, Limerick, Ireland
ivan.ganchev@ul.ie

Abstract. Vehicular Ad Hoc Networks (VANETs) require mechanisms
to authenticate messages, identify valid vehicles, and remove misbehaving vehicles. A Public Key Infrastructure (PKI) can be utilized to provide
these functionalities using digital certificates. However, if a vehicle is no
longer trusted, its certificates have to be immediately revoked and this
status information has to be made available to other vehicles as soon as
possible. The goal of this chapter is to introduce and describe in detail a
certificate revocation mechanism based on the Merkle Hash Tree (MHT),
which allows to efficiently distribute certificate revocation information in
VANETs. For this, an extended-CRL is created by embedding a hash tree
in each standard certificate revocation list (CRL). A node possessing an
extended-CRL can respond to certificate status requests without having
to send the complete CRL. Instead, the node can send a short response
(less than 1 KB) that fits in a single UDP message. This means that any
node possessing an extended-CRL, including Road Side Units (RSUs) or
intermediate vehicles, can produce short certificate-status responses that
can be easily authenticated. The main procedures involved in the proposed mechanism are described in detail. General security issues related
to the mechanism are treated as well.

Keywords: PKI · Certificate revocation · Extended-CRL · MHT ·
VANETs

1 Introduction

In the last years, wireless communications between vehicles attracted extensive
attention for their promise to contribute to a safer, more efficient, and more com-
fortable driving experience in the foreseeable future. This type of communications has induced the emergence of Vehicular AdHoc Networks (VANETs), which
consist of mobile nodes capable of communicating with each other (Vehicle to
Vehicle communication,V2V) and with the infrastructure (Vehicle to Infrastructure communication,V2I). To make this new type of communications feasible,

© Springer International Publishing Switzerland 2014
I. Ganchev et al. (Eds.): Wireless Networking for Moving Objects, LNCS 8611, pp. 282–300, 2014.
DOI: 10.1007/978-3-319-10834-6_15

vehicles are equipped with On-Board Units (OBUs). In addition, fixed communication units Road Side Units (RSUs) are placed along the road. Finally, multi-hop communication based on the IEEE802.11p standard is utilized to facilitate data exchange among network nodes that are not within radio range of each other [1,2].

The open-medium nature of these networks makes it necessary to integrate VANET security mechanisms such as authentication (the assurance to one entity that another entity is who it claims to be), message integrity (the assurance to an entity that data has not been altered), confidentiality (the assurance to an entity that no one can read a particular piece of data except the receiver explicitly intended) and privacy (the quality of being secluded from the presence or view of others) [3].

A generic solution envisioned to achieve these functionalities is based on digital certificates provided by a centralized Certification Authority (CA) [4,5]. This is the approach of the IEEE 1609.2 standard [6], which states that certificates will be used to digitally sign and encrypt the exchanged messages by using the Elliptic Curve Integrated Encryption Scheme (ECIES). Therefore, vehicular networks will rely on a Public Key Infrastructure (PKI) for certificate management. The possibility to assign in the future a personal IPv6 address [7] to each vehicle and embed this address in the vehicle's certificate is also envisaged as a promising proposal for solving many of the security issues existing in these networks.

On the other hand, a critical part of the PKI is the certificate revocation. In general, the revocation approaches for VANETs can be roughly classified as global or local:

- *Local revocation* enables a group of neighboring vehicles to revoke a nearby misbehaving node without the intervention of an external infrastructure at the expense of trusting other vehicles' criteria.
- *Global revocation* is based on the existence of a centralized infrastructure such as the PKI, which is in charge of managing the certificate revocation.

According to the IEEE 1609.2 standard [6], vehicular networks will utilize the global revocation approach based on PKI Certificate Revocation Lists (CRLs). CRLs are black lists that enumerate revoked certificates along with the date of revocation and, optionally, the reasons for revocation. CRLs in VANET are expected to be quite large because this type of networks contain many nodes (vehicles) and also because each vehicle will probably have many pseudonyms[1] to protect the users' privacy. As a result, a VANET CRL might have a size of hundreds of Megabytes [8,9]. The distribution of such a huge data structure within a VANET is a challenging issue that has attracted the attention of many researchers [3,8,10,11]. A general conclusion is that most of the research efforts

---

[1] Certificates with pseudonyms contain a name that a the user assumes for operating in the VANET but that differs from his or her original or true name. These certificates are temporary.

have been put into trying to reduce the size of the CRL, either by splitting or compressing (c.f. Sect. 3).

This chapter explains in detail another approach for reducing the amount of certificate-revocation data, exchanged between VANET nodes. The mechanism described is an adaptation of previous works [12,13] for the VANET scenario. The proposed certificate revocation mechanism is based on the Merkle Hash Tree (MHT) and a model of computation, whereby untrusted repositories answer certificate status queries on behalf of the CA and provide a proof of the validity of the response back to the user. By using this mechanism, two major CRL issues can be tackled: (i) the CA is no longer a bottleneck as there are several repositories that act on its behalf; and (ii) the revocation data can be checked without downloading the whole CRL.

The main idea behind the proposal described in this chapter is to embed a little extra information into the CRL which allow the efficient and timely checking/obtaining the status of a certificate without having to download the entire CRL. This information is not proportional to the number of certificates but it roughly occupies the size of a signed hash value and the fixed overhead of introducing a CRL extension.

More specifically, this chapter proposes a way of efficiently embedding a MHT within the structure of the standard CRL to generate a so-called extended-CRL. For the creation of the extended-CRL, a standard way of adding extra information to the CRL is used. This extension contains all the necessary information to allow any vehicle, or VANET infrastructure element that possesses the extended-CRL, to build the MHT, i.e., a hash tree with the certificate status information of the CRL. Using this MHT tree, any entity possessing the extended-CRL can act as a repository and efficiently answer certificate status checking requests of other vehicles or VANET nodes.

In general, the response with certificate status information is short in size (less than 1 KB), which allows to perfectly fit it within a single UDP message. This makes the distribution of certificate status information more efficient than distributing the whole CRLs (even if they are compressed), thus reducing the amount of data that has to be transmitted over the VANET. The proposed certificate revocation mechanism operates off-line, i.e. no on-line trusted entity (like a CA) is needed for authenticating the responses produced by the repositories (c.f. next section). However, repositories need to have access from time to time to the CA to download the CRL.

The rest of the chapter is organized as follows. Section 2 presents a brief definition of the certificate revocation paradigm along with the corresponding classification of the certificate status checking mechanisms. Section 3 describes the existing global revocation proposals for VANETs. Section 4 explains the operation of the hash tree. Section 5 describes the proposed certificate revocation mechanism and the various procedures involved in it. Section 6 discusses general security issues related to this mechanism. Finally, Sect. 7 concludes the chapter.

2   Certificate Revocation Paradigm

The owner of the certificate to be revoked, an authorized representative or the issuer CA, can initiate the revocation process for this certificate (Fig. 1).

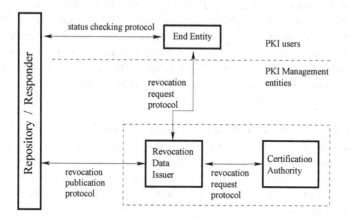

Fig. 1. PKI reference model

To revoke the certificate, any of the authorized entities generates a revocation request and sends it to the Revocation Data Issuer (RDI). The revocation data issuer is a Trusted Third Party (TTP) that has the master database of revoked certificates. The revocation data issuer is also responsible for transforming its database revocation records into "certificate status data". The status data has the appropriate format to be distributed to the end entities and includes at least the following data:

– A *Certificate Issuer* which is the Distinguished Name (DN) of the CA that issued the target certificate(s).
– A *Validity Period* that is the life-time of the status data. Obviously this validity period is much smaller than the validity period of the certificate.
– A *Issuer Name* that is the DN of the TTP that issued the status data.
– A *Cryptographic Proof* that must demonstrate that the status data was issued by a TTP.
– A *Serial Number* of the target certificate(s).
– A *Revocation Date* that is the date when the target certificate was revoked.
– A *Revocation Reason* which is optional. This is used guidance and it can be unspecified, keyCompromise, cACompromise, affiliationChanged, superseded, removeFromCRL, cessationOfOperation or certificateHold.

In the vast majority of the revocation systems, end entities do not have a straight connection to the revocation data issuer. Instead, the revocation data issuer publishes the status data in "repositories" or "responders". The main function of both repositories and responders is to answer requests from end entities concerning the status of certificates (status checking). The difference between them is that the repositories are non-TTPs that store status data pre-computed by the revocation data issuer while the responders are TTPs that have a private key and can provide a signature (serving as a cryptographic proof) for each response. Maintaining the level of security is one of the main drawbacks of using responders, in the sense that the responder has to be on-line, but at the same time it has to protect its private key against intruders. Certificate status checking mechanisms can be classified in different ways [14]:

1. By the type of certificate status checking mechanism:
   - In an *off-line mechanism* the status data is pre-computed by a revocation data issuer and then it is distributed to the requester by a repository.
   - In an *on-line mechanism* the status data is provided on-line by a responder and a cryptographic proof is generated for each request. This provides up-to-date information.
2. By the type of list:
   - *Negative or black lists* contain revoked certificates.
   - *Positive or white lists* contribute valid certificates.
3. By the way of providing evidence:
   - A *direct evidence* is given if a certificate is mentioned in a positive or negative list, respectively. Then, accordingly, it is supposed to be either revoked or not.
   - An *indirect evidence* is given if a certificate cannot be found on a list and therefore, the contrary is assumed.
4. By the way of distributing information:
   - In a *push mechanism* the repository or the responder periodically sends updates to its users.
   - In a *pull mechanism* the user asks the repository or the responder for certificate status data.

It is worth mentioning that certificate status checking is the mechanism that has the greatest impact on the overall performance of a certificate revocation system. Therefore, a certificate status checking needs to be fast, efficient and timely, and it must scale well too. It is therefore necessary to reduce the number of time-consuming calculations like generation and verification of digital signatures, and to minimize the amount of data transmitted.

3   Related Work

This section describes the existing global revocation proposals for VANETs.

Overview of Centralized Revocation Approaches. The IEEE 1609.2 standard [6] proposes an architecture based on the existence of a TTP, which manages the revocation service. In this architecture, each vehicle possesses several short-lived certificates (used as pseudonyms), to ensure users' privacy. However, short-lived certificates are not sufficient because compromised or faulty vehicles could still endanger other vehicles until the end of their certificate lifetimes. Thus, the IEEE 1609.2 promotes the use of CRLs to manage revocation while assuming a pervasive roadside architecture.

Other proposals in the literature also assume the existence of a TTP to provide the revocation service. Raya et al. [3] propose the use of a tamper-proof device[2] to store the certificates. A TTP is in charge of pre-loading the cryptographic material in the tamper-proof device. Thus, when a vehicle is compromised/misbehaving, it can be removed from the network by just disabling its tamper-proof device. To that end, the TTP must include the corresponding revocation information in a CRL. To reduce the bandwidth consumed by the transmission of CRLs, the authors in [3] proposed to compress the CRLs by using Bloom filters[3]. However, this method gives rise to false positives which degrades the reliability of the revocation service.

On the other hand, even compressed, the timely distribution of CRLs to all vehicles is not a trivial process. Some authors [5,10], instead of using a single central authority, have proposed the use of regional certification authorities with developed trust relationships. Papadimitratos et al. [15] suggest restricting the scope of the CRL within a region. Visiting vehicles from other regions are required to obtain temporary certificates. Thus, a vehicle will have to acquire temporary certificates if it is traveling outside its registered region. The authors also propose breaking the CRL into different pieces, then transmitting these pieces using Fountain or Erasure codes, so that a vehicle can reconstruct the CRL after receiving a certain number of pieces. Similarly, in [16], each CA distributes the CRL to the RSUs in its domain through Ethernet. Then, the RSUs broadcast the new CRL to all the vehicles in that domain. In the case when RSUs do not completely cover the domain of a CA, V2V communications are used to distribute the CRL to all the vehicles [11]. This mechanism is also used in [17,18], where it is detailed as a PKI mechanism based on bilinear mapping. Revocation is accomplished through the distribution of CRL that is stored by each user.

Overview of Decentralized Revocation Approaches. Decentralized revocation mechanisms provide the revocation service without assuming the existence of a TTP. Some proposals in the literature divert from the IEEE 1609.2 standard and use on-line certificate status checking protocols instead of CRLs to provide a revocation service in a decentralized manner. This is the case, of the Ad-hoc

---

[2] Tamper-proof devices are designed to resist intentional malfunction or sabotage by any user with physical access to the device.

[3] A Bloom filter is a space-efficient probabilistic data structure that is used to test whether an element is a member of a set.

Distributed OCSP for Trust (ADOPT) [19], which uses cached OCSP responses that are distributed and stored on intermediate nodes. Another group of proposals establishes the revocation service on detecting a vehicle to be misbehaving by a set of other vehicles. Then, the detecting set may cooperatively revoke the credential of the misbehaving node from their neighborhood. Moore *et al.* proposed in [20] a revocation mechanism aiming to prevent an attacker from falsely voting against legitimate nodes. Raya *et al.* in [3] proposed a mechanism to temporarily remove an attacker from the trust list if the CA is unavailable. To do so, the number of accusing neighbor users must exceed a threshold. A similar mechanism based also on vehicle voting is proposed in [21]. Again, by means of a voting scheme, a vehicle can be marked as misbehaving and then removed by its neighbors from the trust list.

Another proposal uses a game-theoretic revocation approach to define the best strategy for each individual vehicle [22]. These mechanisms provide incentives to guarantee the successful revocation of the malicious nodes. Moreover, thanks to the records of past behavior, the mechanism is able to dynamically adapt the parameters to nodes' reputations and establish the optimal Nash equilibrium on-the-fly, minimizing the cost of the revocation.

Finally, there are some hybrid approaches that are neither totally centralized nor decentralized [23–27]. For instance, authors in [28] propose the use of authenticated data structures to issue the certificate status information. Using these schemes, the revocation service is decentralized to transmit the certificate status information but still depends on a CA to decide when a node should be evicted from the VANET.

4   Operation of the Hash Tree

The Merkle Hash Tree (MHT) [29] relies on the properties of the one way hash functions. MHT exploits the fact that a one way hash function is at least 10,000 times faster to compute than a digital signature, so the majority of the cryptographic operations performed in the revocation system are hash functions instead of digital signatures. A sample MHT is presented in Fig. 2.

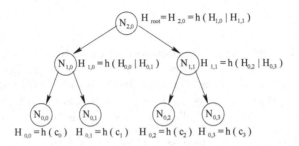

Fig. 2. Sample MHT.

$N_{i,j}$ denotes the j-th node at the i-th level. $H_{i,j}$ denotes the cryptographic variable stored by node $N_{i,j}$. Nodes at level 0 are called "leaves" and they represent the data stored in the tree. In the case of revocation, leaves represent the set Φ of certificates that have been revoked,

$$\Phi = \{c_0, c_1, \ldots, c_j, \ldots, c_n\}, \tag{1}$$

where c_j is the data stored by leaf $N_{0,j}$. Then, $H_{0,j}$ is computed as

$$H_{0,j} = h(c_j), \tag{2}$$

where h is a one way hash function.

To build the MHT, a set of t adjacent nodes at a given level i (i.e. $N_{i,j}$, $N_{i,j+1} \ldots, N_{i,j+t-1}$), are combined into one node in the upper level, denoted by $N_{i+1,k}$. Then, $H_{i+1,k}$ is obtained by applying h to the concatenation of the t cryptographic variables:

$$H_{i+1,k} = h(H_{i,j} | H_{i,j+1} | \ldots | H_{i,j+t-1}) \tag{3}$$

At the top level, there is only one node called the "root". H_{root} is a digest for all the data stored in the MHT.

The sample MHT in Fig. 2 is a binary tree because adjacent nodes are combined in pairs to form a node in the next level ($t = 2$) and $H_{root} = H_{2,0}$.

Definition 1. The $\mathcal{D}$igest is defined as
$\mathcal{D}igest = \{DN_{RDI}, H_{root}, Validity\ Period\}_{SIG_{RDI}}$

Definition 2. The $\mathcal{P}ath_{c_j}$ is defined as the set of cryptographic values necessary to compute H_{root} from the leaf c_j.

Remark 1. Note that the $\mathcal{D}$igest is trusted data because it is signed by the revocation data issuer and it is unique within the tree, while $\mathcal{P}$ath is different for each leaf.

Claim. If the MHT provides a response with the proper $\mathcal{P}ath_{c_j}$ and the MHT $\mathcal{D}$igest, an end entity can verify whether $c_j \in \Phi$.

Example 1. Let's suppose that a certain user wants to find out whether c_1 belongs to the sample MHT in Fig. 2. Then,
$\mathcal{P}ath_{c1} = \{N_{0,0}, N_{1,1}\}$
$\mathcal{D}igest = \{DN_{RDI}, H_{2,0}, Validity\ Period\}_{SIG_{RDI}}$
The response verification consists in checking that $H_{2,0}$ computed from the $\mathcal{P}ath_{c_1}$ matches $H_{2,0}$ included in the $\mathcal{D}$igest:

$$H_{root} = H_{2,0} = h(h(h(c_1)|H_{0,0})|H_{1,1}) \tag{4}$$

Remark 2. Note that the MHT can be built by a TTP (revocation data issuer) and distributed to a repository because a leaf cannot be added or deleted to Φ without modifying H_{root}[4] which is included in the $\mathcal{D}$igest, and as the $\mathcal{D}$igest is signed, it cannot be forged by a non-TTP.

---

[4] To do this, an attacker needs to find a pre-image of a one way hash function which is computationally infeasible by definition.

5   MHT-Based Mechanism for Certificate Revocation in VANETs

5.1   Overview

Our mechanism is a centralized revocation system based on an adaptation of the typical PKI CRL for the vehicular environment. We use a CRL extension to embed a Merkle Hash Tree, which allows us to check certificate status data without downloading the whole CRL.

The mechanism is implemented over a hierarchical architecture that consists of three levels (Fig. 3): the CA is located at level 1, the RSUs are located at level 2, and the OBUs are located at level 3, the bottom of the hierarchy. The main tasks of each entity are presented below:

1. The CA is responsible for generating the set of certificates that are stored in each OBU. It is also responsible for managing the revocation information and making it accessible to the rest of the entities. By definition of TTP, the CA should be considered fully trusted by all the network entities, so it should be assumed that it cannot be compromised by any attacker. In fact, in our proposal the CA is the only trusted entity within the network.
2. RSUs are fixed entities that are fully controlled by the CA. They can access the CA anytime because they are located on the infrastructure side, which does not suffer from disconnections. If the CA considers that an RSU has been compromised, the CA can exclude it from the trust list.
3. OBUs are in charge of storing all the certificates that a vehicle possesses. An OBU has abundant resources in computation and storage, and allows any vehicle to communicate with the infrastructure and with any other vehicle in its neighborhood. Regarding the design of the revocation system, the main issue to address is that the transmission rate between the OBUs and the RSUs for transferring certificate status data might be a bottleneck.

The proposed certificate revocation mechanism consists of three stages. During the first stage of *System Initialization*, the CA creates the "extended-CRL", that is, a CRL in which a signed extension is appended. This extension will allow third non-trusted parties to answer certificate status checking requests in an off-line way when required. Once this *extended-CRL* has been constructed, it is distributed to the RSUs. In the second stage of *Repository Creation*, a non-trusted entity (i.e. a RSU or a vehicle) gets the *extended-CRL* and becomes a certificate status checking repository for other VANET entities. Finally, in the third stage of *Certificate Status Checking*, vehicles can use an efficient protocol to obtain the certificate status information from an available VANET repository. The *extended-CRL* is basically a standard CRL with an appended extension. This extension can be used by non-trusted entities (RSUs and vehicles inside the VANET) to act as repositories and answer the certificate status requests.

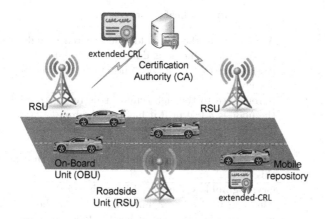

Fig. 3. System Architecture.

The steps followed by the CA are described below:

1. Create a *tbs-CRL* (to be signed CRL), which is a list that contains the serial numbers of the certificates that have been revoked (along with the date of revocation), the identity of the CA, time-stamps to establish the validity period, etc.
2. Create the MHT tree, that is, a MHT that is constructed by using the serial numbers within the previous *tbs-CRL* as leaves of the tree.
3. Calculate the extension, which consists basically of the $\mathcal{D}$igest. Once calculated, append the $\mathcal{D}$igest to the tbs-CRL, generating the *tbs-extended-CRL*. Just recall that this $\mathcal{D}$igest is calculated as the concatenation of the certification authority distinguished number, the root hash and the validity period of the certificate status information, and after that it is signed by the CA. Obviously, the distinguished number and the validity period should be the same than the ones contained in the tbs-CRL. In fact, the MHT tree is just a different way of representing the certificate status information, but the hash tree will be valid during the same time and will provide the same information than the CRL.
4. Sign the tbs-extended-CRL, generating the *extended-CRL*. Note that this second overall signature not only authenticates all the certificate status information, but also binds this certificate status information to the $\mathcal{D}$igest. The *extended-CRL* is only slightly larger than the standard CRL.
5. Distribute copies of the *extended-CRL* to the designated RSUs which are the repositories.

5.2 Responding to Certificate-Status Requests

The MHT embedded in the CRL will help us to efficiently respond to certificate-status requests. Table 1 summarizes the information contained in each leaf of the MHT.

Table 1. Leaf Information.

left child	A reference to the left child. This reference might be `null` if the node is a leaf (the node does not have children).
middle child	A reference to the middle child. This reference might be `null` if the node is a leaf.
right child	A reference to the right child. This reference might be `null` if the node is a leaf or if it has two children.
max	This is the biggest element of the subtree that descends from this node.
min	This is the smallest element of the subtree that descends from this node.
$H_{i,j}$	Cryptographic value stored by each leaf.
Leaf	This is a boolean that indicates whether the node is a leaf or not. If the node is a leaf, it has the following data in addition to the previous fields: − The *revocation date*. − The *revocation reason*. − A *certificate identifier* that is formed by the serial number, a hash of the DN of the certificate issuer (CA) and a hash of the public-key used by the issuer (CA) to sign the certificate.

Figure 4 depicts a sample 2–3 tree that represents a set of revoked certificates $\Phi = \{2, 5, 7, 8, 12, 16, 19\}$.

Note that an internal node has only two or three children. If it has two children, these are the "left" and "middle" ones, and if it has three children these are the "left", "middle" and "right" ones. In other words, an internal node always has "left" and "middle" children. A leaf has no children and $min = max = c_j$. Leaves are ordered in the following way: leaves on the left have smaller numbers than leaves on the right.

As mentioned in Sect. 2, apart from the data that identifies the certificate that has been revoked, revocation systems provide the reason and the date of revocation. We compute the following cryptographic value for each leaf to include the previous information in the MHT:

$$H_{0,j} = h\{CertID \,|\, Reason|\; Date\} \tag{5}$$

As pointed out in Sect. 4, the response varies depending on whether the requested certificate belongs to the MHT or not.

If $c_{target} \in \Phi$, the user needs to be provided with the $\mathcal{P}$ath from the target leaf to the root. For this, a recursive algorithm is provided that starts from the root and goes across the tree until the target leaf is reached. During this trip through the tree, the algorithm finds the $\mathcal{P}$ath for the target leaf.

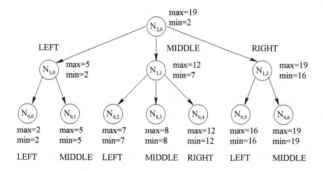

Fig. 4. A sample 2–3 tree

To sum up, when the algorithm has reached a certain internal node denoted by N_i, it decides the next node to go to (denoted by N_{i-1}) and adds the siblings of N_{i-1} to the $\mathcal{P}$ath. The algorithm is presented below in a pseudo-code.

```
While (N_i ≠ leaf){
    If (N_i has two children){
        If (c_target < N_i.middle.min){
            N_{i-1} = N_i.left
            #N_i.middle is included in Path
            N_i.middle ≫Path
        }
        Else {
            N_{i-1} = N_i.middle
            N_i.left ≫Path
        }
    }
    If (N_i has three children){
        If (c_target < N_i.middle.min){
            N_{i-1} = N_i.left
            N_i.middle ≫Path
            N_i.right ≫Path
        }
        Else if (c_target < N_i.right.min){
            N_{i-1} = N_i.middle
            N_i.left ≫Path
            N_i.right ≫Path
        }
        Else {
            N_{i-1} = N_i.right
            N_i.left ≫Path
            N_i.middle ≫Path
        }
    }
```

The above algorithm is illustrated by an example in Fig. 5:

1. Start from the root (Fig. 5# $root = N_{2,0}$, $c_{target} = 16$).
2. Choose next node (Fig. 5# $N_{1,2}$).
3. Add siblings to $\mathcal{P}$ath (Fig. 5# $\{N_{1,0}, N_{1,1}\} \gg \mathcal{P}$ath).
4. Choose next node (Fig. 5# $N_{0,5}$).
5. Add siblings to $\mathcal{P}$ath (Fig. 5# $N_{0,6} \gg \mathcal{P}$ath).
6. End since the target leaf has been reached (Fig. 5# $c_{target} = 16$).

If $c_{target} \notin \Phi$, the two adjacent leaves to the target certificate must be found. Note that if $c_{target} \notin \Phi$ and the same algorithm previously described is followed,

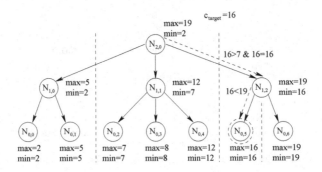

Fig. 5. Example: searching for a revoked certificate

the $\mathcal{P}$ath of the minor adjacent of c_{target} will be found. To find the major adjacent a similar algorithm is needed but using other border-lines. This is why the "Node" object includes the max parameter.

5.3   Adding Revoked Certificates

When a certificate has been revoked, it must be inserted into the MHT. The algorithm that proposed for inserting a revoked certificate in the MHT is depicted below and it is also illustrated by an example in Fig. 6.

1. Start searching the target leaf (Fig. 6a $c_{target} = 9$).
2. Stop searching at level 1. The node at which the search algorithm stops is denoted as $N_{1,j}$ (Fig. 6 $N_{1,j} = N_{1,1}$).
3. If $N_{1,j}$ has "2" children, then
   (a) Insert c_{target} as a child of $N_{1,j}$ in the correct position.
   (b) Update $N_{1,j}.max$, $N_{1,j}.min$ and $H_{1,j}$.
   (c) Recalculate the $H_{i,j}$ from the current leaf to the root (note that the resulting tree is balanced).
   (d) End.
4. If $N_{1,j}$ has "3" children, c_{target} would be the fourth child, which is not possible in a 2–3 tree by definition, then
   (a) Split $N_{1,j}$ (a new node is created). The new node is denoted by $N_{1,j+1}$ (Fig. 6b $N_{1,j+1} = N_{1,2}$).
   (b) The two leaves with the smaller serial number remain as children of $N_{1,j}$, while the other two leaves become children of $N_{1,j+1}$.
   (c) Update $N_{1,j}.max$, $N_{1,j}.min$, $H_{1,j}$, $N_{1,j+1}.max$, $N_{1,j+1}.min$ and $H_{1,j+1}$. The father of $N_{1,j}$ is denoted by $N_{2,k}$ (Fig. 6b $N_{2,k} = N_{2,0}$).
5. Apply the algorithm recursively to insert $N_{1,j+1}$ as a child of $N_{2,k}$.

In the last instance, the root node may be split. In this case, a new root is created whose children will be the old root and the new node. The root splitting is how the tree grows (Fig. 6c).

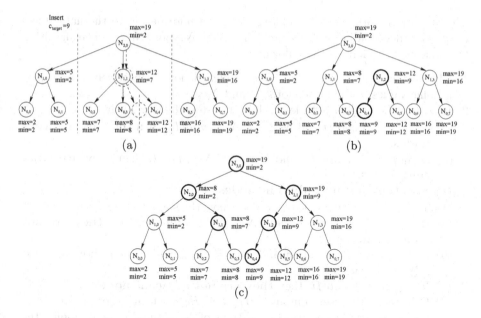

Fig. 6. Example: inserting a revoked certificate (with root splitting)

5.4   Response Verification

To verify a response the user must check that each `TreePath` included in the response is correct to verify a response. In addition, if the target certificate has not been revoked, the user also needs to ensure that the `TreePaths` provided belong to real adjacent nodes.

In first place, to check that each `TreePath` included in the response is correct the user must verify that the `rootHash` computed from the $\mathcal{P}$ath matches the `rootHash` included in the $\mathcal{D}$igest.

However, if a target certificate has not been revoked, this is not enough. The user also needs to ensure that the `TreePaths` provided belong to real adjacent nodes (remember that the repository is a non-TTP, so the user can be misled into believing that a certain pair of nodes within the tree are adjacent leaves).

For example, let's suppose that a user wants to perform a transaction using a given certificate. The certificate is identified by c_{target}. Using the example in Fig. 4, let's assume that $c_{target} = 16$. Note that $c_{target} \in \Phi$, but let's suppose that a malicious repository provides us with the $\mathcal{P}$ath for a couple of leaves that belong to the MHT, claiming that they are adjacent. For instance, let us assume that these leaves are $c_{minor} = 8$ and $c_{major} = 19$. If we only check that $\{c_{minor}, c_{major}\} \in \Phi$, we will think that c_{target} is valid and we will perform the fraudulent transaction.

Thus, an algorithm to check that two nodes are adjacent is also necessary to verify a response. Next, a recursive algorithm is proposed, which verifies, for a given couple of `TreePaths` that they actually belong to adjacent leaves.

The algorithm works without adding any extra information to the data structures. The alleged adjacent leaves are denoted by $N_{0,j}$ and $N_{0,j+1}$. The algorithm for adjacency checking is the following:

1. The user computes $H_{1,m}$ and $H_{1,n}$, which denote respectively the cryptographic values of the fathers of $N_{0,j}$ and $N_{0,j+1}$.
2. If $H_{1,m} = H_{1,n}$, then both leaves have the same father. Then
   (a) If $N_{0,j} = N_{1,m}.left$ and $N_{0,j+1} = N_{1,m}.middle$, then **they are adjacent nodes**.
   (b) If $N_{0,j} = N_{1,m}.middle$ and $N_{0,j+1} = N_{1,m}.right$, then **they are adjacent nodes**.
   (c) Else, **they are not adjacent nodes**.
3. If $H_{1,m} \neq H_{1,n}$, then the leaves do not have the same father. Then
   (a) If $N_{1,m}$ has "2" children and $N_{0,j} \neq N_{1,m}.middle$, then **they are not adjacent nodes**.
   (b) If $N_{1,m}$ has "3" children and $N_{0,j} \neq N_{1,m}.right$, then **they are not adjacent nodes**.
   (c) If $N_{0,j+1} \neq N_{1,n}.left$, then **they are not adjacent nodes**.
   (d) Otherwise, the user computes $H_{2,p}$ and $H_{2,q}$, which denote respectively the cryptographic values of the fathers of $N_{1,m}$ and $N_{1,n}$, and applies the algorithm recursively. In the last instance, the root is the unique common father between the pair of nodes.

Illustrative examples of this algorithm are depicted in Fig. 7.

It must be pointed out that the strength of the above algorithm resides in the position that a certain node occupies relative to its father, in other words whether a certain node is LEFT, MIDDLE or RIGHT. Note that the end user can trust this information since the relative node positions cannot be swapped by a malicious repository because a non-commutative hash function has been used. If the malicious repository modifies the concatenation order, then it will change the cryptographic value of the next step:

$$H_{i+1,k} = h(H_{i,j}|H_{i,j+1}) \neq h(H_{i,j+1}|H_{i,j}) \tag{6}$$

Finally, note that in some cases minor adjacent, major adjacent or both can be missing. For instance,

- If $\Phi = \{\emptyset\}$, i.e. the MHT is empty, then both adjacent nodes are missing.
- If $c_{target} < c_j \ \forall j$, i.e. the serial number of the target certificate is smaller than the smallest leaf within the MHT, then there is no minor adjacent.
- If $c_{target} > c_j \ \forall j$, i.e. the serial number of the target is bigger than the biggest leaf within the MHT, then there is no major adjacent.

A serial number is nothing more than an array of bits. The serial numbers with all bits set to 0 s and 1 s are reserved (not assigned to "real" certificates) to bound the MHT. These "special" serial numbers represent 0 and $+\infty$ respectively, so now each possible serial number has two adjacent nodes independently of the certificates contained by the MHT.

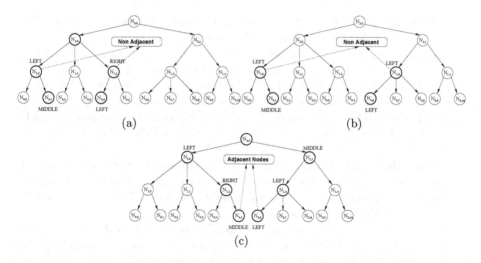

Fig. 7. Examples of adjacent node checking

6 Security Discussions

For a revocation system implementing the mechanism proposed in this chapter to be effective, certificate-using applications must connect to any of the repositories available. In the event that such a connection cannot be obtained, certificate-using applications could implement other processing logic (CRL, OCSP etc.) as a fall-back option.

Another important aspect that the MHT administrators must take into account when deploying the system is that there can be problems with firewalls if the transport mechanism is different from HTTP (many firewalls do not allow anything but HTTP to pass through). In addition, the administrators of the certificate status checking system should not forget that the HTTP transport makes it possible for firewall administrators to configure them to selectively block out messages using specific Multipurpose Internet Mail Extensions (MIME) types. Administrators should also take the reliance of HTTP caching into account because it may give unexpected results if the MHT requests or responses are cached by intermediate servers and these servers are incorrectly configured or are known to have cache management faults. Therefore, deployments should take the reliability of HTTP cache mechanisms into account when MHT over HTTP is used.

On the other hand, possible attacks on the certificate revocation system and their countermeasures must be considered, including:

– *RDI Masquerade Attack:* An attacker or a malicious repository could attempt to masquerade a trustworthy revocation data issuer.
  Countermeasures: This attack is avoidable if the user verifies the signature included in the *D*igest using the correct certificate of the revocation data issuer.

- *Response Integrity Attack:* An attacker or a malicious repository could modify part or the whole of a response sent by legitimate repository.
  Countermeasures: This attack cannot be successfully carried out if the response is verified according to the procedure described in Sect. 5.4. Note that the inherent structure of the MHT together with the response verification algorithm make infeasible to alter an MHT response without making it invalid: the MHT cannot be modified without modifying the root which is signed, and fake adjacent nodes are detected by the algorithm presented in Sect. 5.4.
- *Replay Attack:* An attacker or a malicious repository could resend an old (good) response prior to its expiration date but after the *D*igest has changed.
  Countermeasures: Decreasing the validity periods of the responses will decrease the window of vulnerability.
- *Denial of Service (DoS) Attack:* An attacker could intercept the responses from a legitimate repository and delete them or the attacker could delay the responses by, for example, deliberately flooding the network, thereby introducing large transmission delays. Note that requests do not contain the repository they are directed to, which allows an attacker to replay a request to any number of repositories. Finally, unsigned error responses open up the algorithm to another DoS attack, in which the attacker sends false error responses.
  Countermeasures: The only way to prevent this attack is to increase the redundancy of repositories, which is easy to deploy since repositories are non-TTPs.

7   Conclusions

The certificate revocation service is critical for the efficient authentication in Vehicular Ad Hoc Networks (VANETs). Decentralized approaches based on reputation and voting schemes provide mechanisms for revocation management inside the VANET. However, the local validity of the certificate status information and the lack of support for extending its validity to the global VANET restrain their utilization in real-life scenarios. The IEEE 1609.2 standard suggests the use of Certificate Revocation Lists (CRLs) to manage the revocation data. In this context, the problem is that the traditional way of issuing CRLs does not fit well in a VANET where a huge number of nodes are involved and where several pseudonym certificates and identity certificates are assigned to the same vehicle. This chapter has presented the certificate revocation paradigm and reviewed the main revocation mechanisms proposed in the literature.

A novel certificate revocation mechanism based on the Merkle Hash Tree (MHT) has been then presented and discussed. The mechanism introduces an extension to the CRL allowing any non-trusted third party to act as a repository. The main advantage of this extended-CRL is that the road-side units and vehicles can build an efficient structure based on an authenticated hash tree to respond to certificate status checking requests inside the VANET, thus saving time and bandwidth. Main procedures involved in the proposed mechanism have been described in detail, such as responding to a certificate status request, revoking a certificate, deleting an expired certificate, and response verification. As explained, the proposed certificate revocation mechanism is resistant against malicious behaviors such as Revocation Data Issuer (RDI) masquerading, response modification, replay attacks, and Denial of Service (DoS).

References

1. Bera, R.., Bera, J., Sil, S., Dogra, S., Sinha, N.B., Mondal, D.: Dedicated short range communications (DSRC) for intelligent transport system. In: 2006 IFIP International Conference on Wireless and Optical Communications Networks, pp. 5 (2006)
2. Jiang, D., Delgrossi, L.: IEEE 802.11p: towards an international standard for wireless access in vehicular environments. In: 2008 Vehicular Technology Conference, VTC Spring 2008. IEEE, pp. 2036–2040, May 2008
3. Raya, M., Hubaux, J.-P.: The security of vehicular ad hoc networks. In: Proceedings of the 3rd ACM Workshop on Security of Ad Hoc and Sensor Networks, SASN '05, pp. 11–21 (2005)
4. Hubaux, J.P., Capkun, S., Luo, J.: The security and privacy of smart vehicles. IEEE Secur. Priv. 2(3), 49–55 (2004)
5. Papadimitratos, P., Buttyan, L., Hubaux, J.-P., Kargl, F., Kung, A., Raya, M.: Architecture for secure and private vehicular communications. In: 2007 7th International Conference on ITS Telecommunications, ITST '07, pp. 1–6, June 2007
6. IEEE. IEEE trial-use standard for wireless access in vehicular environments - security services for applications and management messages. IEEE Std 1609.2-2006, pp. 1–117 (2006)
7. Ganchev, I., O'Droma, M.: New personal IPv6 address scheme and universal CIM card for UCWW. In: Proceedings of the 7th International Conference on Intelligent Transport Systems Telecommunications (ITST 2007), pp. 381–386, June 2007
8. Haas, J.J., Hu, Y.-C., Laberteaux, K.P.: Efficient certificate revocation list organization and distribution. IEEE J. Sel. Areas Commun. 29(3), 595–604 (2011)
9. Wasef, A., Shen, X.: Maac: message authentication acceleration protocol for vehicular ad hoc networks. In: 2009 Global Telecommunications Conference, GLOBECOM 2009. IEEE, pp. 1–6, 30 November 2009–4 December 2009
10. Papadimitratos, P., Buttyan, L., Holczer, T., Schoch, E., Freudiger, J., Raya, M., Ma, Z., Kargl, F., Kung, A., Hubaux, J.-P.: Secure vehicular communication systems: design and architecture. IEEE Commun. Mag. 46(11), 100–109 (2008)
11. Laberteaux, K.P., Haas, J.J., Hu, Y.-C.: Security certificate revocation list distribution for vanet. In: Proceedings of the 5th ACM International Workshop on VehiculAr Inter-NETworking, VANET '08, pp. 88–89 (2008)
12. Munoz, J.L., Forné, J., Esparza, O., Soriano, M.: Certificate revocation system implementation based on the Merkle hash tree. Int. J. Inf. Secur. (IJIS) 2(2), 110–124 (2004)
13. Forné, J., Muñoz, J.L., Rey, M., Esparza, O.: Efficient certificate revocation system implementation: Huffman Merkle hash tree (huffmht). In: V Jornadas de Ingeniería Telemática, 09 (2005)
14. Wohlmacher, P.: Digital certificates: a survey of revocation methods. In: 2000 ACM Workshops on Multimedia, pp. 111–114. ACM Press, March 2000

15. Papadimitratos, P., Mezzour, G., Hubaux, J.-P.: Certificate revocation list distribution in vehicular communication systems. In: Proceedings of the 5th ACM International Workshop on VehiculAr Inter-NETworking, VANET '08, pp. 86–87 (2008)
16. Wasef, A., Jiang, Y., Shen, X.: DCS: an efficient distributed-certificate-service scheme for vehicular networks. IEEE Trans. Veh. Technol. **59**(2), 533–549 (2010)
17. Fan, C.-I., Hsu, R.-H., Tseng, C.-H.: Pairing-based message authentication scheme with privacy protection in vehicular ad hoc networks. In: Proceedings of the International Conference on Mobile Technology, Applications, and Systems, Mobility '08, pp. 82:1–82:7 (2008)
18. Armknecht, F., Festag, A., Westhoff, D., Zeng, K.: Cross-layer privacy enhancement and non-repudiation in vehicular communication. In: 4th Workshop on Mobile Ad-Hoc Networks (WMAN'07) (2007)
19. Marias, G.F., Papapanagiotou, K., Georgiadis, P.: ADOPT. a distributed ocsp for trust establishment in manets. In: 2005 11th European Wireless Conference (2005)
20. Moore, T., Clulow, J., Nagaraja, S., Anderson, R.: New strategies for revocation in ad-hoc networks. In: Stajano, F., Meadows, C., Capkun, S., Moore, T. (eds.) ESAS 2007. LNCS, vol. 4572, pp. 232–246. Springer, Heidelberg (2007)
21. Wasef, A., Shen, X.: EDR: efficient decentralized revocation protocol for vehicular ad hoc networks. IEEE Trans. Veh. Technol. **58**(9), 5214–5224 (2009)
22. Raya, M., Manshaei, M.H., Félegyhazi, M., Hubaux, J.-P.: Revocation games in ephemeral networks. In: Proceedings of the 15th ACM Conference on Computer and Communications Security, CCS '08, pp. 199–210 (2008)
23. Wasef, A., Shen, X.: EMAP expedite message authentication protocol for vehicular ad hoc networks. IEEE Trans. Mob. Comput. **12**, 78–89 (2013)
24. Gañán, C., Muñoz, J.L., Esparza, O., Mata, J., Hernández-Serrano, J., Alins, J.: Coach: collaborative certificate status checking mechanism for vanets. J. Netw. Comput. Appl. (2012)
25. Gañán, C., Muñoz, J.L., Esparza, O., Mata-Díaz, J., Alins, J.: Pprem: privacy preserving revocation mechanism for vehicular ad hoc networks. Comput. Stand. Inter. **36**(3), 513–523 (2014)
26. Gañán, C., Muñoz, J.L., Esparza, O., Loo, J., Mata-Díaz, J., Alins, J.: BECSI: bandwidth efficient certificate status information distribution mechanism for VANETs. Mob. Inf. Syst. **9**(4), 347–370 (2013)
27. Gañán, C., Muñoz, J.L., Esparza, O., Mata-Díaz, J., Alins, J.: Epa: an efficient and privacy-aware revocation mechanism for vehicular ad hoc networks. Pervasive and Mobile Computing (2014, in press)
28. Gañán, C., Muñoz, J.L., Esparza, O., Mata-Díaz, J., Alins, J.: Toward revocation data handling efficiency in VANETs. In: Vinel, A., Mehmood, R., Berbineau, M., Garcia, C.R., Huang, C.-M., Chilamkurti, N. (eds.) Nets4Trains 2012 and Nets4Cars 2012. LNCS, vol. 7266, pp. 80–90. Springer, Heidelberg (2012)
29. Merkle, R.C.: A Certified Digital Signature. In: Brassard, G. (ed.) CRYPTO 1989. LNCS, vol. 435, pp. 218–238. Springer, Heidelberg (1990)

Author Index

Printed in the United States
By Bookmasters